ALSO BY ALEX PRUD'HOMME

My Life in France (with Julia Child)

The Cell Game

Forewarned (with Michael Cherkasky)

THE RIPPLE EFFECT

▼ ▼ ▼

THE FATE OF FRESHWATER
IN THE TWENTY-FIRST CENTURY

ALEX PRUD'HOMME

SCRIBNER

New York London Toronto Sydney

SCRIBNER
A Division of Simon & Schuster, Inc.
1230 Avenue of the Americas
New York, NY 10020

First Scribner hardcover edition June 2011

SCRIBNER and design are registered trademarks of The Gale Group, Inc.,
used under license by Simon & Schuster, Inc., the publisher of this work.

For information about special discounts for bulk purchases,
please contact Simon & Schuster Special Sales at 1-866-506-1949
or business@simonandschuster.com.

The Simon & Schuster Speakers Bureau can bring authors to your live event.
For more information or to book an event contact the Simon & Schuster Speakers Bureau
at 1-866-248-3049 or visit our website at www.simonspeakers.com.

Manufactured in the United States of America

1   3   5   7   9   10   8   6   4   2

Library of Congress Cataloging-in-Publication Data

Prud'homme, Alex.
The ripple effect : the fate of freshwater in the twenty-first century / Alex Prud'homme.
p. cm.
1. Water-supply—Forecasting. 2. Fresh water. 3. Water—Pollution. I. Title.
TD345.P77 2011
333.91—dc22
2011008951

ISBN 978-1-4165-3545-4
ISBN 978-1-4391-6849-3 (ebook)

For Sarah, Hector, and Sophia

Contents

THE RIPPLE EFFECT

Take almost any path you please, and ten to one it carries you down in a dale, and leaves you there by a pool in the stream. There is magic in it. Let the most absent-minded of men be plunged in his deepest reveries—stand that man on his legs, set his feet a-going, and he will infallibly lead you to water. . . . Deeper the meaning of that story of Narcissus, who because he could not grasp the tormenting, mild image he saw in the fountain, plunged into it and was drowned. But that same image we ourselves see in all rivers and oceans. It is the image of the ungraspable phantom of life; and this is the key to it all.

—Herman Melville, *Moby-Dick*

Under Pressure

Thirty-five feet down, on the bottom of a concrete tank filled with a million gallons of bitterly cold water, lay a body. The tank's fifty-pound lid was slightly askew; its usually secure bolts were loose or missing. Shards of glass—the remains of a beaker for taking water samples—were scattered across the concrete floor. This was in early February 2005, in a state-of-the-art water purification plant in suburban New Jersey.

The victim was Geetha Angara, a well-liked forty-three-year-old hydrochemist. She was the mother of three, the wife of a banker, had a PhD in organic chemistry from New York University, and had worked at the Passaic Valley Water Commission plant for twelve years. In 2004, the plant underwent a $70 million upgrade, during which a chlorine treatment system was replaced by an ozone-based system. At the same time, Angara was promoted to senior chemist. Her job was to maintain water quality to standards set by the Environmental Protection Agency (EPA) and to oversee the new ozone generators, which would suffer from cracks and other problems. A colleague recalled that during the plant's rededication, Angara was "in such a fabulous mood, [but] other people around her weren't."

An autopsy showed that Angara had been forcibly subdued but that she was still alive when she fell, or was pushed, into the tank. "There was no way out," said Passaic County prosecutor James Avigliano. "The water level was five feet below the opening. It was pitch-dark, ice-cold, thirty-six-degree water. There were no ladders. It was just a horrible way to die. There is no doubt that this is homicide."

The Passaic treatment plant sits on the outskirts of Totowa, a bustling suburb of ten thousand, just west of Manhattan. The plant purifies 83 million gallons of drinking water a day. Although New Jersey has relatively large water reserves, the state's rapid growth has put tremendous pressure on its water supplies. Towns are competing for the same resources, water rates are rising, decades of pollution have poisoned rivers and aquifers, and infrastructure is aging.

As in many states that suffer from similar problems, private water companies sensed an opportunity in New Jersey and began to move in. By the mid-1980s, the Hackensack Water Company controlled hundreds of acres in the watershed of northern New Jersey, supplied water to many towns, and had acquired numerous smaller water companies. When in the early 1990s the company announced it would turn some of its wetlands and forests into housing developments, arguments broke out in town meetings. Local environmental groups—worried that the developments would contaminate the watershed—filed lawsuits to block them. A 1993 settlement preserved 650 of the disputed acres. But in 2000, the company—renamed United Water Resources, and operating in fourteen states—pushed to develop a twenty-acre parcel adjacent to the Oradell Reservoir, near the town of Emerson, and just a few miles from the Passaic Valley water plant. This time, the Environmental Defense Fund, a national environmental group, spearheaded the drive to protect drinking supplies. Both sides were threatening legal action when the giant French water company Suez took a controlling interest in United Water—for $1.36 billion, in mid-2000—and brokered a truce. In December 2001, the borough of Emerson purchased the disputed lot for $7.8 million and turned it into a nature preserve—though the battle still rankles New Jerseyans.

Water is now a big, if unglamorous, business. Disputes over the control of supplies, and the privatization of utilities, have become increasingly common across the country—from Atlanta, Georgia, to Stockton, California—and around the world, from China to Bolivia. In some cases, privatizing water leads to better service; in many cases, it results in higher fees; occasionally, it has led to social upheaval and violence, as people protest the commoditization of an essential resource.

Geetha Angara was proud of her work at the Passaic Valley treatment plant, and she always conducted her water tests conscientiously. On the day she went missing, she was alone by the water tank for only a short time. That afternoon, colleagues noticed an odd sight: an uneaten sandwich on Angara's impeccable desk; they began to search for her but did not call the police for ten hours. The following afternoon, police divers were called in and eventually discovered her radio and clipboard at the bottom of a tank. But Angara's body had migrated from the main tank into a second tank, the "clear well," and wasn't discovered until hours later. Plant administrators worried that the water might have become contaminated and decided to drain the entire 1-million-gallon tank. By the time Angara's body was recovered, chlorine used as a cleansing agent had destroyed any potential DNA evidence.

As news of Angara's death spread in surrounding communities, rumors flew. Officials canceled school, and some local businesses temporarily closed. (A dead body will generally sink as soon as the air in its lungs is replaced by water; once submerged, liquids and feces escape the cadaver, which begins to decompose, rendering the surrounding water unhealthy to drink.) As a precaution against contamination, the Passaic Valley Water Commission issued a "boil order"—a suggestion that the public boil drinking water, to purify it—to seventeen towns. The citizens of Passaic County were forced to confront an uncomfortable fact: their heretofore safe, dependable, boring water supply was not as secure as they had always assumed it was.

Investigators were unable to discover a clear motive for Angara's killing, but they felt sure of one thing: the plant was protected from outside intruders, so she was likely murdered by one of her eighty-five coworkers. All fifty employees present on the day of her death were interviewed and provided DNA samples. Eight of them were deemed of "special interest"; three of them were especially suspect because their stories didn't add up. But without a clear motive or proof of a crime, the investigation stalled in 2006. Detectives were no longer working full-time on the case, though it remained technically open (and therefore I was not allowed to view the voluminous investigative files). The following year, the Angara family filed a wrongful-death suit against the PVWC and a number of individually named supervisors and lab technicians, claiming the water plant—which had a history of accidents involving extremely high levels of chlorine in the water, open and unguarded water tanks, dirty work spaces, a lack of internal security measures, and a record of fifty-five health and safety violations—was a dangerous workplace that the PVWC allegedly knew about but failed to correct. In 2009, a state judge instructed attorneys to mediate the lawsuit. The commission's lawyer declined to comment, other than to say, "The PVWC continues to deny these unproven allegations."

With Angara's death still a mystery, questions remain. Why would someone murder a respected hydrochemist? Did it have anything to do with the quality of water at the plant? Had the water at the PVWC really turned a pinkish color the week before the murder, as Angara had confided to her husband? If so, what did that mean? Did Angara blow a whistle on a colleague? Did the expensive new ozone disinfectant system, which had caused Angara headaches for weeks, have some kind of embarrassing problem? Had she inadvertently stumbled over something illicit, such as a drug deal, or a tryst, as some have alleged? Were any of the more outrageous conspiracy theories—such as the claim, whispered to me in a windy parking lot, that the New Jersey mob had been angered by the PVWC's switch from chlorine to ozone treatment, a move that supposedly curtailed work done by contractors under mob control, and had put out a hit on Angara—true? (No evidence has been presented to back this theory.) One indication that her death may have had something to do with water quality, and not professional jealousy or personal antipathy, was that the EPA sent agents to review PVWC maintenance records. State prosecutors played down the importance of the visit, saying the federal agents "were just dotting their *i*'s and crossing their *t*'s. They found nothing."

To the public, the most pressing question surrounding Angara's death was, how could a body enter the drinking supply in one of the nation's most densely populated regions and remain undetected for a day and a half without sounding an alarm? The answer was that in the PVWC tank, the sensor designed to warn of any change in water displacement wasn't working. So when Geetha Angara fell, or was pushed, into the water tank, no alarm sounded to warn that something weighing 175 pounds had entered the water. It could just as easily have been 175 pounds of cyanide, or a biological weapon, as a body.

This revelation led to further questions. If a body could contaminate 1 million gallons of water with no warning, then what other contaminants might lie unidentified in the drinking supply? In light of the September 11, 2001, terrorist attacks in nearby Manhattan, were the PVWC's treatment chemicals—such as chlorine (a potentially deadly gas that was used as a chemical weapon during the First World War)—used properly and secure?

The PVWC is a typical midsize facility, and one had to wonder, are water supplies at utilities across the country also vulnerable to contamination—whether by natural, accidental, or deliberate poisoning? Who monitors American water, and how good a job are they doing? The issues raised by Angara's death led to broader questions about H_2O and forced people to consider a resource they had never had to think about before.

Water is a deceptively plain substance. Yet it is the basis for life, and is considered an "axis resource," meaning one that underlies all others. Every time we use water—even for the most mundane tasks, such as washing our hands, hosing our lawns, or using electricity—it sets off a ripple effect with wide and deep consequences.

When you wash your hands with antibacterial soap, for example, you flush chemicals in the soap, such as triclocarban (which survive processing at treatment plants), into waterways, where they can disrupt the endocrine system of fish, leaving them vulnerable to disease and death. Such "endocrine disruptors" are also found in children's toys, cosmetics, furniture, and the weed killers many people spray on their lawns. Atrazine, for instance, the nation's second-most-popular herbicide, has been shown in a lab to feminize male frogs, to the point that they can produce eggs and even babies in their testes. Researchers worry that such powerful chemicals could be impacting human health in ways we don't yet understand—perhaps causing feminization or birth defects in people. Another kind of ripple effect is set off when you turn on a lamp or power up your computer: electricity is generated by hydroelectric dams, or by coal, gas, nuclear, or ethanol-fueled plants, which use large amounts of water for the manufacture and disposal of their fuels, for running their works, and for cooling; the construction and operation of energy infrastructure—such as dams, transmission lines, and solar arrays—are water-intensive and impact the environment in countless ways; their use creates greenhouse gases, which affect the hydrologic cycle. And so it goes, on and on, as the ripples of our actions emanate outward, usually without our comprehension and often with unintended hydrological consequences.

In the early 2000s, a rising debate over environmental issues—the impact of climate change, population growth, the competition between resources, and the like—was joined by increasingly pointed questions about water. As if waking from a forty-year nap, Americans began to ask, for the first time since the landmark environmental battles of the late sixties and early seventies (catalyzed, in part, by the burning of the Cuyahoga River and the poisoning of Love Canal): Is our water clean enough to drink? Are we running out of it, or will we be inundated by too much water? How, exactly, are we using it, and what are the repercussions of that use? In short, what do we know about our supplies of H_2O, and what don't we know?

PART I

▼ ▼ ▼

QUALITY

What Is in Our Water?

CHAPTER 1

The Defining Resource

Thousands have lived without love—not one without water.
—W. H. Auden

It is scarcity and plenty that makes the vulgar take things to be precious or worthless; they call a diamond very beautiful because it is like pure water, and then would not exchange one for ten barrels of water.
—Galileo Galilei, 1632

THE PARADOX OF WATER

The received wisdom is that America has some of the best water in the world—meaning that we have the cleanest and most plentiful supply of H_2O anywhere, available in an endless stream, at whatever temperature or volume we wish, whenever we want it, at hardly any cost. In America, clean water seems limitless. This assumption is so ingrained that most of us never stop to think about it when we brush our teeth, power up our computers, irrigate our crops, build a new house, or gulp down a clean, clear drink on a hot summer day.

It's easy to see why. For most of its history, the United States has shown a remarkable ability to find, treat, and deliver potable water to citizens in widely different circumstances across the country. Since the seventies, America has relied on the Environmental Protection Agency and robust laws—most notably the Clean Water Act and the Safe Drinking Water Act, which have been further enhanced by state and local regulations—to protect water supplies. Even our sewer systems are among the best in the world, reliably limiting the spread of disease and ensuring a healthy environment. At least, that is what the water industry says.

To put the state of American water in perspective, consider that by 2000 some 1.2 billion people around the world lacked safe drinking water, and that by 2025 as many as 3.4 billion people will face water scarcity, according to the UN. What's more, as the global population rises from 6.8 billion in 2010 to nearly 9 billion by 2050, and climate change disrupts familiar weather patterns, reliable supplies of freshwater will become increasingly threatened. In Australia and Spain, record droughts have led to critical water shortages; in China rampant pollution has led to health problems and environmental degradation; in Africa tensions over water supplies have led to conflict; and in Central America the privatization of water has led to suffering and violence.

At a glance, then, America seems to be hydrologically blessed. But if you look a little closer, you will discover that the apparent success of our water management and consumption masks a broad spectrum of underlying problems—from new kinds of water pollution to aging infrastructure, intensifying disputes over water rights, obsolete regulations, and shifting weather patterns, among many other things.

These problems are expensive to fix, difficult to adapt to, and politically unpopular. Not surprisingly, people have tended to ignore them, pretending they don't exist in the secret hope that they will cure themselves. Instead, America's water problems have steadily grown worse. In recent years, the quality and quantity of American water has undergone staggering changes, largely out of the public eye.

Between 2004 and 2009, the Clean Water Act (CWA) was violated at least 506,000 times by more than twenty-three thousand companies and other facilities, according to EPA data assessed by the *New York Times*. The EPA's comprehensive data covers only that five-year span, but it shows that the number of facilities violating the CWA increased more than 16 percent from 2004 to 2007. (Some polluters illegally withheld information about their discharges, so the actual contamination was worse.) The culprits ranged from small gas stations and dry-cleaning stores, to new housing developments, farms, mines, factories, and vast city sewer systems. During that time, less than 3 percent of polluters were punished or fined by EPA regulators, who were politically and financially hamstrung.

During the same period, the quality of tap water deteriorated, as the Safe Drinking Water Act (SDWA) was violated in every state. Between

2004 and 2009, a study by the Environmental Working Group (EWG), a nonprofit watchdog organization, found, tap water in forty-five states and the District of Columbia was contaminated by 316 different pollutants. More than half of those chemicals—including the gasoline additive MTBE, the rocket-fuel component perchlorate, and industrial plasticizers called phthalates—were unregulated by the EPA and thus not subject to environmental safety standards. Federal agencies have set limits for ninety-one chemicals in water supplies; the EWG study found forty-nine of these pollutants in water at excessive levels. Translated, this means that the drinking water of 53.6 million Americans was contaminated.

Many people have turned to bottled water as a convenient, supposedly healthier alternative to tap, but a 2008 test by EWG found that bottled water (purchased from stores in nine states and the District of Columbia) contained traces of thirty-eight pollutants, including fertilizers, bacteria, industrial chemicals, Tylenol, and excessive levels of potential carcinogens. The International Bottled Water Association, a trade group, dismissed the EWG report as exaggerated and unrepresentative of the industry, demanding that EWG "cease and desist." EWG stuck to its conclusions and objected to the industry's "intimidation tactics."

The health consequences of water pollution are difficult to gauge and likely won't be known for years. But medical researchers have noticed a rise in the incidence of certain diseases, especially breast and prostate cancer, since the 1970s, and doctors surmise that contaminated drinking water could be one explanation. Similarly, the effect of long-term multifaceted pollution on the ecosystem is not well understood. What, for instance, is the cumulative effect of a "cocktail" of old and new contaminants—sewage, plastics, ibuprofen, Chanel No. 5, estrogen, cocaine, and Viagra, say—on aquatic grasses, water bugs, bass, ducks, beavers, and on us? Hydrologists are only just beginning to study this question.

In the meantime, human thirst began to outstrip the ecosystem's ability to supply clean water in a sustainable way. By 2008, the world's consumption of water was doubling every twenty years, which is more than twice the rate of population growth. By 2000, people had used or altered virtually every accessible supply of freshwater. Some of the world's mightiest rivers—including the Rio Grande and the Colorado—had grown so depleted that they reached the sea only in exceptionally wet years. Springs have been pumped dry. Half the world's wetlands (the "kidneys" of the environment, which absorb rainfall, filter pollutants, and dampen the effects of storm surges) were drained or damaged, which harmed ecosystems and allowed salt water to pollute freshwater aquifers. In arid, rapidly growing Western states, such as Colorado, Texas, and California, droughts were causing havoc.

A report by the US General Accounting Office predicts that thirty-six states will face water shortages by 2013, while McKinsey & Co. forecasts that global demand for water will outstrip supply by 40 percent in 2030.

The experts—hydrologists, engineers, environmentalists, diplomats—have been watching these trends with concern, noting that the growing human population and warming climate will only intensify the pressure on water supplies. Some call freshwater "the defining resource of the twenty-first century," and the UN has warned of "a looming water crisis."

"We used to think that energy and water would be the critical issues. Now we think water will be the critical issue," Mostafa Tolba, former head of the UN Environment Programme, has declared. Ismail Serageldin, the World Bank's leading environmental expert, put it even more bluntly: "The wars of the twenty-first century will be fought over water."

How did this happen? How did the United States, the world's most powerful, wealthy, and technically savvy country, find its water supplies becoming *more*, not less, polluted in the nearly forty years since the Clean Water Act of 1972? How did the nation find itself running dry in some historically wet regions, while suffering devastating floods in historically dry regions? How is water being turned into an expensive commodity, such as oil or gas, and why is it a flash point for conflict? What kind of solutions can we—as individuals, and collectively—build? These were some of the questions that intrigued me, and that this book seeks to answer.

The beginning of the answer lies in a simple, obvious fact: the earth contains the same amount of water it always has—some 332.5 million cubic miles of H_2O—but the number of people using it, how they use it, and where they use it has dramatically changed. While water is the most abundant substance on the planet (it covers 71 percent of the globe), 97 percent of it is too salty for consumption. Only 3 percent of the world's H_2O is fresh, and most of that is frozen: just 0.3 percent of it is accessible and clean enough for people to use.

We recycle and reuse water, but the more times we do so, the more our supplies become "worn-out" and filled with salts, metals, chemicals, and other particulate matter. So water is a limited resource. It is also an essential one.

While bacteria can survive for centuries without water, and desert tortoises can go for years without a drink, and camels can walk the desert for six months without a sip, all organisms eventually require water for sustenance, procreation, and movement. Humans are especially water dependent; in fact, you could say water defines us. A human fetus gestates in amniotic fluid. The body weight of an adult is about 70 percent water (roughly forty-five quarts). Human bones are about 22 percent water. The brain is about 75 percent water, while blood is 82 percent water, and the lungs are 90 percent water. Water carries oxygen to cells, allows us to breathe, lubricates joints, helps to cool the body with perspiration, promotes digestion, and flushes away toxins. People can live without food for a month, but most can survive only a few days without a drink.

Yet humans tend to take water for granted. We pollute it unthinkingly, price it too cheaply, and take too much of it from the environment too quickly—usually in the service of short-term gains. Consequently, freshwater is the earth's most undervalued resource. Since Copernicus, economists and philosophers have observed that while no substance is more precious than water, none is more likely to be free. In *The Wealth of Nations,* Adam Smith famously labeled this the "diamond-water paradox" (aka "the paradox of value"): while water is essential for survival, diamonds—which have only aesthetic value—command a far higher price in the marketplace. Until, that is, water runs out and panic sets in. At that point, humans will do almost anything to get their hands on H_2O. As Benjamin Franklin noted, "When the well runs dry, we know the worth of water."

Although we have not run out of water yet, we are wasting it, contaminating it, and mismanaging it. This is not sustainable.

But not all the news is bad. We are learning to use water more efficiently than ever. We have started to clean polluted wetlands, creeks, and the Great Lakes. We have removed dams from rivers, which helps restore decimated fish populations and parched floodplains. While plenty of states have warred in courtrooms over water rights, even more have hammered out agreements to share water. Spurred by necessity, we have learned to bank huge stores of water underground, and to transform seawater and even human sewage into drinking supplies.

Each of these is an incremental step in the right direction, and together they signal a growing awareness that water fit to drink will be one of the pivotal issues of the twenty-first century.

Once you start paying attention to water, it is revealed to be a vast and constantly changing subject, one that spans issues from the molecular to the cosmic. While this book is not encyclopedic, it attempts to describe some of the most significant water challenges of today and to address the predicaments we will face in decades to come. It ranges from the safety of our drinking supplies, to the rise of nitrogen-fueled dead zones, the fragility of water tunnels and levees, the proliferation of ambitious water pipelines, the conflicts over privatization and bottled water, the "resource wars" centered on water, and the innovations that could save us from drowning or dying from thirst. It explains how we came to this critical juncture and provides a vision of where we go from here.

The scientists, schemers, and pioneers I encountered on the front lines of "the looming water crisis" are attempting to redefine our relationship to H_2O: how it is managed, when and where it is used, who uses it, what quantities are sustainable to use, and why we use it. This book is about the limits—and possibilities—of human reason when applied to water, the clear, odorless, and virtually tasteless resource that defines life.

CHAPTER 2

The Mystery of Newtown Creek

"BLACK MAYONNAISE"

At 12:05 p.m. on October 5, 1950, a huge explosion rocked Greenpoint, Brooklyn. As shards of concrete and specks of tar flew like shrapnel, a ten-foot-wide hole was ripped out of the pavement, twenty-five heavy manhole covers shot into the sky, windows in over five hundred buildings were shattered, and residents stumbled about in an ear-ringing daze. There were a few minor injuries, but, remarkably, no one was killed. After examining the crater and interviewing residents, city investigators concluded that the explosion had been caused by petroleum and other industrial pollutants that had leaked from storage bunkers or deliberately been poured into the neighborhood's soil and water, had pooled underground, and spontaneously combusted. The inspectors issued a report on the blast, noting that chemicals had been leaking from industrial sites in Greenpoint since the nineteenth century. Then they moved on to other things. Nothing was done to clean up the toxins.

The smell of hydrocarbons wafted through the neighborhood; clothes hung out to dry became stained; people and their pets suffered mysterious ailments. Yet, for decades, no one seemed to notice—or, at least, the residents of Greenpoint, who were mostly working-class immigrants from insular Polish, Italian, Irish, and Hispanic communities, never complained.

As the petroleum and other chemicals continued to seep, they tainted much of the soil and groundwater in Greenpoint undetected. Much more obvious was the rainbow-hued oil slick that floated down Newtown Creek, a 3.8-mile inlet of the East River that runs through the neighborhood and defines the Brooklyn/Queens border: it was slowly but plainly transformed into a winding, ink-black question mark in the heart of New York City.

• • •

By 2010, the oil spill beneath Brooklyn was estimated to contain at least 17 million to 30 million gallons of hydrocarbons and other toxic compounds, in pockets up to twenty-five feet deep, though the exact amount remains unknown. At the low end, this estimate represents 6 million more gallons of oil than the 10.8 million gallons of crude spilled by the *Exxon Valdez* in 1989, and 9 million more gallons than the oil spills that coated New Orleans after Hurricane Katrina in 2005. Until April 2010—when the drill rig Deepwater Horizon exploded, spewing 185 million gallons of oil into the Gulf of Mexico—the Newtown Creek oil spill was the largest in US history.

The contaminants that settled onto the creek bed are so thick and viscous that locals call the sludge black mayonnaise. The goop is composed of many different types of hydrocarbons, industrial solvents, and associated chemicals—such as naphtha, the chemical after which napalm is named. Some of the chemicals in Newtown Creek, such as benzene—a by-product of gasoline refining that is widely used by industry—or the gasoline additive MTBE (methyl tertiary butyl ether), are known carcinogens and can cause a host of neurological problems. Investigators have also discovered toxic metals, such as copper and zinc, and compounds associated with gas plants, asphalt companies, hazardous-waste plants, and paint manufacturers, in the water and soil.

Older chemicals such as benzene are referred to as legacy pollutants: compounds that were first manufactured years ago, often at a time when their malign effects were not well understood and regulation was an afterthought. Many legacy pollutants are chemically stable, meaning they don't break down in the environment quickly. They are a festering problem around the world, and there is no simple, cheap way to clean them up. Newer compounds are also found in the creek, such as PCE (perchloroethylene), a colorless liquid used for dry cleaning, and TCE (trichloroethylene), an industrial solvent; both are suspected carcinogens that dissolve in water, and many treatment systems are not equipped to filter them. (PCE and TCE have been identified in the Queens water supply. Whether the Brooklyn spill is the source of the contamination is disputed.)

The longer toxins associated with hydrocarbons and industrial chemicals remain in the environment, the more likely they are to cause health problems. They can have short-term effects, causing nausea and dizziness, or long-term effects, such as developmental problems and cancer.

Since the 1990s, Brooklyn has undergone a renaissance to become one of the most popular places to live on the East Coast. As the Williamsburg neighborhood grew too expensive for artists and musicians, they began to migrate north, into Greenpoint. The city rezoned much of the area around Newtown Creek from light industrial to residential, and by 2008 the gritty neighborhood was rapidly gentrifying. Today, more than one hundred homes and dozens of businesses are built near, or on top of, the oil plume. While some residents worry about their health and property values, others ignore warnings and continue to boat, fish, and occasionally swim in Newtown Creek.

No comprehensive health studies have been done on the neighborhood. Although Greenpoint has a lower overall cancer rate than much of New York City, it has among the highest incidence of certain kinds of cancer, such as leukemia in children and stomach cancer in adults. Anecdotal evidence suggests unusual cancer clusters are nearby. Tom Stagg, a retired police detective who lives there, told *New York* magazine that he had counted thirty-six people with cancer on the block he was raised on. "It's not normal," he said. "I'm sure it's because of the oil spill."

Awareness of the toxic stew in Brooklyn has grown, and anxiety about its effects—on human health, the ecosystem, and property values—has ratcheted up, leading to numerous investigations, new regulations, a record settlement, and two class-action lawsuits. But the enduring mystery of Newtown Creek is, how could such a disaster occur in the heart of the nation's most densely populated city and remain hidden in plain sight for over a century?

To put this question in context, it helps to understand that Americans did not have a reliable supply of clean water, or even a legal right to it, until the twentieth century. For most of the nation's history, people drank whatever water could be found and suffered the consequences.

QUESTIONS OF QUALITY

Water quality refers to the concentration of different constituents found in water, such as oxygen, sediments, nutrients, organisms, toxins, organic matter, and the like.

Freshwater comes from two main sources: surface water (rivers, lakes, and reservoirs) and groundwater (wells or subterranean aquifers). The quality of surface water depends on the composition of the river or lake bed it is in, what substances are washed into the water, and how the water is used. The quality of groundwater depends on the nature of the aquifer from which it is sourced, and what flows into it from the surface. Many other things can affect water quality. The rate of water flow, for instance, affects the physical and chemical aspects of water. Temperature is a key factor: if water becomes too warm or cold, plants and animals die, and as they decompose, water quality is affected—one reason why climate change will affect the purity of drinking supplies almost as much as it will their availability.

Water pollution can be naturally occurring—from microorganisms in soils and wildlife; radionuclides in underlying rock; and fluoride, nitrogen, and heavy metals such as lead, cadmium, arsenic, and selenium. But in many cases, water quality is most affected by what human beings put into it.

In the eighteenth and nineteenth centuries towns grew up along lakes or rivers, and by 1860 a dozen large American cities had substantial water systems, often fed by wooden or clay pipes. But overcrowding and lack of drainage led to outbreaks of lethal diseases such as dysentery, typhoid, and yellow fever. Water supplies became contaminated with sewage and garbage, or bacterial disease; in some cases, the contamination was so severe that wells and pipes had to be excavated and replaced.

As cities rose, engineers became obsessed with building efficient waterworks to supply them. Chicago, for example, was established on the shore of Lake Michigan and grew rapidly, but contaminated water collected beneath its streets, while the city's effluent was dumped into the lake, which was also its drinking supply. Typhoid fever and dysentery broke out, and in 1854 a cholera epidemic wiped out 6 percent of the city's population. (Cholera is a bacterial disease caused by feces in water.) The crisis forced a major overhaul. Municipal leaders installed water pumps, built a new sewer system, and reversed the flow of the Chicago River to carry waste out of Lake Michigan, and the city was much healthier for it.

By 1920, most American cities had efficient water systems, and by 1940 outbreaks of naturally occurring waterborne diseases had sharply fallen. But man-made pollution was another matter, and there were few quality standards to protect people.

In the 1950s and 1960s, Americans, consumed with sending rockets to the moon and coping with the social turmoil of the Vietnam War, paid little attention to what they were pouring into waterways. Twenty-eight chemicals were banned from tap water by federal guidelines in the 1960s, but environmental regulation was mostly left to the states, which were more interested in attracting jobs than in policing agricultural, industrial, and municipal polluters. Between 1961 and 1970, according to the EPA, one community a month suffered from waterborne disease: forty-six thousand people were sickened, and twenty died.

Even so, it took a series of dramatic environmental disasters to focus the nation's attention on water pollution. Among these, the most notorious was the day the Cuyahoga River, near Cleveland, Ohio, burst into flames. The Cuyahoga had grown so polluted with oil and trash that it was lifeless in sections: it "oozes rather than flows," *Time* magazine reported; it was a toxic sump where a person who falls in "does not drown. He decays." The river's surface became coated with a film of industrial waste, which, on June 22, 1969, ignited. The flames rose five stories high and burned out of control until fireboats from Lake Erie doused them.

This was not the first time that a Rust Belt river had ignited, but the Cuyahoga fire galvanized scientists, legislators, and citizens to push Washington to clean up American waters.

By 1970, studies showed that almost half of US drinking water was contaminated. Shocked, millions of citizens demanded the nation's water supplies be protected on the first Earth Day, April 22, 1970. A few months later, Congress and President Richard Nixon established the Environmental Protection Agency (EPA). In 1972, Congress overrode Nixon's veto to enact the Clean Water Act (CWA)—which limits pollution, sets water quality standards, and penalizes violators—into law. The CWA established federal water quality standards that, for the first time, aimed to eliminate toxins and ensure that waters were pure enough to be "fishable and swimmable." In 1974, the CWA was supplemented by the Safe Drinking Water Act (SDWA), which requires communities to deliver clean tap water to residents.

William Ruckelshaus was named the first administrator of the EPA, and one of the first things he did was to fine three large cities—Atlanta, Cleveland, and Detroit—for violating the Clean Water Act; he quickly followed that by prosecuting a number of high-profile industrial polluters, such as Dow Chemical. "I knew that the job of the EPA would be far more contentious in the future if we didn't establish its credibility and its willingness to take forceful—and symbolic—action right from the start," Ruckelshaus recalled forty years later. "The American people had to know we were serious."

In 1978, President Jimmy Carter declared a federal health emergency in the neighborhood of Love Canal in Niagara Falls, New York, when it was discovered that twenty-one thousand pounds of industrial waste had been buried under land on which a school and homes were built. The toxins in Love Canal, which included 248 chemicals such as benzene and dioxin, resulted in miscarriages, birth defects, epilepsy, and retardation. The federal government eventually removed or reburied much of the toxic waste, relocated more than eight hundred families, leveled houses, and sealed the most polluted sections with a barbed-wire fence.

In response to Love Canal, in 1980 Congress passed CERCLA, the Comprehensive Environmental Response, Compensation, and Liability Act—commonly known as the Superfund law—to clean up hazardous-waste sites and hold polluters responsible for the damage. (Using this law, the EPA sued Occidental Petroleum, a subsidiary of which had been responsible for contamination in Love Canal, and in 1995 Occidental paid $129 million in restitution.)

While celebrating the twenty-fifth anniversary of the SDWA in 1999, then EPA administrator Carol Browner announced that, for the first time, municipal water suppliers were required to provide consumer confidence reports, which explained where consumers' water was drawn from and what was in it. This was hailed as a major victory for consumer groups. But a year later, the EPA revealed that 45 percent of the nation's lakes and 39 percent of streams and rivers were "impaired," meaning they were unsafe for drinking, fishing, or even, in some cases, swimming.

The turn of the twenty-first century saw a shift in the US economy, from dirty Industrial Age works to relatively clean businesses such as information technology. Yet many of the nation's waterways remained haunted by their rusty, chemically tainted past. Legacy contaminants from the nineteenth and the twentieth centuries have persisted across the country and continue to impact human and environmental health—from hexavalent chromium (an industrial compound that gained infamy in Erin Brockovich's prosecution of Pacific Gas & Electric) in California groundwater, to perchlorate (used in rocket fuel) in Iowa, uranium in Colorado, perfluorochemicals (PFCs) in Minnesota, and dangerous levels of rust and lead in pipes in Washington, DC.

Even the Potomac—the "nation's river"—was so heavily polluted in the sixties that it was said you could smell the river before you saw it; people were told not to swim in it and to get a tetanus shot if they did. The Potomac has been partly cleaned since then, but it flows into Chesapeake

Bay, a famously rich aquasystem that continues to suffer from monstrous algae growths fueled by pollution, and fish diseases worthy of science fiction, virtually at the feet of the Environmental Protection Agency, Congress, and the White House.

What is happening in Chesapeake Bay has national and global implications. But before I investigated that big story, I took a look at what has happened in my local waters, including Newtown Creek, in Brooklyn. I was surprised by what I discovered in my own backyard.

STANDARD OPERATING PROCEDURE

Newtown Creek is a tidal estuary that once ran through a rich wetland populated by many kinds of birds, animals, and aquatic life. In the early nineteenth century, farmers barged their vegetables to market along Newtown Creek, while aristocrats fished and hunted along its marshy shores. In Greenpoint, named after the broad, wet grassland on the Brooklyn side, land was cheap and taxes were low. As the city expanded, the marsh was filled in, paved over, and built up. By 1860, New York was the nation's leading manufacturing center, and over fifty businesses along Newtown Creek processed kerosene, coal, paraffin wax, naphthas, chemicals, fertilizers, glue, glass, and lumber. In 1867, Astral Oil built America's first large, modern oil refinery there, and as Newtown Creek became the center of New York's petroleum-refining business, it was soon joined by others.

In 1872, John D. Rockefeller's Standard Oil Company arrived in Greenpoint. Originally based in Cleveland, Rockefeller built Standard Oil into a monopoly by acquiring and merging with other companies, including Astral Oil. By 1880, Standard controlled 90 percent of the nation's refinery capacity. Along Newtown Creek, Rockefeller controlled over one hundred stills, which employed two thousand workers and consumed 3 million gallons of crude oil each week.

Pollution around the creek was rampant. When petroleum was transported from distillery to holding tank to wharf to schooner, spillage occurred. Oil evaporated from storage tanks into the air, or leaked into the creek. To maximize profits, companies discarded their unwanted byproducts, which included gasoline in the days before the automobile, in the most expedient way possible—by dumping them into the creek or pouring them onto the land, where they seeped into the soil. By one estimate, three hundred thousand gallons of gas, coke residue (carbon left over from coal or petroleum and used for steelmaking), and other waste was produced along Newtown Creek every week in the 1880s.

"On warm sunny days, a quivering envelope of nauseous fog hangs above the place like a pall of death," the *New York Times* reported in 1887.

Alarmed, the Fifteenth Ward Smelling Committee took a scouting trip aboard a tug up the creek in September 1891. As they worked upstream, around manure scows and cargo ships, they noticed mysterious liquids pouring from factories and saw signs that fertilizer companies were dumping their waste directly into the waterway. Passing the dog pound and sausage factories, they were revolted to see heaps of flesh baking in the open sun. Sludge acid, a tarlike substance produced by refineries, emitted an odor that could "nauseate a horse." The smell grew worse and worse, until they reached the refineries themselves, where "the stenches began asserting themselves with all the vigor of fully developed stenches." The wind blew these odors over neighborhoods in Brooklyn, Queens and Manhattan, prompting people to flee.

In 1919, twenty acres of the Standard Oil refinery burned (allegedly due to arson), releasing millions of gallons of oil. But rather than leak into Newtown Creek, the goop seeped underground, tainting Brooklyn's drinking supply. This happened because residents had pumped so much freshwater from wells that the natural slope of the aquifer (an underground supply of freshwater) had been reversed: it now tilted away from the creek. The oil followed the slope, into the groundwater. By the 1940s, the Brooklyn Aquifer had been pumped so low that seawater had infiltrated and polluted the aquifer further. In 1949, Brooklyn abandoned its aquifer and began to rely on city water, piped from reservoirs over a hundred miles away.

The following year, 1950, the chemical vapors spontaneously combusted underground, signaling that something had gone very wrong. By then, Greenpoint was no longer green: it was a gray Dickensian cityscape of smoke-belching kerosene stills, snaking pipelines, giant petrochemical storage tanks, and greasy wharves. Thousands of people lived in and around the industrial tangle. Newtown Creek was one of the most polluted waterways in the country, but only a few people seemed to care.

QUALITY

"SISTER NEWTOWN CREEK"

In September 1978, a Coast Guard helicopter pilot on a routine patrol over Brooklyn noticed a huge black oil plume emanating from the Meeker Avenue bulkhead along Newtown Creek. He filed a report, and a containment boom—a string of yellow plastic floats designed to restrict the oil to the shoreline, preventing it from washing downstream into New York Harbor—was set. In six months, the boom collected over a hundred thousand gallons of degraded gasoline, fuel oil, and industrial chemicals, some of which dated to 1948. New Yorkers were shocked. A Coast Guard investigation revealed that the entire length of Newtown Creek and a large swath of Greenpoint's soil—an area of roughly fifty-five acres—was saturated by toxic industrial chemicals.

That summer, not long after the Coast Guard's discovery, a city bus driver noticed oil oozing out of the pavement on Manhattan Avenue, a wide industrial street in Greenpoint. He mentioned it to a local nun, Sister Francis Gerard Kress. Sister Francis began to ask people in the neighborhood if they knew anything about the mysterious oil. She was surprised to learn that almost every resident had a story about the black mayonnaise. "Toxic fumes stained their clothes drying on the line outside," she recalled. "It gave people headaches. It made children agitated. The people hated it, but they learned to live with it. They didn't want to cause any trouble."

Although Newtown Creek was viscous with oil, some residents swam there on scorching summer days or ate the fish or crabs they pulled from its murky waters. Sister Francis worried that the spill would endanger people's health, so she mentioned it to the local community board, politicians, and to practically everyone she met. Few of them paid attention.

"They told me I was a nuisance," she said. "But I have Viking blood and decided to look into it anyway."

With the help of sympathetic coastguardsmen, Sister Francis dressed herself in a hazardous-materials suit, climbed over barbed-wire fences into vacant lots, and skirted packs of wild dogs to inspect the creek. The more she saw of it, the more concerned she became. But when Church elders learned that she was agitating for a cleanup, she recalled, they immediately warned her to desist. "The Church banished me from Greenpoint!" Sister Francis declared in a loud voice when I visited her at a church-run nursing home on Long Island, in 2007. She was ninety-two, and wheelchairbound, but recalled every detail of her mission to save Newtown Creek.

Sister Francis continued her activism in secret, but even Greenpoint residents didn't want her to "stir things up." While she made inroads with local politicians and helped individual families, her efforts were largely met with stubborn disengagement. "I've never seen such a community. They *still* need to clean up my creek!" she thundered, insisting that I call her Sister Newtown Creek, as some of her friends still do in Greenpoint. "Think of all the young families living there that could be polluted!"

"TOO MUCH OF A COINCIDENCE"

One of those families, the Pirozzis, lived on Devoe Street, not far from the site of the 1950 explosion. The family's youngest son, Sebastian, was energetic and spent much of his time outside, playing tag and stickball; he played near the creek but not in it. Many of his "old-school Italian neighbors" raised vegetables in their backyards, where the soil and water used to tend the plants may have been contaminated, he recalled.

In the 1970s, five of Pirozzi's neighbors contracted osteosarcoma, a rare form of bone cancer. (It is unclear what causes osteosarcoma, but it is associated with exposure to chemicals. According to the American Cancer Society, osteosarcoma "is not a common cancer," and only nine hundred new cases of the disease are diagnosed annually, on average, in the United States. The *New York Post* reported that in 2006, in New York City, only twenty-four new cases were diagnosed compared to an average of ten thousand new cases of breast cancer diagnosed annually in the city at that time.) Two of Pirozzi's osteosarcoma-stricken neighbors had their legs amputated, and one of them had an arm amputated; a teenage girl whose leg was not amputated died; a friend nearby developed bone cancer in his shoulder and died. Pirozzi's father contracted colon cancer but survived. After the Pirozzis moved from their Devoe Street apartment, the woman who replaced them contracted bone cancer. She fought it for a decade, but the cancer killed her at age sixty-two.

In 1977, when he was fourteen years old, Sebastian Pirozzi was diagnosed with osteosarcoma. The doctors said that his was an extremely grave case. After a year of chemotherapy, his right leg was amputated, and he began an arduous recovery. Since then he has undergone surgeries on his shoulder and knee, had part of his lung removed, and had to cut short a promising career on Wall Street to tend to his health. Pirozzi no longer works and now lives on Staten Island with his wife and three children.

"I used to think my cancer was an act of God. But now that I know more about the pollution, I'm rethinking that," he said. "I'm coping, I guess. But I still have sleepless nights." Although he lacks conclusive epidemiological evidence, Sebastian Pirozzi believes the oil spill and Greenpoint's cancer cluster are linked. "Bone cancer is very rare," he said. "To have all this rare cancer in one place? It's just too much of a coincidence."

The oil underground was invisible and easy to overlook, he said, and no government or oil company officials explained the possible health consequences of industrial pollution. In the 1970s Greenpoint residents "didn't even know what an oil spill was," Pirozzi said. "No one was savvy enough to connect the chemicals to all the sickness. No one was up in arms. You just didn't hear about it."

Pirozzi first learned of the oil spill in 2006, when he read a small newspaper article about it and showed it to his neighbors. "People were amazed— 'How can there be so much oil under our houses and nobody told us?' That really pissed me off," he said. That year, he joined a $58 billion class-action lawsuit brought against ExxonMobil, BP, and other alleged polluters of Newtown Creek by the law firm Napoli Bern Ripka LLP. Most are suing for the loss of their property values, but a few, including Pirozzi, are claiming the spill affected their health.

ExxonMobil took the position that a dense layer of clay beneath Greenpoint stops the oil vapors from rising to the surface. This assumption has been contested by independent geologists, who believe the clay is porous and allows toxic vapors to filter into the air and people's homes. Exxon-Mobil also argued that it was being held responsible for actions taken decades ago, by people who may not have realized how toxic the pollutants were, in an era when regulation was limited. While that may be true, it does not explain why the spill has yet to be cleaned up.

A SECRET REVEALED

On a foggy day in October 2002, Basil Seggos, who worked as the chief investigator of the Hudson Riverkeeper—an environmental group for which Robert Kennedy Jr. is the chief prosecuting attorney—plowed up Newtown Creek in a wooden boat. He was there to discover where people were fishing and warn them against eating anything from the water. As the boat nosed through filth and past abandoned fuel refineries, Seggos noticed oil coating the creek's surface as well as the rocks and old pilings along its edges. "It was thick. It was everywhere," he said, as we retraced his course in the Riverkeeper's thirty-foot motorboat, in 2008. "It was unbelievable to me that a thing this big could be kept a secret for so long."

Intrigued, Seggos dug through old newspaper clippings, contacted city officials, and talked to Greenpoint families. Though he, like Sister Francis, found some residents taciturn at first, the story slowly emerged. What he learned, with the help of Freedom of Information Act (FOIA) requests for documents, was that Mobil Oil—which was descended from Rockefeller's Standard Oil, and which merged with Exxon in 1999 to form ExxonMobil—had allegedly worked out an agreement with the state. If the company assumed responsibility for cleaning up the spill, Riverkeeper charged, then state officials would not subject Mobil to fines or onerous remediation schedules: that way, both sides could avoid a public outcry and a costly legal battle.

Riverkeeper's FOIA requests then turned up ExxonMobil documents they maintained showed that the company was aware that benzene had been leaking into the ground and water for at least a decade, and that the company had dragged its feet on cleaning it up.

In 2004, Riverkeeper and several Brooklyn politicians filed a lawsuit against three oil companies: ExxonMobil, BP, and Chevron. They charged that toxic fumes from the spill had endangered people's health and property. Riverkeeper also alleged that ExxonMobil violated federal environmental laws. Girardi & Keese, the law firm made famous for collaborating with Erin Brockovich to sue PG&E in California, filed a separate case on behalf of five hundred plaintiffs. (These cases were later consolidated.) The oil companies denied the allegations. In 2006, the state's then attorney general, Eliot Spitzer, announced he would investigate the Newtown Creek oil spill. In 2007, his successor, Andrew Cuomo, sued ExxonMobil to force a cleanup. In 2008 the EPA agreed to test four industrial sites along the creek for toxic chemicals.

As in the case of the potentially toxic dust generated at Ground Zero on 9/11, no one really knows how the chemicals polluting Newtown Creek have affected people's health. There is no conclusive link between the oil and chemical spill and human sickness in Greenpoint.

An ExxonMobil spokeswoman pointed out that the company has had no active refinery operations in Greenpoint since 1963 and no terminal operations there since 1993. ExxonMobil's lead counsel on the spill, Peter Sacripanti, said it was not clear where the pollutants originated from, or who was responsible for them, and maintained that ExxonMobil should not be held liable for an environmental mess created at a time when standards were less stringent than they are today. "We do not believe we should be required to compensate the City of New York for someone else's contamination," a company statement read.

After a 1990 consent decree, the company agreed to remediate a portion of the oil beneath Brooklyn by 2007. To do so, ExxonMobil used a system of recovery wells, storage tanks, and groundwater monitors. The wells use a dual-phase recovery system, in which a pump draws down the water table in a specific area while oil is sucked up. The water that is pumped out is treated and emptied back into Newtown Creek; the petroleum recovered is shipped to a refinery in New Jersey, where it is reprocessed for use. (BP ran four additional wells in Greenpoint.)

Environmentalists characterized the remediation efforts as "rudimentary." By 2007, the oil companies had removed a total of nine million gallons of oil. A containment boom at the Peerless bulkhead allowed for the skimming of twenty-eight thousand gallons of oil from the surface of Newtown Creek, but it is hardly an oil-tight barrier—as I witnessed when I toured the creek with Riverkeeper in 2008, and on other visits in 2009 and 2010. Thick, iridescent patches of oil float on the water, especially along the edges, and the smell of hydrocarbons is unmistakable.

In a related but separate case, the city sued oil companies for contaminating groundwater in Brooklyn and Queens. The city's water utility, the Department of Environmental Protection (DEP), has long searched for extra sources of freshwater to supplement its supplies from upstate. The Brooklyn-Queens Aquifer (BQA) could provide a valuable supply for the city in case of drought, a major water tunnel failure, or widespread fire—except that it is contaminated.

In 2007, the DEP issued the "Brooklyn-Queens Aquifer Feasibility Study," which outlined a massive multiphase cleanup of the soils and water beneath Brooklyn and Queens; it envisioned adding some 100 million to 200 million gallons of BQA water per day to the city's drinking water system. (Currently the city uses 1.3 billion gallons of freshwater a day, of which the BQA provides less than 1 percent.) The project has not been funded, but the city has used the tainted aquifer as a legal tool to go after polluters.

In 2003, the city sued twenty-three oil companies over MTBE contamination of the aquifer. MTBE (methyl tertiary butyl ether) is an additive used to oxygenate gasoline, which helps cars burn gas cleanly and reduces tailpipe emissions. MTBEs are highly soluble in water, have leaked from storage tanks across the country, and are suspected carcinogens. The city reached settlements totaling $15 million with all of the companies but one: ExxonMobil.

The city sought $250 million in damages to underwrite a new treatment plant to clean the water in five wells in southeastern Queens. The oil giant denied it was responsible for polluting the BQA, but in 2009 a federal jury found ExxonMobil liable for contaminating the aquifer and said the company knew of the potential for MTBE pollution but had failed to warn the public. The court awarded the city $104.7 million, and New York declared "total victory." Yet even that rich payout is nowhere near enough to clean up the site or compensate Greenpoint residents.

"AN HISTORIC TURNING POINT"

Today Newtown Creek remains mostly lifeless. Experts have deemed it "severely stressed" and say that it is no longer a functioning ecosystem. Seagulls, cormorants, and the occasional heron are seen along its banks, but the water and mud they wade in is noxious. When a dolphin was spotted swimming upstream in the spring of 2010, biologists worried about its health and were relieved when it turned and swam downstream into the relatively clean water of New York Harbor.

Newtown Creek is part of the New York–New Jersey Harbor Estuary, which the EPA lists as an "estuary of national significance." The agency has been sampling the creek's water since the 1980s; when EPA scientists tested the creek bed in 2009, they found sediments along its entire length were impregnated with toxic contaminants.

By 2010, the oil companies ExxonMobil, BP, and Chevron had removed 11 million gallons of oil from the contaminated zone. Depending on which experts you believe, another 20 million gallons of oily pollutants could remain beneath Greenpoint; it is even possible that the vapors trapped underground could explode again. ExxonMobil estimates it will take twenty years to pump the remaining oil out of the ground and water there. But even then, the soil will remain saturated with other toxic compounds, such as xylene, toluene, and methane.

In October 2010, the creek was designated a Superfund site, meaning the federal government will mandate a rigorous cleanup. While the Superfund law allows for the use of federal funds for remediation—which the

EPA estimates will take at least fifteen years and cost over $400 million—most of the cost will be borne by the polluters. Numerous companies are likely to be on the hook, and five of them—ExxonMobil, BP, Chevron Texaco, Phelps Dodge, and National Grid—have already volunteered to underwrite the remediation. A Superfund designation requires years of environmental study of a site before work can begin. Once under way, the cleanup might consist of a light dredging of contaminated soil, which would be replaced with clean fill, or it might require a much deeper cleaning, to thoroughly scour out the contaminants. Either way, the cleanup will only remove toxins from the shoreline and sediments of Newtown Creek. It does not address other, equally pressing, water quality issues, such as storm-water runoff and raw sewage spewing into local waters, which aren't eligible.

As with thousands of other contaminated sites across the country, the only way to completely remediate the black mayonnaise is to excavate the entire polluted zone, including the creek bed, the shoreline, and much of the neighborhood, and replace it with clean fill. This would be massively expensive and would require the government to condemn a large swath of Greenpoint. It will never be practical to entirely rid Greenpoint of industrial pollutants.

More likely, the polluted zone will be partly cleaned, and the remaining pollutants will be capped and left alone. This solution is far from perfect—it will allow toxins to continue to leak into the water and the soil—but it is a pragmatic compromise similar to those instituted in New York Harbor and the Hudson River. Wildlife has returned to those waterways, which remain polluted by PCBs and mercury, making their fish and ducks unsafe to eat.

As the seriousness of Brooklyn's environmental pollution became clear in the first decade of this century, Greenpoint residents, local environmental groups, Riverkeeper, the borough of Brooklyn, and Attorney General Cuomo increased pressure on ExxonMobil to accelerate and expand its cleanup efforts. Finally, in mid-November 2010, the company agreed to settle with Cuomo (by then the state's governor-elect); speed the cleaning of the water, soil, and air in Greenpoint; and pay $25 million in penalties, damages, environmental restoration fees, and future costs. It was the largest single payment of its kind in state history.

ExxonMobil officials said they were "pleased" that the settlement resolved numerous legal actions and vowed the company would "remain in Greenpoint until the remediation effort is done—and done right." Paul

Gallay, the Hudson Riverkeeper's executive director, hailed the settlement as "an historic turning point," which it was. Yet it did not resolve the two class-action suits, in which residents such as Sebastian Pirozzi are seeking billions of dollars' worth of restitution for harm to their property values and for potential health costs related to the oil spill.

"After all we've been through, I hope we can [resolve] the lawsuit soon," said Pirozzi. "It's taken so long. But whatever happens, it's not going to change my cancer. I still have some bitterness about that."

THE WORST OIL SPILL IN HISTORY

On April 20, 2010, the Deepwater Horizon, a drill rig contracted by BP to prospect for oil miles beneath the Gulf of Mexico, suffered a catastrophic blowout and exploded in a giant fireball that could be seen from thirty-five miles away. The disaster killed eleven men, sank one of the world's most sophisticated drilling platforms, and spewed at least 2.5 million gallons of oil per day into the Gulf—equivalent to an *Exxon Valdez* spill every four days. Eighty-six days later, BP managed to cap the well. The Coast Guard predicted it could take years to remediate the giant oil slick, which threatened seashores in Louisiana, Mississippi, Alabama, and Florida, and freshwater supplies as it entered tributary rivers. The Justice Department initiated a criminal investigation to determine if environmental laws had been violated, and BP's CEO was forced to resign.

The BP oil spill has been widely described as "the worst environmental disaster in the nation's history." Given the gravity and magnitude of the calamity, it is tempting to accept this headline, but it is not entirely accurate.

We tend to think of oil spills as dramatic events—crude carriers impaled on Alaskan rocks, a blowout shooting geysers of oil into the Texas desert, a burning platform sinking into the Gulf of Mexico. But these cases are the exception rather than the rule. Spectacular disasters such as BP's Gulf spill divert our attention from slower-moving, nearly invisible disasters, such as the pollution of Newtown Creek, which can prove even more insidious in the long run because they are less likely to be cleaned up.

The worst oil pollution caused by humans originates not in a single giant disaster but in millions of tiny leaks from the cars, trucks, motorcycles, lawn mowers, boats, planes, snowmobiles, and other machines we use every day. Gasoline that spills during refueling, or oil that drips from an engine, falls to the ground, where it is eventually washed into sewers or creeks that flow into rivers, lakes, or the ocean. The cumulative effect of these millions of tiny leaks is even worse than that of the sinking of the Deepwater Horizon.

According to *Oil in the Sea III*, a respected 2003 report by the National Research Council, humans spill more than 300 million gallons of oil into North American waters every decade, which is nearly double the highest estimate of the BP spill. Worldwide, the report said, some 4 billion gallons of oil leaks into the world's oceans every decade, more than twenty-five times the highest estimate from the BP tragedy. (Natural seepage of oil is another major problem and could be as much as 493 million gallons a decade in North American waters alone, according to the report.) Neither government nor industry track such small-scale spills, and woefully little research has been done on their health and environmental impacts. What is known is that small amounts of oil-based products contain toxic compounds that kill marine life and cause cancer in humans.

Likewise, it is easy to forget that across the country, thousands of industrial spills, many left over from a less regulated time, continue to poison groundwater, leak toxins into rivers and lakes, and impact human and environmental health in ways that are difficult to define or even to imagine.

These cases are reminders of the unintended consequences of man's progress, moral lessons about our long-term impact on the environment for short-term gain. Yet, in an ironic twist, and in defiance of easy categorizing, some of the nation's most polluted rivers and lakes contain the promise of rescue and redemption.

CHAPTER 3

Going to Extremes

THE RIVER NEXT DOOR

Don't drink too much Housatonic River water. Don't swim in it for long. Don't dig your hands into the river's muddy banks and put your fingers into your mouth, as children like to do. While you are welcome to catch the river's plentiful fish for sport—brown and rainbow trout, large- and smallmouth bass, northern pike, perch, bluegill, catfish, suckers—don't eat them. The same goes for the ducks, weasels, and other animals that live along the riverbanks. The Housatonic contains some of the highest levels of PCBs (polychlorinated biphenyls) of any river in America—or in the world.

The Housatonic River flows 149 miles, from the Berkshire Mountains of western Massachusetts, down the length of Connecticut, to the coast, where it empties into Long Island Sound and the Atlantic. For centuries, the Mohican and Schaghticoke Indians, and the creatures they subsisted on—squirrels, ducks, wild turkeys, turtles, frogs, and catfish (which were slathered in mud from the river bottom and baked over a fire)—lived on the Housatonic. The river is bucolic, and its pristine-looking waters draw legions of canoeists, fishermen, and campers. But the river's clarity is deceiving.

Between 1932 and 1977, the General Electric (GE) plant in Pittsfield dumped or leaked thousands of pounds of PCBs into the Housatonic. Exactly how many pounds is disputed. GE has acknowledged that the plant discarded almost forty thousand pounds of PCBs into the river, which, the company is quick to note, was legal at the time. But others, including two former senior GE employees, and the watchdog group Housatonic River Initiative (HRI), believe the actual amount was at least 1.5 million pounds, and probably more. (Neither of these estimates include the other toxic substances—such as benzene, chlorobenzene, trichloroethylene, and methyl chloride—that GE buried around town.) Most of the Housatonic, from GE's now shuttered plant in Pittsfield down to the river's outfall in Long Island Sound, is tainted by PCBs.

PCBs are synthetic oils, made by heating benzene with chlorine; they are part of a class of chemicals known as congeners, which were once nearly ubiquitous industrial solvents, coolants, and lubricants. From 1903 to 1979 PCBs were used as fire retardants and hydraulic fluids, and in joint compounds, waterproofing, plastic manufacturing, surgical implants, and carbonless carbon paper.

Because they weigh 35 percent more than water does, PCBs don't float in an obvious slick on the surface, like the oil in Newtown Creek. They drop to the bottom of a waterway, cling to sediments, and enter the food chain through aquatic plants and invertebrates. PCBs are classic legacy pollutants: they do not break down readily in H_2O and can persist for years. After contaminated cooking oil poisoned thousands of residents in Japan and Taiwan, many countries banned PCB use in 1977. It took another two years before Congress banned PCB production and distribution in the United States. The compounds are now outlawed in most nations. But it is estimated that over 1.5 billion pounds of PCBs still linger in the environment. They have been detected in a broad variety of animal species and even in rain-forest tribes and Eskimos, who have never used them.

As they work their way up the food chain, PCBs bioaccumulate in the tissue of fish, amphibians, mammals, and birds. Predators at the top of the food chain—such as eagles, orca whales, or humans—carry the highest levels of toxins. Doctors call the load of pollutants that accumulates in animal tissues the *body burden.*

Prolonged exposure to PCBs can cause severe acne and rashes and has been linked to childhood obesity and diabetes. PCBs may damage the liver, cause hormonal disruptions, and impact fertility. In high doses, PCBs cause cancer in animals, and they are regarded as probable carcinogens in people; they are especially linked to cancers of the liver and biliary tract.

The maximum allowable exposure level of PCBs in humans is two parts per million (ppm). The Housatonic's fish contain PCB concentrations of up to 206 ppm, which are among the highest levels ever recorded. Housatonic ducks showed average PCB levels of 100 ppm, levels rarely seen anywhere else in the world. One of the first ducks trapped near Pittsfield registered a PCB count of an astonishing 3,700 ppm, and its carcass was treated as "flying hazardous waste." Even small amounts of PCBs are dangerous. In one study, half the mink puppies fed Housatonic fish with PCB levels of only 4 ppm died quickly, and the surviving pups eventually developed jaw lesions, tooth loss, anorexia, and then died.

A 2009 EPA study of the Housatonic concluded, "Fish, other aquatic animals, and wildlife in the river and floodplain contain concentrations of PCBs that are among the highest ever measured. . . . Natural recovery from this contamination . . . will take decades if not hundreds of years."

About forty miles south of Pittsfield, the Housatonic passes through the small town in northwest Connecticut where my parents have a house. Here, the river sweeps beneath a red covered bridge, past boulder-strewn banks and verdant hills. Despite warning signs posted on trees, my friends and I spent countless hours canoeing and fishing a ten-mile stretch of "the Housie" and occasionally swam in it and ingested its water. But it was not until I wrote this book that I realized how contaminated the river is. Nor did I understand why GE's legendary chairman, Jack Welch, fought the cleanup of the Housatonic, and the nearby Hudson River, in New York, so hard for so long.

In 1903, GE, which had been founded by Thomas Edison a few years earlier, bought the Stanley Electric Company and began to manufacture three important product lines in Pittsfield: electrical capacitors and transformers, military ordnance, and plastics. For the next seven decades, Pittsfield was a one-company town, and the GE plant expanded to over 5 million square feet of buildings on a 254-acre site. "The GE" employed eighteen thousand people during the Second World War—75 percent of the local workforce—and as many as sixty-five hundred in the 1980s. But in the 1990s, the company began to shut down its Pittsfield operations and sent work to its plants in the South or overseas.

GE first used PCBs in Pittsfield in 1932, as an insulating fluid in its electrical equipment. But the plant produced so much PCB-contaminated oil that workers ran out of places to bury it on company grounds. Numerous pipes dumped PCB-laden water and oil into the ground, storm drains, and nearby Silver Lake, as well as directly into the Housatonic River. PCBs and other chemicals were poured into metal drums and buried off-site. PCB-laced oil was sprayed onto dirt roads as a dust suppressant. Wooden blocks soaked with PCBs were dumped into a nature preserve, Brattle Brook Park. Still, the PCBs kept piling up.

The Harvard School of Public Health sounded an alarm about the possible adverse effects of PCBs in 1937, but the companies that produced and used the chemicals ignored the warnings, and government regulators never addressed the question seriously. In the 1940s, a few Pittsfield residents complained about the PCBs, but most locals remained unaware of the problem or were unwilling to criticize the region's biggest employer. GE assured citizens that Pittsfield would not be harmed, a message it repeated for decades.

In the 1950s, GE offered the residents of Pittsfield free "clean fill," which was really fuller's earth, a Kitty Litter–like substance used to absorb spilled PCBs. All that the recipients of the fuller's earth had to do was to sign a waiver agreeing that they had received clean fill and would not hold GE liable for any health problems resulting from it. They happily did so—unaware that it was toxic, according to HRI—and used the fill in construction projects or to enhance their lawns and gardens.

In the 1970s Massachusetts health authorities discovered that milk from cows grazed along the banks of the Housatonic near Pittsfield was contaminated by PCBs. GE bought portions of two farms built on the river's floodplain. Four decades later, signs are still posted along the river, warning of PCB pollution and advising people not to consume the Housatonic's fish, waterfowl, frogs, and turtles. Yet some people ignore the signs and eat the local fish and ducks anyway—a practice, the EPA said, that makes them a thousand times more susceptible to serious medical problems.

In 1997, GE ran ads that said, "There have been a lot of studies of long-term worker exposure to PCBs, and they show overwhelmingly that even workers who had close contact with PCBs day after day showed no unusual health problems."

That year, it was discovered that the soil in a playground in a largely African American neighborhood of Pittsfield was laced with PCBs. The revelation made headlines across the country. Then Lakewood, a neighborhood mostly populated by Italian American families, was discovered to contain extremely high levels of PCBs. One house lot was found to have 44,000 ppm of PCBs: GE bought the house, tore it down, and fenced off the lot. But the greatest indignity was Hill 78, once a five-acre ravine next to Allendale Elementary School. Beginning in the 1930s, GE began shoveling PCB-laced earth into the ravine until it grew into a tall mound. The pile remains today, looming about forty feet over the school. Soil samples from inside Hill 78 register PCB levels of 120,000 ppm. The soil around the school has been excavated and "capped" with untainted soil, but traces of PCBs have been found in air filters inside the school's buildings, according to HRI. In the 1990s, the EPA said it would clean Hill 78, but in 2000 the agency suddenly reversed course. Not only would Hill 78 remain as it was, the EPA said, but PCBs dredged from the Housatonic would be added on top of it.

As GE began to lay off workers and pull out of town, some Pittsfield residents rose up to protest the toxic legacy it had left behind.

"THE WORST THING
THAT EVER HAPPENED TO PITTSFIELD"

On a brisk November afternoon in 2009, Tim Gray pulled his blue minivan to a stop along the Housatonic River in Pittsfield and pointed upstream at the hulking shell of the old General Electric plant. "When the EPA and the Massachusetts Department of Environmental Protection (DEP) people first got here, the situation was so out of control that they became shell-shocked," he said. "That plant was literally marinating in toxic chemicals. The regulators had no idea what to do. They weren't evil people, it's just they had never seen anything like it before. When a few of us tried to help, they didn't want to hear from us."

Gray first encountered PCBs in 1976, when, as an undergraduate studying natural resource science at the University of Massachusetts–Amherst, he and some friends tested the Housatonic's water and discovered PCBs in the river below the GE plant. His research was ignored, but, indignant about the pollution, Gray, now a soft-spoken greenhouse operator, helped form the Housatonic River Initiative, won allies, and kept shouting from the rooftops until his foes had no choice but to listen.

Gray and his neighbors, many of whom were former GE employees, are working-class people who live along the Housatonic. As they see it, GE made a mess of the river and should clean it up. "We want our grandkids to have 'a fishable, swimmable' river, like the Clean Water Act says," Gray explained. "It's pretty simple—or, at least that's what we thought when we started this thing."

HRI has been a constant thorn in the side of both GE and Massachusetts regulators, using its own experts to show that GE dumped far more PCBs into the river than it claimed; that PCBs have leached under the river and can evaporate into the air; that over eight hundred barrels filled with PCBs were dumped into the Pittsfield landfill; and that ducks poisoned in Massachusetts can fly into Connecticut.

This enrages local boosters. Pittsfield is the county seat, a city of forty-five thousand set in the foothills of the Berkshire Mountains. The region is gentrifying from a rural agricultural and industrial zone into a popular destination for urban transplants and arts institutions. But the legacy of GE's pollution is a shadow that looms over the aspirational dreams of developers and politicians.

The aquifer beneath Pittsfield holds a vast store of water, but it is heavily contaminated by industrial chemicals, including PCBs, and cleaning it would be prohibitively expensive. Instead, the city draws drinking water from nearby reservoirs, which are clean. But the tainted groundwater could impede future growth, as could HRI's constant harping about the Housatonic.

One former mayor of Pittsfield called Tim Gray "the worst thing that ever happened to Pittsfield," among other names. But such attacks only stiffen HRI's resolve.

Standing in his kitchen, Dave Gibbs, a rangy former crane operator at the GE plant who is now the president of HRI, said, "The company never said nothin' to me—or any of the other workers—about the danger in those chemicals. *Nothin'!*"

Gibbs lives off Newell Street, with a view of the GE plant from his backyard. For years, a grassy field there was used by GE as a chemical dump. The *Boston Globe* unearthed a 1948 memo showing that GE officials were worried about residents' growing opposition to the burial of PCBs: "This is the last section anywhere near the plant where we can dump most anything," one company man confided to another. "I would hate to have them take it away." In 2000, EPA inspectors discovered dozens of old capacitors, corroded barrels filled with PCBs, and what Gibbs calls "a Campbell's soup of dioxins, ethylene, solvents, and other toxic chemicals" buried in the field. When GE contractors excavated the field, Gibbs and his wife clandestinely videotaped the contractors crushing barrels and spreading chemicals as they worked.

The top two feet or so of earth in Gibbs's yard was scraped away and replaced by clean fill. But Gibbs doesn't believe it helped. The field behind his house yielded PCB levels of three hundred thousand parts per million, he said, "which is basically pure product." Though it is impossible to prove a link to the PCBs, Gibbs's dog developed a rare blood vessel cancer and died, and several neighbors—including his parents, sister, and aunt—contracted leukemia and other cancers, and several of them died. Gibbs and at least 150 other residents who live along the Housatonic in

Berkshire County have PCB levels higher than the EPA limit of 2 ppb in their blood.

"You lied to me, General Electric!" Gibbs shouted from his deck. "Now my job is to find some very sharp sticks and poke you in the eye."

In 1991, the federal EPA began legal proceedings to define the scope of the Housatonic's pollution by GE. The company steadfastly maintained that its dumping of PCBs was legal and safe, and refused to acknowledge it was responsible for cleaning the river. Nevertheless, the EPA found that exposure to PCBs led to "increases in cancer mortality in workers," while experts worried that major storms or floods could spread PCBs widely and in uncontrolled ways. In 1996, the government sued GE, and the following year placed the Housatonic and Pittsfield on the Superfund National Priorities List—a preliminary step the government takes before designating a contaminated site ready for Superfund cleanup, which acts as a stern warning to alleged polluters. In a settlement, GE begrudgingly agreed to clean a half-mile stretch of the Housatonic below its Pittsfield factory.

One major roadblock was Jack Welch. A Massachusetts native, Welch began his storied career at GE in the Pittsfield plant in 1960, as a $10,000-a-year engineer; he later rose to become the plant's manager. In 1998, when Welch earned $83.6 million a year as the company's chairman and CEO, he testified, "PCBs do not pose health risks. Based on the scientific evidence . . . we simply do not believe that there are any significant adverse health effects."

The EPA argued that the PCBs should be scraped out of the Housatonic and sealed away in a landfill, but Welch vehemently disagreed. He hired scientists and lawyers and spent years challenging the need to remove the contaminated mud from the river bottom—an expensive, technically challenging process. The company's lawyers devised a clever argument that it repeated as often as possible: dredging up PCBs would only stir them into the water column and cause more health problems than if they were left alone; if left buried in the river's sediment, the PCBs would biodegrade over time.

HRI and others disputed this logic (the EPA notes that the type of PCBs found in the Housatonic take "hundreds of years" to degrade), yet regulators were unable, or unwilling, to force the company's hand.

GE used the same argument to deny that it was responsible for cleaning another load of PCBs—at least 1.3 million pounds' worth—that the company had dumped into the Hudson River, in New York, between 1947 and 1977. The Hudson is an estuarine river, with a rich fishery famous for its runs of striped bass and shad. But in 1976, all fishing was banned in the Hudson's upper reaches, due to concerns over toxins in the sediment and fish. In 2002, the EPA issued a Record of Decision, which defined 197 miles of the Hudson a Superfund site (the largest in the nation), and required GE to undertake a massive restoration effort.

Although the Superfund law holds polluters retroactively responsible for any cleanup, GE maintained that the PCBs in the Hudson were better left undisturbed, and delayed the case for years. Between 1990 and 2005, activist shareholders discovered that GE had spent $122 million on political donations, lobbyists, scientific experts, and lawyers—such as Harvard Law School's constitutional expert Laurence Tribe—to avoid dredging the Hudson.

In 2001 Jack Welch retired and was replaced as GE chairman by Jeffrey Immelt, who agreed to work with the EPA to dredge the Hudson clear of PCBs. In May 2009, a dredge lowered a blue clamshell bucket into the river near the town of Moreau, New York, and brought up the first scoop of toxic mud, which it deposited in a hopper barge. Once dewatered at a $100 million GE treatment plant, the contaminated Hudson mud was wrapped in plastic and shipped by rail to a dump in West Texas. By the time it is finished in 2015, GE's remediation of the Hudson will be the most complex and expensive environmental cleanup in history. The first phase will remove 22 tons of the pollutant from the river; the second phase will remove 102 tons. Federal officials say the program will cost $750 million, though industry experts estimate the total cost will be "much larger than that."

Money helps to explain GE's recalcitrance: the company is wholly or partially responsible for 175 Superfund sites across the country, according to *Harper's*. If it is forced to clean up the Hudson and the Housatonic, then GE could well be obliged to pay for expensive cleanups elsewhere.

Cleanup of the Housatonic has gone more slowly, with much less fanfare than the larger Hudson case. By 2008, GE had spent $250 million to clean a two-mile section of the river below its Pittsfield plant. The EPA maintains that the two miles of dredged river will not become recontaminated by PCBs, but that seems like wishful thinking. PCBs remain in the river's banks, in its wide floodplains, and in storm drains that empty into the river. Silver Lake, which feeds the Housatonic, and Woods Pond, through which the river flows, remain polluted by PCBs. And the 147 miles of river south of the cleaned zone remain contaminated, mostly at dam sites, where PCBs collect. In preparation for a second phase of remediation, GE proposed a set of Corrective Measures, which outline ten different options for cleaning the "rest of river" downstream of the remediated zone. One plan calls for PCB-laden mud to be dredged from the river and its flood-plains, loaded into trucks, and deposited in landfills or local ponds over the next fifty years. This scenario scares local people. But a coalition of environmentalists, sportsmen, and environmental groups complain that GE's plan is outdated and hugely expensive, could remove the dredged material by railway instead of trucks (as is done along the Hudson), and is akin to a blunt instrument that will damage wildlife and will not guarantee the removal of PCBs.

Instead, activists propose a ten-point plan that emphasizes careful, cost-minded planning, environmentally sensitive remediation of PCBs in only a few sites at a time, and postfact evaluations of the effectiveness of the cleanup.

"We've made progress, but there's just so much more to do," sighed Tim Gray. "I doubt this river will ever be 'fishable and swimmable' in my life-time, if ever."

He was cautiously optimistic that President Obama's EPA would push GE to undertake a more extensive cleanup than President Bush's did. But GE will likely resort to its by now familiar strategy: drag out the case for as long as possible, use up HRI's limited resources, and bog down regulators. If that fails, the company could take the case to the US Supreme Court, where Chief Justice John Roberts has proven to be industry-friendly.

As in the case of Newtown Creek, the only "permanent solution" for cleaning the Housatonic is to dig up all of the buried chemicals; treat all of the polluted water, sediments, and floodplains along the entire length of the river; and replace the soil with clean fill so that no PCB contamination is left. Even Tim Gray doesn't believe such comprehensive remediation is possible. What he does envision is something nearly as radical: turning Pittsfield's misfortune into its salvation.

Industrial pollution is a national—and global—problem, and as Gray sees it, this presents an unusual opportunity. He envisions transforming Pittsfield from a down-on-its-heels Industrial Age shell into a booming, Silicon Valley–like hub for the study of pollution control, a magnet for academics and businesses to pursue innovative remediation technologies. Gray has already investigated a number of novel techniques, such as using bacteria or earthworm enzymes to "digest" pollution. Why not scale this research up a hundredfold and turn it into a revenue producer?

"I could really see turning all the negatives into a big positive for the region," he said. "I mean, why not—all we need is funding."

Standing in front of Pittsfield's dark, haunted GE plant, the idea seems quixotic, at best. But Gray is not delusional. Similar initiatives to turn industrial toxins into profits have taken root in places even more blighted than Pittsfield—such as Butte, Montana.

THE SILVER LINING TO A DARK PIT

From the late nineteenth through much of the twentieth centuries, the Anaconda Copper Mining Company extracted tons of silver and copper from mines bored around Butte, known as "Mining City" and "the richest hill on earth." But the company also dumped tons of mine tailings (waste rock) and heavy metals directly into Silver Bow Creek, which flows into the Upper Clark Fork River, creating a poisonous plume 150 miles long. ARCO, the Atlantic Richfield Company—now part of BP—bought Anaconda in 1977. In 1982, as copper prices dropped, it shut down the company's Berkeley Pit and removed pumps that had kept it dry. Since then, about 2.6 million gallons of water have flowed into the thirty-nine-thousand-foot-deep pit every day.

The water in the pit is oxblood red at the surface, a color derived from iron and manganese; deeper down, the water turns a lime green, from heavy copper compounds. The water is also suffused with heavy metals and toxic chemicals, including arsenic, lead, cadmium, zinc, and sulfuric acid. It is, in essence, an acid lake.

In 1995 a flock of 342 snow geese landed on the poisonous lake, and every one of them died. ARCO blamed the death of the geese on a "grain fungus," but the theory was widely ridiculed; tests showed that the acidic water had eaten away the epithelium that lines the esophagus and then attacked the birds' internal organs. Since 1998, BP-ARCO and regulators from Montana Resources have used a pontoon boat on the lake and an observation shack overlooking the pit; using shotgun blasts and "wailers" that emit predator calls and loud electronic sounds, they scare birds away from the lake. The system has been relatively effective, though dead birds continue to be found in the pit. One day in November 2007, thirty-six ducks and geese and one swan landed on the lake, but the bird patrol was blinded by snow and fog; all of the birds died.

As the copper mines began to shut down, the Anaconda smelter closed in 1980. Butte slipped into decline, and the population drained away. Starting in the 1970s, a group of enlightened residents—led by Donald Peoples, a former football coach and mayor—branded Butte the "Can-do City" and worked to replace three thousand lost jobs. In 1989, Peoples joined Mountain States Energy (MSE), a fifteen-year-old civil engineering company that treated Butte's toxic pit as a laboratory for developing new pollution cleanup processes and businesses. The company worked with the US Departments of Energy (DOE) and of Defense to engineer new ways to safely store industrial and military waste. It developed a plasma furnace that cooks toxins down to a sludge that hardens into an inactive substance. And it runs the Mine Waste Technology Program for the DOE: "The need is great," MSE's website proclaims. "Remediation cost for abandoned mines are estimated between $2 billion and $32 billion." MSE has clients in Japan and South Korea and is courting business in Europe.

By 2007, the Berkeley Pit had filled with 37 billion gallons of toxic seepage. Researchers had assumed the waters were too poisonous to support life and were shocked to discover the presence of more than a hundred types of microbes—fungi, bacteria, and algae—that had adapted to the extreme conditions. The organisms, known as extremophiles, are believed to be unique to the pit. They are being closely studied because some of them inhibit the growth of cancer cells in a laboratory setting; they have also shown the potential to inhibit enzyme reactions associated with multiple sclerosis and Huntington's disease. As unlikely as it may seem, Butte's extreme water pollution—and perhaps Pittsfield's—could one day lead to profits or even to breakthroughs in health care.

CHAPTER 4

The Number One Menace

POINT/NONPOINT

The nature of water pollutants has changed in recent decades, but regulators have not kept pace, and the public and the environment are vulnerable to new kinds of contamination.

In contrast to the obvious "point-source" pollutants of last century—the classic industrial pipe spewing brown filth into pristine waterways such as Newtown Creek or the Housatonic River—the greatest source of water pollution today is the more diffuse "nonpoint-source" pollution known as *storm-water runoff*. This term describes pollutants of many kinds, from many sources—motor oil, paint, sewage, fertilizers, insecticides, pharmaceuticals, and other contaminants—that are washed off the land by rain, snow, or mist and into water supplies.

This represents a reversal. In 1970, the EPA estimated that 85 percent of water pollution came from obvious point sources, such as factories or wastewater treatment plants; only 15 percent came from nonpoint sources, such as poultry farms, suburban lawns, or city streets. By 2010, point-source pollution had been significantly reduced, thanks largely to the Clean Water Act (CWA). Now point-source pollution accounts for only 15 percent of water contamination, while nonpoint sources account for 85 percent.

But EPA regulations have not adapted to this shift. The traditional top-down regulations of the CWA are not well suited to control runoff across a watershed. Storm-water runoff is especially difficult to identify and remediate because it is so diffuse, washes across wide swaths of landscape, and pollutes water in myriad ways. This holds as true for rural citizens who draw water from a single well as it does for urban dwellers who rely on vast systems of pipes, pumps, and reservoirs.

It was long assumed that well water was better protected from contamination than surface water. But that is not always the case. Ninety-six percent of all health violations occur at small water systems, according to the EPA, and those who use private wells are most vulnerable to contamination.

While wells are relatively cheap to build, they can be polluted by impurities, such as bacteria, viruses, parasites, fungi, fertilizers, volatile organic compounds (such as methane or formaldehyde), and naturally occurring arsenic or uranium. Frequently they are polluted by agricultural runoff, such as manure, pesticides, and nutrients.

Approximately 43 million Americans—15 percent of the population—get their drinking water from "self-supplied sources," which usually means wells. But the Safe Drinking Water Act does not protect wells that serve twenty-five or fewer people; in those cases, homeowners are responsible for the quality of their own water (and should test it). The quality of that water depends on what is happening around the well, which homeowners cannot always control.

"NOT A MATTER OF CONVENIENCE"

In February 2004, just after Samantha Treml turned six months old, her doctor suggested that her parents, Scott and Judy Treml, test their well water. The Tremls live in a rural area near the town of Luxemburg, about fifteen miles east of Green Bay, Wisconsin. Using a testing kit, they sent a sample to a state lab. A few days later they received the results: the water was free of harmful bacteria and chemicals, and perfectly safe for Samantha to drink.

Three weeks later, on the evening of February 22, Glen Stahl, who runs a large feedlot nearby, with about nine hundred cows—a so-called CAFO, or concentrated animal feeding operation—began to spread liquid manure on the field across the road from the Tremls' house. Stahl wasn't spreading the manure as fertilizer; his large storage pits had filled to nearly overflowing, and he was spreading the manure simply to get rid of it. At the time, this was a common and legal practice.

That day, eighteen inches of snow lay on the ground, but the temperature had risen to forty degrees and the snow was melting. As the snow melted into water, it carried Stahl's manure into a ditch, where it pooled and seeped through cracks in the bedrock into the groundwater, which flowed west, toward the Tremls' well. When Scott Treml asked Stahl to stop spreading manure, the farmer cursed and said he had permission to spread from the Wisconsin Department of Natural Resources (WDNR), the state environmental regulatory agency. Stahl continued to spray for three days, eventually coating the field with eighty thousand gallons of liquid feces.

On February 29, Judy Treml filled her bathtub for six-month-old Samantha; the water looked clear and was odorless. The following evening Judy turned on her kitchen tap. Instead of clear water, a thick brown liquid that smelled of fresh cow dung sputtered out. Repulsed, she jumped back and asked her husband to call the WDNR.

"Judy, I already tried," he said. "They don't care."

Scott had called David Bougie, the WDNR enforcement agent responsible for Stahl Farms. Bougie visited the field across from Treml's house and judged that there was no evidence of manure runoff. Calling other DNR officers, Scott was told by one, "I'm a very busy man . . . call someone else," and by another, "If you think that's bad, I've actually seen straw coming out of someone's kitchen tap." At a public meeting, Bougie would say only, "Glen Stahl's spreading met the conditions of his permit" and refused to take regulatory action. Feeling "utterly helpless," the Tremls walked away. Just then, a man who worked for the local government pulled them into his office and showed them a map of the field Stahl had sprayed. A shallow, fractured bedrock, known as karst, lay just beneath the surface of much of the field. Karst is porous and allows water, and the things it carries, to seep underground. State guidelines now restrict the spreading of manure on fields overlying karst.

On March 5, Scott Treml opened the door to Samantha's room to discover that the baby's hair, face, ears, body, and crib were coated in vomit and diarrhea. By the following evening, Samantha was growing listless, and the Tremls rushed her to the emergency room. The ER doctor judged that Samantha had been infected by *E. coli* from her Sunday-night bathwater.

E. coli is the common abbreviation for *Escherichia coli,* a rod-shaped bacterium that originates in the lower intestines of warm-blooded organisms. It is transmitted by animal or human feces. Some strains of *E. coli* can be beneficial to the host, but virulent forms, such as the O157:H7 strain, can cause painful cramps, diarrhea, kidney failure, or even death. Coliforms are a family of bacteria including *E. coli*; they are also associated with animal or human excrement and cause gastroenteritis. According to the EPA, the safe limit for both *E. coli* and other coliforms is zero. In Wisconsin, *E. coli* bacteria present in water at 1,000 parts per milliliter are sufficient to close a public beach. The manure flowing from the Tremls' tap had an *E. coli* count of 2,800 parts per milliliter and coliform at 9,800 parts per milliliter. Tests of the Tremls' well by the state hygiene labs confirmed that the water was contaminated by both *E. coli* and other coliform bacteria (which can be present even in clean-looking water).

"I was devastated," Judy recalled. "I had unwittingly exposed my baby to *E. coli* because I didn't have any knowledge that manure applied to the land could contaminate our drinking water."

In the hospital, the doctor explained that Samantha faced four possible outcomes: she could be sick for a few days, then recover; she could suffer kidney damage, then recover; she could suffer permanent kidney damage, which would require a transplant; or she could die.

As Judy Treml considered this, she suddenly felt woozy and was admitted to the ER, infected by the same bacteria that had sickened her daughter. At home, her two older daughters and Scott had also been stricken.

Every member of the Treml family eventually recovered, but in April 2004, with the help of Midwest Environmental Advocates, Wisconsin's only pro bono environmental law firm, they filed a notice of their intent to sue Stahl Farms for violating the Clean Water Act. The state Department of Justice also filed suit against Stahl, who had allowed manure to leak from his feedlot for twenty years while receiving more than $10,000 in state assistance to prevent environmental pollution. In January 2006, a US federal court judge approved a settlement under which Stahl's insurance company paid the Tremls $80,000 in damages. Stahl agreed not to spread manure on the field across from the Tremls' house from December through March, the period of highest risk for groundwater contamination.

Testifying before Congress about water quality in the fall of 2009, Judy Treml asked, "What's it going to take for the WDNR to enforce the Clean Water Act? I hope for our state that a death, or several deaths, isn't what it takes!"

Regulating and stopping agricultural runoff is not easy. In tight-knit farm communities, confronting neighbors is socially awkward. State regulators are torn between maintaining water quality and being sensitive to farmers, who provide food, jobs, and community leadership, while Congress has allowed large farms to "self-police," a rule that has proven ineffective.

Most farmers care deeply about the land and do not intentionally pollute. But, according to the EPA, agricultural runoff is now the single biggest source of water pollution in America. Pathogens such as *E. coli* are responsible for 35 percent of the nation's impaired waterways, and large "factory farms" are one of the most common sources of pathogens.

An estimated 19.5 million Americans are sickened each year from waterborne bacteria, viruses, or parasites, including those from animal and human sewage, according to a 2008 study by the scientific journal *Reviews of Environmental Contamination and Toxicology.*

In the United States, farmed animals produce more than 1 billion tons of manure per year. As the population, and its demand for food, continues to rise, the amount of cow, pig, goat, and poultry excrement continues to grow and to infiltrate water supplies.

The problem is not limited to Wisconsin. The Chesapeake Bay and the Gulf of Mexico—two of the most ecologically rich aquasystems in the world—have been badly contaminated by agricultural runoff. In California, up to 15 percent of wells in farming regions have water pollution above federal thresholds. In Arkansas, Maryland, and Oklahoma, residents and regulators have charged that poultry farmers have polluted important drinking supplies. Runoff from dairies and farms had such a devastating effect on Lake Okeechobee and the Everglades that the South Florida Water Management District has spent $2 billion to build forty-five thousand acres of "filter marshes" to remove some of the phosphorus flowing into the water.

Under the ideal cycle, manure is used to fertilize crops, which are in turn used to feed the cows. This was the traditional, holistic model used on small family farms. But the number of small family farms has steadily declined since the Second World War—as of 2002, only 25 percent of US farms were considered family farms—while the number of CAFOs has steadily risen, due largely to their economies of scale.

Farming is a significant industry. In 2008, US farms held 96 million head of cattle, 68 million pigs, 9 billion broiler chickens, and 446 million laying hens. Cattle farming was a $48.6 billion business, while milk production was valued at $34.8 billion, broiler production at $23.1 billion, and poultry egg production at $8.2 billion. The incentive to expand these profit centers is large, but they have a significant health and environmental cost.

Cows are relentless eaters, and a cow's digestive system, with its series of four stomachs, produces a steady stream of manure. Dairy cows are often fed a high-protein diet, which increases milk production and results in liquid manure that is easier to spray than solid manure. A single lactating Holstein emits 150 pounds of waste every day—usually two-thirds wet manure and one-third urine. This is equivalent to the daily waste of eighteen people. A large farm with four thousand cows will produce some 200 million pounds of manure a year.

Wisconsin had 19 CAFOs in 1992; by 2009, the number had leaped to 185, and the WDNR had 50 new applications under review. In January 2010, state regulators green-lit Wisconsin's biggest CAFO yet: Rosendale Dairy, a $70 million operation that will house eight thousand cows and produce 92 million gallons of manure a year—which is more biological waste than every city in the state other than Madison and Milwaukee produce in a year.

The largest dairy in the world is Threemile Canyon Farms, a few miles from the Columbia River, near Boardman, Oregon. The farm promotes itself as "sustainable" and "green" and claims it contains forty-one thousand head of cattle, though news reports say the farm contains fifty-five thousand cows and is permitted to contain ninety thousand. This industrial-scale operation is jointly owned by A. J. Bos, of Bakersfield, California, who runs one of the largest dairy operations in the country, and R. D. Offutt, of Fargo, North Dakota, one of the largest potato growers in the United States. Threemile Canyon produces an estimated half a million tons of manure per year.

At times, CAFOs produce so much liquid manure that it overwhelms a farmer's ability to store it; in that case, he will usually spread it on fields to get rid of it. Not infrequently, this excess manure is washed off the land by precipitation. Glen Stahl apparently faced this situation when he sprayed eighty thousand gallons of liquid cattle feces on the field next to the Tremls' house.

Aside from pathogens such as *E. coli,* manure also contains nutrients, such as phosphorus and nitrogen, that, in excess, can create havoc in the ecosystem. Phosphorus is a common supplement used to stimulate milk production; but many farmers add more phosphorus than necessary, just to "make sure" their cows lactate productively. Nitrogen originates in cattle feed, such as distillers' grains, the waste left over from corn fermentation, which supplies dairy cows with protein. (Distillers' grains cause cows to produce greenhouse gases—including ammonia, methane, and other volatile compounds—which has stirred a debate over agricultural air pollution.) Cattle in the United States excrete some 3 million pounds of phosphorus and 8 million pounds of nitrogen a day.

When manure is spread on fields, crops absorb some of these nutrients, but the majority is washed off the land into waterways. This can cause human health problems, such as cyanosis, in which the hemoglobin in blood is deoxygenated (commonly known as the blue baby syndrome, because tissues low on oxygen fill with dark, deoxygenated blood, which gives the skin a blue cast). Moreover, excess nutrient flows in agricultural regions—from the Great Lakes to the Sacramento Delta—have caused vast algal blooms, which block sunlight and absorb oxygen, creating lifeless underwater deserts known as dead zones.

While researchers look for new ways to use manure, such as converting it into gas to produce electricity (Threemile Canyon has built a pilot manure "digester" that traps methane gas for use as fuel), water experts say the best way to reduce agricultural runoff is to strengthen pollution laws and empower regulators to enforce them. As the law stands now, the EPA cannot shut down a farm or block it from expanding, even when its manure runoff threatens water supplies.

Despite its known hazards, agricultural runoff is poorly regulated. The Clean Water Act is focused on the quality of water in pipes and ditches and does not address more complex scenarios, such as when manure sprayed onto a field seeps into groundwater. This type of nonpoint-source pollution is governed by state laws, which are often weak or not well enforced. What's more, many farmers do not file the requisite paperwork and are rarely fined for polluting water. Under President George W. Bush, regulations were loosened to allow farms to "self-certify" that they would not pollute; many experts were not surprised when this resulted in an increase in agricultural runoff.

The EPA has instituted special rules to regulate runoff from the thousands of large CAFOs (defined by the EPA as a farm that keeps more than 700 dairy cows, 1,000 cattle, 2,500 swine, 55,000 turkeys, or between 30,000 and 125,000 chickens) that are cropping up across the country. Yet those rules have done little to stem the tide of manure that is infiltrating water supplies.

Moreover, the agricultural lobby has blocked efforts to regulate runoff that causes water pollution. In Brown County, Wisconsin, for example, officials instituted new rules to limit dairy operations and prohibit the spraying of manure during high-runoff months. But farm lobbyists inserted a provision requiring the state to finance up to 70 percent of the cost for some farms to follow the regulations, which made the program prohibitively expensive.

Other nations have grappled with these issues, and some have pioneered tough regulation. Holland instituted policies in the 1980s to limit the size of livestock farms, capping the amount of manure allowed per hectare; if a Dutch farmer wants to produce more manure than his allotment, he must buy more land to accommodate extra cows. While such an approach could theoretically work in the United States, in practice the agricultural lobby would certainly oppose it.

In the 1970s, Congress identified CAFOs as polluters to be regulated under the Clean Water Act. But the biggest facilities were able to avoid government regulation by claiming they do not discharge pollutants into waterways protected by the CWA. Incensed, a coalition of environmental groups sued the EPA in 2009 to force regulators to monitor the effects of factory farms on waterways more closely. Gathering more—and higher-quality—data, the environmentalists hope, will eventually lead to tougher regulations and better water protection. The EPA has settled the suit and committed to finalizing new rules by 2012.

Urban dwellers hear of these battles over manure and assume that they don't affect them; after all, they don't draw water from wells, don't live next to CAFOs, and don't understand how agricultural runoff could possibly impact their water supplies. But it does.

When she testified about water pollution before Congress in 2009, Judy Treml pointed out that Stahl's manure runoff was not simply her problem: the creek he polluted flows into the Kewaunee River, which supplies Lake Michigan, the third largest of the Great Lakes. Twelve million people live along the shores of the lake, including in major cities such as Milwaukee and Chicago. Lake Michigan was badly polluted during the Industrial Age but has recently been the focus of intensive cleanup efforts. This has put the states around it—Wisconsin, Illinois, Indiana, and Michigan—in an ironic predicament: while they have made costly and largely successful efforts to clean up the lake, they have simultaneously provided incentives for farms to grow, which creates more agricultural runoff.

"It makes no sense to clean up a lake only to have all the water that drains into it polluted," Treml told Congress. She added that as a homeowner, a taxpayer, and a mother, she was astounded by the lack of regulation for agricultural runoff: "It's not a matter of convenience," she said. "We need water to survive."

QUALITY

Cities face another set of runoff problems even more daunting than those faced by rural communities. With much of their surface area paved, cities do not absorb precipitation well. The thousands of pipes, valves, and pumps of city sewers are often old, leaky, and overwhelmed, especially during an intense storm burst or a prolonged rain. Furthermore, the demand on city systems to separate water from human and industrial effluent is much higher than on rural systems. Sewage treatment requires enormous amounts of energy, which is costly and adds to climate change—which ultimately creates more runoff. Most of the nation's sewer network was built in the nineteenth and twentieth centuries and has been compared to a ruptured appendix—an overburdened system that is struggling to function and remain clean.

CHAPTER 5

The Treatment

THE ART AND SCIENCE OF CSOS

It was midevening in January 2010 when a light snow turned to rain over Manhattan at just the moment when people began to wash their dinner dishes, do laundry, take showers, and flush toilets in earnest. Within minutes, thousands of gallons of storm-water was rushing off the city's nonabsorbent sidewalks, parking lots, and buildings and cascading into the sewer system. Sweeping along whatever was in its path—salty grit, candy wrappers, paint, antifreeze, leaves, abandoned toys, styrofoam cups, drug paraphernalia—the storm water dropped into a matrix of 550 pipes running beneath the streets, where it mixed with untreated feces and industrial wastes and swooshed south with gathering momentum.

As the slurry of waste rose and rose, its flow accelerated from a gentle 2.5 feet per second to a raging 9.5 feet per second, scouring sediment out of the pipes and straining the venerable system. It moved from small waste pipes eight inches in diameter, into progressively larger pipes, and then into a main seventeen feet in diameter, which channeled the water downtown to a large pumping station on East Thirteenth Street at Avenue D. There, giant pumps whirred and the sewage and storm-water mix was sent beneath the East River to Brooklyn, where it was captured by the city's newest and biggest sewage treatment plant, the Newtown Creek Wastewater Treatment Plant (NCWWTP).

This is no ordinary sewage plant. A futuristic collection of sleek gray buildings, green towers, and giant silver egg-shaped digester tanks, the NCWWTP rises incongruously from the brown-gray industrial tangle along the same waterway poisoned by the black mayonnaise of industrial pollutants. The Newtown Creek plant is a dramatic sight. Designed by the Polshek Partnership, the white-shoe architectural firm responsible for the

Clinton Library and other notable buildings, it is often wreathed in steam and occasionally erupts as methane gas is flared off. At night, the treatment plant and its giant silver "eggs" are bathed in a fantastical blue glow, from a lighting scheme designed by Hervé Descottes of L'Observatoire International, in Paris. One Greenpoint resident aptly described the plant as looking like a gleaming hunk of twenty-first-century space station that crash-landed onto Brooklyn's nineteenth-century waterfront.

The Newtown Creek plant services a large J-shaped drainage area that starts below Seventy-Fourth Street on Manhattan's Upper East Side, flows south through Chinatown, past Wall Street, and bends east under the river to encompass North Brooklyn. The drainage includes 1.33 million people spread over twenty-five square miles. Because it collects water from such a wide area, a mere one-eighth of an inch of rain translates into 63 million gallons of excess water flowing into the system, while an inch of precipitation results in 504 million extra gallons of storm water.

"That's a lot of water," said Jim Pynn, the plant's lean and garrulous superintendent. "A slow, steady rain is easier for the system to absorb than an intense storm. It only needs to be rainin' hard for twenty or thirty minutes before we have to use the throttles"—meaning the system has reached capacity.

New York's "combined" sewer system—considered state-of-the-art when it was built in the mid-nineteenth century—collects both runoff and sewage in one set of pipes. (There were no wastewater treatment plants at the time, and there was no reason to use separate sewage and storm-water pipes, as modern systems do.) To avoid massive backups during storms, which could flood streets and basements with toxic sewage, relief valves, called outfalls, allow the excess sewage to flow into local waters.

By the time the sewer pipes reach the Newtown plant, they are buried forty-five feet beneath the surface. On a "dry weather day," when the skies are clear, it requires only four pumps to lift an average of 310 million gallons of wastewater per day from the pipes. But during a heavy rainstorm—when five inches of water falls in thirty minutes, say—all ten of the plant's giant pumps are put to work and can lift up to 700 million gallons of water (usually composed of 450 million gallons of storm water and 250 million gallons of sewage) in twenty-four hours, treat it, and release it into New York Harbor.

As the wastewater pouring into the plant reached 700 million gallons that January night, Pynn grew concerned that the heavy flow was becoming dangerous: at that velocity, he said, "the water can literally erode away the sewer pipe." He ordered the throttling of eight gigantic gates—four at the Thirteenth Street pump house in Manhattan, four at the NCWWTP in Brooklyn—which diverted, or "tipped," the wastewater into outfalls around the city: raw sewage began to spew into New York Bay.

Such an event, known as a combined sewer overflow (CSO), is distressingly common. As little as one-twentieth of an inch of rain can be enough to cause the sewers to overflow, according to Riverkeeper. The city reports that 460 CSOs discharge more than 27 billion gallons of untreated wastewater into New York Harbor every year.

The effluent from CSOs has been found to contain human feces, high levels of coliform bacteria, forty types of disease-causing pathogens, viruses, industrial solvents, debris, metals, nuisance levels of "floatables," pesticides (such as malathion, an insecticide used to combat West Nile virus and the suspected cause of massive lobster die-offs in Long Island Sound), and the like. CSOs can result in water quality problems, low levels of dissolved oxygen, and nose-wrinkling odors. They have closed beaches, polluted drinking water, hindered navigation, and damaged aquatic habitats.

There are 490 outfall pipes spread around the city's five boroughs, and the Newtown plant has access to 55 of them. Pynn tries to keep untreated sewage away from already severely polluted waterways—such as Newtown Creek, the Gowanus Canal, and Jamaica Bay—reasoning that "a healthy body of water, like the Hudson, East River, or New York Bay can handle the overflows. The water is cleaner to begin with, with more dissolved oxygen in it, which helps to break down the raw sewage in twenty-one days just as well as this plant does in six hours."

By that night in January 2010, New York had 8.3 million documented residents, making it the nation's largest city, and, with twenty-seven thousand people per square mile, by far its most densely populated. Such an "ultra-urban" setting has little space for artificial runoff controls, such as catch basins and canals. Nor is there much room to collect storm water underground, as the city's subsurface is honeycombed with tunnels, ducts, and pipes that convey subways, electricity, natural gas, phone lines, television cables, steam, and water. New York's main line of defense against storm-water runoff remains its aging sewer system.

QUALITY

A WAKE-UP CALL

New York was one of the first major American cities to build a sewer system. Construction began in 1849, when the city had about half a million residents. Water and sewage conduits were made of hand-laid ceramic tile and brick, some of which remain in use. As they age, the oldest pipes are insufficient to keep up with the city's rising demand, and some of them are leaking. In 1856, the city's new pipes began to dump raw sewage directly into local waterways, including Newtown Creek. It took decades, and millions of dollars, for New York to build its current fleet of fourteen sewage plants, but the system's Achilles' heel is the "combined" pipework.

New York is not alone with this dilemma. An estimated 4 percent of the nation's twenty-five thousand municipal sewer systems use combined systems like those in New York. These are mostly in older cities in the Northeast, the Great Lakes, and in the Pacific Northwest. Newer cities equip themselves with separate pipe systems to capture and transport storm water and sewage water, to avoid CSOs.

Despite stricter laws and advances in water treatment in the 1990s, biological outbreaks have occasionally flared up, at least in part due to sewage infiltrating drinking supplies. In 1993, for example, both Washington, DC, and New York City were forced to issue temporary "boil orders" for tap water, in order to kill *E. coli* and *Cryptosporidium* (a parasitic microorganism), respectively. That same year 69 people died and an estimated 403,000 were sickened by a *Cryptosporidium* outbreak in Milwaukee tap water, in the largest recorded outbreak of waterborne disease in US history. A year later, Las Vegas suffered the nation's second-largest outbreak of *Cryptosporidium,* which killed 43 people and sickened 132 more. Between 2001 and 2006, another eighty-five minor outbreaks of waterborne illness may have been partly the result of sewage contamination.

It rains or snows in New York City every three and a half days on average, providing forty-four inches of precipitation a year. Before the city's surfaces were sealed by concrete and tarmac (which began two centuries ago), rain filtered into the soil and wetlands and was sucked up by vegetation. But as New York City expanded, impermeable streets and buildings increasingly covered absorbent earth. Between 1970 and 2000, more than nine thousand acres of land were paved over. Even the soil in some city parks and athletic fields has become so tightly compacted by heavy use that it is nearly impermeable. And in the twentieth century, 90 percent of New York's spongy wetlands were destroyed to make room for development. As a result, most of the city's precipitation washes directly into the sewers.

On an average sunny day, New York City residents discharge about 1.4 billion gallons of sewage, made up of household waste, street runoff, and industrial effluent, into more than seven thousand miles of sewer pipe. The system was carefully designed so that most of this wastewater flows by gravity alone. After being processed at one of fourteen pollution control plants, the treated effluent is flushed back into local rivers and the harbor. In a downpour, New York's sewage system can absorb the crucial first five minutes of sustained rain—the "five-minute flush"—when storm water surges through the pipes and rushes into treatment plants. But if the rainfall is sustained or arrives in an intense burst, trouble can quickly build up in the system.

A drought in 2002 kept CSOs to a minimum and local waters were relatively clean. But the rainy summers of 2003 and 2004 caused so many CSOs that New York waters were declared unhealthy, and beaches were repeatedly closed. The swimming leg of a triathlon was canceled due to the pollution from CSOs.

Most notorious was the sultry afternoon of August 14, 2003, when a massive power outage—caused by surging electricity demand, computer malfunctions, and power lines snagged in trees in Ohio—led to a rolling blackout that knocked out electricity to roughly 45 million people in the Northeastern and Midwestern United States, and another 10 million in Canada. In New York, most of the city's wastewater treatment plants used backup generators to keep functioning. But at two plants, the generators did not work, and 30 million gallons of untreated human waste was illegally discharged into the city's waters. This led to a massive increase of fecal coliform in New York Harbor and Long Island Sound and forced the closing of most city beaches. The lack of functioning generators and the discharge of sewage violated both federal and state laws. To avoid prosecution, the city had to admit it erred and was put under court supervision. City officials said that workers had repeatedly tried to have the generators repaired, but the job was never accomplished.

New Yorkers questioned whether they had been unfairly singled out, noting that a plant in Cleveland discharged at least 60 million gallons of raw sewage into the Cuyahoga River, Lake Erie, and other waterways during the blackout, while in Detroit, citizens were advised to boil their water after the city's sewer plants lost power. Neither of those cities faced prosecution. (Regulators ignored the protest.)

New York's sewer system is designed to accommodate a so-called five-year storm—a rainstorm so severe that it is predicted to fall only twice a decade. But lately weather patterns have been shifting. In 2007 alone, the city experienced three intense twenty-five-year rainstorms—storms so extreme they are predicted to occur only four times per century—which flooded subways and highways and threatened to shut down the city.

At a time when national attention was beginning to focus on the long-term effects of climate change—greater heat, more frequent and intense hurricanes, rising seas—sewage experts viewed the storms of 2007 as a wake-up call.

THE SECRETS OF SEWAGE

Sewage treatment is the generic term for the removal of contaminants from runoff and domestic wastewater via chemical, biological, and physical processes. The result is a waste stream of treated effluent and solid waste, or *sludge,* which is often filled with contaminants and toxic compounds of an almost unimaginable variety. The main objective of sewage treatment is to clean water to the point that it can be discharged back into the environment. Americans produce about 18 million tons of feces a year, and treatment plants process about 34 billion gallons of wastewater per day, according to the EPA.

Treatment in sewage plants mimics natural cleansing processes: typically, bacteria consume organic contaminants, and sunlight helps break down pollutants; when wastewater is mixed with large volumes of freshwater, it is diluted. Similarly, most pollution control plants in the United States use three stages of treatment: primary (sewage is held in tanks, where heavy solids settle to the bottom while lighter solids and oil float to the surface and are removed), secondary (the removal of dissolved or suspended biological matter, a job often performed by microorganisms), and tertiary (the disinfection of treated water by chemicals such as chlorine by ultraviolet light, or by microfiltration). By the end of this "treatment train," water is usually clean enough to be discharged back into a river, bay, or wetland, where it mixes with freshwater. Or it can be used as nonpotable gray water to irrigate parks or golf courses. If it is cleaned thoroughly enough, treated effluent is sometimes injected underground, to recharge groundwater stores that are eventually used to supply drinking water (as I will discuss later).

A sewage treatment plant was first built on the edge of Newtown Creek in 1967, to the standard of the day. This meant it used a two-step treatment process to remove 65 percent of the waste from the water passing through its system before flushing it into New York Harbor. In 1972, the federal Clean Water Act was passed, which required the removal of 85 percent of waste from treated water. The new standard rendered the plant out of compliance and set the stage for its reinvention. The Newtown plant's reconstruction began in 1998 and was supposed to be completed by 2007 but was delayed; it is now scheduled to be finished by 2015, at a cost of some $5.2 billion. At peak times, a thousand workers from twenty-five prime contractors and hundreds of subcontractors try to push the project ahead as fast as possible.

On the cold day in February 2008 that I toured the plant with Jim Pynn, the Newtown Creek Wastewater Treatment Plant was still a dusty construction site. The property was originally owned by ExxonMobil, and the first priority was to excavate 750,000 cubic yards of oil-contaminated soil and replace it with clean fill. When it is fully operational, the plant's digesters will hold 3 million gallons of sewage and process some 1.5 million gallons of sludge a day.

As Pynn weaved through a maze of silver and yellow ductwork, past settling tanks, blowers, methane-gas extractors, control rooms full of gauges and flashing computer screens, and tanks of chemicals labeled HAZARDOUS, he regaled me with tales of the things he has raked out of the sewers: turtles, fish, eels, and all manner of aquatic life. "I never found an alligator—it's an urban legend that they live in New York's sewers," he said, though he and his colleagues have recovered a working camera (which took photos as it bounced around inside sewer pipes), thousands of counterfeit dollars bundled together, drug and sex paraphernalia, teddy bears, and "basically anything you could imagine that anyone would chuck into a toilet or a sewer grate."

The primary design and cleansing feature of the plant is eight huge egg-shaped stainless steel sewage "digesters." The digesters soar 145 feet high and bulge 80 feet wide. They were based on a German design, fabricated in pieces in Texas, transported across country by rail and truck, and welded together onsite in Brooklyn. Each egg required four and a half months of welding to assemble. When empty, an egg weighs 2 million pounds; when full of sludge, each can weigh as much as 33 million pounds; they rest on a slab of concrete nine feet thick. The NCWWTP uses an "activated sludge process" that is popular in Europe but is used in only a few US cities. It works like this: raw sewage is piped into the plant, passes through screens into grit chambers (these remove silt, gravel, coffee grounds, and egg-shells, which cause wear and tear on pumps), then on to aeration (where microbes eat the "solids," aka feces), and settling tanks (where fine air bubbles mix the microorganisms, causing the oxidation of organic matter); finally, the effluent is disinfected with sodium chloride and discharged.

The Newtown plant releases its effluent into a twelve-foot-wide, forty-eight-hundred-foot-long outflow pipe that drops steeply underground and emerges under the shipping channel in the East River. Out there, the current is fast; the treated sewage effluent passes through diffusers to spread the muck out, so no visible boils or slicks occur on the surface. The Hudson River and East River flow into New York Harbor, which opens up to the Atlantic Ocean.

In the meantime, sludge (organic material) is skimmed away from the effluent and "digested" inside the plant's giant eggs. Inside the digesters, bacteria, heat, and a lack of oxygen break down the sludge; after fifteen days, what remains is water, carbon dioxide, methane gas (which is burned off), and digested sludge. The eggs' oval shape helps to concentrate grit at the bottom of the tank, aids in mixing the sludge for improved "digestion," and helps to concentrate methane gas at the top of the tank. By using this process, which avoids the traditional primary settling tanks, the city figures it will save taxpayers about $2.5 billion.

Effluent from sewage plants is a big contributor of nitrogen to New York's waters, as is the case with treatment plants across the country. A heavy nitrogen load leads to hypoxia—a lack of dissolved oxygen—the death of fish, and the growth of algae. Nitrogen is a growing threat to major bodies of water, such as Chesapeake Bay and the Gulf of Mexico, and the EPA has placed New York under a nitrogen-reduction order.

The four wastewater treatment plants that sit along the East River, including the one on Newtown Creek, discharge 482 million gallons of treated water into the river every day; this water is 85 percent clean and accounts for about 50 percent of the nitrogen load in Long Island Sound, according to the DEP.

The Clean Water Act of 1972 was designed in part to improve the nation's sewer controls and protect human and environmental health. Yet, despite $60 billion in upgrades to sewer systems in the 1970s and 1980s, CSOs continue to pose a major water pollution concern for 40 million people in thirty-two states.

BUILDING A "POROUS CITY"

In 1994 the EPA established a national framework to lessen the effects of CSOs. It recommended that the public be given ample warning when over-flows occur, and that sewer pipes be designed in such a way that they do not become blocked. In 1996, EPA budgeted $44.7 billion to implement a nationwide CSO Control Policy, a comprehensive set of water quality standards, and in 2000 the Clean Water Act was amended by Congress to reduce sewage overflows. Some cities made great progress. San Francisco eliminated seven outfalls and reduced overflows into San Francisco Bay and the Pacific Ocean by roughly 88 percent. Saginaw, Michigan, spent $100 million to eliminate twenty of its thirty-six outfalls and reaped a 75 percent reduction in annual CSO discharge. Portland, Maine, eliminated twenty-five of thirty-five outfalls, and saw an 80 percent reduction in CSOs.

But fixing large infrastructure is physically daunting, politically chal-lenging, and extremely expensive. A decade after Congress amended the Clean Water Act, hundreds of sewer systems remained out of compliance.

No national records document how many people have been sickened by CSOs, but there is anecdotal evidence. When local sewers overflowed in Milwaukee, the journal *Pediatrics* reported in 2007, the number of chil-dren suffering from diarrhea rose. In 2008, the *Archives of Environmen-tal and Occupational Health* estimated that as many as 4 million people are sickened every year from swimming in California waters tainted by pathogens linked to sewage.

These are cautionary tales, especially given that between 2006 and 2009, a third of major US sewer systems (more than ninety-four hun-dred, including those in San Diego, Houston, Phoenix, San Antonio, Philadelphia, San Jose, and San Francisco) reported violating environ-mental laws. In addition, thousands of smaller wastewater treatment systems operated by factories, mines, towns, colleges, and even mobile-home parks have broken the law. But few of the violators—less than one in five, according to a *New York Times* analysis of EPA data—were sanc-tioned or fined.

• • •

Since the 1970s, New York City has invested about $35 billion to maintain and improve the quality of its waterways and has focused on developing systems that capture CSO overflows before they are discharged into the harbor, store them until after a storm has passed, and only then send the excess water on to treatment plants.

Although rain causes Pynn headaches—and has turned him into a devotee of the Weather Channel—it is also his ally: rainwater is high in dissolved oxygen, which helps to break down pollutants. As a result of concerted cleanup efforts, the quality of New York Harbor and Hudson River water has improved significantly in the last two decades, he said, and "oxygen levels have returned nearly to their natural state." Even so, parts of the New York waterfront, including Newtown Creek, remain polluted and unsafe for recreation, especially after heavy rainstorms.

John Lipscomb, a Riverkeeper boat captain, said that city studies claiming that local waterways are cleaner are flawed because they show only average water quality; what is more important, said Lipscomb, is the quality of water at specific locations. That kind of detailed analysis is becoming more important as the city opens the plant to the public, including nature trails, art installations, and a grand stairway leading from the plant down to the polluted water of Newtown Creek. "We're going from the bad old days to a hopeful future where we're inviting people to the water," said Lipscomb. "But we don't have the information that the public really needs to make an educated decision on whether they're gonna fish there, whether they're gonna eat that fish, whether they're gonna climb down that ladder and get in the water."

As of 2010, Newtown Creek is listed by the EPA as "unclassified water," which, Pynn explained, means it is not suitable for recreational use. "We're tryin' to educate the public and promote the *concept* of fishing—as a sport," he said. "But we don't want people actually *eating* fish out of Newtown Creek."

Even with expensive improvements to the city's sewer system, "there's no way to completely stop CSOs," Pynn acknowledged. He explained that New York will have to rely on its combined sewer pipes for the foreseeable future because replacing them with a "two-pipe" system would be expensive and unpopular and would require entire neighborhoods to be excavated.

Environmental planners point to basic steps to control storm-water runoff and CSOs. New York City has allocated millions of dollars for "green" infrastructure projects, instituted new laws that give tax credits for green roofs, and required that new parking lots include landscaped areas to absorb precipitation. The next step is to plant more trees and use permeable pavement and sidewalks. These relatively cheap fixes will help recharge aquifers and enhance overall environmental quality. More ambitious plans include building large rooftop or subterranean cisterns, which collect rain and storm-water runoff and release it slowly—as has been done in the new Brooklyn Bridge Park. This takes pressure off the sewer system and cuts down on the amount of pollutants swept into waterways.

Other cities are taking similar steps. Philadelphia, for instance, has one of the nation's oldest sewer systems, which is notorious for backing up and causing floods along the Delaware and Schuylkill Rivers. But over the next two decades, it plans to reinvent itself as a "porous city." With a $1.6 billion investment, the city will plant thousands of trees, build rain gardens and urban farms, and create permeable basketball courts and parking lots that allow rain to slowly sink into gravel beds and eventually into the groundwater supply.

The volume of water flowing through sewers will increase this century, as more people produce more sewage and global warming causes more rainfall. But we have ignored our sewage infrastructure for decades, and now systems across the country are relying on outdated technology. It is a serious and growing problem. President Obama's fiscal stimulus bill of 2009 set aside $6 billion to improve water systems, and legislation on Capitol Hill includes millions of dollars in water infrastructure grants. But those funds will not be sufficient. According to estimates by the EPA and the Government Accountability Office, upgrading the nation's sewer systems will require $400 billion by 2020.

"People wonder where their water is comin' *from*, but they never think about where it *goes*, and what it takes to clean it," said Jim Pynn, waving at Newtown Creek plant's giant sewage digesters. "But wastewater treatment is absolutely vital. Imagine what would happen if this place stopped working one day? Let's just say it wouldn't be pretty."

CHAPTER 6

Brave New World

Trying to solve these [modern pollution] problems with the 1972 Clean Water Act is like trying to use a 1972 auto repair manual to repair a 2008 electric hybrid.

—Paul Freedman, vice president
of the Water Environment Federation

SEEKING A PARADIGM SHIFT

When the Clean Water Act was signed into law by President Nixon on October 18, 1972, it was hailed as landmark legislation. Over the next three decades, the law led to tangible, significant improvements in the quality of American water. By its spelling out exactly what kind of effluent could be discharged into which waterways, and in what quantities, and by its clearly defining penalties, many rivers and watersheds were cleaned up. But today the CWA and SDWA are fast becoming obsolete. While they remain the nation's primary legal defenses against water pollution, hundreds of new chemicals are entering waterways every year, and many of them are not regulated or even tested.

Lake Erie—the fourth largest of the Great Lakes—had become so grossly contaminated in the 1960s that it was declared "dead." But as a result of the CWA, the Safe Drinking Water Act (signed into law by President Ford in 1974), and years of expensive remediation, the lake now supports a fishery worth several hundred million dollars a year. Lake Erie's comeback is remarkable and a major environmental victory, one the EPA points to with justifiable pride. Yet, as is the case with many of the EPA's water-quality improvements, its success is qualified.

The CWA was updated and enhanced by major amendments in 1977

63

and 1987; the SDWA was amended in 1986 and 1996. But since then, those groundbreaking laws have slowly slipped from the minds of Congress and the public, and neither has been significantly updated in years.

Today Lake Erie still suffers from legacy pollutants and storm-water runoff, but it is also afflicted by new problems—including invasive species such as grass carp and zebra mussels, and so-called emerging contaminants, a new class of pollutants that includes synthetic estrogen, pharmaceuticals, narcotics, antimicrobial soaps, and lawn-care products. Most of these contaminants are unregulated, and little is known about how toxic they might be to human and environmental health.

In 1999–2000, scientists at the US Geological Survey (USGS)—the Department of Interior's scientific bureau—began the first large-scale examination of emerging contaminants in 139 streams across the country. They discovered a broad range of residential, industrial, and agricultural chemicals, including human and veterinary drugs, natural and synthetic hormones, detergents, plasticizers, insecticides, and fire retardants. One or more of these chemicals were found in 80 percent of streams sampled; half the streams contained seven or more chemicals; about one-third of streams contained ten or more chemicals.

The study of these new compounds is a scientific frontier, one that is raising complex new questions about water quality: How does antibacterial soap impact the algae fish feed on? What effect do Prozac, heroin, and perchlorate have on insects, crabs, and bass? What is the cumulative effect of a "cocktail" of such pollutants on humans?

For now, the answer to such questions remains elusive.

As the nation grows increasingly concerned about health care, hydrologists, medical researchers, and government officials are wary of this Brave New World of contaminants and are wrestling with ways to regulate them. There are no easy answers, but one thing has become clear: the CWA and SDWA are not suited to the job.

"Trying to solve these [modern pollution] problems with the 1972 Clean Water Act is like trying to use a 1972 auto repair manual to repair a 2008 electric hybrid," Paul Freedman, vice president of the Water Environment Federation, a nonprofit technical and educational group, warned Congress. "It just doesn't work."

For a vivid example of what Freedman means, consider that over sixty thousand different types of chemicals are used in America every year, yet the EPA has assessed the toxicity of only a few of them. By 2000, the EPA's list of regulated chemicals had steadily climbed to ninety-one, but then the list suddenly stopped growing. Since then, roughly seven hundred new chemicals have been introduced to the marketplace every year, but the agency has not added a single new substance to its restricted list.

In 2003, environmentalists pressured the EPA to update its list, but the agency—led at the time by Christine Todd Whitman—refused, saying this "would not provide a meaningful opportunity for health-risk reduction." Environmentalists charged that this was disingenuous and that the EPA had been cowed by the Bush administration, which had, critics alleged, capped the list of restricted substances to ingratiate itself with the powerful pharmaceutical and chemical industries. The White House ignored the criticism. After clashing with President Bush over other pollution issues, most notably air quality, Whitman resigned from the EPA in June 2003.

By 2009, government scientists had evaluated 830 of the pollutants most frequently found in water supplies. They discovered that while many chemicals are benign, some are linked to serious diseases—including leukemia, brain and breast cancer, Parkinson's, Alzheimer's, asthma, autism, and birth defects—even in small amounts. But, as of this writing, the EPA has yet to add any of these chemicals to the list of ninety-one that are restricted.

What's more, experts charge, the process by which EPA evaluates and restricts chemicals is flawed. Rather than classifying groups of chemicals, which would be efficient, regulators assess them case by case, which is laborious and expensive. The technology to evaluate chemicals by group has existed for years, but the funding, manpower, and political will have not.

"We simply do not have the scientific capacity to test every individual chemical used in the US," Dr. Jeffrey K. Griffiths, associate professor of public health and of medicine at Tufts University, who is an adviser to the EPA Drinking Water Committee, told Congress in 2009. "This is disgraceful . . . the process for identifying pollutants is flawed. . . . We have institutionalized an approach . . . that, in my opinion, will not protect the public unless it is changed. . . . We need a paradigm shift about water."

"A SLEEPING GIANT"

As the US population ages, more people are using medications with greater frequency. The pharmaceutical industry introduces new drugs every year; it is also pushing for the use of old drugs in new ways and for the expansion of drug use by children. As a result, increasing numbers of prescription drugs and common household health products are being detected in our water supplies.

No government regulations limit the amount of pharmaceuticals allowed in drinking water, and many public water systems have not been tested for them. Extrapolating from those that have been tested, the US Geological Survey has estimated that 46 million Americans drink water containing detectable amounts of pharmacological agents. There is no conclusive evidence that such chemicals are harmful to humans, and the EPA says that discharge of pharmaceuticals by manufacturing plants into wastewater treatment plants is well controlled. But it also admits that it has no oversight of discharges from individual homes or medical businesses.

That's one reason why a national association of wastewater agencies warns that "pharmaceuticals are a potential sleeping giant."

In January 2010, New York attorney general Andrew Cuomo announced a settlement with five health-care facilities—two hospitals and three nursing homes—in upstate New York that had been flushing painkillers, antibiotics, antidepressants, hormones, and other drugs down toilets and sinks. Drugs disposed of this way usually flow to sewage treatment plants or septic systems. Most treatment plants—even those that use chlorine disinfectants—don't consistently remove pharmaceuticals, and septic systems have no means of removing the drugs. Once they had been introduced into the water system, trace amounts of the pharmaceuticals were discovered in the New York City watershed, which provides drinking water to 9 million people. Alarm bells went off. Each facility was fined between $3,500 and $12,000 for its violations and agreed to dispose of excess pharmaceuticals at waste-management plants. But this was unusual; most states have not researched "drug dumping," and few health facilities have been fined for it, even as flushing pharmaceuticals down the drain has become common practice.

While reducing the amount of drugs dumped into water systems by health-care facilities is good policy, far more pharmaceuticals end up in our tap water when people excrete the small percentage of a drug that doesn't metabolize in the body. Nearly all Americans excrete man-made chemical compounds or wash them off in the shower or flush them down the toilet. Ever more pharmaceuticals and personal-care products, or PPCPs, which include such substances as suntan lotion, perfume, and antibacterial soap, are being detected in wastewater treatment plants or in groundwater and septic systems.

One of the most common drugs found in biosolids—a residue produced by sewage treatment plants that is used as a farm fertilizer—is triclocarban, an antibiotic that is added to antimicrobial soaps. In most cases, triclocarban appeared in small amounts, but several lab samples showed triclocarban present at levels as high as 440 parts per million, which, according to *ScienceNow*, is almost ten times higher than ever reported in biosolids before. The question this raised is, do antibiotics harm aquatic life or soil microbes? The answer remains as yet unknown, but the EPA is examining it.

In 2008, the press began to report extensively on the drugs found in drinking water, raising public concern. The Associated Press (AP), for instance, ran an investigative report headlined "Drugs Found in Drinking Water," which included a string of disturbing factoids: in Southern California, antianxiety and antiepileptic drugs were found in drinking supplies; Tucson found three medications in its drinking water; Washington, DC, tested positive for six drugs; Philadelphia discovered a staggering fifty-six pharmaceuticals or by-products in its treated drinking water. Of thirty-five watersheds tested by scientists for the AP, twenty-eight had pharmaceuticals in them. The story also noted that bottled water companies that use purified tap water—a common practice for popular brands such as Pepsi's Aquafina, Coca-Cola's Dasani, and Nestlé's Nestlé Pure Life—do not test for pharmaceuticals.

There is a certain irony here. Decades ago, the normal practice was to dispose of drugs in the trash or burn them. But with the outcry against air pollution, most hospitals shut down their incinerators, while landfills grew more discerning about what sort of drugs they would accept. With disposal options narrowed, hospitals began to dump old or unused drugs down their toilets and sinks and to recommend that patients do the same. The AP estimated that the health-care industry sends at least 250 million pounds of pharmaceuticals down the drain every year.

Hospital waste carries more antibiotics and germs than domestic waste. This worries researchers, who fear that "drug dumping" into water systems could lead to genetic mutations that create antibiotic-resistant germs. This is not purely dystopian paranoia. A study done by the University of Rouen Medical Center in France found that of thirty-eight wastewater samples, thirty-one of them had the ability to mutate genes.

Spurred by the AP report, the public roused politicians to take action on drugs in water supplies. Philadelphia called for federal intervention. Phoenix said it would wait for the EPA to issue federal standards, but after an outcry decided to test its water quality immediately. In California, regional water managers formed task forces and implored customers, "Don't stop drinking your tap water. It's okay to drink."

Many utilities were caught off guard by the AP report and felt it was sensational. In Las Vegas, J. C. Davis, of the Southern Nevada Water Authority, told me, "That story was shameless self-promotion by the AP. This is difficult science, and that report set us back five years. We test our waters and clean them to a very high degree, and then the AP comes along and just beats us to death. I'm livid!"

In 2008, Congress held hearings on drug waste in water supplies and angrily demanded regulatory action by the EPA. In 2009, the agency began to research the question of establishing national standards, while some states debated whether to reopen landfills for drug disposal. EPA spokeswoman Roxanne Smith said landfilling hazardous drugs poses little threat to the public, yet pharmaceuticals leach from landfills into waterways, either through leaks or the intentional release of treated seepage; researchers have detected trace amounts of ibuprofen and carbamazepine, a seizure medication, in water near landfills.

Incineration "is considered a BMP [best management practice] for today," says Laura Brannen, of Houston's Waste Management Healthcare Solutions, "because we don't really know what the hell to do with the stuff." Others point out that incineration allows some contamination to escape into smoke and ash. Rain then "scrubs" pollutants from the atmosphere and drops them back into the water system.

New technologies—such as using microwaves, electrical arcs, or caustic chemicals to destroy old medications—might help ease the strain.

Occasionally, when public ire grows loud enough, politicians and medical professionals have suggested that the pharmaceutical industry—which, after all, profits handsomely from drug manufacturing—should bear some responsibility and help to underwrite the disposal of drug waste. Some legislators have even called for fining companies that refuse to take back old drugs. The industry has stonewalled these efforts, replying that "without sufficient evidence of harm" the cost of drug disposal outweighs the potential benefits.

HIGH WATER

In the mid-1990s, Dr. Ettore Zuccato and his colleagues at the Mario Negri Institute for Pharmacological Research, in Milan, wondered if the Po, Italy's largest river, would be filled with pharmaceuticals. Zuccato had come across a scientific paper by Thomas Ternes, a young German researcher at the University of Mainz, who had discovered clofibric acid, a cholesterol-lowering drug, in groundwater beneath a water-treatment plant. Other European researchers had found traces of ibuprofen, antibiotics, and chemotherapy drugs in drinking-water sources. "Whatever people ingest, they excrete, and that ends up in the water," said Zuccato. Because commonly used therapeutic drugs are hardy and metabolize through the body in specific ways, Zuccato figured he would have a good chance of identifying them in river water.

To test his idea, Zuccato and his team took samples from a number of sites along the Po and passed them through a mass spectrometer, a long cylindrical instrument that can detect billionths of a gram of a substance per liter of water. When they tested the river for thirteen known drugs—such as erythromycin, naproxen, and sulfasalazine—they identified trace elements of all of them. The results were also consistent with known prescribing patterns (meaning the ratio of drugs in the water reflected the frequency with which each was prescribed) and were considered an accurate and objective record. They also identified metabolites of clofibrate, a powerful drug that had been withdrawn from the market years earlier yet still lingered in the ecosystem. After further study, the Negri team concluded that even trace elements of pharmaceuticals in drinking water—present at only a few parts per trillion—"can significantly inhibit embryonic cell growth in vitro." This was a worrisome finding and caused a stir: the Italian study was published in the *Lancet* and picked up by other media around the world. Yet it would prove to be a mere preview to a far more sensational story.

Studies in Germany confirmed Zuccato's findings, and later studies in the United States discovered that recycled water contains small amounts of pharmaceuticals and steroids—antibiotics, birth-control hormones, anticholesterol drugs, Valium, and Viagra, among others. Some of these drugs are resistant to our most advanced three-stage treatments, which, to some minds, raises questions about the safety of using recycled gray water, which is increasingly being mixed with natural supplies.

While scientists doubt that trace amounts of pharmaceuticals have any impact on human beings, little is known about how a cocktail of many such drugs might work in concert, or their effects on wildlife—frogs that ingest Prozac, say, or mosquitoes exposed to antiseizure drugs, or fish that swim in synthetic estrogen (which might be one cause of intersex, in which male fish grow eggs or female ovarian tissue—a phenomenon I will discuss in the next chapter).

At one site along the Po River, Zuccato's team noticed something strange: a high concentration of the antiasthma drug salbutamol. "There was no obvious reason for this," Zuccato told me. "Health records indicated that incidence of asthma in the area was normal."

The scientists began to interview the local cattle and pig farmers. Within days, they had an answer: the farmers had been using salbutamol (a human drug) illegally as a promoter of muscle growth in their livestock. The mass spectrometer allowed the scientists to identify, accurately and objectively, how much of the drug had been used.

The Mario Negri Institute is a small private pharmacological institute named for the jeweler who funds it. At a meeting in 2005, Zuccato was discussing his research with his team when his boss, Dr. Roberto Fanelli, wondered, "If we can determine how much unrecorded use of a *legal* drug there is, can we do the same for an *illegal* drug?"

Zuccato thought for a moment, then said he could probably devise a test for cocaine, a narcotic that has become increasingly popular in Western Europe.

In the spring of 2005, Zuccato's team took samples from the Po River and measured the level of benzoylecgonine (BE), the major metabolite of cocaine (BE cannot be produced by other means), in the water. They were astonished by what they found: "Cocaine use was far, far greater than we had anticipated," Zuccato says.

Italian officials had estimated that the 5 million inhabitants of the Po River valley used about fifteen thousand doses of cocaine per month. (A typical line is about fifty to seventy-five milligrams of cocaine.) But Zuccato's test revealed that the real number is over forty thousand doses per day. "The economic impact of trafficking such a large amount of cocaine—at least fifteen hundred kilograms per year—is staggering," says Zuccato. "This amounts to about 150 million dollars in street value. Not to mention the legal issues, social impact, and long-term health problems associated with such an [addictive] drug."

Zuccato published his results in an international scientific journal in August 2005. Although most of Europe was on vacation, the phone in his lab began to ring and ring. "I was almost overwhelmed by calls and e-mails from almost every corner of the globe," he said with a rueful smile. "Journalists and scientists from the US, Europe, Australia, Japan, and South America called me all the time for more details." Newspapers ran sensationalist stories with headlines such as "Italian River Flows with Cocaine." Zuccato even received a query from "someone in Colombia," the suspected source of much of Italy's cocaine. One frequently asked question was "Can I use your machine to get cocaine out of the water?" (The answer is no.) Bloggers grew intrigued, and one labeled Zuccato's work a "Giant Piss Test."

In November 2005, the *Sunday Telegraph* invited Zuccato and his team to London, to test the water in the Thames River. The paper was especially interested in discovering how much cocaine was in the river next to the Parliament building. When the paper ran its story, "The Thames: Awash with Cocaine," it misinterpreted Zuccato's data, claiming, inaccurately, that "Londoners snort more than 150,000 lines of the class A drug every day." The story ran on the front page under a photograph of Kate Moss, the supermodel who had just emerged from a scandal, and rehab, after being photographed snorting cocaine. What the Negri team had actually written was that they detected 49,066 doses of cocaine in the Thames on the day of the test. Zuccato's team was incensed by the *Telegraph* story and turned down "hundreds" of subsequent requests for print and TV interviews about it. But they kept working.

Since then, they have used their cocaine test in Lugano, Switzerland, and in Milan, and are now comparing the data they collected in Italy, England, and Switzerland. They are working on tests to detect cannabis, ecstasy, LSD, amphetamines, and heroin, among other drugs. They are observing the effects of narcotics on fish cell-lines, and in combination with pharmaceuticals, to see what effects such drugs might have on humans.

In the United States, antinarcotic officials have quietly been analyzing sewage and wastewater across the country for the by-products of illegal drugs, including in major cities such as San Diego, Washington, DC, and New York, since 2006.

Water quality is affected by drug use in other ways, too. According to the Office of National Drug Control Policy (ONDCP), marijuana farmers hack fields out of national-forest land to make room for their plants, leading to erosion, water pollution, and habitat destruction. The production of methamphetamines, or meth, relies on toxic chemicals such as lye, red phosphorus, and hydriodic acid. The ONDCP estimates that for every pound of meth, five or six pounds of hazardous waste are produced, much of which is tossed into wells, onto farmland, or down mine shafts, creating broad public health risks. In California, chemicals from meth labs have killed livestock, polluted streams, and destroyed forests.

By the turn of the twenty-first century, experts understood that a broad array of pollutants affect our waterways—from age-old contaminants such as bacteria, sewage, lead, and rust; to the rising problem of nutrients from agricultural runoff; to the latest emerging contaminants such as industrial chemicals, estrogen, pharmaceuticals, and narcotics. Some waterways suffer from all of these contaminants at once, and scientists are only now beginning to investigate the effect of such cocktails on aquatic and human life.

Ironically, one of the nation's most dire and complex cases of water pollution has occurred in Chesapeake Bay, which lies almost literally at the feet of the White House and federal regulators, in Washington, DC.

CHAPTER 7

From the Chickens
to the Crabs

In the Chesapeake Bay, "oysters lay as thick as stones and posed a hazard to navigation."

—Captain John Smith, 1608

INTERSEX AND DEATH IN THE CHESAPEAKE

If you measure every wrinkle and crenellation around the rim of the Chesapeake Bay, the shoreline runs ten thousand miles long. By comparison, the California coast extends eight thousand miles, and the coast of Maine runs for just thirty-five hundred miles. The Chesapeake is constantly refreshed by two large rivers, the Potomac and Susquehanna, and by a vast watershed that drains an area stretching across 64,299 square miles, including the District of Columbia and parts of six states—West Virginia, Delaware, Maryland, Virginia, Pennsylvania, and New York. With protected inlets, a shallow depth that averages only twenty-one feet, and a biologically rich mixture of fresh and salt water, the bay is known for having one of the most prolific fish, oyster, and crab populations in the world.

But the bay's fantastic natural bounty and prime location ultimately worked against it. By the start of the twenty-first century, the region had become heavily populated and polluted, and the bay's aquatic life was spiraling into a steep decline. The Chesapeake's malaise is not unique, but it is extreme. Because it is such an ideal natural fishery, biologists point to the bay as a paradigm of how an ecosystem can be affected by many different types of pollution, in many ways, which accumulate over many years.

Fish, sensitive to changes in their environment, are excellent "indicator species" that reflect the overall health of a water system. The World Wide Fund for Nature reports that fish populations in rivers and lakes have dropped by 30 percent since 1970. This is a bigger loss than that of animals in savannas, temperate forests, jungles, or any other substantial ecosystem. Just as the health of the Chesapeake's fisheries is a clear indicator of the overall health of the bay's aquasystem, so the state of the bay is a proxy for what is happening to other water supplies and the creatures who rely on them. We know there is a grave problem with the water in Chesapeake Bay; the question is how and why this happened, and what to do about it.

In the spring of 2002, huge shoals of dead fish, primarily smallmouth bass, suddenly floated to the surface of the South Branch of the Potomac River, in West Virginia, about two hundred miles upstream from Washington, DC. Fishermen noticed that many of the bass had painful-looking lesions along their sides. They alerted the West Virginia Division of Natural Resources (DNR), which asked the US Geological Survey to investigate.

That summer, a USGS fish pathologist named Dr. Vicki Blazer led a team of scientists to collect fish in the river and to search for clues to what was happening to them. Out on the South Branch of the Potomac, Blazer found that the best fish to study were moribund bass—fish that were sick and on the verge of death but not yet dead. To collect bass humanely, DNR scientists working with Blazer first stunned them with an electro-shock in the river, which caused the fish to float to the surface, where they were collected and put into buckets of water dosed with an anesthetic. Working quickly, the biologists observed the outside of the fish, noting any lesions or other abnormalities. They took blood samples, and samples of the mucus that coats the fish's skin and scales. The mucus is the fish's first layer of defense against infection. If the flora in the mucus is normal, it will inhibit pathogens; if the flora is abnormal, it is a sign that the fish's health is compromised.

"Before big fish kills, we've seen a change in the mucous flora," Blazer explained. "It indicates contaminants in the water."

The fish were dissected in the field. Biologists noted whether a fish's liver looked too pale, the spleen was too big, or whether parasites were in the tissues.

Back at her lab in Kearneysville, West Virginia, Blazer and her colleagues examined bass tissues in thin slices under a microscope. They discovered that some bass had bacterial lesions, others had fungal lesions, and some were afflicted by parasites. The lesions had no single cause, suggesting that the fish were immunosuppressed, meaning their immune systems weren't working properly.

Then came the shocker. When they sliced open the testes of the bass and examined them under the microscope, Blazer and her colleagues discovered clusters of immature eggs nestled where only sperm should be. This condition, not apparent to the naked eye, is known as intersex, or TO, which stands for "testicular oocytes," or testis-ova.

This abnormality had been reported in Western Europe ("intersexual" fish were first reported in Europe in 1923 and in Britain in the 1940s), and it had cropped up sporadically in heavily populated regions of the United States. But this was the first time intersex fish had been identified in the Potomac, where they were found in unusually large clusters in the sparsely populated region along the South Branch. "TO is a clear sign of ecological damage in the bay's water," Blazer said. "It's really strange."

In the spring and summer of 2003 and 2004, her team discovered more intersex bass on the Upper Potomac, near Sharpsburg, Maryland, and along the Shenandoah River. "There was a gradation," said Blazer. "The South Branch, which is fairly sparsely populated, did not have as heavy a prevalence of intersex and fish kills as the Shenandoah did, which is more heavily populated and has more agriculture."

In 2005, Blazer found that over 80 percent of the male smallmouth she had trapped in the Potomac, the Shenandoah, the Monocacy, and in Conococheague Creek were affected by intersex, including every single male bass at four of her six test sites. Since then, intermittent fish kills have occurred around the watershed, but "feminized" bass have continued to appear year after year, most often in the spring pre-spawn period.

Intersex occurs in fish species around the world: white perch in the Great Lakes, white suckers in Colorado, spottail shiners in the St. Lawrence River, shovelnose sturgeon in the Mississippi, sharp-tooth catfish in South Africa, three-spine stickleback in Germany, barbel in Italy, and roach fish in Britain. There have also been reports of panthers with atrophied testicles; intersex alligators, mice, and frogs; seals with suppressed immune systems; and female polar bears that have developed penislike stumps. (In a condition known as imposex, which is an abbreviation for "the imposition of male sex characteristics on female organisms," female snails and other invertebrates have, on rare occasions, developed male organs.)

In September 2009, the USGS released the most comprehensive study of intersex yet, which revealed that it affects species across the country—

in the Columbia, Colorado, Mississippi, Rio Grande, Apalachicola, Savannah, Chattahoochee, and Gila Rivers, among others. The only basin in which researchers did not find at least one intersex fish was the remote Yukon, in Alaska, where there are few people. Of the sixteen fish species biologists examined at 111 sites, intersex was most common in bass: a third of all male smallmouth bass and a fifth of all male largemouth bass were found to be intersex.

What could cause male bass to develop eggs? In the scientific literature, effluents from wastewater treatment plants in England, and runoff from paper mills in Canada, have been the primary focus of research. But when Blazer tested fish and water chemistry upstream and downstream of treatment plants on the Monocacy River and Conococheague Creek—both tributaries of the Potomac—"there was no significant difference between the two," she said, indicating that something else was to blame. She noticed "these were all heavy agricultural areas. More and more I began to think agricultural runoff was driving this."

A broad spectrum of man-made compounds is suspected of contributing to intersex, but a prime suspect is high levels of estrogen in the water. Natural estrogens are sex hormones, which help to modulate animals' immune response. Synthetic estrogens come from pharmaceuticals such as birth-control pills, or agricultural runoff loaded with pesticides, or industrial runoff laced with plastics. Also, a group of compounds are known as estrogen mimics, the chemical structure of which allows them to act like estrogen. These range from herbicides to personal-care products such as antibacterial soap and even perfume. Indeed, so many chemicals show varying degrees of estrogenic activity that methods to identify them are still being developed.

Estrogen is a normal hormone, but when high levels of it or estrogen mimics are present, scientists believe that they bind to estrogen receptors on numerous cells within the body and disrupt the endocrine system. That system of glands controls the release of hormones and is a key regulator of growth, development, metabolism, and tissue health. If the endocrine system is disrupted, an animal can suffer lesions, cancer, and numerous health problems in its reproductive, immune, and nervous systems.

In 2007, in an effort to understand intersex better, a Canadian scientist named Karen Kidd added a small amount of ethinyl estradiol, one of the active ingredients in birth control pills, to an experimental lake in Canada. It caused the feminization of most of the male fathead minnows in the lake. Over a number of generations, Kidd showed, the minnows were not able to reproduce successfully, and the population was nearly wiped out. "That was really scary," Blazer recalled. In a 2009 study, Kidd found that once she stopped dosing the lake with estrogen, the fathead minnow population rebounded.

"The issue is, if these chemicals are affecting the endocrine systems of fish, which are basically the same as the endocrine system of humans, then couldn't we face some of the same negative health effects as fish?" Blazer wondered. "I think the answer is yes, we could."

A growing body of evidence suggests that certain man-made chemicals released into the water and the air have led to a surge in serious health issues, such as breast cancer, leukemia, asthma, neurodevelopmental disorders, and physiological changes. According to Dr. Philip Landrigan, the chairman of the department of preventive medicine at Mount Sinai Medical Center, in New York, the risk that a fifty-year-old white woman will develop breast cancer has spiked from 1 percent in 1975 to 12 percent in 2009 (although some of this increase is likely due to better detection). Similarly, childhood leukemia is increasing by 1 percent a year, while asthma rates have trebled since 1980, and obesity and diabetes are on the rise.

It is well documented that Western women are beginning puberty earlier and going through menopause later. In 1800, American girls had their first period at age seventeen. By 1900, that had dropped to fourteen. By 2000, it was twelve. Studies have linked early puberty to exposure to PCBs, industrial chemicals, and pesticides. Although the evidence is not conclusive, doctors are particularly concerned about the role of endocrine disruptors, which may fool the body into undergoing hormonal changes early.

Endocrine disruptors are found in many everyday items, including cleaning products, pesticides, flooring, air fresheners, and plastics (especially plastic containers numbered 3, 6, and 7, which are associated with potentially harmful toxins).

Beyond early puberty, the incidence of intersex humans may, in fact, be on the rise. In 2000, Anne Fausto-Sterling, a biology professor at Brown University, conducted the leading study on the frequency of intersexuality and found that 1.7 percent of the population develops in a way that deviates from the standard definition of male or female. Based on this figure, intersexuality is far more common than Down syndrome or albinism. The issue was thrust into the spotlight in 2009, when an eighteen-year-old South African track star named Caster Semenya won the women's world 800-meter title by a wide margin—over two seconds—at the World Championships in Athletics in Berlin. After her win, competitors questioned Semenya's gender: she has a husky voice and a muscular body, and her rivals complained, "She's not a woman; she's a man." After an eleven-month absence and much debate, Semenya was allowed to race again in 2010. At the same Berlin track she won the 800 meters again. Another outcry ensued, and her competitors demanded that officials define what constitutes an acceptable biological baseline for female athletes.

Fish are most susceptible to endocrine disruption when they are still in their eggs in river sediments or are very young and still undergoing sexual differentiation. If human babies are exposed to endocrine disruptors when they are at a similar stage of development—in utero, or when they are very young—then they, too, could theoretically suffer immunosuppression or possibly intersex.

This is such new science that little hard evidence exists to link the incidence of intersexuality in fish to that in humans. For now, it remains an intriguing question.

"For me that is the issue," Vicki Blazer said. "Are we exposing our children to those sorts of chemicals when they are most susceptible? And if we are, what are the effects?"

AQUATIC BOMB

A river is like a urinary tract. To Bob Hirsch, this is not a joke, it is a statement of fact. As he explains it, doctors study a patient's urine to find out what is happening in a person's body. Similarly, he said, "River water is the urine of the landscape. And we in the hydrologic community look up and down our rivers to see what's in them in terms of sediments, chemistry, pollution—in other words, to understand what's really happening to the quality of our water." With a grin he added, "I guess you could call people like me 'the nation's urologists.'"

When I met him in 2008, Dr. Robert M. Hirsch was fifty-nine years old and, as chief hydrologist of the US Geological Survey, arguably the US government's leading water expert. (He has since voluntarily stepped down from that leadership role to return to his first love, hydrologic research for the USGS.) With a lithe bulk, receding dark hair, and a bushy gray beard, Hirsch's fuzzy robustness lends him the aspect of an old-time scientist-explorer. It's easy to picture him in a sepia-toned photograph standing next to the legendary one-armed bearded scientist-explorer John Wesley Powell—the second director of the USGS, and one of Hirsch's heroes.

The USGS, generally known as the Survey, was founded in 1879 to "classify the public lands." The only scientific bureau in the Department of the Interior, USGS had some ten thousand employees by 2009. It plays a leading role in studying the nation's waters but also has a broad portfolio that covers biology, geology, and geography. I noticed a pronounced esprit de corps among USGSers; many of them are lifers, and even those who have moved on to other things continue to proselytize on the agency's behalf.

On this warm June morning, Hirsch stood ankle-deep in the brown swirl of Muddy Creek, a slim, lazy watercourse in Mount Clinton, Virginia, at the southern end of the Shenandoah Valley. The Blue Ridge Mountains rose to the east, the Alleghenies to the west; the verdant, gently rolling hills were planted with neat rows of corn; animals wandered around small barnyards. There were no belching smokestacks, traffic-clogged highways, putrid hog-waste lagoons, or noxious mounds of garbage here. It was difficult to believe that the most toxic thing for miles was the bucolic stream we were standing in.

In 1996, Muddy Creek failed Virginia's fecal coliform water-quality standard, violated the nitrate public-drinking-water standard, and had excessive levels of phosphorus and sediments. It was placed on Virginia's List of Impaired Waters. A more recent report found Muddy Creek to be suffused with "elevated nitrogen concentrations" and "fecal bacteria." Locally, it has been called "the most contaminated stream in Virginia."

Muddy Creek is part of the Chesapeake Bay watershed. The creek flows into the Shenandoah River, which merges with the Potomac, which empties into the bay. As the water moves downstream, it picks up nutrients and toxins until it hits the Chesapeake's ecosystem with the impact of an aquatic bomb.

"See that? That's a typical indicator of excessive nutrients," Hirsch said, bending to point out strands of bright green algae growing along the sides of Muddy Creek. "Hypoxia—the depletion of dissolved oxygen in the water, which occurs when the algae die—associated with agricultural runoff is a major water-quality issue. Not only here but around the world."

Scientists have been studying the water quality of streams like this one in the Chesapeake Bay watershed since the 1980s, when they began to notice large algae blooms, which blot out sunlight and suck up oxygen in the water, killing all other aquatic life. This excessive plant growth is called eutrophication, and it is a growing concern worldwide. It leaves behind vast swaths of lifeless water, commonly referred to as dead zones. "We've come to realize that eutrophication is one of the most important questions facing the hydrologic community today," Hirsch mused in a deep baritone. "Scientists have studied it for fifty years and have a pretty good handle on its causes and effects. Typically, it's caused by some combination of excessive nitrogen and phosphorus in the water. But even with this knowledge, it remains a difficult problem to solve."

But clearly, the problems of big, conspicuous places such as Chesapeake Bay begin in small, seemingly innocuous places such as Muddy Creek.

THE INTEGRATORS AND THE REGULATORS

Since the 1990s, the quality of Muddy Creek has significantly improved, thanks to a concerted effort by farmers, and state and federal assistance. While its fecal coliform count has decreased by 44 percent, Muddy Creek is still listed as "slightly impaired" and is likely to remain that way.

One likely source of the creek's contamination was staring me in the face. On the opposite bank, a cluster of horses whisked their tails and eyed us curiously from behind a fence. Up the hill a herd of black cows wallowed in a cool mudhole; as they relieved themselves into a ditch, the runoff carried their manure straight downhill into the creek. Across the road, a herd of goats scampered across a field, scattering manure bomblets as they went. A tractor snorted in the distance.

Almost every vista in the Shenandoah Valley includes a farmhouse, and appended to virtually every one was at least one—but more often two, three, or a half dozen—long, low, windowless sheds. Undistinguished beige structures, they housed chickens or turkeys.

The Shenandoah Valley has nine hundred poultry farms, and in 2000 they held 265 million broiler chickens, 25.5 million turkeys, and 824 million eggs. A giant bronze turkey statue, mounted on a stone base, declares Rockingham County, a two-hour drive from downtown Washington, DC, to be Virginia's "turkey capital." At the same time, Rockingham's farmland is increasingly being plowed under for new highways, developments, and big-box stores. Each of these is equipped with hard roads, roofs, and parking lots, which hasten storm-water runoff.

In the 1800s, farmers in Rockingham County kept simple chicken coops in their backyards. As the population grew, so did the poultry business. In the 1920s, Charles W. Wampler Sr., "the father of the modern turkey industry," raised the first flock hatched in an incubator and matured in confinement here. By the 1940s and 1950s, large poultry-feed companies began contracting with farmers to share profits from raising birds in exchange for feed. Over time, manufacturers and feed distributors consolidated. Today five large, fully integrated poultry companies, or integrators, process and market poultry in the Shenandoah Valley on a giant scale: Cargill Turkey Products, George's Foods, Perdue Farms Inc., Pilgrim's Pride Corp., and Tyson Foods Inc.

Think of this poultry production system as a protein conveyor belt. Integrators produce chicks in large incubators (no hens are involved). When they are hardly a day old, the chicks are shipped on consignment, a thousand at a time. The farmers raise the chicks until they've "grown out" into mature birds, which takes six to eight weeks. During that time, the farmers are responsible for the health and feeding of the birds, and the disposal of their waste. The chickens are raised on feed and medications mandated by the integrators. The birds are housed by the tens of thousands—roughly one chicken per three-quarter square foot—in poultry sheds. Standard sheds house 27,200 birds; some hold 42,000. Small poultry operations have one or two sheds; bigger ones have up to ten, fifteen, or even twenty-five sheds. After about seven weeks, the grown chickens are retrieved by the integrators and sent to a plant for processing into plastic-wrapped skinless breasts.

As I learned about the poultry industry, I began to see Rockingham County through a darker lens. What appeared to be small family farms and simple chicken shacks were revealed to be more akin to a stage set for industrial-farming operations. The bright little signs posted by every driveway—Perdue, Tyson, Cargill—are placed there so that the feed trucks know where to deliver their proprietary loads, but they are also heralds of corporate turf.

Each integrator has its own feed recipe, which is fiercely protected as a trade secret and subject to little government oversight. The farmers don't know what's in the feed, consumers don't know what's in the chicken they eat, and hydrologists don't know what kinds of chemicals are being washed from chicken manure into waterways.

"Farmers have no rights," said Carole Morison, who grew over 6.25 million chickens for Perdue, starting in 1986. She finally quit the business in 2008, after Perdue insisted she upgrade her two chicken houses, at a cost of $150,000, and she refused. "There's no equality between the company and the farmer—those aren't *our* chickens, they are *theirs*. The integrators hold title to them as long as they are alive. But if a chicken dies, which happens, it's our problem. The only things the farmer owns are the mortgage, the dead chickens, and the manure."

Once the integrators take a shipment of chickens away, the tenant farmers must "scrape out" their chicken sheds: they shovel the litter—an odoriferous mound of guano mixed with the sawdust or peanut hulls used for bedding—into big piles. Tractors spread the litter across acres of row crops, as fertilizer. This is an ancient, and seemingly holistic, method of farming. But the sheer volume of poultry waste in the Shenandoah Valley has overwhelmed the ability of crops and the soil to absorb it. The inevitable result is that it seeps into local waterways.

According to the Chesapeake Bay Foundation, an environmental group, Rockingham County has more excess manure on its animal farms than any other county in the nation. This agricultural pollution is immeasurably worsened by the large number of septic systems and "straight pipes" from area homes, which dump human sewage into the ground and eventually into the water table. A 1999 USGS survey found that nitrate concentrations in the Delmarva Peninsula, in Maryland, were among the highest in the country. In 2008, chicken farms there produced an estimated 1.5 billion pounds of manure, which was reportedly more than the annual human waste of New York, Washington, DC, San Francisco, and Atlanta combined.

Bill Satterfield, executive director of the Delmarva Poultry Industry, defends the integrators. In a 2009 essay titled "Every Day Is Earth Day for Delmarva's Chicken Industry," he wrote, "To single out the broiler industry as 'the bad guy' in the Chesapeake Bay region is simplistic and sensationalistic and not based on the facts." He has said that the poultry industry aggressively reduced nutrient pollutants in the previous decade. Because groundwater moves slowly, the effect of farming practices from thirty or forty years ago "may have allowed nutrients to get into the aquifers." But, he added, simply because the USGS study found the highest concentrations of nutrients near poultry farms doesn't necessarily mean the farms are the source.

"I'm not sure what these studies indicate," he told the PBS news show *Frontline*. "Is it nutrients from a chicken, from a fox, from Canada geese, from ducks, from cats, from dogs, from humans, from septic systems? . . . If we're going to talk scientific data, let's not jump to conclusions."

The question of who is legally responsible for the chicken manure is murky. Poultry industry spokesmen, such as Satterfield, maintain that the manure belongs to the growers, who are happy to use it as fertilizer. "The manure is considered a resource, actually," Jim Perdue, chairman of Perdue Farms Inc., told *Frontline*. "We're trying to help [the farmers] understand what the EPA wants . . . the farmer puts the litter on his land, and that's a nutrient management plan, and we're not involved in that, you know? If he puts chemicals on his land, he's responsible for what he does."

Nevertheless, Carole Morison, who lives on the Delmarva Peninsula, told me, "Nobody educates farmers about water pollution. I've never had anyone come here and say, 'What we're doing is not good for the environment.' Never. Not once." Rather, Perdue's representatives would tell her about legislation proposed to limit industry practices and focus only on the negatives. "This law will run you out of business," they'd say. The only "education" she got, Morison said, was when Perdue gave her the phone number of legislators they wanted her to complain to.

Agribusiness has powerful, well-funded lobbyists and is notoriously resistant to regulation. Poultry farming is just one part of a much larger agribusiness matrix that includes feed and fertilizer companies, irrigation-pipe and tractor makers, CAFOs, and so on. The integrators have warned that if environmental regulations become too tough in Maryland, Delaware, or Virginia, they will move their job-producing, tax-generating operations to more lenient states, such as Kentucky. Thus far, the threat has worked to minimize government oversight.

Leon Billings, a Maryland legislator from 1991 to 2003, said, " 'Big Chicken' . . . hired the top guns in the lobby community in Annapolis, and they made every effort to prevent us from enacting tough regulations on agriculture."

Federal regulators such as the EPA have allowed integrators to monitor their own agricultural runoff on what is essentially a voluntary basis, which clearly doesn't work. Moreover, policing runoff into the Chesapeake has been hampered because Washington, DC, and the six states in the bay's vast watershed—West Virginia, Delaware, Maryland, Virginia, Pennsylvania, and New York—have different laws and customs.

"There are laws on the books, but there is no enforcement," said Carole Morison. "It was very discouraging. The regulations get so watered down and full of loopholes they're not worth the paper they're written on."

"THE NEXT GLOBAL WARMING"

As the poultry litter and other fertilizers flow into surface and groundwater, they carry heavy loads of nitrogen (fertilizers) and phosphorus (pesticides) with them. With help from rains, snowmelt, and spring flooding, surface and groundwater spread these chemicals far and wide. Or so the theory goes; as Bob Hirsch said, scientists have many clues but don't yet fully understand the spread of eutrophication.

Nitrogen and phosphorus are basic aspects of the food chain, but scientists suspect that when they mix with water and sunlight—especially in a fecund place such as the Chesapeake Bay—the result is superstimulated algae growth and expanding dead zones.

The buildup of nitrogen, in particular, is emerging as what experts such as Hirsch call "the next global warming." Nitrogen is an inert gas that makes up about 78 percent of the earth's atmosphere, but it has more reactive forms, one of which is made into fertilizers for food production. Some 90 to 120 million tons of nitrogen are created every year by natural processes, such as nitrogen-fixing bacteria and lightning strikes. Humans manufacture another 190 million tons a year and also convert nitrogen gas into ammonia, which is turned into fertilizer.

Humans have been applying nitrogen-based fertilizers to cropland since the 1950s, and the effect has been dramatic. They have provided remarkable crop yields that have helped to fuel the Green Revolution and stave off mass famine in places such as India and Mexico. But too much nitrogen can "burn" crops, kill off beneficial microorganisms, and deplete minerals in the soil; and it can lead to cyanosis, the "blue baby" syndrome. Farmers commonly overapply nitrogen fertilizer as a precaution against poor yields and to give their crops an added growth boost.

Carole Morison admits that she and her husband spread so much chicken manure on their fields that the land became oversaturated. When they had soil samples tested for nitrogen and phosphorus, they were told their levels were so high that they didn't need to fertilize again for another fifteen years. "I bet most of the land on the Delmarva Peninsula is in the same condition," Morison said. "If we were still raising chickens, what would we do with the extra manure? There's nowhere to put it."

THE MYSTERY OF THE SHENANDOAH

A river is the report card for its watershed.
—Alan Levere

Muddy Creek spills into the South Fork of the Shenandoah River, which is where Bob Hirsch and I floated downstream in 2008 as part of a flotilla of dark green canoes filled with scientists. The Shenandoah is a midsize, fairly shallow, and ledgy river, with water colored a light brown, like weak tea. It flows north for 150 miles, from Virginia into West Virginia, and then into the Potomac River at Harpers Ferry.

I canoed with Jeff Kelble, the Shenandoah Riverkeeper, and right away we saw telltale signs of pollution: bright green algae streaming beneath us, clumps of foam on the river's surface, cows grazing along the water's edge, a small lumber operation, piles of garbage spilling down eroded banks. "Every spring since 2004 we've seen a jump in the number of dead fish, or fish with sores on their skin," said Kelble. By 2008, the spring fish kills had eliminated an estimated 80 percent of adult smallmouth bass and a number of other species from the river. A task force has found few concrete answers to explain why the Shenandoah, in particular, has been hit so hard, and why the fish kills have targeted just the adults from a few species.

Of all the rivers in the Chesapeake Bay watershed that Vicki Blazer has studied, the Shenandoah has the highest incidence of intersex bass, with testicular oocytes (the immature eggs) found in 80 to 100 percent of male fish trapped in the river. The Shenandoah, Blazer noted pointedly, is surrounded by farmland.

In 2006, the conservation group American Rivers listed the Shenandoah as the "fifth most endangered river in the United States" (after the Pajaro, Upper Yellowstone, Willamette, and Salmon Trout Rivers) due to three factors: an overabundance of nitrogen and phosphorus; industrial discharge; and a murkiness caused by erosion from livestock, plowed fields, and construction sites that blocks light and burdens aquatic life. Advisories warn against eating the river's fish, which may be contaminated by mercury, spilled by the DuPont plant in Waynesboro over half a century ago, and by PCBs, which were released by the Avtex Fibers Plant in Front Royal, which was shuttered in 1989.

Kelble was an affable thirty-four-year-old, with dark hair and a boyish face. After graduating from Tufts, he worked as a Shenandoah River fishing guide. The action was so good that he quickly attracted clients from around the world. His wife opened a little B&B. The good fishing lasted for eight years, and then his livelihood began to die off.

In 2004 and 2005, 80 percent of the Shenandoah's smallmouth bass and redbreast sunfish died after developing lesions that looked like cigar burns. Since then, the river's annual mortality rate for smallmouth bass has fluctuated, and Kelble worries about their "chronic health issues." Juvenile bass are growing bigger more quickly than ever—reaching twelve inches in about half the time it took before 2004. Some biologists theorize that the fish kills have left fewer big predators and have changed interspecies competition for food.

Scientists from several agencies have conducted water quality studies in the Shenandoah, looking for signs of a virus, bacteria, or man-made contaminants. But if there is one cause of fish deaths, it remains a mystery.

Kelble suspects that arsenic, which occurs naturally but is also present in herbicides and pesticides, is likely to blame. Critics say that much of the inorganic arsenic in the region comes from Roxarsone, a feed additive that the industry claims is used to control intestinal parasites in poultry and promote food safety. "That's a lie," said Kelble. "According to the FDA, it's really used to promote weight gain in chickens and give the meat color."

Roxarsone contains a relatively harmless form of arsenic. But once chickens excrete it, bacteria break it down and it releases an inorganic form of arsenic, which is an immune-system suppressor in fish and a poison that can lead to nausea and cancer in humans. Scientists like Keeve Nachman at the Johns Hopkins Center for a Livable Future have pushed for the banning of Roxarsone from US poultry feed, as the European Union has done.

But the poultry industry strenuously denies that Roxarsone is responsible for fish kills. The Poultry & Egg Institute says "the benefits of Roxarsone . . . far outweigh the concerns." Hobey Bauhan, of the Virginia Poultry Federation, said that arsenic levels from chicken litter (11.7 parts per million) fall well below the EPA's standard for land-applied biosolids (75 parts per million). And Richard Morris, who uses poultry litter to fertilize his fields about a mile west of the Shenandoah River, told *Blue Ridge Outdoors* magazine that while the litter washes into his pond, it supports plenty of twenty-inch bass. Kelble counters that farm ponds hold largemouth bass, which are resilient; the Shenandoah's smallmouth bass, however, have been dying in large numbers. Speaking for many farmers, Morris said of the fish kills: "If someone proves it's poultry litter, which I doubt will happen, then [farmers] and [integrators] will do everything they can to stop it."

Kelble isn't persuaded: "This is a business that's electing to continue introducing a known carcinogen and toxic substance onto the land, and it gets into the water. That is a problem. We need to stand up for the river."

The Shenandoah feeds into the Potomac—"the Nation's River"—which wends for 383 miles, from the Appalachian Mountains, through Washington, DC, to Point Lookout, Maryland, where it empties into Chesapeake Bay. Some 5.24 million people live in the Potomac watershed, a number expected to grow another 20 percent, to 6.25 million, by 2020.

QUALITY

Intensive development around Washington has led to impermeable roads and buildings, which create "a waterslide for pollutants" into the bay.

The 2002 National Water Quality Inventory noted that of the approximately ten thousand stream miles in the Potomac watershed, more than thirty-eight hundred miles were deemed "threatened" or "impaired." In 2007, the Potomac Conservancy, noting the persistence of these "disturbing trends," gave the river a D+ for cleanliness. By 2010, the grade had improved to a C, which represents "moderate ecosystem health."

Much of the river's pollution originated with human sewage, and cleaning the Potomac required expensive upgrades to water treatment plants such as the Blue Plains Advanced Wastewater Treatment Plant, just south of the capital. Blue Plains is a massive plant, capable of treating some 370 million to 1.076 billion gallons of sewage a day for the District of Columbia and parts of Maryland and Virginia. In 1979, Blue Plains underwent a $1 billion upgrade, which added new technologies such as BNR, or biological nutrient removal, which uses bacteria and other organisms to consume sewage. (It was such a success that over a hundred other treatment plants around the bay were also upgraded.)

The clean water laws of the 1970s had clearly defined criteria, with deadlines and enforcement penalties spelled out. But in 1981, Ronald Reagan ushered in the era of deregulation and a massive reduction in funding for the EPA. Under Reagan's Secretary of the Interior, James Watt, and his EPA administrator, Anne Gorsuch, regulatory oversight was sharply curtailed, and the EPA relied on industry to voluntarily police itself—in what has been called a "grand experiment." It was a miserable failure. Around Chesapeake Bay it led to confusion, inaction, and countless missed deadlines.

Today, the lofty goals of the 1972 Clean Water Act—to clean up all water pollution by 1985—remain unattained, even in the waters at the feet of the nation's capital. Groups such as the Chesapeake Bay Foundation hold fund-raisers to "Save the Bay" and urge lawmakers to craft meaningful environmental laws. But up to half the pollution flowing into the bay remains essentially unregulated, and the effects on aquatic life have been devastating.

"WELCOME TO THE DEAD ZONE"

The day in 2008 when we sailed across the bay, from Rock Creek to the Delmarva Peninsula, both in Maryland, it was bright and hot, and the

Chesapeake's water looked syrupy. We were aboard *Adventure Bound,* a thirty-six-foot sloop, captained by Earl Greene, a cheerful mustachioed raconteur who has sailed all over the world. At the USGS, he works on groundwater hydrology. There was not a whisper of wind, so Captain Greene didn't bother to hoist the sails. It took *Adventure Bound* a couple of hours to motor across the bay.

It had recently rained, and we sliced through a patch of brownish water—"probably caused by storm-water runoff from construction sites," said Captain Greene. Bob Hirsch and I sat in the cockpit with a group of scientists, eating blueberry bagels and sipping orange juice.

As the Chesapeake widened before us, the water turned from brown to gray-green. Captain Greene pointed to a patch of reddish algae, called Mahogany Stain, which is the result of overnitrification. The stain kills rockfish (striped bass), often carries coliform bacteria that cause painful sores known as fisherman's disease, and has led to beach closures. "We're seeing more and more suspended solids in the water, which block sunlight," said Greene. "Sea grasses need clear water to photosynthesize in sunlight. But now a lot of those grasses, which provide oxygen and hiding places for little fish, are dying."

Scott Phillips, a USGS hydrologist, added, "The bay is a pretty tough place, but it's up against a big enemy. It's like a fighter that keeps getting knocked down and standing up. But by the seventh knockdown, it might not be able to stand up and recover to the way it was in the 1950s."

"Welcome to the dead zone," someone said.

A dead zone is an area where oxygen levels are low, or hypoxic, a condition caused by excess nutrients in the water. Nitrogen and phosphorus are the two primary nutrients for microscopic organisms called phytoplankton. In small quantities phytoplankton are invisible to the eye, but in large numbers they cause algae blooms that cloud the water red, green, yellow, or brown and block sunlight from other underwater plants. When the phytoplankton die, they are eaten by bacteria, which uses up much of the oxygen in the water. Fish and crabs either leave the area or suffocate. Worms and clams emerge from their sedimentary hideaways in an attempt to reach oxygen. Other animals lower their metabolism and simply shut down. Those that can't move die.

Thus, the excess nutrients mount a double attack: they promote phytoplankton growth, which blocks sunlight and destroys plants and grasses that provide food and habitat for marine creatures; and the bacteria that feed on dying phytoplankton suck away oxygen normally used by fish and crabs. Once every bit of oxygen has been used up, a new suite of bacteria bloom, often producing a strong sulfurous odor.

To Hirsch, the Chesapeake Bay is something like a giant petri dish in which multiple diseases are festering. "Most people don't understand what's happening here," he said. "But they do like [to eat] their rockfish and oysters and crabs. And those creatures are all being affected by the water quality of the bay. It's in big trouble."

Rockfish, also known as striped bass, a black-and-white-striped sport fish, are fun to catch and delicious to eat. But in the mid-1980s, the Chesapeake's rockfish were being overfished, and a moratorium was imposed. By 1995, the population had revived—in what wildlife experts hailed as "a rare triumph"—and the fishing ban was lifted. In 1997, though, pods of dead and diseased rockfish appeared in the bay, forcing beach closings and threatening a fishing industry worth $300 million a year. The rockfish suffered from painful-looking lesions—similar to those on the freshwater bass in local rivers—and from mycobacteriosis, a wasting disease that causes fish to lose weight and is the result of bacteria in the water. (It can cause skin infections in humans.) What sorts of bacteria are causing mycobacteriosis, and how they ended up in the Chesapeake, is the subject of ongoing investigations.

Even more distressing, the Chesapeake oyster, a quintessential part of local culture, is facing catastrophic population declines. Since the Civil War, a large percentage of the oysters eaten in America were the teardrop-shaped Atlantic oysters, *Crassostrea virginica,* from the Chesapeake. Oysters spawn in the warm season (hence the injunction against eating the bivalves in months that don't feature an *r* in their name), by releasing gametes into the water, which fertilize when opposite gametes meet. A female Atlantic oyster can exude ten thousand to 60 million eggs, only a fraction of which will find a mate. This haphazard procreation strategy makes it essential for oysters to be bedded near one another. Once gametes connect and form a larva, it drifts and uses cilia to "swim" in tidal currents. When the larva has grown to about three hundred microns, it extends its foot onto a hard, chalky surface and grows into a spat. The zone it prefers is just under the water surface, which holds the maximum amount of oxygen and food particles.

Chesapeake oysters have long been farmed by "watermen," who used sailboats and long metal tongs or power dredges to rake them off the bottom. Traditionally, the bay was considered a "public fishery," meaning anyone with a license could harvest oysters from state-owned flats. Catch size and limits were set but not always maintained. This led to overfishing, which wore down the population. Disease further eroded stocks. After years of decline, oysters began to grow too far apart for their gametes to connect regularly, and those larvae that did survive had difficulty finding hard surfaces to grow on. The population began to crash. Today, the watermen's harvest is estimated at only one-tenth of 1 percent of what it was in 1900.

Few species filter nitrogen from the water as efficiently as oysters. "The oyster is pretty particular about what it eats, but it's not particular about what it filters," Bill Goldsboro, a senior scientist with the Chesapeake Bay Foundation, said. A single oyster can filter about fifty gallons of water per day. A few decades ago, the Chesapeake had enough oysters to filter the entire bay every week. Today, that same task would take the existing population a full year.

Restoration efforts have been under way for years but have shown only glimmers of success. Over the summer of 2009, a surprising bit of good news came from the mouth of Virginia's Great Wicomico River. An experiment that began in 2004, using broad beds of oyster shells that raised oyster seedlings above the sediment, resulted in a promising comeback. The experimental "oyster cities"—comprising 185 million oysters on eighty acres of raised beds, created by the US Army Corps of Engineers—contain the largest reestablished population of native oyster species in the world. Scientists from the Virginia Institute of Marine Science believe the Wicomico could prove a model for revivals elsewhere. The looming question for researchers, though, is disease. In 1996, a healthy spawn of oysters in the river was eventually wiped out by disease. What happens in the next few years will be critical to *Crassostrea virginica*'s long-term recovery.

With all due respect to the oyster, the blue crab is Chesapeake Bay's most delectable and famous seafood. But since 1990, the bay's blue crab stock has dipped 65 percent. While the number of crabs in the bay has always had cyclical ups and downs, it has never before stayed so low for so long. Marine biologists say that the number of spawning crabs dropped to 100 million in 2007 and estimate that if the population dips below 86 million, the blue crab could be doomed.

The declining crab population is due in part to overfishing, but the main culprit remains the dead zones, which scientists estimate rob the bay of some eighty-three thousand tons of fish and other ocean life each year, which is enough to feed half the crabs caught each year. Dead zones usually occur only in the summer, when sunshine and warm water power the algae blooms, but this could change as the effects of global warming spread.

The watermen call dead zones "bad water," and they compare notes on where algae are blooming and where the crabs go afterward. "In the summer, you'll pull the [crab] pots up, they've got algae and mud all over them. The bad water comes in and coats everything and the crabs can't stand it," Paul Kellam, the captain of the *Christy,* told the *Washington Post.* His nineteen-year-old deckhand, Randy Plummer, said, "I want to make a living on the water. But there ain't no future in it. Everybody knows that."

At the end of our two-hour cruise, Captain Greene berthed *Adventure Bound* at a marina on the Delmarva Peninsula, in Maryland. In a restored inn overlooking the bay, we were served a sumptuous lunch of crab cakes—the signature dish of the region. They were large and moist, and as we smacked our lips and savored every last crumb, the chef emerged from the kitchen. He beamed as we applauded his work. Then the party began to break up.

Hirsch glanced out at the bay, framed in a window, and pulled the chef aside. "Just out of curiosity," he asked, "where does your crabmeat come from?"

Without a trace of irony, the chef replied, "Indonesia."

THIS TIME IT WILL BE DIFFERENT

In 1983, the EPA announced an ambitious cleanup initiative to clean Chesapeake Bay of pollutants by 2000. The program was heralded as a model remediation program, but the result is a case-study of just how difficult pollution control can be. The six states that drain into the bay and Washington, DC, missed their first deadline, so the EPA set a new deadline for 2010. By then, $5 billion had been spent on pollution controls but nitrogen had been cut by only half the required amount and phosphorus levels had risen higher in eight of Chesapeake Bay's nine major tributaries. The EPA did not punish the states for missing their targets, and while the states did impose tighter regulations on sewage plants, they did not crack down on pollution from farms or city sewers. The Obama administration's ongoing attempts to force the states to take responsibility for reviving Chesapeake Bay have been met with fierce resistance and apathy. The core problem was the human fear of and resistance to change, which was encouraged by entrenched financial interests and abetted by a lack of political will. The bay states have different fishing regulations, their officials do not coordinate well, and their legislators are reluctant to get tough on small farmers and commercial fishermen (about one thousand watermen ply the bay, and many other jobs depend on them), especially during a recession or in an election year. Environmental groups, such as the Coastal Conservation Association (CCA), have pushed for capping fish catches and lobbied politicians to list oysters as an endangered species. But so far that has not happened.

On September 11, 2009, President Obama declared Chesapeake Bay a "national treasure" and unveiled sweeping plans for the federal government to take over efforts to restore its waters, including proposals to strictly regulate agricultural runoff, curtail development, and protect crab and oyster fisheries. It appeared to be one of the few high-profile victories for the EPA, and its new administrator, Lisa P. Jackson, during Obama's first year as president. But Washington has a reputation for making bold statements that aren't translated into meaningful action. Those working to protect the bay know its problems are complex and resistant to quick fixes.

In 2009, a pair of Maryland lawmakers introduced the Chesapeake Clean Water Ecosystem Recovery Act, which would funnel some $2.25 billion over six years into cleaning up the estuary. The bill languished for months, taking a backseat to debates over health care and the war in Afghanistan, until the spring of 2010, when BP's Gulf of Mexico oil spill generated wide interest in environmental cleanup programs. The new bill would fund the EPA's efforts to cut the amount of nitrogen entering the bay by 30 percent by 2025; states that do not meet their goals could lose millions of dollars in Clean Water Act grants, which, in Virginia alone, for example, amount to some $24 million.

But concerns over state and federal debts have undermined the bill, and agricultural and builders' associations have pushed back. The American Farm Bureau, in particular, has opposed it, saying that provisions of the bill requiring farmers to fence off cattle, cover manure pits, and install vegetation that slows storm-water runoff would be too expensive for its members.

Dick Brame, a CCA fisheries scientist, described the Chesapeake's ecosystem as "a patient that is dying of arterial bleeding, but he also has cancer. The arterial bleeding in this case is overexploitation of species. The cancer underneath is the continuing decline of water quality. If you can't stop the bleeding, the cancer doesn't matter. But if you do, you still have to deal with the cancer."

CHAPTER 8

The Missing Greenhouse Gas

A BIGGER PROBLEM THAN CARBON

"By the way, dead zones aren't just a local syndrome," Bob Hirsch said on our last day of touring the Chesapeake Bay watershed. "You see it in much bigger river systems, like the Mississippi and Atchafalaya. It's a global problem—a *growing* global problem."

In 2004, the UN reported 146 dead zones worldwide. By 2008 there were 405. These areas affected a total of more than 245,000 square kilometers, which is roughly the size of the United Kingdom. They are found in the Baltic Sea (now hypoxic year-round), the Black Sea, the Adriatic, and off the coasts of South America, Japan, Australia, and the United States. They can appear in the salt water of Long Island Sound and the freshwater of Lake Champlain—both popular recreation areas where water quality has been seriously degraded. The dimensions of dead zones change over time, according to wind, weather, and nutrient flows. Some are small, perhaps one square kilometer, while others, such as the persistent dead zone off the coast of Oregon, measure three hundred square miles.

"We believe that nitrogen is the main problem," said Hirsch, who is frustrated by the lack of research on the subject. "A lot of people are focused on CO_2 these days—we hear about carbon emissions, carbon footprints, carbon trading, carbon caps, carbon sequestration, you name it—which is all well and good, don't get me wrong. But when it comes to discussing big environmental issues, carbon tends to 'suck all of the oxygen out of the room.' There's little discussion of other issues, like nitrogen—which is arguably an even bigger problem than carbon."

Some scientists have labeled nitrogen a "missing greenhouse gas" because it is not one of the four gases (carbon dioxide, methane, nitrous oxide, and sulfur hexafluoride) and two groups of gases (hydrofluoro-carbons and perfluorocarbons) named in the Kyoto Protocol, the global accord on climate change.

Mankind is changing the way certain elements move around between soil, rock, living things, water, and air. We have caused the most significant changes by our heavy reliance on nitrogen and carbon. "In our focus on climate change, driven mostly by carbon, we shouldn't lose sight of the way we are changing the nitrogen cycle," Hirsch said. "In fact, while carbon in the atmosphere has increased by about thirty-five percent over the past century, nitrogen flowing down the Mississippi River has increased two hundred percent."

America's biggest dead zone lurks in the Gulf of Mexico, a result of the outflow of the Mississippi River. "It's bad enough that little Muddy Creek impacts Chesapeake Bay," Hirsch said. "But think of what happens when the Mississippi and Atchafalaya flow into the Gulf of Mexico. Those are much bigger systems, by several orders of magnitude; the effects of nitrogen and phosphorus runoff on them is that much bigger, too."

At 2,320 miles, the Mississippi River—"the Big Muddy"—is the second-longest river in the United States; when it combines with the Missouri, it creates the biggest river system in North America. The Mississippi's watershed, its size exceeded only by those of the Amazon and the Congo, drains 41 percent of the continental United States, or 1.245 million square miles, drawing water from parts of thirty-one states and two Canadian provinces before the big river empties into the Gulf of Mexico, about a hundred miles downstream of New Orleans.

Every year farmers apply approximately 7 million metric tons of nitrogen, in fertilizers, to the Mississippi Basin. (This number does not include nitrogen from human sewage, animal manure, the atmosphere, or natural deposits from woodlands.) According to a USGS study, nine states—Illinois, Iowa, Indiana, Missouri, Arkansas, Kentucky, Tennessee, Ohio, and Mississippi—account for 75 percent of the nitrogen and phosphorus flowing into the Gulf from the Atchafalaya and Mississippi River Basin. Agriculture accounts for an estimated 70 percent of nitrogen delivered to the Gulf; about 9 percent originates in urban areas.

Nitrogen is "slippery," meaning it is mobile in the environment; rather than sticking to the soil, where the farmers want it, as much as 20 percent of the fertilizer is washed off the land and flows downstream to the Gulf, where instead of producing corn it stimulates algae growth. Wetlands help to filter and absorb some of this runoff, but they have largely been filled in and destroyed by man. In the Midwest, about 85 percent of wetlands have been drained and filled in to create farmland or room for development.

Fossil fuels burned by cars, factories, and power plants are another major problem, creating low-lying smog and high-altitude air pollution. When it rains, nitrogen oxide is scrubbed from the air, drops to the ground in acid rain, and is eventually washed into freshwater ways and the sea.

Carried into the Gulf of Mexico on warm, fresh Mississippi and Atchafalaya currents, nutrients collect near the Gulf's surface, where sunshine causes the massive algae monster to bloom. When those algae die, they settle into the deeper, colder salt water, where they decay and use up all of the oxygen near the bottom. Down there, the algae create the Gulf dead zone, which has averaged 6,046 square miles since it was first mapped in 1985. The lack of oxygen in the Gulf's deep waters makes it impossible for fish and other aquatic life to survive.

When conditions are right, the eutrophication in the Gulf of Mexico can grow to Frankensteinian proportions. In 2002, a record algae bloom created a dead zone of 8,500 square miles, which is slightly larger than the state of Massachusetts. In 2008, the dead zone was slightly smaller, thanks to the water-mixing effects of Hurricane Dolly. In 2010, the BP oil spill from the sinking of the Deepwater Horizon caused further environmental destruction.

The Gulf's dead zone depletes about 212,000 metric tons of biomass, which serves as food for brown shrimp. Robert Diaz, a marine biologist at the College of William & Mary, estimates that this is enough to feed 75 percent of the brown shrimp usually caught in a season. "If there was no hypoxia and there was that much more food, don't you think the shrimp and crabs would be happier?" he said. "They would certainly be fatter." The Gulf's shrimp population has plummeted, causing the Louisiana fishing industry, the nation's second largest, to crash.

QUEEN OF THE DEAD ZONE

In the first decade of the twenty-first century, a combination of vastly increased corn and soybean production in the Mississippi watershed—much of which is slated for what Hirsch deems "the great ethanol fuel experiment, a very misguided experiment in my view"—and terrible flooding in the Midwest, which washed many pollutants into the system, worried experts. Some fear that the Gulf's dead zone could expand to as much as ten thousand square miles.

Nancy Rabalais, executive director of the Louisiana Universities Marine Consortium, described it this way: "Think of a giant corridor from Des Moines to Chicago, and you [put] a great big piece of Saran wrap over all that area and sucked all the oxygen out. You would have a big problem."

Rabalais, known as the Queen of the Dead Zone, was the first to map the Gulf of Mexico's hypoxia, in 1985. Every summer she sets out into the Gulf aboard the research vessel *Pelican* to chart the spread of algae.

One of the biggest challenges to denitrification is the politics of agriculture in the United States, she says. The Mississippi Basin encompasses many communities, each with its own agenda and set of conditions; without much federal leadership on the issue, it is difficult to build consensus, fund programs, and turn ideas into action. "Des Moines is willing to filter their drinking water to an extra degree just to be able to flood their water supply with more-than-normal levels of fertilizer," Rabalais said. "Look, you just can't have all these states and all these communities knowingly overfertilizing their land because they want a bumper crop every year. That's just all kinds of bad."

In response to growing alarm, the EPA and other federal and state agencies drafted a plan to shrink the Gulf's dead zone to 1,930 square miles by 2015. The EPA calls the plan "urgent." Yet, funding and political will seem to have dissipated. "It's so much talk and not enough action," Rabalais complained to the *New York Times*. "Because you're not just going up against the agribusiness lobby, but also the livelihood of farmers. It is not exactly popular in the Midwest."

Economists have suggested using a cap-and-trade system for nitrogen polluters, based on that used for carbon—an approach to control pollution by setting limits, or a cap, on how much pollution can be emitted by factories. Companies that are big polluters can buy additional pollution credits from those that pollute less; in effect, buyers pay to pollute and the sellers are rewarded for reducing emissions.

Some nations are exploring so-called geoengineering solutions: large-scale human intervention into natural systems, such as bubbling air into bays, to stir up the hypoxic water. Biotech companies are trying to engineer technologies to keep nitrogen fixed in the soil. Others are trying to develop nitrogen-use efficiency (NUE) technology, which allows plant roots to absorb more nitrogen before it gets washed away.

One option that Bob Hirsch favors is the imposition of strict TMDLs, or total maximum daily loads. A TMDL is a pollution budget: if a body of water remains polluted even after point sources, such as sewage plants and factories, have been cleaned up, then regulators allocate the maximum load of pollution that comes from each part of the watershed, allowing quality standards to be met. TMDLs are a provision of the Clean Water Act; many of them have been calculated and put into place, but they remain only goals with no easy way to enforce them. If it were granted authority, the EPA would oversee TMDLs and be able to fine polluters who flout the standards.

But no hydrologists, biologists, activists, or politicians really know whether such measures will solve the dead zone puzzle. Humans have put nutrients into the soil for centuries, and by now they have penetrated deep into groundwater and sediments. Even if new sources of nitrogen are removed, the old stores will continue to be released over time. Since 1950, the amount of nitrogen applied to the land in the Mississippi River Basin has grown by more than a factor of ten. "If you stopped applying nitrogen to the land surface today—magically put an end to all of the pesticides and fertilizers, which you can't—it would still take decades before you'd see significant reductions of nitrogen in Chesapeake Bay or in the Gulf of Mexico," said Hirsch.

But he finds room for cautious optimism. "Seven million metric tons of nitrogen is applied to the land in the Mississippi Basin every year. But the amount that flows into the Gulf is only about one to one and a half million metric tons," he says. "What happened to the rest of it? Clearly, there's a lot of natural processing occurring along the way, such as storage or denitrification. These numbers suggest there's something we can do about nitrates because nature is doing a lot to eliminate them." In other words, man can learn to imitate nature's nitrogen-scrubbing processes.

Consider denitrification, for example. When water with a heavy nitrate load flows through groundwater that has lots of carbon and little oxygen, the bacteria turn it into harmless nitrogen gas. By enhancing this natural process, people can greatly reduce the problem of too much nitrogen.

An accident around the Black Sea offers a mixed lesson on the revivification of dead zones. After the dissolution of the Eastern Bloc, Black Sea nations with centrally planned economies could no longer afford to use manufactured fertilizers. (And they don't use the nitrogen-heavy feed for their animals that American farmers do.) Within seven years, the nitrogen load flowing into the Black Sea had dissipated and most of the dead zones disappeared; now the depleted fisheries are reviving. Which has been excellent for environmental health but devastating to local farmers and regional economies. Some argue that if the amount of fertilizer applied to the Mississippi River Basin was dramatically cut, it would help to reduce the Gulf's dead zone, but at the cost of US farmers' export of grain, a major crop. This is just one example of how complex the politics of dead zone cleanup can be—a situation that will almost certainly be exacerbated as the effects of the BP oil spill are felt in the Gulf, while the human population continues to grow, and demand for food—and clean water—intensifies.

CHAPTER 9

One Step Forward,
Two Steps Back

WHO IS MINDING THE WELL?

In December 2009, after a series of blistering news reports—in the *New York Times,* the *Washington Post,* and the Associated Press—about the rise of water pollution in recent years, the House Committee on Transportation and Infrastructure held hearings on water quality, which revealed a deepening rift between federal and state lawmakers.

"States are doing a good job of enforcing provisions of the Clean Water Act and should be commended given the many constraints such as small budgets and an expanding number of polluters," said Tom Porta, an environmental official from Nevada. CWA violations, he said, "represent a small part of the compliance picture."

But many congressmen were unconvinced by this and said they were shocked to learn that water pollution was such a big problem thirty-seven years after the CWA was signed. "I don't think anyone realized how bad things have become," said Representative James Oberstar, a Minnesota Democrat. "The EPA and states have completely dropped the ball."

The question of what role the Environmental Protection Agency and its leader, called an administrator, should play has been a sore point in Washington for years.

Since its heyday in the seventies, the EPA has suffered a long, slow decline. Underfunded, overly politicized, and widely dismissed as toothless, the agency shed water-pollution experts and became increasingly ineffective during the administration of George W. Bush. During his presidency EPA regulators took a hands-off approach to municipal water systems and tried to nudge repeat polluters to comply with the Clean Water Act and Safe Drinking Water Act rather than punish them with fines. This approach proved ineffective at stemming pollution, and agency employees grew cynical and demoralized.

Part of the problem was (and is) that EPA regulators lack jurisdiction to prosecute many major pollution cases. This is the result of rulings that have left it unclear which waterways are protected. An estimated fifteen hundred major pollution cases were not prosecuted in recent years because of confusion over jurisdiction, according to the *New York Times*. Most notorious was the muddying of the Clean Water Act by the US Supreme Court.

In 1995, in Midland, Michigan, developer John Rapanos filled fifty-four acres of wetland with sand to build a mall. He had not filed a permit, but argued the land was not technically a wetland, and that he didn't need a permit. The US Army Corps of Engineers denied him a permit to build, and the EPA charged Rapanos with violating the law by filling in the wetland. The Clean Water Act protects "navigable waterways," and Rapanos said his property was twenty miles from the nearest navigable waterway. In enforcing the law against Rapanos, the EPA had interpreted the law broadly, to include wetland areas connected by tributaries, as it had traditionally done. State officials, and even Rapanos's own environmental consultant, agreed with the EPA. Rapanos was convicted of two felonies for violating the law and faced millions of dollars in fines.

But Rapanos appealed his case up to the Supreme Court. In June 2006, five of the justices agreed to void the rulings against Rapanos. Four conservative justices argued in favor of a restricted interpretation of "navigable waters," while four liberal justices argued in favor of the EPA's interpretation. Justice Anthony Kennedy did not fully join either side and argued for a case-by-case evaluation. The result of the *Rapanos* case was general confusion as to what legally constitutes a wetland and how to enforce the law.

In 2007, the US Chamber of Commerce complained that because of the *Rapanos* ruling, some sixteen thousand permits for projects around streams had been delayed because developers were unsure of their rights.

On the other hand, EPA's chief enforcement officer, Assistant Administrator for Water Granta Nakayama, wrote in an internal memo (leaked to Greenpeace) that the *Rapanos* decision "ignores longstanding ecosystem . . . protection," was causing "jurisdictional uncertainty," and "a significant impact on enforcement." Nakayama concluded that the decision had "negatively affected approximately 500 enforcement cases" in nine months. Not long after Nakayama's memo came to light, Representative

Henry Waxman revealed that the EPA had dropped or delayed more than four hundred cases involving illegal pollution from industrial discharges and the like. (John Rapanos never admitted to breaking the law. But by 2008 he had paid a $150,000 civil penalty and agreed to spend another $750,000 to re-create the wetlands he had destroyed.)

Rancor over the Rapanos case continues to fester, not the least among EPA regulators. "We are, in essence, shutting down our Clean Water programs in some states," Douglas Mundrick, an EPA lawyer in Atlanta, told the *New York Times*. "This is a huge step backward. When companies figure out the cops can't operate, they start remembering how much cheaper it is to just dump stuff in a nearby creek."

Part of the problem was that EPA officials lacked meaningful enforcement tools or were pressured not to use the ones they had. Peter Silva, assistant administrator for water, defended the EPA's regulatory actions—known as administrative and judicial referrals—saying they rose from 4,478 cases in 2004 to 5,875 in 2008. But a study of CWA enforcement by Jay Shimshack, an economist from Tulane University, found that while EPA is allowed to fine polluters up to $50,000 per day for illegal discharges, actual fines were much lower. Between 2001 and 2008, the median amount of EPA penalties for water pollution was $3,000, and these fines often targeted multiple violations over several months. "Environmental monitoring and enforcement has been falling over time," Shimshack wrote.

The most basic problem for the EPA, though, is a lack of public support for pollution control. While most Americans support the idea of environmental protection in the abstract, many resist—sometimes fiercely—government oversight of their water use. People who tell pollsters they are in favor of reducing the human "footprint" on the environment are often unwilling to pay for cleanup and conservation measures. Where the payer (the current generation) is not the same as the beneficiary (future generations), "the American people are ideological liberals and operational conservatives," wrote former EPA administrator William Ruckelshaus in the *Wall Street Journal*.

Even when state governments enact tough environmental laws, they don't always appropriate enough money to enforce them, while local courts often refuse to prosecute water contamination cases as fully as they could. But, then, legislators and courts simply reflect the public's will.

As he campaigned for the presidency, Senator Barack Obama vowed to reinvigorate the EPA. Upon his election, he announced a new era of "scientific integrity," "rule of law," and "transparency" at the agency—implicit rebukes of the Bush administration's poor environmental stewardship. He backed his words by raising the EPA's annual budget from $7.7 billion in 2008 to nearly $10.5 billion a year in 2010, the largest budget in the agency's history. And in January, 2009 he swore in Lisa P. Jackson as the first African American woman to head the EPA.

But even before Jackson's swearing-in, the EPA was faced with a crisis.

At 1:00 a.m. on December 22, 2008, a massive dike at the Kingston Ash plant, a Tennessee Valley Authority (TVA) facility, ruptured, unleashing a toxic wave of some 1.1 billion gallons of coal slurry and water. Of the 5.4 million cubic yards of coal ash released, about 3 million cubic yards flowed into the Emory River, polluting it and downstream rivers. The ash also destroyed three homes, disrupted electrical power, ruptured a natural gas pipeline, covered roads and railroad tracks, and caused dozens of people to be evacuated. It was the largest coal ash spill in US history, and the cleanup will cost an estimated $1.2 billion.

EPA investigators found that the ash spill had swept numerous poisons—including arsenic, cobalt, iron, and thallium at dangerous levels, as well as naturally occurring radioactive materials, such as radium—into the Emory River. But the agency does not classify coal ash as a toxin, a situation that hobbled EPA regulators: how could they fine or punish the TVA if the dangerous pollutants it spilled were not classified as such?

The question was made even murkier by its timing: the Kingston spill took place in the last days of the Bush White House, and before President Obama had sworn in Lisa Jackson as the EPA's new administrator.

Jackson, forty-six at the time, and a Princeton-educated chemical engineer, had worked for sixteen years as an EPA scientist before overseeing enforcement of water and land-use laws for the New Jersey Department of Environmental Protection (NJDEP). At her confirmation hearing in January 2009, a few weeks after the Kingston spill, she said she intended to review whether coal ash should be treated as hazardous waste. But while the agency announced proposed new regulations in May 2010, it deferred answering the key question of whether to treat coal ash as hazardous waste, drawing criticism from the environmental community.

The Kingston disaster was a trial by fire for Jackson, and her response—well-intentioned rhetoric followed by inaction—became a symbol of the political difficulty of environmental protection and of what Jackson's critics perceived as her weakness.

While some hailed her as "one of EPA's most progressive administrators," critics from both the right and left questioned Jackson's fitness for the EPA's top post. "Under her watch, New Jersey's environment only got dirtier, incredible as that may seem," said Jeff Ruch, executive director of Public Employees for Environmental Responsibility (PEER), referring to Jackson's previous job at the NJDEP. "If past is prologue, one cannot reasonably expect meaningful change if she is appointed to lead EPA," Ruch wrote to President Obama.

Jackson had worked as an EPA staff scientist in Washington, DC, and New York City. In 2002, she moved to the NJDEP and headed several high-profile cases—including the landmark Highlands Water Protection and Planning Act, which preserved 860,000 acres slated for development and protected freshwater supplies for 5.4 million people. She proved herself a quick study and was hired by New Jersey's then governor John Corzine as his chief of staff in December 2008; two weeks later, she was tapped by Obama for the EPA.

But, according to PEER's reports, Jackson did such a poor job of regulating toxic Superfund sites at the NJDEP that the Bush EPA felt compelled to intervene. In a separate case, Jackson's unit discovered that a day-care facility housed in a former thermometer factory was exposing toddlers to mercury pollution, but failed to alert parents for more than three months. (Jackson did not respond to my requests for an interview.)

In her first months as administrator, Jackson seemed to confirm the suspicions of critics such as PEER's Jeff Ruch when she stumbled over the charged question of mountaintop coal mining. In this practice, tops of mountains are blasted away to reveal subterranean coal seams. Under the controversial "fill rule," the fractured rock waste, which can be toxic, is often bulldozed into local rivers, killing fish and making the water undrinkable.

Early in her tenure at EPA, Jackson approved over two dozen permits for mountaintop coal mining that were holdovers from the Bush administration. Environmentalists were aghast. "This mining is devastating Appalachia," declared Robert F. Kennedy Jr., Riverkeeper's chief prosecuting attorney. "Everyone expected Obama to do something about it. Instead they're saying, 'We're going to let this happen.'"

A year later, Jackson admitted those quick approvals were a mistake. "In hindsight, I certainly wish we could have gone through a longer process," she told *Rolling Stone*. In the meantime, she had put seventy-nine permits for mountaintop removal on hold, pending a review to ensure that each complied with the Clean Water Act. In an unprecedented move, the EPA revoked a permit for the Spruce No. 1 Mine, Appalachia's largest mountaintop-removal operation, which had sought permission to destroy seven miles of West Virginia streams.

In her first year on the job, Jackson seemed to find her footing in Washington, and water quality emerged as an important theme for her. She declared that enforcement of the Clean Water Act was "a priority," while acknowledging that the EPA had fallen "short of this administration's expectations. . . . The time is long overdue for EPA to reexamine its approach."

She vowed the agency would establish strict new benchmarks for state regulators, compel companies to submit electronic pollution records so violations could more easily be detected, and target enforcement of the most egregious contamination cases. Jackson said that EPA regulators would refocus on nonpoint polluters, such as CAFO feedlots, mines, wastewater treatment plants, and building sites. Jackson also worked with Congress on legislation to require chemical manufacturers to prove that their compounds are safe before they enter the environment, saying, "Safety standards . . . should rest on industry." The EPA targeted 104 chemicals for regulation under the Safe Drinking Water Act, a move that would more than double the 91 toxic substances currently regulated.

In 2010, Jackson announced a new strategy to limit contaminants in drinking water. Instead of assessing pollutants one by one, as in the past, the EPA said it intends to address contaminants in groups, promote new treatment techniques, use multiple statutes to protect water supplies, and build better state and local partnerships.

Despite these promising efforts, resistance to environmental regulation remains strong. The agriculture industry, for example, worried that tougher regulations would be difficult and expensive for small farmers to comply with and might even drive them out of business. In signing the Clean Water Act, "Congress did not intend [the act's reach] to be unlimited," averred Don Parrish, a lobbyist for the American Farm Bureau Federation.

And powerful politicians—most notably Senator James Inhofe, Republican of Oklahoma, the ranking member of the congressional Committee on Environment and Public Works—said that the EPA's rules were already too difficult for operators of small water systems to comply with.

Gene Whatley, executive director of the Oklahoma Rural Water Association, which represents 458 rural systems, told Inhofe's congressional committee, "Many of the regulations and water quality standards are unnecessary, and the benefits and regulations do not justify the cost. This is a significant problem for small systems."

Rural water suppliers were worried they wouldn't be able to afford or comply with increasingly restrictive laws, Whatley said. At one Oklahoma water plant, the cost of water treatment chemicals rose from $1,800 a month to $18,000 a month, which Whatley blamed on more stringent EPA rules. Using their limited funds to keep up with "unnecessary regulations," Whatley said, left small operators unable to afford other important projects, such as upgrading their water treatment facilities.

But Jackson wasn't just pressured by Republicans: coal-state Democrats, such as Representative Earl Pomeroy of North Dakota and Senator John D. Rockefeller of West Virginia, attempted to weaken the EPA's authority to restrict climate-polluting gases. David Obey, the chairman of the House Appropriations Committee, exempted Great Lakes shippers from strict EPA restrictions on diesel emissions from lake shipping. The move—reportedly a favor done for a diesel-fuel refinery in Obey's district—undermined an antipollution measure designed to save twelve thousand lives a year.

By 2010, some of the environmentalists who'd questioned Jackson's fitness for the job had been won over. Buck Parker, the former head of Earthjustice, told *Rolling Stone,* "She's fantastic . . . one of the bright lights of the administration." But Jeff Ruch of PEER told me it was too soon to appraise Jackson. Pointing to her "opaque" promises and her "waffling" on mountaintop removal, he said that many of Jackson's pronouncements "appear to be more hype than reality. Many of the plaudits she has received have been for low-hanging fruit. On issues requiring heavy lifting the jury is still out."

CHAPTER 10

Time of Waste

When you put your hand in a flowing stream, you touch the last
that has gone before and the first of what is still to come.

—Leonardo da Vinci

WASTE NOT, WANT NOT

In the twenty-first century, the nation is faced with a set of new conditions: the population continues to grow, the climate is warming, and
demand for freshwater is surging, yet supplies are generally static or are
dropping. Many experts fear that this century will prove to be an age of
scarcity. We have responded by searching for new sources of water, which
has led to innovations and forced the issues of water quality and quantity
to converge more tightly than ever.

One effect of this new sensitivity to quantity has been a surge of research
and investment in recycling. Just as severe water pollution in the Berkeley Pit led people in Butte, Montana, to create new remediation technologies, so has water scarcity led to technical invention. By 2010, more than
a billion people worldwide lacked safe drinking water, and the demand
for efficient water treatment systems was rapidly expanding: *Global Water
Intelligence* magazine estimated the water treatment market will grow 18
percent between 2010 and 2016.

Perhaps no water treatment initiative is more counterintuitive, or divisive, than turning sewage—one of man's most ancient and intractable
water pollution problems—into a solution. Wastewater, of all things, is
being hailed as a potentially significant source of "new" freshwater.

• • •

QUALITY

Victorian London was the first place in which as many as 2.4 million humans were densely packed into a thirty-square-mile urban zone. In the last week of August 1854, many residents of Golden Square, a dank slum, suddenly became ill, and some of them died writhing in pain. Their symptoms included stomachaches, cramps, diarrhea, a terrible thirst, and vomiting. Seventy deaths occurred in twenty-four hours, most within five square blocks, while hundreds more—entire families, often—were infected by the mysterious disease. Known as cholera, the illness had been feared in Britain since devastating outbreaks in the 1830s and 1840s, one of which killed almost seventy-five hundred Londoners within two years. But no one knew how cholera was transmitted. Most experts suspected it was airborne, passing from one person to another by coughing or breathing.

John Snow, a private doctor, had a novel theory: he believed that cholera was transmitted by contaminated drinking water. He studied water samples under a microscope and plotted the patterns of cholera death on a map. His "Ghost Map" showed the disease radiating from an epicenter at the Broad Street pump, which drew from a well beneath Golden Square. Authorities shut down the pump, and within days the cholera epidemic disappeared.

In pinpointing the locus of the outbreak, Snow had pioneered the science of epidemiology. An assistant curate later discovered that the outbreak had been triggered when a sick baby's diapers were thrown down the well, infecting the water. Shortly after Snow created his Ghost Map, an Italian researcher named Filippo Pacini identified the cholera bacteria itself, *Vibrio cholerae,* which circulates from one person's feces to another person's stomach, and back again. Although he published his findings, Pacini's work was ignored until 1884.

From that point on, the elimination of human and animal waste from water supplies was one of the central goals of water treatment around the world, and one of the most important efforts in the history of public health. Yet today, much of our freshwater is mixed with treated sewage; some of it is used for irrigation, and some of it we drink.

THE WATER FACTORY

A deeply embedded human trait is to be revolted by the idea of drinking sewage, and there are sound reasons for this. As John Snow discovered nearly two centuries ago, wastewater contains many contaminants that can lead to serious illness. But domestic sewage includes runoff from sinks, washing machines, and lawns; only 10 percent of household wastewater comes from the toilet, and most of that does not include solids. In other words, household effluent is about 99 percent water, which can safely and economically be recycled.

Although many people are not aware of this, water systems across the country take drinking water from rivers or lakes, then discharge treated wastewater back into those same water bodies; the water flows downstream, and at the next community the cycle is repeated; and so it goes, again and again. Up to half the water in American rivers is recycled this way.

At its northern reach, the Mississippi supplies drinking water to St. Paul, Minnesota, then carries the city's effluent downstream. By the time it has traveled over a thousand miles south to New Orleans, the river has flowed through the "kidneys" of over a dozen cities before emptying into the Gulf of Mexico. Likewise, the Colorado River is used both for drinking water and to flush away treated sewage by more than two hundred communities, including Las Vegas, Phoenix, and Los Angeles.

The effluent in a river such as the Mississippi or Colorado doesn't go directly into people's taps, of course. Once it leaves a sewage plant, the treated sewage is swept along by river currents and is heavily diluted with clean, naturally supplied water. Sunlight, and time spent mixing and settling, degrade pollutants further. At the next town, treatment plants filter and disinfect the water to a high quality and often mix it with other supplies before piping it into people's homes. To ensure quality, the EPA requires utilities to monitor pathogens and report any abnormalities, and most do so with admirable efficiency.

Though properly recycled water has proven safe for people to use, it doesn't make sense to use water that has been laboriously and expensively cleaned to drinking water standards to fill toilets or irrigate gardens and golf courses.

In the 1960s, concerned about dwindling water supplies, hydrologists in arid states suggested using recycled water for those purposes. They separated treated water into two classes: water clean enough to drink, and "gray" water clean enough that it could be used for such things as irrigation. (Technically, gray water is household wastewater that does not contain sewage, while *blackwater* is wastewater that contains sewage. Both can be treated and reused.)

A gray water movement sprang up in dry and increasingly populated Southern California. Since 1994, the state has been a leader in developing large-scale treatment systems for oil refineries and communities. The seventeen thousand citizens of Arcata, for example, rely on a townwide gray water system for nondrinking use. Frustrated by California's byzantine plumbing codes, "graywater guerrillas" have created illegal but efficient systems made of PVC pipes, buckets, gravel, and cattails that send sink and dishwasher runoff into toilets and lawns.

"In a drought-prone region like ours, it doesn't make sense to use potable water to irrigate," explained Michael Markus, general manager of the Orange County Water District (OCWD). Recycled water helps to conserve drinking water and reduce energy use.

Orange County lies south of Los Angeles and gets only fourteen inches of rain a year, on average. Though it once had plentiful groundwater, supplies began to drop in the 1950s. The depletion of aquifers—originally by irrigators, and recently by urbanization—has lessened the hydrostatic pressure underground. Ocean water has seeped as far as five miles inland to fill the void, and the salt water has contaminated freshwater supplies.

Two-thirds of the county still relies heavily on groundwater, but southern Orange County must import 90 percent of its drinking water from Northern California's Sacramento Delta, or from the Colorado River, to the east. Both sources are hundreds of miles away and are already overused; importing their waters is expensive and energy-intensive.

In 1976, Orange County opened Water Factory 21 in Fountain Valley, the first treatment plant to use reverse osmosis to purify household wastewater to drinking-water standards. But it wasn't used for drinking. It processed recycled sewer water into highly treated water that was injected into wells along the coast, forming a hydrologic barrier against saltwater intrusion.

In other places, recycled water has been used to make ice for skating rinks, or artificial snow, or to water the greens at golf courses such as Pebble Beach, home to the US Open. But that was just the beginning. For years, recycling advocates have pushed to use highly treated sewage (they prefer the term *wastewater*) as a new drinking supply. The technology is proven and is being used in a limited way. It has been highly controversial but may also be a harbinger of things to come for the rest of the nation. The question is, if current trends continue, will we have a choice?

FROM THE TOILET TO THE TAP

How exactly do we turn human waste into drinking water? Praised as "showers to flowers" technology by its supporters, and derided as "toilet to tap" by its opponents, this transmutation process has set off a furor in California while slowly gaining acceptance elsewhere.

In El Paso, Texas, recycled water supplies 40 percent of the city's tap water. In Fairfax, Virginia, recycled water provides 5 percent of the city's drinking supplies. Counties in Florida and Georgia are evaluating the idea. In other parts of the world, the showers-to-flowers experiment is well under way. Windhoek, Namibia, for instance, is one of the driest places on earth and is the only major city to rely solely on treated wastewater for its drinking supply. Singapore uses ultrapurified sewage water to supply its high-tech industry. Arid nations such as India have already invested in advanced water treatment systems, while Israel and Australia are studying the idea closely.

By the mid-1990s, the Orange County Water District was facing continued problems with saltwater intrusion, increasing demand for its treated wastewater. County planners decided to replace Water Factory 21 with the larger, more advanced Groundwater Replenishment System, which produces 70 million gallons of highly treated wastewater per day, some of which is pumped into the aquifer and eventually added to Orange County's drinking supply.

The practice remains highly controversial, but, said OCWD's Markus, "We got into this out of necessity, not choice. . . . We live in a desert, but a lot of people here don't seem to realize it. We have very little water, and the concern is that our periodic droughts will grow more extended. We realized we needed to find a more reliable supply."

By 2007, the population of Orange County was surging toward 3 million and facing two related problems: soaring water demand and an increasing amount of sewage. In 2007, water consumption in the central and northern parts of the region was half a million acre-feet a year. By 2020, the population is projected to increase by 20 percent, and water consumption will climb to six hundred thousand acre-feet a year. (An acre-foot of water is 325,851 gallons, which is the amount that would cover an acre of land with one foot of water.) County managers solved their problems with one masterstroke: turn the bothersome sewage into a new supply of drinking water.

In January 2008, Orange County opened the $481 million Groundwater Replenishment System (GWRS), the world's most ambitious sewage-water purification project, on the site of Water Factory 21. The GWRS collects wastewater from twenty-two cities—including Santa Ana, Newport Beach, Fullerton, and Costa Mesa—and, after an initial cleansing at a conventional two-stage sewage treatment plant next door, pushes the effluent through fine reverse-osmosis membranes, doses it with hydrogen peroxide (an oxidizer), and disinfects it under ultraviolet light to kill any microbes and pathogens. The result is "the cleanest water there is," said Mike Markus of OCWD.

The GWRS's treated water does not flow directly into people's taps, though it is clean enough to do so. Instead, it is pumped fourteen miles north into a series of recharge basins in Anaheim. There, it mixes with natural supplies, storm-water runoff, and water diverted from the Santa Ana River, which eventually percolates down through layers of sand, clay, and rock into deep aquifers. Months later, the mixture is pumped back up and sent to 2.3 million customers.

The GWRS plant produces 23.5 billion gallons of water a year. "It's a water supply we can't get anywhere else," said Markus. "It's a big, big advance in water treatment."

The toughest hurdle for reclaimed toilet-to-tap water is not microbial, financial, or technical: it is emotional. The "yuck factor" led to screaming headlines and became a divisive political issue, especially in San Diego and Los Angeles, the state's two biggest cities.

"Your golden retriever may drink out of the toilet with no ill effects. But that doesn't mean humans should do the same," declared the *San Diego Tribune*. In 2006, the paper and the city's mayor criticized the idea of adding recycled sewage to the city's water supply as too costly and an unnecessary risk to public health.

Inveighing against the "toilet-to-tap boondoggle," opponents labeled recycled sewage "an option of last resort" because "many uncertainties are associated with assessing the potential health risks of drinking reclaimed water."

Daniel Okun, distinguished professor of environmental engineering at the University of North Carolina, told the *New York Times Magazine* that treated sewage water "may contain trace elements of contaminants. Reverse osmosis [filtering] and UV disinfection are very good, but there are still uncertainties." Mary Quartiano, a spokeswoman for the Revolting

Grandmas, a San Diego civic group, said she opposed the plan because "I just look at what goes down my toilet."

San Diego imports about 85 percent of its water. In 1999, and again in 2007, the City Council promoted a $200 million sewage-reclamation project that would produce 21.2 million gallons of water a day. The city's two relatively new treatment plants (which already transform wastewater into recycled water for irrigation and industrial use) work at only one-quarter of their capacity and could easily produce potable water. While the plan made sense on paper, public aversion to toilet-to-tap water overwhelmed the technical, fiscal, and environmental virtues of the initiative.

In 2007, when Bruce Henderson, a former city councilman, described water reclamation as a form of "economic racism" that "the affluent . . . can opt out of. They can just drink bottled water," the initiative was killed.

In 2000, a similar public outcry forced Los Angeles to abandon a $55 million project that would have provided enough water for 120,000 homes.

But David Spath, who once headed the California health department's drinking-water division, said that while some concerns about using reclaimed water are legitimate—treatment equipment can malfunction, for instance—the risks are "no greater, and probably in some cases better, than in what people may be drinking from river systems around the country." Most California environmentalists, such as the San Diego Coastkeeper, support the initiative. City planners have noted that in the long run, toilet-to-tap water is going to be cheaper and have a smaller carbon footprint than pumping water from hundreds of miles away.

THE TEST CASE

Orange County managed to avoid the yuck-factor trap by conducting extensive public outreach—"a battle for minds"—before proposing its enhanced reclaimed-water system on the grounds of Water Factory 21. The mission was led by Ron Wildermuth, a retired navy captain who had served as the public relations officer for General Norman Schwarzkopf during the first Persian Gulf War. After two years of handing out free pizza and talking to everyone from local garden clubs to leading politicians, OCWD had worn down virtually all opposition. With backing from city councils and state and federal politicians, Orange County's GWRS was green-lit in 2001, winning $92 million in local, state, and federal grants.

The timing was fortuitous. Since the mid-1960s, the Metropolitan

Water District (the Met), the regional water wholesaler, had supplied Orange County with sixty-five thousand acre-feet of water a year. But in 2007, water imports from the overstretched Colorado River and Sacramento Delta were severely restricted, and the Met was forced to drastically reduce the amount of water it could guarantee for delivery. Had Orange County not built the GWRS, which opened in 2008, it would have been left high and dry. (The Met has awarded GWRS an $85 million operational subsidy for reducing its dependence on imported water.)

The Groundwater Replenishment System is a collection of low-slung modernistic buildings, with tan concrete walls, big white holding tanks, and gray pipes. It uses a multistaged "treatment train" to produce "ultra-pure" water. First, sewage is processed by the county's treatment plant, next door. (The residue left over from processing sewage is flushed out to sea, where it is diluted.) Then the treated wastewater passes into the GWRS, where microfiltration removes any bacteria, protozoans, and suspended solids; reverse osmosis removes viruses, dissolved minerals, and pharmaceuticals; any remaining microscopic organic compounds are removed by oxidation, which disinfects the water. Just about everything in the water is removed. Indeed, the GWRS's water is so pure that minerals must be added back into it lest the treated water leach calcium out of the cement mortar that lines water pipes, weakening them.

The GWRS's water is cleaner than natural water supplies. Even so, it is against state regulations to send treated wastewater directly into people's taps (known as direct potable reuse). Why? There are technical reasons, but essentially, Markus sighed, because "the public is simply not ready yet."

If current social and environmental trends continue, recycled sewage will undoubtedly be flowing directly into people's taps within a few years—in Orange County, at least, if not in San Diego. "I believe it will become a reality in the not-too-distant future. Maybe ten years from now," Markus predicted in 2009. "We hardly have enough water to keep up with the growth we have already. We're severely challenged, and with all the new problems it's only going to get worse."

Markus was talking about Orange County, but his words hold true for every community. What might be called the Age of Easy Water—an era of plentiful, reliable supplies of clean water, accessible to population centers—is drawing to a close. The drama behind this headline is playing out in sometimes surprising ways and places, from deep beneath New York City to the high, parched valleys of Nevada to the fragile Sacramento Delta in California. People everywhere are facing a new hydrologic reality.

PART II

DROUGHT

A Creeping Disaster

CHAPTER 11

Water Scarcity

And it never failed that during the dry years the people forgot about the rich years, and during the wet years they lost all memory of the dry years. It was always that way.

—John Steinbeck, *East of Eden,* 1952

PLUMBING THE EIGHTH WONDER OF THE WORLD

On a cold, bright afternoon in March 2007, I walked across a busy construction site on a windy corner of Eleventh Avenue, on the far west side of midtown Manhattan, stepped aboard an orange steel elevator cage, and dropped into an enormous hole in the ground. The hole, called Shaft 26B, was the main portal to a new subterranean labyrinth, City Water Tunnel No. 3. Pressed around me were half a dozen men dressed, as I was, in yellow slickers, muddy rubber boots, and orange hard hats. "The tunnel can be dangerous," said Ted Dowey, the project's executive construction manager. "It can flood. Water pressure can hemorrhage a pipe. And there's groundwater seepage through the rock—about two hundred thousand gallons a minute along the nine-mile tunnel. If you don't pump it out every day, the water'll shut it down."

Dowey slammed the gate shut. "Okay!" he said. The construction elevator shuddered disconcertingly, and with a grinding noise began to drop. We passed through a couple of inches of asphalt, perhaps a foot of concrete, several feet of brown dirt, then continued down through sixty stories of dark gray granite called Manhattan schist, 450-million-year-old metamorphic rock that is flecked with mica and prized for its ability to support one of the densest clusters of skyscrapers in the world. At two hundred feet down, the hole at the surface through which we could see blue sky was reduced to the size of a quarter, and the light was growing murky. By three hundred feet down, we were completely enveloped in a warm, humid blackness. By five hundred feet, I heard the sound of dripping water. After a long four-minute ride, Dowey said, "Almost there!" A single dim light-bulb rose up from below, like some kind of phosphorescent deep-sea fish, then a bell rang, and the cage bounced to a stop. Dowey opened the gate, and we filed out into a world of smudged light, ankle-deep water, and soft gray mud. We were roughly 580 feet underground, inside New York City's most urgent water supply project.

At this depth, I sensed the weight and density of the city's bedrock. My eyes slowly adjusted to the gloom, and I saw muddied yellow drill rigs mounted on Caterpillar tracks. The rigs were armed with twin hydraulic bits and stood next to a long, mud-spattered conveyor belt. Giant air ducts and thick, looping power lines carrying 13,200 volts of electricity to power the tunnel-boring machine snaked along the wall beneath a line of dim bulbs. In either direction, the massive tube seemed to recede to infinity.

Dowey, a tall, lean man with a dark goatee, pointed straight ahead, along the tunnel. "That way is north," he shouted over the roaring fans that supplied fresh air. "From here, the tunnel runs straight uptown to Sixty-Eighth Street, with no stop signs." Then he turned downtown. "Let's go this way and see if we can find some sandhogs." *Sandhogs* is the nickname for the tunneling specialists who have excavated New York's subways, sewers, and skyscraper foundations since the mid-1870s, when they dug out the caissons for the Brooklyn Bridge.

Manhattan is a relatively dry island in a relatively wet region. Viewed through the lens of water supply, New York City has more in common with dry Western cities such as Denver, Phoenix, and Las Vegas than it does with most places in the East. Just like those cities, New York has responded to its water demands by building a gigantic siphon to bring water into the city from rural sources far away.

Tunnel No. 3 is a project of the New York City Department of Environmental Protection (DEP), which comprises the largest and most complex municipal water system in the country—known to many engineers as "the eighth wonder of the world." The DEP's exquisitely engineered network of dams, reservoirs, aqueducts, and tunnels draws from a watershed stretching across 1,972 square miles—an area about the size of Delaware—and contains 580 billion gallons of water. The distribution system supplies roughly 1.3 billion gallons of freshwater to 8 million city dwellers and 1 million suburbanites every day. The DEP system encompasses sixty-five hundred miles of water mains and sixty-six hundred miles of wastewater pipes; 95 percent of the water it carries flows dozens of miles into the city by gravity alone. Dropping from aqueducts as high as fourteen hundred feet above sea level down to pipes a thousand feet below sea level, the water builds up so much pressure that when it reaches Manhattan's water mains, where it flows at roughly ninety-five pounds per square inch, it will rise to the sixth floor of most buildings unaided by pumps. Pressure in the system is so great that in some parts of the city it must be lowered mechanically by regulator valves.

New York City's water system was well designed and robustly built but has grown leaky and decrepit with age. Parts of the system are 140 years old and require significant upgrades. The city's drinking supply has had a higher profile under Mayor Michael Bloomberg, but much of the system suffers from years of underinvestment and deferred maintenance, and the DEP faces a growing list of problems: infirm dams and seeping water tunnels, sewage overflows and industrial water pollution, pressure from development and gas drilling in the watershed, tension between rural communities and the city over control of water, competition with neighboring states for future drinking supplies, and worries about the impact of climate change on water quality and quantity.

Aging infrastructure is a growing problem nationwide, but the decline has occurred largely out of sight, both literally and figuratively. The American Society of Civil Engineers (ASCE), the nation's oldest engineering society, has reported that much of the nation's hydro-infrastructure is on the verge of failure. In its 2009 Report Card, ASCE gave the nation's infrastructure a D, or "Poor," grade, and waterworks earned some of the worst grades of all: the nation's dams were given a D, while drinking water, wastewater treatment plants, inland waterways, and levees all received grades of D-minus, meaning they are dangerously compromised.

In New York, DEP engineers are especially concerned about the state of the city's two main water arteries—City Water Tunnels No. 1 and No. 2.

Tunnel No. 1 was completed in 1917. It runs eighteen miles, from Hillview Reservoir in Yonkers (now a large city in Westchester County, two miles north of Manhattan), through the Bronx, across the Harlem River, down the west side of Manhattan, under Central Park, over to the Lower East Side, and across the East River to downtown Brooklyn, where it terminates at Schermerhorn Street and Third Avenue. Most of Tunnel No. 1

lies about 250 feet deep, and it carries 500 to 600 million gallons of water a day. But it began to leak even before it was officially turned on. Since then, new types of concrete and grout have been developed specifically to patch New York's water tunnels.

Tunnel No. 2, completed in 1936, carries 700 to 800 million gallons of water per day. It begins at Hillview Reservoir and runs through the Bronx, before bending south under the East River to Astoria, Queens, and running along the length of Brooklyn to New York Bay, where it connects to the Richmond tunnel, a five-mile spur that carries water to Staten Island. Tunnels No. 1 and 2 were connected at the Battery, on the southern end of Manhattan, to form a continuous loop.

Both tunnels have been in continuous service since the day they opened, delivering the vast majority of the 1.3 billion gallons consumed daily in the city. But the two original water tunnels have grown fragile and now leak a large amount of water. The city does not provide total estimates for leaks, though it admitted that the Delaware Aqueduct was leaking between 10 and 36 million gallons of water per day before repairs in 2008. I have been told by a person close to the DEP that for years the city hardly bothered to measure its water use and had no idea of how much water was being lost. In the early 2000s, the DEP improved its water metering, regularly checked its pipes with sonar, and used temperature and pressure sensors to identify leaks. But it is virtually impossible to pinpoint a leak unless someone complains about it. In 2007, 159 leaks—most in small pipes feeding buildings or houses—were identified by complaining citizens, and the repairs saved an estimated 4.6 million gallons of water a day. (The EPA estimates that 1 trillion gallons of water are wasted every year in the United States—due to leaking pipes and fixtures and aging infrastructure.)

Tunnels No. 1 and No. 2 are essential to the city and cannot be taken out of service for inspection and repair until Tunnel No. 3 is completed in 2020. If either tunnel No. 1 or No. 2 collapsed, millions of people would lose water. If both suffered major breaches at the same time, New York City would effectively be shut down. Mayor Bloomberg has called the tunnels "very vulnerable" and said, "The city could be brought to its knees if one of the aqueducts collapses."

Some engineers believe that Tunnels No. 1 and No. 2 are in such poor shape that the water pressure inside may be the only thing holding them intact; if the pressure lessens, weak sections could cave in. Other experts fear the possibility of an earthquake, and geologic fault lines do cross

Manhattan. If one, or both, of the city's main water tunnels collapsed, the city would return to its natural state: essentially a dry, rocky island. There would be no tap water and no fire hydrants; dehydrated people would fan outward as people searched for a drink; those who hoarded enough water to stay would be dirty; disease and fire would spread. The Empire City would become a parched shell of its former self.

But a more immediate concern is terrorism. In 2003, Richard Fitzsimmons Jr., the business manager of the sandhogs' union, Local 147, told the *New Yorker*, "If you attacked the right spots . . . you could take out all the water going into New York City." When I asked another senior sandhog about this, he said, "Well, it would be very, very difficult. But, yes, it's possible."

The construction of City Tunnel No. 3 was authorized in 1954, and by the late 1960s city engineers—called pencils by the sandhogs—had drawn up plans for much of it. But ground wasn't broken until January 1970. At the time, the DEP figured the project would cost $1 billion to complete.

More than half a century after its planning, the tunnel is still under construction. Tunnel No. 3 is scheduled to be fully operational by 2020, at a total cost of $6 billion, making it the largest capital construction project in the history of New York City. Stage 1, which runs from the Bronx into Manhattan and cost $1 billion, went into service in 1998. Stage 2, which will complete the tunnel's passage through Manhattan and link Brooklyn to Queens, will begin operation in 2013, at a projected cost of $2 billion. Stages 3 and 4, which will connect Tunnel No. 3 to the Kensico Reservoir and add another thirty miles of tunnel in Queens and the Bronx, are in the final planning stages and are estimated to cost $3 billion. When it is completed, Tunnel No. 3 will extend over sixty miles, from Hillview Reservoir in Yonkers, south through the Bronx and down the length of Manhattan, and into Brooklyn, Queens, and Staten Island. A key element of the new system is that valves for the new tunnels are housed in a series of underground distribution chambers, which allow for maintenance. The largest of these is the system's command center, the Van Cortlandt Park Valve Chamber, a 620-foot-long, 42-foot-wide, 41-foot-high vaulted room hidden twenty-five stories beneath Van Cortlandt Park, in the Bronx. It contains eight-foot-wide conduit pipes with meters that measure water flow, seventeen steel lateral tunnels, nine vertical shafts, two giant manifolds, and thirty-four precisely designed valves made of stainless steel, rather than bronze, in Japan. Once the new system is complete, DEP engineers will be able to use these valve chambers to route water around any problematic sections of tunnel, ensuring that the city's water supply is never interrupted. For security reasons, the exact location of the DEP's valve chambers is not publicized; they are extremely difficult to access and designed to withstand a nuclear blast. Aboveground, the Van Cortlandt Park Valve Chamber is marked only by a small guardhouse and a door leading into a grassy hillside, which masks one of the most critical pieces of infrastructure in the city.

Nearly six hundred feet belowground, Ted Dowey sloshed ahead of me through the muddy, cold, ankle-deep water of Tunnel No. 3. After fifteen minutes, we came to a junction in the railroad tracks and saw a half dozen shadowy silhouettes moving in the gloom: sandhogs. Large men, dressed in orange or black hard hats and yellow slickers, hogs always work in "gangs" of six, for safety and efficiency, and often develop specialties, such as drilling, electrical work, or dynamiting rock.

Tunnel No. 3 turned forty years old in 2010, and some hogs and pencils have spent their entire careers working on it. The hogs are a tight-knit fraternity, mostly of Irish or Grenadian descent (islanders from Carriacou—one of the Grenadine islands, in the Caribbean—are particularly well represented), with a few men of Italian or Hispanic origin. There are no female sandhogs. The only woman I saw on my trip underground operated the elevator cage in Shaft 26B. Families of sandhogs intermarry, hand positions down through generations, are superstitious about the dangers of their job, and are well compensated. Standard pay is $35 to $38 an hour, and experienced hogs can make $100,000 to $120,000 a year.

Hogs have their own language, rituals, and specialized tools—spud wrenches, sinking hammers, jackleg drills, drift pins, lump hammers, scaling bars, side cutters, flashlights, dynamite, "battleships" (buckets), "rabbits" (sponges), and "muck sticks" (shovels). Before the advent of automated tunnel-boring machines, which went into use in 1992, Tunnel No. 3 killed twenty-four men in twenty-five years. No sandhogs have died in Tunnel No. 3 since Anthony Oddo was crushed by a sixteen-ton winch that tumbled down a 503-foot-deep shaft in Queens, in 1993. But it remains a dangerous place.

Building their aqueducts two thousand years ago, Roman engineers used fire and water to crack rock and removed the shards with horse-drawn wagons. Building the first stage of Tunnel No. 3, sandhogs relied on technology only marginally better: dynamite, picks, and brute force, or "drill and blast."

Since 1992, hogs have used tunnel-boring machines (TBMs), better known as moles, to drill through the rock. A typical mole is seventy feet long and trails another seven hundred feet of equipment, including a machine shop and a dining car. The machine weighs 230 tons and has to be lowered into a shaftway in pieces by a special crane and assembled underground. Computer-operated and laser-guided, the mole is outfitted with giant hydraulic arms that grab the tunnel walls and propel its cutting face into the granite. At its front is a round shield studded with twenty-seven cutting blades, each of which weighs 350 pounds. While the hydraulic rams push the snout of the machine into the rock face, the shield spins and the blades shred the schist with a deafening cacophony. A conveyor belt carries the resulting gravel away to the rear and unloads it into muck cars. The muck is hauled to the surface and trucked to a landfill in New Jersey.

Before 1992, it took eighty sandhogs a full day to drill and blast through twenty-five to forty feet of bedrock. Now, a mole cuts through fifty-five to a hundred feet in the same time.

Tunnel No. 3 has taken six times longer to build than either of the first two tunnels, mostly because of financial and political, rather than geological, challenges. In the early 1970s, cost overruns totaling millions of dollars led to a lawsuit by the city against a consortium of contractors, which delayed work. In the mid-1970s, the project was again halted while the city extracted itself from bankruptcy. In 1981 work resumed sporadically. But by then, New York's increasing thirst had led the DEP to send 60 percent more water through Tunnels No. 1 and No. 2 than they were designed for. Meanwhile, corruption plagued the Board of Water Supply, a now defunct body that oversaw construction, further slowing progress. Worried that Tunnel No. 3 was suffering death by a thousand cuts, city executives beseeched federal officials to step in and finance the project; Washington declined. In the 1990s, work again resumed, but NUMBY, or "not under my backyard," protests erupted in Manhattan and Queens, where residents held signs aloft saying DON'T GIVE US THE SHAFT! to protest the building of access shafts and the use of dynamite in their neighborhoods.

Finally, in 2001, Mayor Bloomberg took a personal interest in Tunnel No. 3. He told a 2006 press conference that his administration had devoted $4 billion to the new tunnel, or "double what's been invested by the last five administrations combined." During his mayoralty, progress on the tunnel has remained steady, as has his worry about the city's water supply.

The pressure to finish Tunnel No. 3 as quickly as possible is high. Beginning in 2004, the hogs tunneled five days a week, in three shifts a day, in "maximum effort," said Ted Dowey. In any twenty-four-hour period, about 165 men were in Tunnel No. 3, shuttling between work sites by six diesel locomotives.

As my tour of Tunnel No. 3 came to an end, Dowey explained that about six more years of work lay ahead: the DEP would have to line the tunnel with concrete, sterilize it so that it can carry drinking water, hook it up to many trunk lines, fit it with instruments and sensors, and connect it to the command center under Van Cortlandt Park. (By 2010, the excavation of Stage 2 was complete, and the hogs were working one shift per day, mostly in the Distribution Chamber.)

We rode the elevator cage back up Shaft 26B to the surface and emerged, blinking in the sharp light and cold air. As we stepped out of the cage, a fresh crew of sandhogs trooped aboard. There was some jovial shouting, one man made a quick sign of the cross, the cage door slammed shut, and within minutes the men had disappeared down the giant hole.

THE URBANIZATION OF WATER

While the fragility of its water system is a pressing concern to New York, other large cities face even greater and more immediate hydrological challenges.

In 2000, the world had 18 "megacities," with populations of 5 million to 10 million (depending on different definitions), or more. In 2007, 336 cities worldwide had populations of 1 million or more. According to the UN, in 2008, for the first time in history, more people lived in urban areas than in rural ones.

As of 2010, China alone had at least 43 cities with populations greater than 1 million; by 2025, according to *Foreign Policy*, that number will grow to 221. Seventy percent of Chinese will live in cities of at least 1 million by then, and 44 Chinese cities will have populations of at least 4 million.

Yet some of the world's biggest cities have already suffered unprecedented water shortages. In 2007 and 2008, Barcelona, Spain, and Melbourne, Australia, faced drought emergencies. Cities in Brazil and South Africa, nations already rife with social unrest, suffered numerous brownouts because reservoir levels were too low for hydroelectric turbines to spin properly. Mexico City, having drawn down the large aquifer beneath its streets, began to subside: sidewalks caved in, walls buckled, sinkholes appeared and occasionally swallowed cars and buildings.

As water use shifts from mostly rural use to urban use, and drought is on the rise, farmers in the American West have begun to cut down nut trees, fallow land, and sell off their water rights to expanding cities. To some longtime irrigators, water has become more valuable than crops.

In California, a drought in 2008 prompted farmers such as Bruce Rolen, a Sacramento Valley rice farmer, to fallow his fields. Instead of planting in April, he sold his irrigation water on the open market, where prices jumped from about $50 per acre-foot to as much as $200 an acre-foot. "It just makes dollars and sense right now," Rolen said. "There's more economic advantage to fallowing than to raising a crop."

As dry regions become even drier, and populations continue to grow, unprecedented ecological disasters could follow. One foreshadowing of this harrowing scenario is unfolding in Perth, Australia. In recent decades the metropolitan area around Perth has seen its population surge past 1.5 million at the same time that precipitation has tapered off. Water planners fear that unless drastic action is taken, Perth could become the world's first "ghost city"—a large, modern metropolis that will have to be abandoned due to a lack of water. This apocalyptic vision was unthinkable just a few years ago. A similar situation could be facing such cities as Las Vegas or Phoenix, in the American Southwest, which is already the hottest and driest part of the country, where cities are continuing to expand into the increasingly arid desert.

MODERN WATER USE

In the last half century, America's total water use has risen steadily: from 150.7 billion gallons per day (Bgal/d) in 1950 to 410 Bgal/d in 2005, according to the USGS. (Water use peaked in 2000 at 413 Bgal/d and has since leveled off, thanks to greater efficiency.) Eighty percent of this water was taken from surface supplies and 20 percent from groundwater supplies. Just four states—Florida, Idaho, Texas, and California—accounted for more than a quarter of all water withdrawals in the United States.

While urban demand for water is growing, the biggest users of water in the United States, and worldwide, are irrigated agriculture and power plants that run tons of water through giant cooling towers to dissipate the heat built up in electrical generation. In 2005, irrigation in the United States accounted for 201 Bgal/d, equivalent to 62 percent of the nation's total freshwater withdrawals. Thermoelectric power generation used 201

Bgal/d, or 48 percent of fresh and saline water, which was mostly used by steam-driven turbine generators and cooling towers and then returned to the environment. Combined withdrawals for domestic use, livestock, aquaculture, and mining represented just 3 percent of US water withdrawals, or less than 13 Bgal/d in 2000, the USGS reported.

But these numbers are educated guesses. No one knows exactly how much water Americans use because it often goes unmeasured. In most states, a landowner can drill a domestic well without a permit and use as much water as he wants. Some states don't require permits for commercial wells that withdraw less than 36 million gallons a year. Few states require smart water meters that measure the volume of water used in real time and transmit it to utilities—which is important to quickly detect leaks and waste, and to help boost efficiency. Without knowing how much water is being used, it is difficult to manage existing supplies, or to plan for future demand.

Because we don't measure the water we use carefully, we use it thoughtlessly. The EPA estimates that in the United States 7 billion gallons of clean drinking water is lost to leaking pipes every day; industry uses inefficient cooling towers at coal-fired power plants; homeowners insist it is their "right" to maintain water-hungry lawns in desert states; while farmers pump down groundwater supplies to irrigate thirsty crops such as corn or cotton instead of growing "dryland" crops such as nuts and fruits.

In the developing world—particularly in China, India, and Southeast Asia—rising economic success has led to bigger populations and more meat-centric diets, which increase demand for water. By the end of the twentieth century, virtually every accessible source of freshwater on the planet had been used, diverted, or altered by man. Rivers, lakes, and aquifers were drained, and at least half of the world's wetlands had been damaged or filled in, which caused greater storm-water runoff and allowed salt water to pollute freshwater aquifers. Humanity's nearly unslakable thirst is threatening to outstrip the earth's ability to supply water in a sustainable way.

Borrowing from the notion of peak oil—a point at which the supply of oil is outstripped by human consumption—academics worry that the earth could be reaching a point of "peak water." While experts don't usually predict a massive hydrological apocalypse, they point out that local water crises exacerbate many other social conflicts. They warn that two major trends, population growth and climate change, will accelerate water scarcity in coming decades, setting off a ripple effect of changes.

THE POPULATION AND ITS APPETITES

It is tempting to say that human overpopulation is the greatest threat to the planet's carrying capacity (the maximum population an area can support in a sustainable way), but that's not the whole story.

By 2025, demographers estimate, global population will increase to nearly 8 billion. By 2050, it will have risen by another 1.3 billion people. Water demand will rise exponentially as the standard of living in developing nations improves.

According to the National Center for Health Statistics, more babies were born in the United States in 2007 than in any other year in American history. The 4.3 million births that year even eclipsed the number of births in 1957, at the height of the baby boom. It is estimated that the US population will increase by over 100 million people in the next thirty to forty years. The water footprint of 100 million more Americans will be enormous. But it will pale in comparison to the water stress that will be felt in the developing world.

Most of the additional 2 billion people who are expected to join the global population by 2025 will come from developing nations that are already burdened by a lack of clean drinking water and effective sanitation. To feed an additional 2 billion people, the UN estimates, will require as much as 60 percent more water than is currently used by agriculture (assuming no changes in efficiency). But almost every available water source has already been tapped, and many have been overused.

Absolute numbers of people don't influence water demand as much as changing diet and lifestyle do. Irrigated agriculture accounts for about 70 percent of the world's freshwater use, but different diets consume different amounts of water. The largely vegetarian diets of Africa and Asia use about 2,000 liters of water a day, while the carnivorous Euro-American diner requires 5,000 liters a day (and another 100 to 250 liters of water per day for drinking and washing).

As developing nations aspire to first-world status, global diets are becoming more meat-oriented, and thus more water-intensive, due to the water required to raise animals. In 1985, a typical Chinese person ate about 20 kg of meat per year; in 2009, he ate 50 kg. This shift represents 390 cubic kilometers of water (1 cubic kilometer of water is 1 trillion liters) per year, which is nearly the total use of water in Europe, according to the *Economist*.

If global trade patterns better reflected the amount of water required to manufacture food and other products, many economists believe that water would be used more efficiently and that people would make better-informed decisions about what they buy.

The subtler point is that wealthy societies use more resources and create more pollution than poor ones do. The onus to change how water is used, therefore, rests with those who use it most. But people don't like change, and convincing them to forfeit old entitlements will be difficult. As the effects of climate change are felt, however, change will be thrust upon us.

Climatologists predict that drought will increase in many of the world's most densely populated regions this century, and that global warming is the second major trend that will significantly impact water supplies.

IN HOT WATER

In 2008, the UN's Intergovernmental Panel on Climate Change (IPCC), which shared the 2007 Nobel Peace Prize with former vice president Al Gore, identified areas of the world at risk from drought. As expected, the report identified parts of the developing world, especially equatorial Asia and Africa, as especially vulnerable to prolonged aridity. The 1984–85 drought in the Horn of Africa, the East African peninsula that encompasses Ethiopia, Somalia, Eritrea, and Djibouti, led to 750,000 deaths. But the IPCC also pointed to the American South and West as prime targets for increased heat and water stress.

In 1998, according to a NASA study, losses from a severe drought and heat wave that swept from Texas and Oklahoma eastward to the Carolinas caused some $40 billion in damage and killed two hundred people, surpassing the losses of the San Francisco earthquake in 1989, Hurricane Andrew in 1992, and the Mississippi River floods in 1993. (NASA uses satellite data and computer models to study the causes of past droughts, such as the 1930s Dust Bowl, to predict future weather patterns.)

Even places that have long been wet have recently become hotter and drier. In 2008, the water in the Great Lakes dropped to levels that impeded shipping. Dredging, which is expensive and environmentally destructive, was required to keep channels open. In the summer of 2009, Seattle, Washington, which is reputed to be one of the wettest cities in America, had no measurable rainfall for thirty days in a row, worrying city leaders.

DROUGHT

Atlanta, Georgia, faced a terrible drought between 2005 and 2009, which threatened to dry up its main reservoir, Lake Lanier. Experts fear these cases could be early warning signs of an increasingly arid future in both dry regions, such as the Southwest, and historically temperate ones, such as Georgia.

Man cannot manufacture "new" water, nor can he destroy the planet's existing supply; when water leaves one place, in one phase (solid, liquid, gas), it simply goes elsewhere, often in another phase: ice melts into liquid water, which evaporates into gas, and so on. As a result, global warming will not change the amount of water in the world, but it will change the distribution of water, which will have many consequences.

Drought, unlike other extreme shifts in weather, such as tornadoes or hurricanes, tends to tighten its grip slowly and inexorably. Some equate it to a python's squeezing its prey to death, and scientists refer to it as a "creeping disaster" because drought can deepen over many years, and its effects are not felt all at once.

There is a difference between drought and climate change. Drought is a period of months or years when a region has consistently below average precipitation. Climate change is a change in weather patterns over time, from decades to millennia; the change can be in the average weather for a region, or in the distribution of extreme weather events.

"Some places used to getting [water] won't, and others that don't, will get more," said Dan Nees, a water-trading analyst with the World Resources Institute. "Water scarcity may be one of the most underappreciated global political and environmental challenges of our time."

As temperatures rise, experts say, the demand for water will increase, storms will become more intense, and droughts and floods will occur with greater frequency. Many hydrologists believe evidence suggests that global warming is speeding up the hydrologic cycle—the rate at which water evaporates into the air and falls to the ground as rain or snow. The implications of this are enormous: as the climate warms, there will be more rain and less snow; diminished snowpack will lead to changes in runoff patterns and water supplies; increased evaporation will lead to less soil moisture, which causes greater erosion, an influx of invasive species, and the spread of pathogens.

Climate change will also change the life cycle of plants, particularly trees. With plentiful rain, plants undergo a growth spurt; in dry periods, they wilt. The extra biomass that results from a growth period creates dry tinder, which can lead to highly destructive forest fires. And it entices insects that attack large swaths of woods, such as the bark beetles that have notoriously decimated 3.5 million acres of pine forests in northwestern Colorado.

USGS scientists who conducted a fifty-year survey of forests in the western United States and Canada found that average temperatures in the West rose by more than one degree over the last few decades, and that trees were dying twice as quickly in 2008 as they did in the 1970s. The die-off in old-growth forests had eclipsed the growth of new trees. Because forests act as "carbon sinks," this has a double impact: plants take in carbon dioxide and release oxygen as they grow, which removes carbon from the atmosphere, but when a tree dies or burns, the carbon it has stored is released back into the air, which helps to warm the planet.

Though most experts tend to focus on how climate change will affect water quantity, hydrologists such as USGS's Bob Hirsch point out that it also profoundly affects water quality. Higher water temperatures, more frequent storms, and shifts in flows affect aquatic life, pollution levels, oxygen content, and turbidity, among other things. While Hirsch agrees the planet is warming, he says, "Scientific evidence about the specific ways it is changing our water resources is still very unclear."

The 2008 IPCC report highlighted concerns about equatorial regions, particularly in sub-Saharan Africa, where climate change is adding to desertification. The UN has warned that basins of the Nile, Niger, Volta, and Zambezi Rivers are all potential flashpoints for violence over water supplies. Hydrologists, academics, and diplomats worry that in coming years water disputes could devolve into wars among historical rivals—between China and India, or India and Pakistan, over the Himalayan glaciers, for example; or between Turkey, Syria, and Kurdistan over the Tigris and Euphrates Rivers; or between Egypt and its neighbors over control of the Nile.

The IPCC report also noted the diminishing snowpack of the Sierra Nevada in northeastern California, and the overuse of the Colorado River. The Colorado begins as snowmelt trickling off the Rocky Mountain snowfields, provides water for 30 million people in seven states and Mexico, and has suffered from drought since 2000. If the Colorado River continues to decline at a time when more Americans than ever are moving to cities in the desert West, the IPCC cautioned, then social, economic, legal, and environmental havoc could follow—especially in a place such as Phoenix, Arizona, which is the hottest city in the hottest state in the nation.

CHAPTER 12

The Age of Perpetual Drought

God has cared for these trees, saved them from drought, disease, avalanches, and a thousand tempests and floods. But he cannot save them from fools.

—John Muir

"GROUND ZERO FOR CLIMATE CHANGE"

At dawn on August 23, 1905, a naked man stumbled out of the Sonoran Desert, in Arizona, and collapsed at the feet of a scientist who had ventured out to study biology and meteorology. The Sonoran is an exceptionally hot, dry place, where temperatures can spike to 121 degrees in midsummer, and where there is almost no humidity and little shade. The scientist, W. J. McGee, had set up camp at Tinajas Altas, a collection of small pools that provided the only drinking water for miles. The naked man looked familiar, but his body was so withered and scratched that it was difficult for McGee to believe it was the same boisterous forty-year-old he'd met only a few days earlier.

The man was Pablo Valencia, a sailor turned gold prospector. He and his partner, Jesus Rios, had introduced themselves to McGee when they stopped to water their burros at Tinajas Altas on the way to their gold claim, near the Mexican border. When they reached the claim, the men discovered they were low on water, and Valencia sent Rios back to McGee's camp, to resupply. But in the rush of departure they failed to set a meeting place. When Rios returned to the claim, Valencia was nowhere to be seen. Rios again returned to McGee's camp, and for five days the two scoured the desert for the missing Valencia. Valencia, meanwhile, was wandering the desert in search of a way to quench his thirst. He managed to stumble across nearly forty miles of scorched sand with nothing to drink but his own urine, which he carefully hoarded in a canteen, plus a few drops of liquid he squeezed from the body of a scorpion he'd caught.

At dawn on the seventh day, McGee heard a strange noise, "like a cow bellowing" in the distance. He rushed out of his tent to find the wasted prospector weaving unsteadily toward him. McGee and Rios took Valencia in and nursed him back to health. He "was well and cheerful," McGee wrote, "though his stiff and bristly hair, which had hardly a streak of gray a fortnight before, had lost half its mass and turned iron gray."

Once he returned to civilization, McGee wrote an analysis of Valencia's extreme dehydration entitled "Desert Thirst as Disease." It is a closely observed record of what happens to the human body when it runs out of water:

> Pablo's . . . formerly full-muscled legs and arms were shrunken and scrawny; his ribs ridged out like those of a starveling horse . . . his lips had disappeared as if amputated, leaving low edges of blackened tissue; his teeth and gums projected like those of a skinned animal, but the flesh was black and dry as a hank of jerky; his nose was withered and shrunken to half its length; his eyes were set in a winkless stare . . . his skin generally turned a ghastly purplish yet ashen gray . . . the heartbeat was slow, irregular, fluttering, and almost ceasing in the longer intervals between the stertorous breathings.

When we imagine the worst-case scenario for climate change, this is one possible image: all of us reduced to Pablo Valencias, lost in a desert without a drop to drink.

In Phoenix, Arizona, which rises from the Sonoran in "the Valley of the Sun," not far from where Valencia wandered, such a fate is more than idle speculation. For three months a year, average high temperatures in Phoenix surpass one hundred degrees. There is less than 10 percent humidity, and rainfall averages only seven inches a year.

According to the National Weather Service, the average temperature of Phoenix has risen five degrees since 1960. Every summer, about eight hundred Phoenicians are hospitalized with heat-related problems; some of them, usually the very young or old, die. A report published by the *Arizona Republic* predicts that average temperatures in Phoenix could rise by fifteen to twenty degrees over a generation, due to the "urban heat-island effect"—i.e., the more blacktop highways, parking lots, air-conditioned office towers, and sports stadia that are built in the desert, the more heat will be trapped in the valley, raising temperatures to blast-furnace heights. Most credible scientists believe this shift is due to climate change.

Life in Phoenix can be viewed as a kind of experiment in extreme living, like a dress rehearsal for life on Mars, or perhaps for a future America beset by regions of extreme heat and dryness. "Having already seen an increase . . . in our average temperatures," the *Tucson Citizen* reported in 2009, "we are at ground zero for climate change."

When there is a lot of moisture, trees grow thick rings; when it is dry, the rings become thin. Looking at wood samples from around the West, paleoclimatologists from the University of Arizona have been able to track the region's long history of droughts, some of which lasted for twenty to thirty years.

About a thousand years ago, the Hohokam Indians settled in the Salt River Valley, just outside present-day Phoenix. Using stone hoes, they scraped an ingenious irrigation system out of the desert—185 miles of canals that watered crops on two hundred thousand acres. As Jared Diamond showed in his book *Collapse,* irrigation entails a number of risks; most important, if a society becomes reliant on irrigated agriculture, it will suffer disproportionately when hit by drought. The Hohokam tribe's population grew to an estimated 250,000 at its peak in the 1400s. But by the 1500s, archaeological evidence shows that the Hohokam began to quit their large settlements and scatter. Scientists conjecture that it was a lack of water, perhaps a "megadrought," or a combination of drought and flood, that led to their demise.

In the 1580s, tree rings show, a severe drought extended from California to the Carolinas. More recently, a Southwestern drought that began in the late 1940s ran until 1957. President Eisenhower declared New Mexico a disaster area, Arizona suffered from forest fires, trees began to die off, and ranchers were forced out of business.

Signs indicate that Arizona forests, stressed by rising temperatures, are dying again. During a drought in 2002, the Rodeo-Chediski wildfires—the first started by an arsonist, the second by a stranded motorist—combined in central Arizona to scorch 467,000 acres, an area the size of Phoenix. Fed by high winds and tinderbox-dry woodlands, it was the worst forest fire in the state's history, and it set off a soul-searching debate. Scientists were concerned about the health of Arizona's ecosystem, politicians and environmentalists battled over logging, and the fire helped usher in controversial policies, such as the Healthy Forests Restoration Act, which President George W. Bush signed into law in 2003.

In the aftermath of the fires, insects moved in, causing further damage to the trees. Some experts fear that if the trend continues, the forest ecosystem of Arizona could reach a tipping point and collapse.

Studies show a steady decline in precipitation across the Southwest in recent decades. Climate models for the region have predicted a deepening strain on water supplies in coming years. Some say the change could lead to aridity akin to that experienced during the Dust Bowl.

In 2007, Dr. Richard Seagar, of the Lamont-Doherty Observatory at Columbia University, analyzed what nineteen global climate models projected for the future of the Southwest. The models showed the region will become more arid this century as a consequence of rising greenhouse gases. Seagar also studied historical records and discovered that Southwestern droughts usually resulted from the cyclical variations in tropical Pacific Ocean temperature. During El Niño events (a periodic warming of the eastern Pacific), the Southwest typically has more rain and floods, while during La Niña events (the cooling of the eastern tropical Pacific), there is typically below-average precipitation. The recent drying of the region is likely due to a series of La Niñas since the 1997–98 El Niño, but it is also probably due to emerging climate change. According to Seagar's report, "human-induced aridifications" will become noticeable in the first half of this century.

I asked Seagar if he really believed that "a perpetual drought" was possible in the Southwest, as he had written. He shrugged and replied, "You can't really call it a *drought* because that implies a temporary change. The models show a progressive aridification. You don't say, 'The Sahara is in drought.' It's a desert." If the models are right, then the American Southwest could face a permanent drying out. The effects of El Niños and La Niñas will continue to be felt, but the wet years will become less wet while the dry years will become more dry.

"We are very confident about the realism of these model projections," Seagar said. "Federal and state governments need to start planning for this right now."

Australia, the driest inhabited continent in the world (Antarctica is drier), has felt the effects of climate change earlier than most other nations, and its experience holds lessons for places such as the American Southwest and equatorial Asia and Africa. At first, Australians reacted to shift-ing conditions with stubborn refusal to change, but as weather patterns became increasingly extreme in the early 2000s, they had no choice but to resort to innovative solutions.

THE BIG DRY

Goulburn, New South Wales, Australia's oldest inland city, is usually a lush green from an annual wash of twenty-six inches of rain. With a popula-tion of twenty thousand, Goulburn sits 120 miles southwest of Sydney, in a pastoral region that celebrates its heritage with the world's largest cement sculpture of a sheep, "the Big Merino." But, in the first decade of the twenty-first century, Australia suffered the worst drought in its recorded history.

By 2002, 99 percent of New South Wales—the country's most populous state, located on its southeastern flank—was suffering from a lack of water. By late 2006, average rainfall in South Australia was the lowest since 1900. That year, Goulburn saw only fourteen inches of rain, and its rolling hills turned a depressing brown. By late 2008 and early 2009, temperatures hit 109 degrees in Melbourne and 114 degrees in Adelaide, the highest on record since the 1950s. It was so hot that railroad tracks buckled, wildfires sparked and burned out of control, power plants were idled due to a lack of water, and, unable to rely on air-conditioning, people resorted to wear-ing clothes they had cooled in the freezer.

Communities in the outback were devastated. Livestock markets were overwhelmed by ranchers trying to unload sheep and cattle that they could no longer afford to feed. Production of Australia's three main crops—wheat, barley, and canola—was cut by 60 percent. Rice, a thirsty crop that Australia usually produced at a rate of 720,000 tons a year, for export to Asia, was almost wiped out: farmers harvested only 18,000 tons of rice in 2008. In some areas of the country, the price of water increased sevenfold.

Between 2001 and 2006, 10,500 families quit farming. Others suc-cumbed to even darker despair. "Every four days a farmer in Australia is committing suicide," said Charlie Prell, a fourth-generation Goulburn farmer. "I haven't contemplated that myself, but it destroys the soul."

The Murray-Darling River Basin is known as Australia's "food bowl." The Murray-Darling is also the country's most important river system, transecting the country's southeast and drawing from a watershed roughly the size of Spain and France combined. In the winter of 2006, tributaries of the Murray-Darling stopped flowing altogether. Although flows resumed late the following year, some fifty thousand farmers were affected, food prices skyrocketed, and inflation loomed.

By early 2008, rains returned to parts of eastern Australia and even threatened to flood some towns. But the Murray-Darling remained in drought, and experts fretted over the long-term repercussions. Some climate models predicted that the trend will continue, and that rainwater flowing into the basin will decline 70 percent by 2030. Many Australians feared that their hot, arid decade, what they call the Big Dry, was "the new normal."

The Big Dry may have been caused by a combination of shifting weather patterns, such as El Niño and La Niña, and the southern oscillation (changes in air surface pressure). In 2010, Australian researchers blamed climate change, writing in the journal *Nature Geoscience* that the Big Dry was likely due to "anthropogenic [man-made] climate shift."

Whatever the precise cause, the effects of the drought were greatly worsened by poor planning, outdated infrastructure, and an unwillingness to adapt to changing conditions. Industry was reluctant to change its practices, and rural irrigators vied with city dwellers over water rights. Aborigines feared a "cultural genocide" if the drought forced them out of the bush.

In 2002, farmers were using so much water from the Murray River that it no longer reached two big lakes that flow into the Indian Ocean. As a result, the lake levels dropped, evaporation accelerated, and the remaining water began to accumulate silt and salts. By early 2009, the lakes had sunk to a meter (3.2 feet) below sea level. Further evaporation could expose mud on the lakes' bottoms to the air, which would release sulfuric acid and a host of poisonous metals into the atmosphere. If this happens, the lakes will turn into what experts have termed irrecoverable "toxic swamps."

One option is to flood the dying lakes with seawater, to prevent acidification—a drastic measure that would destroy the freshwater ecosystem, disrupt bird migrations, and leave behind a salty residue. "It will end up being a dead sea," said Dr. Paul Dalby, an independent Australian water consultant. "The options are toxic swamp, dead sea, or pray for rain."

In a 2009 speech in Atlanta, Georgia, Dalby warned the United States, "Australia is where America could be in a few years. . . . Climate change is not necessarily a slow and gradual process. There are valuable lessons to be learned from the Australian experience. You can be forewarned and forearmed about how to deal with [climate change] before it arrives, and perhaps not go through so much of the pain that we had."

DROUGHT

One positive consequence of the Big Dry, he said, was that Australian farmers had learned new tricks. They now cover their crops with mulch and use underground irrigation systems to reduce evaporation. More significantly, farmers won the right to use a certain amount of water free, and a trading system now allows them to sell or buy those rights (called usufructuary rights) from each other. This market-based approach allowed resources to go to the most productive use. Profitable growers could use more water, while farmers with marginal yields could still make a living by selling their water. The allotments shift, depending on the weather. In some areas, irrigators are restricted to 18 percent of their allocation during the drought.

Australian vintners, who export some $1 billion worth of wine a year, have been especially innovative; as grape supplies drop, prices have risen overall. Water is reserved for older vines, which produce more profitable grapes. Newer vines are shorn of all their leaves, wrapped in bandages, and kept barely alive with minimal irrigation. When more water is available, the newer vines are allowed to flourish.

Australia has yet to reconcile that while it is the driest continent, it remains one of the world's biggest exporters of "virtual water," or the water used to grow exportable crops. Invented by Professor John Anthony Allan, of King's College, London, virtual water is a way to assess how much water is used to produce commodities. The water used to grow wheat, for example, is said to be "virtual" because once the wheat has been grown and is shipped to market, it no longer contains the actual water used to raise it. Measuring virtual water helps judge which crops are best suited to a given climate. Cotton, rice, corn, and alfalfa are water-intensive crops and are not as well suited to arid regions as are fruits and nuts.

Though new regulations in areas such as virtual water await political action, Australians took steps to reinvent their irrigation system. In 2009, Australia's prime minister, Kevin Rudd, launched a $1.3 billion plan to limit the amount of water extracted from the Murray-Darling Basin, buy water rights from farmers, begin monitoring water use, integrate ground and surface water supplies, impose rationing, raise water prices, ban car washing and garden watering, and invest in water infrastructure.

"For the first time the cities are focused on their worries about the future water supply," New South Wales Senator Bill Heffernan said in 2006. "Everyone has taken for granted that you turn the tap on and water comes out. I think they now can see that that might not necessarily be the case."

• • •

In the United States, the relationship between climate change and water supply has not become a politically salient topic. During the Bush years, Congress bickered over legislation aimed at reducing greenhouse gases, such as the carbon cap-and-trade proposal, which would put a price on carbon emissions and allow permits to emit the gases to be auctioned. Cap and trade is the mechanism most favored by the Obama White House for limiting carbon emissions. In March 2009, the EPA administrator, Lisa Jackson, released an official opinion stating that global warming poses a danger to public health. Congress began to lay the groundwork for legislative changes, which many in the GOP contended were based on flawed science. The conflict made a consensus impossible, and in July 2010 legislation designed to limit global warming died in the US Senate.

Despite the political gridlock, the scientific consensus is that global warming will profoundly affect the water supply in coming years and will force people to make difficult decisions about how to manage it. The demands of urban and rural users and the ecosystem will have to be balanced. As the population soars, we will need to ensure long-term food and energy supplies. To adapt to new conditions, we will need to develop new strategies and technologies.

Many of the water policies of the twentieth century will become obsolete in the twenty-first. But before addressing new approaches for the future, I went to the desert West, to see how we collected, transported, and used water in the past.

Nations have traditionally responded to a lack of water by building hydro-infrastructure, from digging simple ditches to erecting vast dams, to capture runoff in wet periods and store it for times of need. The next conceptual and technical leap was to devise ways to move water from its source (a river, lake, or aquifer) to where it was in high demand (a farm, a factory, a growing city). In America, especially in the West, grandiose schemes to relocate water supplies via man-made rivers—aqueducts or pipelines—have long been an obsession. More often than not, such "water conveyance" schemes have proven controversial. The steady growth of population and climate change will only sharpen the disagreement.

CHAPTER 13

Revenue Streams

As it happens my own reverence for water has always taken the form of this constant meditation upon where water is, of an obsessive interest not in the politics of water but in the waterworks themselves, in the movement of water through aqueducts and siphons and pumps and forebays and afterbays and weirs and drains, in plumbing on the grand scale.
—Joan Didion, "Holy Water," *The White Album*

THE JOYS AND SORROWS OF CONVEYANCE

In America, *the West* refers to those states west of the hundredth meridian of longitude. Heading south from the Canadian border, the hundredth meridian cuts through North Dakota, South Dakota, Nebraska, Kansas, Oklahoma, and Texas. To the east of that line, average annual precipitation is over twenty inches, and crops don't usually require irrigation. To the west, the land is mostly arid, and irrigation is essential.

In its water laws, the United States has long existed as two separate nations. Because water is mobile, varies in supply and location, and can be used in different ways (hydropower, irrigation, or recreation), it is notoriously difficult to regulate. Most Eastern states employ riparian ("along the bank of a river") water rights, based on British common law, while many Western states rely on the right of prior appropriation, based on Spanish precedent, with roots in Latin law. Each state uses its own variation of these basic principles, and some, such as California, use elements of both systems.

In the East, riparian rights permit the use of water found on, beneath, or next to a property. The rights cannot be sold or transferred except to a neighboring property; the water cannot be transferred out of the watershed; and the use of the water must be "reasonable." The latter is a notoriously imprecise term. What is reasonable depends on many factors, including how much precipitation has fallen, how quickly aquifers refill, or the opinions of other water rights holders. The decision about who gets to use how much water is usually judged by a court, unless a state creates a regulatory agency to determine the "reasonableness" of the water use. (Many Western states claim ownership of groundwater and allocate it through a system of appropriations.)

The nuances of Western water talk have roots in the nineteenth century, when forty-niners prospected their way across the West, while farmers and ranchers dug miles of irrigation ditches, drove Indians off water-rich land, and swiped water from one another regularly. Under the Western doctrine of prior appropriation, a person acquires property rights in water by converting it to "beneficial use," which usually means farming, ranching, or mining.

The rule of thumb for Western water is "first in time, first in right." If Farmer A claims the use of an aquifer before Farmer B, then Farmer A has the first, or superior, right to the water, even if Farmer B lives closer to the aquifer. (These claims can be inherited by Farmer A's descendants.) Subsequent users can use remaining water for their own beneficial purposes, provided that they do not encroach on the rights of "senior" users. This imprecise legal framework has reliably led to conflicts ever since its inception. It presumes that water is a commodity that is distinct from the land it is found on or under, can be mortgaged or sold like other property, and can be transported out of the watershed, often via pipeline.

One of the most controversial water-conveyance schemes in US history was promoted in the 1970s and continues to crop up: to divert water from the Columbia River—the largest river in the Pacific Northwest, which flows from British Columbia, Canada, down through Washington and Oregon to the Pacific—to the dry Southwest. Promoters of this plan argued that it would be entirely beneficial, as the Columbia's freshwater was being "wasted" as it flowed into the Pacific Ocean. This claim is one that is frequently invoked by backers of diversion projects, but it overlooks the impact a massive drawdown of river water would have on the people and the complex ecosystems that depend on existing river flows. If the Columbia's flows are diverted on a large scale, many users would be affected: power generation by nuclear plants and the fourteen dams on the river's main stem—and the many other dams on its tributaries—would be disrupted; so would shipping, transportation and recreation; and so would ecological health, especially among anadromous fish, such as salmon, which migrate from the Pacific upstream to freshwater and are a food source.

Another grandiose conveyance scheme is known as NAWAPA, for the North American Water and Power Alliance, a plan conceived in the 1950s by Donald Baker, a Los Angeles engineer, to divert water from Alaska and western Canada to the United States and perhaps Mexico. And NARA, the North American Recycling Alliance, envisions harnessing billions of gallons of the freshwater that discharges into James Bay, which is part of Hudson Bay in eastern Canada, shipping it to the Great Lakes via a tunnel, then distributing it throughout the United States and Canada. The idea has flared up periodically but is considered by most water experts to be impractical.

But many smaller water-conveyance projects are under way in the West, some of which have proven successful and nearly all of which have led to disputes.

Regulatory approval for a new pipeline is often the key to promoting real estate development. Since the 1980s, as increasing numbers of people relocated from the wet Northeast to the dry Southwest, economic and political pressure has built on local governments to approve new water pipelines. The rising costs and divisive politics of water have increasingly led state agencies to partner with private investors, or to step away altogether, allowing private water companies to build water pipelines of their own. Such projects enable developers to build where there is little or no water; they bring water to the people, instead of the other way around. The effect has been to promote the growth of cities in dry regions—such as Sparks, Nevada, St. George, Utah, and Yuma, Arizona—which were once considered too dry to sustain large populations.

According to the EPA, the United States and Canada now have approximately 1 million miles of pipeline and aqueducts, enough to circle the earth forty times, and entrepreneurs have filed applications to build more.

Some cities have a nearly magnetic attraction for those who dream of building water pipelines. Such a place is Denver, Colorado. The city and its suburbs are expanding, as are Boulder and Fort Collins, to the north, and Colorado Springs, to the south. These cities are all located on the Front Range, the dry eastern side of the Continental Divide (so-called because it marks the line that separates the watersheds of the Atlantic Ocean and Pacific Ocean). While 88 percent of Colorado's population is on the eastern side of the Divide, most of its water lies on the western side.

In 2009, Denver had 610,345 residents, making it the nation's twenty-fourth most populous city and the second-largest city in the Mountain West, after Phoenix. Denver's twelve-county Combined Statistical Area had about 3.1 million residents. And the eighteen-county Front Range Urban Corridor had an estimated population of 4.3 million. Denver Water, the city's water supplier, is one of the oldest water utilities in the West. It operates a complex system of reservoirs, canals, tunnels, and treatment plants to supply water to over a million people.

Transmountain diversions such as Roberts Tunnel, a twenty-three-mile-long pipeline bored through the Rockies, bring water from the Western Slope to Denver and its satellites on the Front Range.

Such major infrastructure does not come easily or cheaply. While national water fees average about $458 per residence a year, some of Denver's expanding suburbs charge $10,000 or more for providing water to a new home. The town of Louisville charges $20,000 per house, and Broomfield charges $24,424 per house per year. Such high fees have many causes, most notably Colorado's uniquely rigid water-court system. And as suburbs such as Thornton and Aurora reach farther and farther afield for water, they have resorted to using agents to acquire millions of dollars' worth of land, held predawn meetings with water brokers, traded water-use credits with towns hundreds of miles away, and reseeded thousands of acres of farmland as native grassland, all to protect their water sources.

"Do I choke at the price of it?" asks Peter Binney, Aurora's utility director. "Yes. But it's the cost of doing business."

While the region's growing demand for water is straining municipal supplies, hydro-entrepreneurs see it as a golden opportunity. Many dream of bringing water to the Front Range from sources far away through pipelines.

Since the mid-1980s, Dave Miller, a retired air force colonel, has pushed a plan to divert water from the Gunnison River, in west-central Colorado, to Denver; in 2005, a federal judge ruled against him, but he has not given up. In 2003, a study of the Western Slope defined five potential pipeline sites, with costs ranging from $3 billion to $15 billion; none of them have been developed, so far, but their supporters continue to push them.

Bob Moran knows a lot about these pipeline controversies, in part because his father was a major player in one of them back in the 1950s. But he also lives in Golden, just outside Denver, which is the busiest water market in the United States. "Most of the big Western rivers have their headwaters in Colorado," he explained. "There are more water lawyers—and water fights—in Colorado than in all of the other states combined."

Bob Moran is a hydrogeologist, though I prefer to think of him as an Indiana Jones of freshwater. In a typical year he will travel to half a dozen states, from New Mexico to Alaska, and several nations, from Ghana to Indonesia to Romania, conducting hydrological mapping, assessing water quality, and liaising among regulators, attorneys, and policymakers. After a stint at the USGS in the 1970s, he became an independent water consultant. His clients include players from across the water spectrum—industry, government agencies, nongovernmental organizations (NGOs), tribes, environmentalists, and private investors. Some of the latter have what Moran terms a "*special* interest in hydrology." These men tend to be wealthy, influential, secretive, and ambitious.

"There was this one guy—well, this is a wild story," he began, and he launched into a tale about a mysterious billionaire's pipeline dreams. Then Moran invited me to go have a look for myself, to see what had become of Baca Ranch and its legendary aquifer.

"WATER IS GOLD"

What makes the desert beautiful is that somewhere it hides a well.
—Antoine de Saint-Exupéry

On a hot day in August 2007, Bob Moran and I drove about 125 miles south, mostly on rural roads, from his house in Golden, just west of Denver, to the town of Crestone, in the San Luis Valley. The valley, which stretches for eight thousand square miles, from central Colorado into northern New Mexico, is a wild and beautiful place that has long attracted dramatic personalities.

In 1978, a Canadian billionaire named Maurice (pronounced "Morris") Strong bought Baca Ranch—two hundred thousand pristine acres in the middle of the San Luis Valley—for a "fire sale price," according to *Forbes*, from the oil refining consortium Tosco. Strong and his Danish wife, Hanne, fell in love with Baca and made it their permanent home. At first they planned to grow quinoa and to build a small brewery on their property. But then they discovered the aquifer, which, they later maintained, they had no idea was there when they bought the place. Given that the valley's water supply had been studied for years by private and government hydrologists, as well as mineral and energy companies, this assertion strains credulity.

The southern part of the valley drains into the Rio Grande, but much of the northern part of the valley is a thirty-four-hundred-square-mile area called the Closed Basin. Within the Closed Basin lies the Unconfined Aquifer, whose water is connected to streams and lakes on the surface. Beneath that is a layer of impermeable clay, and then bedrock. Six miles beneath the earth's surface is the Confined Aquifer, which is not connected to the surface water. The Confined Aquifer is a magnificent water supply that seems to make people go crazy. When USGS hydrologists surveyed the valley in 1971, they calculated that at least 2 billion acre-feet of water was stored in its upper six thousand feet of sediments. This is equivalent to fifty times the combined capacity of Lake Powell and Lake Mead, the enormous reservoirs built on the Colorado River. Depending on snowmelt, Baca Ranch itself receives an additional twenty thousand to thirty-one thousand acre-feet of surface water every year.

As a former oilman, Maurice Strong knew the resource business, and no one had to point out to him the commercial potential of the water under his ranch. He has predicted that by the year 2031 freshwater will be so scarce that in arid parts of the world it will be rationed by armed guards.

In the mid-1980s, the suburbs around Denver were one of the fastest-growing regions of the country. But their growth was limited by water. Some towns were willing to pay up to $7,000 per acre-foot for a reliable supply. At those prices, Strong was sitting on top of something like $14 trillion in water.

In 1986 he formed American Water Development Inc. (AWDI), with backing from the Vancouver billionaire Sam Belzberg and others. One of the first things AWDI did was to hire a young consultant from Denver named Bob Moran to assist in evaluating the quality and quantity of water in the Baca, and to interpret satellite images of the valley. Moran explained to AWDI's lawyers that while there was plenty of water there, it had spent so much time working its way through heated rock deep underground that it was infused with dissolved salts and other pollutants. Moran's recommendations to AWDI were confidential, but Strong clearly considered questions about water quality a mere bump in the road.

"It was a very interesting project, and Strong was a very mysterious man," Moran told me. "He never said much. He had this little smile. You could never tell exactly what he was thinking, but, clearly, he was thinking *big*."

Maurice Strong grew up in the Depression years in Oak Lake, Manitoba. According to legend, he graduated from high school at age fourteen, hopped a train, then worked for the merchant marine along the Canadian coast. In Alberta, he worked as a financial analyst for the oil and gas business. By twenty-five he was vice president of Dome Petroleum. By thirty-one, he was president of the Power Corporation of Canada. By forty, he was a millionaire. Later, he founded the Canadian International Development Assistance program and led Petro-Canada.

Strong has aged into a short, plump, silver-haired eminence with a soft voice, an occasional stutter, and a deferential manner—"a kind of negative charisma," as one acquaintance put it. A self-declared environmentalist, Strong organized the first Earth Summit, in Rio de Janeiro, for the United Nations, in 1992. It was the largest summit in history at the time, and its purpose was to convince delegates from 178 nations to embark on "a new era of collective security" by replacing military buildups with environmental protections. At the UN, Strong worked as senior adviser to former secretary-general Kofi Annan until 2005, when Strong resigned in the aftermath of the Iraqi oil-for-food scandal.

One evening in 1978, a gray-bearded shaman appeared at Hanne Strong's door at Baca Ranch and introduced himself as Glenn Anderson. "I've been waiting for you," he said. "I predicted in the sixties that a foreigner would come here and build an international religious center. What took you so long?" Mrs. Strong listened carefully. She had been raised in a moneyed family in Copenhagen. During the Second World War, her mother helped the Danish Resistance smuggle Jews out of Germany. From childhood, Hanne believed she could see angels and recall past lives. She sensed she had once been a Native American, and so she had traveled to the United States to find her ancestral home.

After hearing Glenn Anderson's prophecy, Hanne decided to turn Baca Ranch into an interfaith religious sanctuary. According to accounts she has given reporters, Hanne believes that a new Dark Age is coming, and that thanks to environmental degradation the earth's population will shrink to about 400 million. To prepare for the coming apocalypse, she decided to build a seed bank in her basement and turn San Luis Valley, which she calls a "birthplace of ancient souls," into a repository of world knowledge. In 1998, Hanne established the Manitou Foundation, which funds various religious orders. Today, Tibetan Buddhist monks, Carmelite nuns, Hindu gurus, humanists, an alternative community, a camp for Native Americans, wiccans, shamans, and a few stray cowboys (including a Japanese bison herder) have established themselves around Crestone, a former ghost town that now boasts a health food store, organic farms, and a bar. It is an unlikely seeming place for a water war.

At about 8,000 feet above sea level, the San Luis Valley is hot and dry, with grassy flatlands, caldera mounds, sagebrush, yucca, juniper, and scrub pine. The average rainfall is only seven and a half inches a year. Rising majestically from the desert floor are a set of enormous tan waves that undulate against the cerulean sky. These are the Great Dunes, the tallest sand dunes in North America, some peaking at 750 feet high. The sand here originated hundreds of miles away, on the Rio Grande and in the San Juan Mountains. It was lifted by winds and swept across the Rockies, then trapped here by the Sangre de Cristo Mountains. The water underlying the sandy landscape nurtures the dunes and keeps them stable. In 1932, President Herbert Hoover declared them the Great Sand Dunes National Monument.

Maurice Strong planned to pump up some of the Baca's water—twenty-five thousand to two hundred thousand acre-feet per year—and send it through a fifty-mile pipeline to a river that would carry it north to Denver and its suburbs. Annual revenues for AWDI were projected to be $175 million to $1.4 billion.

Though the San Luis Valley is one of the poorest regions in Colorado, farmers there had some eighty thousand acres of potatoes and carrots under cultivation. They feared AWDI's pumping would lower the water table. Greg Gosar, an organic farmer, predicted, "They're going to dry up this valley . . . and make obscene amounts of money doing it. . . . Unfortunately, greed isn't illegal in America." The Rio Grande Water Conservation District, the largely tax-funded entity responsible for managing the valley's water, sued AWDI in state water court. Environmental groups joined the opposition. Admirers of the Great Dunes feared that drying up the valley would hurt the sandy waves. A group called Citizens for San Luis Valley Water held bake sales to raise funds to fight Strong's plan. Cars in the valley, even the police cars, wore anti-AWDI bumper stickers. A videotape was handed around, accusing Strong of being part of an "international conspiracy" to take over the world, and of warehousing millions of dollars' worth of US currency in Canada to prepare for a new global order. Then the National Park Service objected to Strong's planned water pipe.

Stung by the criticism, Strong objected to the accusations of greed. "We love this valley. We live there," he said. But his financial partners were growing increasingly uncomfortable with Hanne, who herself had become an obstruction to Strong's ambitions. She declared to journalists that beneath the valley floor lay a sacred lake lined with crystals; a powerful energy field protected the lake from evil channelers from Vancouver who had launched a massive psychic attack on the Baca. "I know one thing for sure," she said. "This water will never leave the valley!"

US Geological Survey hydrologists had discovered that the water under the San Luis Valley is part of a vast underground system that flows from Canada through Colorado, New Mexico, and Texas into Mexico. Made up of multiple connected aquifers, it is one of North America's largest stores of groundwater. Strong's plan to siphon off much of the water midstream had caught the attention of state and federal regulators.

In May 1994, after eight years of controversy, the Colorado Supreme Court denied AWDI pumping rights and granted a motion filed by Strong's opponents to recover $3.1 million in legal and scientific costs. Strong's lawyers appealed to the US Supreme Court, which declined to hear the case. (After a protracted negotiation, Strong reportedly retained certain rights to Baca's water and was paid $1.2 million by the water company.) Strong threw in the towel. He resigned as chairman of AWDI and donated his company shares to a foundation.

One of the loudest voices of opposition to AWDI had come from Gary Boyce, a local rancher. Born into modest means, Boyce had left the San Luis Valley to work at equestrian stables across the country. He became an expert in training racehorses, and his grateful clients guided Boyce into a series of lucrative investments. After he married, he bought the fifty-five-hundred-acre Rancho Rosado, next to Strong's Baca Ranch, and moved back to the beautiful valley.

In 1995, AWDI put ninety-seven thousand acres of Baca Ranch up for sale. The Nature Conservancy bid on it, but Boyce won the parcel for about $16 million. Boyce's partner in the deal was Farallon Capital Management, one of the world's largest hedge funds, based in San Francisco. (It would later come to light that Farallon's Vaca Partners put up all of the $8 million in equity and $8 million in loans used to purchase the ranch.) The following year, Boyce incorporated Stockman's Water Company and declared his intention to pump water from the valley. His neighbors were stunned. Asked by reporters how he could protest AWDI's water project one minute and promote his own pumping scheme the next, Boyce just smiled and said, "Water is gold."

Now the Baca's water was worth even more than when AWDI was trying to commercialize it. Between 1990 and 2000, a million people had moved to Colorado's Front Range. Douglas County, between Denver and Colorado Springs, was the fastest-growing county in the nation, not to mention one of its driest. Stockman's Water Company proposed to deliver 150,000 acre-feet of water to the region annually, for a cool $750 million a year.

To blunt criticism, Boyce claimed that his pumping plan was totally different from Strong's because he would take only "a small percentage" of the water from the Confined Aquifer. If any of his neighbors was hurt by his water pumping, Boyce promised, he would compensate them. To mollify environmentalists, he said he would establish a wildlife refuge and protect his two fourteen-thousand-foot peaks from development.

Once again, the Rio Grande Water Conservation District rallied the troops, painted signs, held bake sales, called legislators, and went to court to block two ballot initiatives backed by Stockman's Water Company. They accused Boyce of "water mining"—the depletion of groundwater faster than nature can replenish it—and warned of the dangers of "out-of-state investors." The dispute had a distinctly ad hominem edge. Lewis Entz, the local state representative, characterized Boyce as "a drugstore cowboy" driven by revenge: "He's still mad at the potato farmers because they had a few more dollars to spend than he did when he was a kid. He's bitter and vindictive. So now he's gonna get even with us spud farmers come hell or high water. It's a personal deal with him."

Boyce, blowing cigar smoke, smiled wryly. "That's the way they are down in the San Luis Valley. Those kinds of [attacks] have always worked for them. . . . What you've got is a bunch of corporate farmers who are taking advantage of the system. I'm simply saying that's not right."

In 1998, state attorney general Ken Salazar—a fifth-generation native of the San Luis Valley, and now President Obama's interior secretary—strongly opposed Boyce's initiative. That year, a law passed by the Colorado legislature and the defeat of Boyce's ballot initiatives ended Stockman's Water Company's bid to export the valley's water. Boyce blamed "uninformed voters" who did not understand the complex issues. Lewis Entz had another explanation: "When people come down here and try to start trouble, we work them over."

In April 2001 Boyce and Farallon agreed to sell their Baca holdings to the Nature Conservancy for $33 million. This was more than twice what they had paid for it only six years earlier and would have represented a 40 percent profit. But in January 2002, a union report noted that Farallon's Vaca Partners was 50 percent owned by Yale University. This revelation hit like a mortar round. Yale was excoriated for a "secret investment" in a project many people deemed morally compromised. The story set off a pyrotechnical display of criticism, made national headlines, and embarrassed the university.

Yale agreed to donate $4 million to the Nature Conservancy from the university's profits from the sale of its Baca holdings. But in early 2004, Yale reneged, saying it would reduce its charitable donation to $1.5 million. Students wrote impassioned editorials in protest, pushed the university to define its ethical investing, and picketed the university's investment office. In the end, Yale donated $1.6 million in profits from the ranch sale to the Nature Conservancy. (Thereafter, Yale stopped including the names and addresses of companies it invests in on its tax returns.)

In September 2004, the Nature Conservancy led the federal acquisition of the 151-square-mile, 97,000-acre parcel of Baca Ranch, for $33 million. The Great Sand Dunes was officially designated America's fifty-eighth and newest national park. One section of the park was deemed so ecologically sensitive that it was designated the Baca Wildlife Refuge and closed to the public. At last, the water under Baca Ranch appeared to be protected forever. To tap into the Baca's aquifer, the federal government must apply for water rights from the Colorado state court. "There will be no change in the way the water is used," said Charles Bedford, the Nature Conservancy's state director. "There will be no pumping."

But as he squinted up at the Great Dunes in August 2007, Bob Moran said, "I wish I could be so optimistic. Maybe I have a touch of my dad in me. But I've seen enough to know how the world works. Politicians come and go, laws change. Nothing is permanent—especially when it comes to water. Someone is always going to try to game the system."

As I later discovered, Lexam Explorations, a Canadian energy company, had announced the previous December that while the federal government owned the surface of the park, Lexam and its partner, ConocoPhillips, had owned the mineral rights beneath the surface long before the park was protected. Under Western law, this gave them "senior" rights to the underground resources. Lexam also had a surface-use agreement in place, meaning they were allowed to drive heavy equipment into the preserve and drill in the area deemed so ecologically sensitive that the public is not allowed to visit it.

In drilling for gold in 1992, Lexam had discovered oil and gas reserves on the western flank of the Sangre de Cristo Mountains. Oil and gas drilling uses lots of water and often spews toxins into the environment. The company planned to drill two fourteen-thousand-foot test wells in the Baca Wildlife Refuge and said on its website that "the potential of the prospect is promising."

Valley citizens, Indian tribes, historians, and environmentalists were outraged. In 2008, over forty-seven thousand public comments were filed about the plan. The San Luis Valley Ecosystem Council filed a lawsuit charging that the US Fish and Wildlife Service had a duty to protect the refuge, to involve the public in the discussion, and to establish environmental safeguards.

In November 2008, the Fish and Wildlife Service ruled that Lexam's drilling would have "no significant impact." But environmental groups used a Freedom of Information Act request to obtain communications between regulators, Lexam, and their consultants and charged the company had exerted "inappropriate influence" on the environmental assessment of the site, "including specific wording edits . . . and inappropriate exchange of information." In 2009, a US district court judge issued a preliminary injunction against drilling in the refuge, and settlement talks got under way. In 2010, the litigation was ongoing, though Lexam appeared willing to sell its Baca mineral rights to the government for some $9.7 million, allowing them to be retired and presumably protecting the refuge and its water supply once and for all.

If that happens, it will be a significant victory for those who would protect water supplies over those who would profit from them. But in the history of the American West, it has been far more common for the pipeline dreamers and profiteers to triumph. No case exemplifies this more starkly than Los Angeles's notorious "water theft."

CHAPTER 14

Drain

The first rule of water is that it flows uphill, towards money and power.

> —Edward Moran, attorney general of Mono County,
> California, to his children, circa 1954

"THE MOTHER'S MILK OF LOS ANGELES"

A desert is a place that gets ten inches of rainfall or less a year. Los Angeles receives an average of eight inches of rain per year and was built on a coastal desert where native water supplies can support perhaps a million people, at best.

In 1898 Frederick Eaton, an engineer and politician from a prominent Pasadena family, was elected mayor of Los Angeles. He appointed his friend William Mulholland, an Irish-born self-taught water engineer who had once been an itinerant ditchdigger, superintendent of the Los Angeles City Water Company, which later became the Los Angeles Department of Water and Power (LADWP). The two men envisioned turning the growing city—a hot, dry oil and railroad and ranching hub of about one hundred thousand strong in 1900—into a major metropolis, a glorious new city that would rival New York and Chicago as a center of commerce and power. All that Los Angeles required to grow was water.

The closest major water reserves lay over two hundred miles to the northeast, in the Owens Valley, where snow melts off the mountains in great quantities. Known as the Switzerland of California, the Owens Valley runs about seventy-five miles long and stretches between the eleven-thousand-foot Inyo Mountains to the east and the fourteen-thousand-foot Sierra Nevada to the west. The Owens River runs down the length of the valley, collecting water as it goes. At the southern end of the valley is Owens Lake, a broad, shallow body of water fed by the Owens River.

At the turn of the century, the Bureau of Reclamation, the federal agency responsible for water management in the West, was planning to build an irrigation system there, to aid Owens Valley farmers. But Eaton and Mulholland, backed by a syndicate of powerful investors including Harrison Gray Otis, the publisher of the *Los Angeles Times,* and his son-in-law and successor, Harry Chandler, had another, secret plan: to build a massive aqueduct to suck water from the high Owens Valley down to coastal Los Angeles.

Eaton, whose family had founded Pasadena, pulled strings in state political circles and met with President Theodore Roosevelt's advisers in Washington, DC, to quash the Bureau of Reclamation's irrigation plan. At the same time, Eaton quietly bought up water rights and large parcels of land in Owens Valley, with the idea of selling them to Los Angeles for a vast personal profit.

When the city's secret aqueduct plan was revealed in 1905, the farmers, ranchers, and miners in Owens Valley rose up in protest. But it was too late. Eaton and his friends had used a combination of bribes, intimidation, and legitimate purchases to seize control of the valley's water rights. Over the next twenty-five years, Los Angeles gained control of nearly a quarter of the Owens Valley.

While valley residents grew alarmed by the city's takeover, Eaton, Chandler, and Otis persuaded the citizens of Los Angeles that an aqueduct was necessary to ensure the survival of the city. They used all manner of persuasion, including planting false stories in the *Los Angeles Times* that gave the impression the city was facing drought, and forbidding people from watering their lawns, all the while lowering the city's water supply by dumping it into sewers. What the conspirators didn't say was that Owens Valley water would not only feed the city but would also be used to irrigate the San Fernando Valley, a semidesert region just north of Los Angeles that was not legally part of the city. Otis, Chandler, and others bought up large parcels in the valley and pushed for the bond that would fund the construction of the aqueduct. In the summer of 1906, President Roosevelt allowed the aqueduct to cross federal lands. The following year, spooked by the idea that they were running out of water, Angelenos voted to approve $22.5 million in bonds to build a 233-mile-long aqueduct to bring water from Owens Valley to the city.

William Mulholland oversaw the construction of the Los Angeles

Aqueduct, which became the world's longest at the time. Starting in 1908, the project took five years and required over two thousand workers and the boring of 164 tunnels to drain water from the elevated Owens Valley to the San Fernando Valley and the city, at sea level. When Owens water first spilled into the San Fernando reservoir, north of Los Angeles, on November 5, 1913, Mulholland famously declared, "There it is. Take it."

In 1915, Los Angeles annexed the mostly rural San Fernando Valley, more than doubling the size of the city. With Sierra Nevada runoff flowing through the aqueduct, the arid San Fernando region was transformed into a major center of corn, cotton, citrus, and walnut growing. By 1960, the valley had over a million inhabitants; by 2007, the valley's population had reached 1.7 million.

The aqueduct also had a major impact on Owens Valley. The city's water withdrawals drained the hundred-square-mile Owens Lake and desertified the valley's land. As a result, most farming and ranching became impossible there. Owens Valley residents rebelled and began to sabotage the aqueduct. In the "civil war" of November 1924, a group of enraged citizens dynamited the Lone Pine spillway gate, which controlled water flow in the aqueduct, seized control of another large water-control gate, and dynamited the aqueduct where it crossed Jawbone Canyon. No one was arrested. Over the next three years, which included a drought in the summer of 1926, the fight over Owens Valley water simmered, and ranchers occasionally opened sluice gates to divert the flow of water back into the valley.

In 1927, as Los Angeles continued to ignore the pleas of valley residents for more water, angry ranchers again dynamited sections of the aqueduct. The city's leaders responded by dispatching a force of private detectives. A half dozen ranchers were arrested, but the case was dropped for lack of evidence. By 1928, Los Angeles had gained control of 90 percent of the water rights in Owens Valley, which effectively ended most agriculture, ranching, and mining there.

This California "water war" formed the basis for Roman Polanski's classic film noir of the seventies, *Chinatown,* which starred Jack Nicholson as a private investigator who becomes embroiled in machinations over Los Angeles's theft of water from a rural valley. In the movie's dark vision, power brokers consider water a resource so vital it is worth stealing and killing for.

The water Mulholland and Eaton brought from the Owens Valley to Los Angeles created vast fortunes for a few, encouraged the proliferation of irrigated orchards and other agriculture in the San Fernando Valley, and led to suburban sprawl. Los Angeles's growth became self-perpetuating: the availability of water created demand for more housing and jobs, which naturally created demand for more water. By 1924, Owens Lake had been sucked dry, while almost all of the Owens River and groundwater along the length of Owens Valley were being diverted into the Los Angeles Aqueduct. To reach more water, planners at the Los Angeles Department of Water and Power dreamed of extending the aqueduct farther north, tunneling a pipeline through the Mono Craters to tap the watershed around the high, mysterious Mono Lake.

Said to be the oldest lake in North America, and one of the oldest in the world, Mono is a large and strangely beautiful lake fed by streams and rain. An endorheic lake, meaning it is self-contained and does not flow into rivers and the ocean, it has slowly been evaporating since the Pleistocene epoch. Sedimentary records indicate that the lake we see today is the same body of water that has occupied the Mono Basin since its formation some 730,000 years ago.

Like the Great Salt Lake or Pyramid Lake or the Salton Sea, the waters of Mono Lake have become hypersaline. Filled with dissolved carbonates, sulfates, and sodium salts of chlorides, they are rich in borate and potassium. The carbonates render the lake highly alkaline; with a pH of 10, about the same as household glass cleaner, its waters have a viscous look and a slippery feel, like soapy water, and the bitter-tasting brine will destroy clothing.

Due to a salinity of between 5 and 8 percent—double the oceans' salinity—the lake's waters are inhospitable to fish and most other creatures, but Mono holds an enormous population of brine shrimp and alkali flies. More than seventy species of migratory and nesting birds feed on the shrimp and fly blooms. (Experts say that if the lake's salinity increases to 13.3 percent, the shrimp population will collapse.)

To L.A.'s water planners, the supersaline waters of the lake were not of immediate value, but its many clear tributary streams were a valuable prize.

According to the California historian William Kahrl, Mulholland's agents had scouted Mono Basin as a new water supply and even acquired a few water rights there as early as 1913. But Los Angeles was competing with local power companies, farmers, miners, and even the city of San Diego for Mono's water. In 1920, Mulholland and his friend Arthur Powell Davis, head of the federal Reclamation Service, concocted a deal whereby Reclamation engineers would prepare detailed plans for an extension of the Los Angeles Aqueduct to the Mono Basin—work that Los Angeles would pay for and retain control of—in the name of irrigating the Owens Valley and the possible construction of hydroelectric dams. Under this pretext, Mulholland gained political cover from his competitors and access to land for an extension of his aqueduct.

To the LADWP, characterizing Mono as "lifeless" or "a dead sea" helped deflect interest from the lake's water and made the case for diverting its tributary streams for its own purposes. Los Angeles engineers initiated a project to "reclaim" the basin's "wasted" waters and declared that "to salvage the water in Mono Basin being lost in the saline waters of Mono Lake" was a noble cause. In 1930, Los Angeles voters approved a $38 million bond issue to extend the city's aqueduct into Mono Basin. As in the Owens Valley, Los Angeles's agents bought out property owners, brought lawsuits, condemned property, and used whatever means they could to grab the water rights in the Mono Basin. With those rights secured, in 1934 they began to build the Mono extension of the Los Angeles Aqueduct.

In 1941, after six years of backbreaking work by eighteen hundred men, a tunnel connecting the Mono and Owens Valleys was completed. It extended the length of LADWP's aqueduct to 350 miles. As water from the tributary streams feeding Mono Lake was diverted south to Los Angeles, the effect was dramatic: within a few years, the volume of Mono Lake was cut in half and the salinity of its water doubled. Algae, the base of the lake's food chain, could no longer photosynthesize efficiently. Islands that were once important nesting sites became peninsulas accessible to predators; bird populations were wiped out or driven away. As the lake bed was exposed, winds swept particulates into the air, causing bronchial problems for people nearby. But Mono County was sparsely populated and hundreds of miles from Los Angeles. As water levels dropped, few noticed or cared—except for those who lived there.

The water table of the Owens and Mono Basins has always fluctuated several feet with the seasons, but in the spring of 1953, Mono County grew exceptionally dry. This was odd, because the snowpack and rainfall had been normal that year. In the early 1950s, Edward Moran, father of the Denver-based hydrogeologist Bob Moran, was the attorney general of Mono County. He grew curious about the mysterious drying of his jurisdiction and began to nose around.

Ed Moran spoke to local ranchers and miners, who told him that almost every drop of water in Mono Basin was being diverted. Hiking the steep-sided watershed around the town of Lee Vining, which overlooks the lake, Moran discovered that nearly every little spring and creek that hydrated Mono Basin was being tapped, and wells had been dug around the lake's perimeter to access seeping groundwater.

"Holy shit, Los Angeles is stealing all our water!" Moran said. Far from being cowed by this discovery, Moran—the son of an Irish cop in San Francisco, a man who enjoyed a good fight—was thrilled. "My dad was like a kid in a candy shop at Mono," recalled Bob Moran. "It was the biggest case of his career."

"Water is the mother's milk of Los Angeles," Ed Moran instructed his children. "No water, no L.A. People never understood this fact, and they still don't."

He decided to open the city's eyes.

In early 1954, Ed Moran filed suit against Los Angeles, claiming that the city was taking far more water from the Mono Basin than it was legally allowed. That spring he won a significant legal victory against the LADWP, his son Bob recalled, which required the city to pay Mono County's taxes. (The details of this case remain murky.) "He was asking tough questions: Who thought it was a good idea to drain Mono, and who really benefits? Where is that water going, and how are those withdrawals sustainable? What happens if the basin is totally drained?" said Bob Moran. "My father managed to make a lot of very rich and powerful people in the city very uncomfortable."

On March 5, 1955, Ed Moran met with state legislators in Sacramento, then had lunch with his cousin. Late that afternoon, he climbed behind the wheel of his car and set out on the long drive home. Sometime that evening, the car veered from the road and plunged off a cliff, killing Ed Moran instantly. He was thirty-eight years old. There were no witnesses. But there were plenty of conspiracy theories about what happened that night. "My father had made a lot of enemies, and there were hints of foul play—'He was done in by the water barons.' It was right out of *Chinatown*," Bob Moran said. "Some of my family still believe that romantic version of the story, but after all these years I don't."

Given the history of violence and political machinations over water in the Golden State, it is certainly possible that Ed Moran was done in by sinister forces. But given that the Mono case had already been resolved, and Ed Moran had gained prominence as a result, it seems more likely that his death was an accident. The larger point, Bob Moran said, is that Los Angeles's water extractions depleted the Mono and Owens Basins and left simmering tensions up and down Highway 395, the nerve stem of eastern California, nearly a century after the water wars.

I witnessed this tension firsthand. Driving through the town of Bishop one day in 2008, I happened across a colorful mural of a landscape painted on the side of a home-decorating store. The top of the mural, titled *Drain,* shows the lush Owens Valley, while at the bottom it depicts a rusty pipe labeled LADWP sucking the water, and, metaphorically, the color, out of the landscape. As I stood there, a big white pickup truck with LADWP stenciled on the door slowed and a meaty hand was stuck out the window, the middle finger raised at *Drain.* The driver gunned his engine and disappeared in a cloud of dusty rancor.

The hundred-square-mile Owens Lake once featured steamships, towns, mills, and mines and provided a rich habitat for birds, fish, and other aquatic life. Today, it has been so thoroughly drained by Los Angeles's water takings that it is little more than a wide gray sandlot called a playa. Winds kick up huge clouds of superfine dust (smaller than ten microns in diameter), salt, arsenic, and alkalies into the air and carry them across the Mojave Desert. These dust storms are said to remove 4 million tons of dust from the lake bed every year, making Owens Lake the single largest cause of particulate pollution in the nation and regularly violating federal air-quality standards. The dust storms rise as high as 13,500 feet and affect an estimated forty thousand people downwind. Dust from the lake bed has coated three national parks, shut down the China Lake Naval Weapons Center, and caused wide criticism of Los Angeles's environmental stewardship.

Since 2001, as part of a contentious settlement agreement with valley citizens, the LADWP has built a $500 million sprinkler system to flood twenty-seven square miles of the bed of Owens Lake ankle deep with water—not to restore the lake but to control the dust. In December 2006, by court order, Los Angeles, after missing thirteen deadlines, finally restored 5 percent of the Owens River's flow. As he turned a knob that opened a new steel gate in the aqueduct, allowing icy emerald-green water to flow into the river for the first time since 1913, Los Angeles mayor Antonio Villaraigosa alluded to Mulholland's famous line by declaring of the water, "Here it is. Take it back!"

The river now runs about two to six feet deep and flows smoothly south for sixty-two miles. It takes about sixteen days for it to meander through the Owens Valley floodplain, before it pours into storage ponds on the northern edge of dusty Owens Lake. There, four 600-horsepower pumps draw the water up and discharge it back into the concrete and steel aqueduct, where it continues its journey to Los Angeles.

When I visited the Owens River, just a few months after Mayor Villaraigosa's rewatering ceremony, Michael Prather, a botanist who worked tirelessly for the dust mitigation agreement, drove me along Owens Valley in his rattling pickup truck. "The wildlife and native vegetation are making a slow comeback," he said, explaining how the thin film of water from the river and the sprinklers on the bed of Owens Lake have had a rejuvenating effect. "The really good news is, the migrating birds have found us again." He raised his binoculars to peer at gulls, teal, scaup, sandpipers, and blackbirds wheeling in the distance.

During the fall and spring, the shallow waters in Owens Lake come alive with algae and brine flies, which supply food for some fifty thousand migrating birds. Peregrine falcons feed on the birds. Audubon California has designated the lake and its resurging wetlands one of the state's most important birding areas. Since then, the project has expanded to encompass thirty of the lake's hundred square miles and added another nine square miles of ponds in 2010; record numbers of birds, of over a hundred species, were counted at the lake in 2008. But California was in its second year of drought, and questions were being raised about the necessity of LADWP's dust-mitigation efforts. The project had suffered cost overruns and used sixty thousand acre-feet of water a year, which was worth some $54 million and was enough to supply sixty thousand households. Critics thought the money and water could be better spent elsewhere.

By 2009, Los Angeles had become a megacity with 3.8 million residents, in a broad combined statistical area that had swelled to 17.8 million people—thanks in good part to the water drained from Mono County. The city is also hydrated by water from the Sacramento Delta, channeled south by the California Aqueduct, and by the Colorado River, channeled west by the Colorado River Aqueduct.

If current growth rates continue, it is estimated that Los Angeles's population will reach 33 million by 2020. Where is the water to supply such a megalopolis going to come from?

"REMEMBER THE OWENS VALLEY!"

It is difficult to overstate the significance that Westerners ascribe to the debate over Los Angeles's water grab. The tension over Owens Valley remains a potent symbol for people across the West, who invoke it, and the movie *Chinatown,* to resist the expropriation of rural water to fuel urban growth.

In 1990, citizens in the Sierra foothills rallied to oppose the East Bay Municipal Utility District, near San Francisco, from piping water from the Mokelumne River, declaring, "This county can't let itself be turned into a twenty-first-century Owens Valley so residents of the East Bay can wash their cars in pure mountain water."

In northeastern California, residents of Honey Lake Valley fought against the development of a pipeline just over the border, in Nevada. The $100 million project would pump water from the aquifer beneath Fish Springs Ranch in a 28.6-mile-long pipe, up a steep mountain, to new housing developments around Sparks, outside Reno. "Natives, fearing that history may repeat, have begun to fight," the *Sacramento Bee* reported. "We all know what happened in the Owens Valley. The fear is here." After several aborted attempts to develop a water pipeline, the owners of Fish Springs Ranch, Dr. Harry Brown and Franklin Raines, made a deal in 2002 with Vidler Water Company, a private water development firm, to develop the deep aquifer beneath the ten-thousand-acre ranch. As he toured me along the nearly completed pipeline in the spring of 2008, Brown scoffed at his opponents' claim that pumping water from Fish Springs Ranch would affect the aquifer in California. "Taking water from our valley will not affect them in the slightest," Brown thundered. "This has nothing to do with Owens Valley!"

Shortly after my visit, the Bureau of Land Management agreed with Brown and green-lit the pipeline, which was completed in 2009 and is now in service.

The most ambitious water-conveyance project in America today is a plan to suck water from desert valleys in rural Nevada down to Las Vegas through a pipeline nearly as long as the Los Angeles Aqueduct. The project has been brewing for years, has cost millions of dollars, has turned neighbors against each other, and has even embroiled Senate Majority Leader Harry Reid in a sharp dispute between the city and his former allies in rural communities. Of all the water schemes currently being debated, the Las Vegas plan has the closest parallels to the Owens Valley, despite what its backers maintain.

CHAPTER 15

The City That Wasn't Supposed to Be

There is no lack of water here [in the Southwest], unless you try to establish a city where no city should be.

—Edward Abbey

THE SIMPLE MATH OF DROUGHT

Lake Mead, the largest man-made reservoir in the United States, is surrounded by steep cliffs that come in many shades of ruddy brown, except for a strange white band that runs along their base, just above the waterline, encircling the lake like a noose. Known as the bathtub ring, the white band is the result of the cliffs being submerged in calcium-rich water, which bleached out the color. But starting in 1999, the Southwest was gripped by the worst drought in five hundred years; over the next decade the reservoir's water level dropped more than one hundred feet, and the bathtub ring grew steadily wider and more ominous.

Lake Mead was formed in 1935, when Hoover Dam impounded the Colorado River in Boulder Canyon, containing up to 9.3 trillion gallons of water when full. Ninety-seven percent of the lake's water comes from the Colorado River; the remaining 3 percent comes from the Muddy and Virgin Rivers, and from a wetland called the Las Vegas Wash. Mead was built to supply water to Nevada, Arizona, and California; to generate electricity; to prevent flooding during wet years; and to create a recreational area. Mead's chief beneficiary is Las Vegas. The lake provides 90 percent of the city's water, and experts worry that Las Vegas's near total reliance on a single troubled source makes it vulnerable to a crippling drought.

DROUGHT

When I took a boat ride around Lake Mead in the spring of 2008, the drought was in its eighth year, and the white bathtub ring extended a startling 102 feet up the cliff face. The water level had dropped from 1,215 feet in 2000 to 1,095 feet in 2008, its lowest elevation since 1964. If the lake sinks below 1,050 feet, the water level will be beneath the intake valves—a state known as dead pool—and Las Vegas will lose up to 90 percent of its water supply. If that happens, people would have to abandon the city, the glittering Strip would go dark, and the desert would reassert itself.

"It's simple math: there is no way to meet one hundred percent of people's demand with only ten percent of the water supply," said Pat Mulroy, general manager of the Southern Nevada Water Authority (SNWA), the water agency for Clark County, when we met in June 2008. "If this drought continues much longer, it will change the West. It will change the way we use water. It will change the way we live."

Trim and energetic, with a barking voice that cleaves through the most lugubrious water debate, Mulroy is a polarizing figure. The nation's most prominent water manager, Mulroy is a longtime political ally of Senate Majority Leader Harry Reid and has herself been rumored as a gubernatorial candidate. She has been dubbed the Water Witch, Water Czarina, the Chosen One, and with many other less charitable nicknames.

"We grew out of the desert," she said. "This is the city that wasn't supposed to be."

For Mulroy, the possibility of a crippling drought has an obvious solution: not to limit the city's growth or raise water rates or conserve water more aggressively, as many outside experts have suggested, but to find a new source of water. She thinks she has found one. Mulroy has proposed building an enormous pipeline to pump billions of gallons of "unused" water from remote valleys in central-eastern Nevada almost three hundred miles south to Las Vegas.

According to many valley residents, Mulroy's plan—which they refer to derisively as Pat's Pipe—is the biggest water grab since William Mulholland turned the Owens Valley into Los Angeles's private watering hole. The ranchers, along with a broad, loosely organized coalition of sportsmen, environmentalists, endangered-species regulators, Indian tribes, and Utah politicians, have been fighting Pat's Pipe for nearly twenty years.

"Why does Las Vegas need more water? Simply to fuel more growth," said Dean Baker, a slim, hawk-faced sixty-eight-year-old rancher, whose property sits over an important aquifer in remote Snake Valley, near the Utah border. "If Mulroy starts pumping our valley, the water table will go down and we'll have some real, serious problems. It's a lot like what happened in the Owens Valley."

DOUBLE PLUMBING TREASURE ISLAND

Nevada is the driest state in the nation. Lying in the rain shadow (where mountains block wind and rain, casting a dry "shadow" behind them) of the Sierra Nevada, it receives only seven inches of precipitation a year on average, and drought is a regular feature of life. Las Vegas—which is tucked into a sliver of territory in the southeastern corner of the state, between Death Valley and the Grand Canyon—receives only four inches of rain a year. It is the driest city in the driest state in America. But it wasn't always that way.

Las vegas is the Spanish phrase for "the meadows," or "the alluvial plain." In 1829, a party of Spanish explorers gave the name to a green oasis they found in a hot, dusty valley. The springs at Las Vegas had so much natural water pressure that they were said to erupt from the earth "in geysers." In the first half of the twentieth century, enough water was in the aquifers beneath Las Vegas that kids swam in the springs, and lawn sprinklers were ubiquitous. But as the city expanded, groundwater levels dipped. By the 1950s, the water beneath the valley had been pumped out so thoroughly that the land began to subside, and parts of Nellis Air Force Base caved in. The hotels and casinos and golf courses that came to define Las Vegas proliferated, but most of the springs had run dry by 1962. From then on, the city relied on Lake Mead, which is to say the Colorado River, for 90 percent of its water.

The Colorado begins as snowmelt trickling out of a remote part of the Never Summer Range, in the high Rocky Mountains. A cold and clear rivulet up there, above the tree line and two miles above sea level, it descends through gorges to become a thundering red-brown colossus that flows 1,450 miles south, providing water for over 27 million people in seven states, several Indian reservations, and Mexico. For centuries, the river flowed all the way to the Sea of Cortés (aka the Gulf of California), its nutrients creating a rich ecosystem in the warm, protected seawater between the Baja Peninsula and the northwest coast of Mexico. But in the last century, the river was so overused that now it reaches the sea only in exceptionally wet years.

A 2008 study by the Scripps Institution of Oceanography, one of the nation's oldest earth-science research centers, made a startling assertion: overuse of the Colorado River, combined with drought, has created a net deficit of almost 1 million acre-feet (about 3.25 million gallons) of water per year. That is equivalent to the water supply for 8 million people. "There is a 50 percent chance Lake Mead . . . will be dry by 2021," the report concluded. Using the same data, the federal Bureau of Reclamation, which manages Lake Mead, paints a slightly rosier picture and predicts the Colorado will face water shortages 58 to 73 percent of the time by 2050. Regardless of the details, one thing is certain: the river is in trouble. Lake Mead is dropping, and Nevada's growth—particularly Las Vegas's unbridled expansion into the desert—is restricted by a lack of water.

Of the seven states that signed the Colorado River Compact, a landmark agreement on the allocation of the river's water, Nevada has always received the smallest portion. In 1922, when the original deal was struck, the state had few residents, but as Nevada grew so did its water needs. In 1910, the permanent population of Clark County, in southern Nevada, was 3,321. By 2010, it was 2 million. The entire state has only 2.72 million residents, meaning that Las Vegas is the economic and political engine that drives Nevada. In most cases, Las Vegas gets its way. And so it has been, more or less, with Pat Mulroy's pipeline.

In 1978, when she was twenty-five years old, Pat Mulroy was hired as a $13,000-a-year junior management analyst by Richard Bunker, the Clark County manager, a top political office. "I thought I died and went to heaven," recalled Mulroy, who had been raised in Germany by an American father and a German mother. Bunker is a Mormon who doesn't gamble or drink, yet has become one of the state's top casino lobbyists and a major force in state politics. Mulroy proved so effective that she was sent to Carson City to lobby for Clark County before the state legislature. It wasn't glamorous work, but it taught her how to create legislation and get it passed. In 1989, Mulroy was named general manager of the Las Vegas Water District.

In 1991 the district and seven other water companies that service Clark County formed a cooperative for regional water issues called the Southern Nevada Water Authority, or SNWA. Pat Mulroy helped to champion the idea, and she was named the new agency's general manager. Abhorring waste, she embarked on an ambitious water-conservation program. Lawns, which are not native to the desert and require vast amounts of water to maintain, were her first target. One study showed that 65 percent of the water flowing to Southwestern suburbs was used to maintain lawns and wash cars. "People move here from all over, and they bring every water-sucking plant in the world—bluegrass from Kentucky, magnolias from Florida, roses from England, lawns from Chicago," Mulroy said, rolling her eyes. "Newsflash: we live in a *desert*. If you choose to live in a desert, then use appropriate landscaping. This need to conquer nature, the unwillingness to live within the confines of the environment, has got to change."

In 2002, she instituted a "cash for grass" incentive program to curtail lawns and employed water police to ticket excessive watering. People hated the program at first, but SNWA's carrot-and-stick approach eventually removed over 60 million square feet of grass—enough, Mulroy claims, "to lay a strip of sod roughly one-third of the way around Earth." An SNWA study found that 76 percent of the water used by Las Vegas went to maintaining lawns; the number has now dropped below 70 percent. Mulroy put golf courses on a water budget and forced them to rip out most of their nonfield turf, such as grass on parking-lot dividers. Now, many of them use artificial turf on nonplaying surfaces and have their own weather stations, computerized humidity sensors, and water-recycling facilities.

Mulroy's next crusade was what she called "the war of the fountains [small, decorative displays] and water features [the dramatic water shows along the Strip]." Many of Las Vegas's hotels and casinos use large, ornate water features, such as the Bellagio's famous "dancing fountains." These spray gorgeously to entice people inside, but they evaporate many gallons of water in the hundred-plus-degree days of summer. Spraying water in the desert is a deliberately theatrical gesture, one that sets the tone for the entire city: "This is a city built on fantasy, where the normal rules don't apply," it seems to say. The water features are an obvious target for conservationists, yet Mulroy contends that hotels and casinos use water efficiently. "The much maligned Strip uses only three percent of our water [when recycling is taken into account] while providing jobs to tens of thousands of Nevadans," she said. "If you were to shut off the canals at the Venetian and the fountains at the Bellagio, you would affect the mainstay of our economy. The casinos are the largest economic driver in the state, by far. Why would you *not* invest three percent of your water in making them attractive to tourists?"

When Steve Wynn, the legendary casino and hotel developer, was building Treasure Island, a hotel-casino with a nautical water feature that included a "sea" in which a life-size replica of a pirate ship does battle with a naval frigate, he wanted to know how to maintain the illusion of an ocean in the desert. "Double-plumb Treasure Island," Mulroy replied. "Use gray water in your features." And so he did. Treasure Island (now owned by MGM) recycles wastewater from the showers and sinks in its three thousand rooms in a reverse-osmosis facility, then pipes it to the hotel's water feature. As a result, Wynn became an important ally for Mulroy, an advocate for water conservation in the gaming and hotel industries, and a proponent of the pipeline plan.

Each year, the SNWA spends about $3.5 million to run ads that encourage residents to conserve water by planting native species (xeriscaping), using low-flow showerheads, covering swimming pools (to avoid evaporation), watering their grounds at night, and so on. To a degree, the effort has paid off. Between 2002 and 2008, the population of Las Vegas grew by four hundred thousand people, yet water consumption dropped by 18 percent, or 15 billion gallons, thanks to conservation. "If you do the slide-rule math, Las Vegas could keep growing and growing because we constantly reuse our water," Mulroy insisted.

In spite of these rosy numbers, however, Las Vegas continues to use more water per day than many other cities with tenuous drinking supplies. According to the SNWA, Las Vegans used about 254 gallons of water per capita per day (gpcd) in 2009. Mulroy has set a goal of 199 gpcd by 2035. But other cities have already done much better: Long Beach uses 105 gpcd; San Diego, 150 gpcd; and Albuquerque, 175 gpcd.

A survey shows the top one hundred private water users in the Las Vegas valley—including many of the casino owners and real estate developers who have strongly supported Mulroy's pipeline—use enough water for nearly two thousand homes. One property, owned by the sultan of Brunei, uses 17 million gallons of water per year, and Mulroy herself used six hundred and fifty-two thousand gallons in 2010 (when she suffered "a substantial leak"). A 2007 study by the Pacific Institute, an Oakland, California, think tank, found that a more aggressive conservation program could save Las Vegas the same amount of water that the pipeline would take from rural basins. Mulroy vehemently disagrees with those conclusions, complaining that the institute focused on "indoor conservation"— more efficient toilets and showers—where "the relative gain is marginal" and doesn't alter the essential problem: "you cannot create more water."

Water rates in Las Vegas are comparatively low, which critics say encourages demand and furthers growth. In summer months, a Las Vegan household typically uses seventeen thousand gallons of water per month and pays $36.64, or about two cents per ten gallons, according to SNWA. Average use in the winter is eleven thousand gallons, costing $21. But critics such as UC Berkeley resource economist David Zetland contend that low water rates are self-defeating. "Many people blame the 'shortage' of water in the southwest US on overpopulation . . . this critique is not valid for water (the shortage is because demand exceeds supply at low LOW prices)," Zetland writes in his Aguanomics blog. Reducing development, he says, will reduce water demand: "One way to do this . . . is to raise water prices—if it's too expensive to do business or live in Las Vegas, people will move to places where it's cheaper."

Mulroy takes exception to that: "Pricing alone will not effectuate more conservation. It is one of several tools we use. But Las Vegas is a very affluent community. For the sultan of Brunei, it doesn't matter what we charge him. On the other hand, I have a problem with affixing high water rates on the backs of the little guy who can't afford it."

In other words, raising water prices is politically risky. As is the suggestion that land-use policy and water-use policy be more directly linked. Currently, a development is proposed and then water is found to supply it. Critics say this formula has it backward: new building should take place only if there is enough water to support it. Mulroy dodges this question, saying that her only job is to supply water, not restrict Clark County's growth.

"We're expecting one hundred million more people in this country by 2040," she said. "Everybody talks about 'controlling growth.' Well, tell me, where do we want people to go? You could shut the town down, I guess, but I don't know of any metropolitan area in a no-growth mode. It's not *whether* Las Vegas grows, it's *how* we grow. If we are smart about our water and waste, this community can grow forever."

It's an intriguing thought, but it may be a wishful one. The earth has a fixed supply of freshwater: to manage it sustainably, man will have no choice but to link land use and water use more intentionally and to radically shift the way urban centers are planned. As the examples of Perth, Australia, Barcelona, Spain, Atlanta, Georgia, and other drought-stricken cities have shown, water supply will increasingly limit growth—especially in regions such as southern Nevada, which are in the bull's-eye for aridification by global warming.

In October 1998, the water in Lake Mead reached a nearly all-time high of 1,215.76 feet. A year later, the Colorado River Basin slipped into the first year of what would become an extended drought. In 2000, the flow

DROUGHT

of water into the basin, the so-called inflow, was 62 percent of its sixty-five-year average. In 2001, the inflow dropped to 59 percent of average. In 2002, it was 25 percent of average, the lowest inflow ever recorded along the Colorado River. Since then, flow rates have fluctuated up and down, and by 2007 Mead and its sister reservoir, Lake Powell—where the Glen Canyon Dam impounds the Colorado on the Utah/Arizona border, two hundred miles upstream from Mead—were at 50 percent of capacity.

When I interviewed Mulroy in 2008, she had decided that incremental steps were insufficient to stave off "disaster" in Las Vegas. "It's time to begin looking at our water resources in a more holistic fashion," she said. By which she meant, the answer was to build a pipeline to transfer billions of gallons of "rural water" from Clark, Nye, Lincoln, and White Pine Counties down to the city. The pipe would supply about 25 percent of the water Las Vegas currently takes from the Colorado River. In the event that Lake Mead falls to dead pool, Mulroy said, the pipeline would provide enough water to allow the city to survive, as long as strict conservation measures are followed.

The plan is technically feasible, but it is expensive, divisive, and carries heavy environmental risks. The debate over Pat Mulroy's pipeline has crystallized a question that is becoming increasingly important in the New West: what is water really worth?

AN "INSURANCE POLICY"

Las Vegas sits at the intersection of three deserts. To the south is the Sonoran, to the west is the Mojave, and to the north lies the Great Basin. The Sonoran and Mojave are "hot" deserts, where the temperature can rise to 120 degrees on a summer day, and fall to 10 below zero on a winter night. The Great Basin, which covers most of Nevada and part of Utah, is a "cold" desert surrounded by snowy peaks. During the spring snowmelt, those peaks release billions of gallons of water into the carbonate aquifers of the Great Basin, a vast endorheic watershed (one that doesn't flow to the sea) that extends between the Wasatch Mountains to the east, to the Sierra Nevada to the west, and from Utah into Nevada. Hydrologists have had their eye on that water for years.

In the mid-1980s, when many of the wells in the Las Vegas valley began to go dry, a USGS groundwater specialist named Terry Katzer had a brain-flash: what if Las Vegas could tap into the aquifers beneath the sparsely

167

inhabited valleys of the Great Basin Desert? John Bredehoeft, who was in charge of Western water for USGS at the time, cautioned that water stored in aquifers is protected. "Taking water out of storage is mining," he reminded Katzer, according to the *Las Vegas Sun*. Water mining, pumping water faster than it is replenished, is illegal in Nevada. The Great Basin's porous limestone and dolomite aquifer allows groundwater to flow from valley to valley, for hundreds of miles. Bredehoeft and other experts believed that the hot playas above them have no water to spare. What little water they do have is already spoken for, by ranchers, flora, fauna—and, not incidentally, Utah. If water is mined from one valley, it will suck water from other valleys, which could potentially destroy springs and creeks, kill off plants and animals, and spark a border war between Las Vegas and Salt Lake City.

But Katzer's idea had caught the eye of Pat Mulroy. In October 1989, the Las Vegas Water District quietly filed applications with the state engineer for "unclaimed, unused" groundwater in thirty basins in rural east-central Nevada, as an "insurance policy against drought." This represented about 840,000 acre-feet of water, an amount believed to be the equivalent of half the unclaimed water in the state. It was the single biggest groundwater claim in the history of Nevada.

Rural people had no idea that the city was laying claim to the water beneath their ranches until the filings were announced in local newspapers. "It was a dirty trick!" state senator Virgil Getto complained to the *Las Vegas Sun*. Critics of the plan began to organize protests.

Mulroy ignored them, and between 2006 and 2009 SNWA spent $78 million to buy seven ranches in White Pine County, along with their water rights. In Nevada, water rights are assigned for a purpose, in this case cattle ranching and alfalfa growing. To use its new water supply, the SNWA had to go into ranching.

"Watching the city try to run four thousand sheep?" Dean Baker deadpanned. "That'll be . . . *interesting*."

SECRET WEAPONS

All of the water in Nevada is owned by the state (citizens purchase the right to use it): if the state engineer grants the SNWA permits to build the pipeline, and Mulroy can mollify her many critics and convince regulators that draining the valleys won't harm endangered species, then, she says, it will take about ten to fifteen years to build her "in-state groundwater project," as she insists on calling the pipeline. The pipeline itself will take only three years to build. The first leg will extend north from Las Vegas to Delamar and Dry Lake Valleys, the first two "stepping-stone" basins from which groundwater will be pumped. The pipe will then reach into Cave Valley, Spring Valley, and ultimately up to Snake Valley, where Baker's ranch is. When the project is finished, the system of pipes, pumps, and storage reservoirs will stretch about 300 miles and cost between $2 billion and $3.5 billion. Opponents say the project will cost far more and deliver far less water than the SNWA claims.

The two basins with the most potential to supply Las Vegas with water are in White Pine County: Spring Valley and Snake Valley. In July 2006, SNWA bought the Robison Ranch in Spring Valley for an attention-getting sum of $22 million. Before long, almost every ranch along the valley floor had sold out to the SNWA.

The SNWA applied to the state engineer for a permit to suck more than 16 billion gallons of groundwater a year from Snake Valley, which is enough to service one hundred thousand average Las Vegas homes. The agency has characterized this water as "unused." To do so with a straight face, it has relied on Western water law to argue that native plants, such as greasewood, are not "legally entitled" to the valley's water as they have no "beneficial use." Greasewood, which serves as forage for cattle and deer, is a phreatophyte, a class of plant with long roots that stretch deep underground. Las Vegas's plan is to target "weeds" such as greasewood: pumping hard and fast would kill them off; once the plants are gone, the city will use the snowmelt previously claimed by the plants. But not only does greasewood support animal life, its sturdy roots hold the earth in place. Killing off the phreatophytes could lead to dust storms that might rival those blowing off the Owens and Mono lake beds.

At Dean Baker's ranch in Snake Valley, he and I climb into his old SUV and motor slowly over the bright desert until we stop at a shallow sandy bowl. "This used to be Antelope Corral," Baker explains. Because of a drought, he said, "It's drier now than it ever was." A ragged muddy hole about a foot deep has been scraped out of a gully by thirsty badgers and coyotes. "This used to be a pond," he says, kicking at the talc-dry dust with the toe of his cowboy boot, revealing the bleached shells of freshwater snails. "And all around here was meadow. Now these sand dunes are the biggest source of dust in the valley. If they start pumping here . . ." He doesn't finish the sentence, but the implication is clear.

Halfway across the valley we cross an invisible borderline into Utah and pull to a stop at Needle Point Spring. In 1939, the Civilian Conservation Corps excavated the spring, and every year a trough and a nearby pond filled with water to slake the thirst of cattle and wild horses. In the summer of 2001, the spring level suddenly dropped a couple of feet and the trough went dry. A dozen wild horses died of thirst nearby. A federal study concluded that the likely cause was that a ranch about a mile away had increased the pumping of groundwater for irrigation that year, lowering the water table. To Dean Baker, the lesson is that "even a little extra pumping lowers the water level. So how is it we are supposed to have enough water to supply the city of Las Vegas? The pipeline will make this valley into an environmental nightmare—that will be Harry Reid's legacy."

Once, Dean Baker and Senator Harry Reid were trusted allies. Reid, who was named Senate majority leader in 2007, was born in Searchlight, a mining camp south of Las Vegas, in 1939, the son of an alcoholic miner (who committed suicide) and a mother who was a laundress for brothels. After suffering a hard-knocks childhood, he converted to Mormonism, earned a law degree, and became the right-hand man to the popular governor Mike O'Callaghan. Reid was elected to the House of Representatives in 1982 and to the Senate in 1986. In 1985, Reid helped to promote Great Basin National Park, a seventy-seven-thousand-acre preserve famous for the Lehman Caves and ancient stands of bristlecone pine. The park had been debated for sixty years; Nevada had no national park, and Reid was determined to fix that. He had the support of a wide coalition of environmentalists and urbanites. The biggest hurdle was water. Local ranchers such as Dean Baker worried that a park designation might curtail their access to aquifers and opposed it. But when Reid gave his word that the ranchers' water supply would be protected, they relented, and the park was signed into existence in 1986. It was, Reid has said, one of the biggest victories of his career.

But in 2000, Harry Reid sided with Pat Mulroy in support of the SNWA pipeline. To the people of White Pine County, this was regarded as a deep, personal betrayal. "Harry Reid gave his word that draining down our water won't be his legacy," Baker said in a cold fury. "But he got himself in too deep."

Mulroy has a starkly different view of the senator: "Harry Reid is our secret weapon. As he's moved up in seniority in Washington, Nevada's become more respected." Reid has raised the SNWA's profile and helped it negotiate permission from the formerly distrustful Department of Interior for the pipeline to cross federal lands. Mulroy has many other influential supporters, including casino operators, developers, and politicians such as Governor Jim Gibbons, who initially opposed SNWA's plan but now supports it.

Dean Baker doesn't have Mulroy's connections, but he, too, has powerful allies. They include environmentalists, Indian tribes, and even the least chub—a tiny fish found in only a few desert springs and which is under consideration for listing as an endangered species. That ruling could thwart SNWA's water-siphoning plan, which could wipe out the fish's habitat. And Dean Baker has a secret weapon of his own: the State of Utah.

The Great Basin aquifer flows from Utah into Nevada under Baker's ranch. If Las Vegas pumps water out of Snake Valley, it could draw down the reserves of Utah ranchers, just a few miles away. The ranchers, many of whom are wealthy, politically connected descendants of early Mormon settlers, have not been shy in expressing their extreme opposition to Las Vegas's pipe. The ripples of their displeasure washed all the way to Washington, DC, where, in 2000, Congress required Nevada and Utah to enter into an agreement before any water was exported from their shared aquifer under Snake Valley.

"Utah," Mulroy said, has "stonewalled" Las Vegas's pipeline. But Utah's opposition wasn't simply a principled defense of its farmers; Utah would like to build a 158-mile pipe of its own, which would suck water from Lake Powell and send it through southwestern Utah, then up to St. George, a retirement mecca and one of the fastest-growing cities in the nation.

Behind closed doors, representatives of the two states tried to forge what appeared to be a quid pro quo: if Nevada backed Utah's bid for a St. George pipeline (which would require a federal right-of-way ruling), then Utah would back SNWA's pipeline to Snake Valley. But the negotiations dragged. In 2006, Pat Mulroy declared that the longer Utah waited to endorse SNWA's pipeline, "the more uncomfortable it will become for Utah. If they can do it to another state, they can have it done to them, too." Offended, Utah refused to sign a water-sharing agreement with Nevada. Mulroy dismissed this as petty and said, "Our main driver for developing groundwater is for drought protection."

In 2010, the two states were still squabbling. Mulroy sniped that Salt Lakers didn't know how to spell the word *conservation*, while Utahans scoffed at Mulroy's offer to swap Snake Valley water for a greater allotment of Colorado River water: "It's a good news bite, but it's not possible [under the Colorado Compact] and she knows it," said a government official.

A MODEL

In the early 1980s, when Timothy Durbin was head of USGS's California office, he modeled the effects of pumping water from the Owens Valley. In 2001, he joined Terry Katzer at the SNWA as a groundwater consultant. When he forecasts the effect of transporting water out of the Great Basin, Durbin told the *Las Vegas Sun*, "The Owens Valley is a model of what to expect."

Las Vegas has applied to withdraw ninety thousand acre-feet a year of water from Spring Valley. To simulate what effect such withdrawals might have, Katzer and Durbin created a computer model that showed the valley's water table would drop two hundred feet or more over seventy-five years. This would kill off the greasewood, as planned. But it could also dry up thousands of acres of federally owned land, destroy endangered species and other animals, and close down ranches founded by Nevada's pioneer families. Suddenly, the comparisons to Owens Valley didn't seem so far-fetched.

The Nevada state engineer is the arbiter of whether the pipeline project can move ahead. Once an applicant files for water rights, the state engineer has eight months to review the claim, hear objections, and render a decision. The amount of water awarded is determined by whether withdrawals will affect existing water rights holders, and how much withdrawn water will be replaced by rain and snowmelt.

In 2007, Durbin testified before Nevada state engineer Tracy Taylor but didn't mention the results of his model because, he told the *Las Vegas Sun*, no one asked about them. Taylor granted Las Vegas the use of forty thousand acre-feet of Spring Valley water a year, for ten years. (The city is required to monitor its withdrawals and file an annual report. After a decade, the withdrawals can be raised to sixty thousand acre-feet a year, unless they cause problems.)

After the hearing, Durbin said, he felt great remorse for what he had left unspoken. In 2008 he once again appeared before Taylor, only this time he represented a group of pipeline critics. He put the results of his groundwater model on the record. To his surprise, the SNWA hardly reacted. Only later did he realize why: they had already gotten what they wanted—approval to pump water from the valleys—and had no incentive to call attention to his damning projections.

Pat Mulroy shrugs off Durbin and Katzer as "two consultants" and their research as "just a model."

Opponents to the SNWA pipeline, such as the Great Basin Network, relied on Simeon Herskovits, a slim, bushy-haired, and bespectacled environmental attorney from Taos, New Mexico, to press their case. In 2007, Herskovits challenged a state senate ruling that had denied pipeline protesters a hearing within a year of the close of the protest period, as is required by law. When his motion was denied, he appealed the case up to the Nevada Supreme Court.

Over the next two years, the SNWA won a string of victories. In 2008, State Engineer Taylor granted Las Vegas almost nineteen thousand acre-feet of water from its first three claims in Cave, Dry Lake, and Delamar Valleys, south of Snake Valley. In the summer of 2009, as the fight over Snake Valley escalated, so did Mulroy's rhetoric. She declared that if the SNWA board voted to halt the pipeline, the result would be "an absolute hole" in Las Vegas's water supply by 2020. She said that without a secure water supply, Nevada would have a difficult time recovering from the recession. Without a backup supply, she warned Las Vegans, "You're going to live like Amman, Jordan. You're going to get water once a week . . . [if] you don't have water in hydrants, you can't put out a major fire."

In the end, Taylor granted Las Vegas about half the rural water it wanted, some 6 billion gallons annually. And in August 2009, Utah governor Gary R. Herbert agreed to allow the SNWA to pipe thirty-six thousand acre-feet of water a year from the Great Basin to Las Vegas. Pat Mulroy had won. After twenty years of cajoling, maneuvering, spending, and compromising, the SNWA had at last secured the right to build its pipeline.

Two months later, the victory began to unravel.

In October 2009, Nevada district judge Norman C. Robison struck down Tracy Taylor's rulings on three of the four rural basins—Cave, Delamar and Dry Lake Valleys—along Las Vegas's pipeline. The state engineer had "acted arbitrarily, capriciously and oppressively," Robison wrote. Allowing such significant withdrawals requires "specific empirical data," he wrote, but Taylor was "simply hoping for the best while committing to undo his decision if the worst occurs." The SNWA countercharged that Judge Robison, who lives in rural Nevada, was "flat-out wrong" and was biased against the city: "We believe the judge ignored the evidence and improperly substituted his opinion."

In late January 2010, the Nevada Supreme Court ruled unanimously that Tracy Taylor and state engineers who preceded him had violated the due-process rights of hundreds, perhaps thousands, of Great Basin residents. When Las Vegas filed applications for rural water rights in 1989, more than eight hundred "interested persons" had filed protests. But the number of protesters had risen to over three thousand by 1990, when the protest period closed. In 2005, the state engineer denied the protesters' request to reopen the protest period, and the pipeline's critics, represented by Simeon Herskovits, took the matter to the state supreme court. In January 2010, the court ruled for the protesters, throwing the future of Las Vegas's pipeline into question. Utah suspended its water-sharing agreement with Nevada "indefinitely," saying that the ruling "significantly changes the landscape."

Although the pipeline project did not die, the January 2010 reversal was its most stunning setback yet. Pat Mulroy, who had staked her considerable reputation on the pipeline and had already spent an estimated $180 million to develop it, called the supreme court's decision "disappointing." The SNWA said it would ask the court to reconsider "because we believe the justices may not fully appreciate the far-reaching ramifications of their decision."

Up in White Pine County, opponents cheered the latest twist in the saga. In 2010, the SNWA's request for another hearing was scheduled to be returned to Judge Robison. The Nevada legislature, which was struggling with budget shortfalls, said it would not have time to focus on the pipeline until its 2011 session.

"THE WORLD HAS CHANGED"

In February 2009, Lake Mead was at 46 percent of capacity: the water level had dropped 5 feet lower than a year earlier and 118 feet below its high point a decade earlier. In February 2010, heavy rains swept across the West, which decreased demand for irrigation water in California and Arizona and helped to raise Lake Mead by more than a foot. The Bureau of Reclamation declared 2010 a "normal" water delivery year, which gave the impression that the decade-long drought was about to end. But that was not the case. The more important indicator—snowpack levels in the Utah mountains that feed Colorado River tributaries—stood at about 70 percent of average, which did not portend well.

If the drought does not break, and Lake Mead's water level dips below the critical dead-pool level of 1,050 feet, the consequences for Las Vegas, and much of the West, could be catastrophic. But few people actually want to see Las Vegas dry up and blow away, so if the Colorado River Basin hits critical lows, then Congress will likely come to the rescue with federal assistance. Just what that might entail remains unanswered. (Mulroy has suggested a "dramatic" replumbing of the nation's water system in which Midwestern floodwater would be sent to the parched West, a subject I will return to later.) Furthermore, the "hotel-casino complex," as locals refer to Nevada's biggest businesses, is highly unlikely to allow Las Vegas to die of thirst. As Las Vegas mayor Oscar Goodman succinctly put it, "The bottom line is that we'll never run out of water as long as we can pay for it."

Yet Mulroy worries that her opponents don't take the looming crisis seriously enough. "People refuse to change their habits until they absolutely have to—which in this case will be too late," she insists. "We'll have no choice" but to build the in-state project. But Peter Gleick, of the Pacific Institute, disagrees: "Rather than looking outward to take water from rural counties, Las Vegas could look inward and figure out how to use water more effectively."

The threat that a major city could be relinquished to the dust, heat, and tumbleweeds has proven sufficiently apocalyptic to spur a search for creative new solutions to drought.

In 2005, well before the Great Basin court ruling, Pat Mulroy announced that desalination, the purification of salty or otherwise dirty water for drinking, would play a significant role in Nevada's future. But with further study, Mulroy conceded that the plan was technically and politically complex and in the end left Nevada dependent on the overextended Colorado. She later said that while desal remains a viable option, "one tool in the toolbox," it is not a solution.

In a 2007 agreement between the Department of Interior and the seven Colorado Basin states, a new set of guidelines was established on how to share the Colorado River in case of extreme drought. If Lake Mead drops to an elevation of 1,075 feet above sea level, the first "shortage declaration" will be triggered, which will cut water deliveries to Nevada by thirteen thousand acre-feet a year, or enough water to supply twenty-six thousand average Clark County homes. (Arizona would be shorted more than ten times that amount.)

To buy time, the SNWA has initiated a series of stopgap remedies. By 2014, the agency hopes to have completed a "third straw," a new pipeline, that will reach deeper into Lake Mead than the two existing pipes, at a cost of roughly $1 billion. It has snapped up water leases for the Muddy and Virgin Rivers, which are tributaries of the Colorado. It has worked with California and Arizona to build a new reservoir in Southern California, called Drop 2, to store excess water from the Colorado and capture runoff; controversially, Drop 2 will also restrict flows into Mexico. If the

SNWA needs emergency water, it will swap its portion of Drop 2 water for a greater percentage of the other states' Colorado River water. And Nevada has paid Arizona $100 million to "bank" 1.25 million acre-feet of water in massive underground aquifers.

Yet all of these plans rely on the Colorado River, which remains badly overstretched.

On July 24, 1983, Lake Mead reached a record elevation of 1,225.85 feet above sea level, and engineers feared that the concrete of Hoover Dam's spillway would buckle (it did not).

At 11:30 a.m. on October 17, 2010, the water level in Lake Mead dipped to 1,083.18 feet above sea level, its lowest point since Hoover Dam impounded the Colorado River seventy-five years earlier. This record-low watermark was set during the region's eleventh year of drought, when demand for water was surging across the West. As Nevadans erected new casinos, Californians washed their cars, and Arizonans strolled green golf links in the brown desert, most were unaware of, or unconcerned by, the drying reservoir. But a few were alarmed. "This strikes me as an amazing moment," said Barry Nelson, a senior policy analyst for the Natural Resources Defense Council. "It's three-quarters of a century since they filled [Mead]. And at the three-quarters mark, the world has changed."

The predominate image of Las Vegas is of the glittering Strip, but in reality that represents a thin slice of the metropolitan area. Drive just a mile or so in any direction from the soaring, flashy epicenter, and you will notice that the city spreads low and wide, with acres of stucco tract housing extending into the desert. When you reach the city's outer rim, where developments often come to an abrupt halt in the middle of dusty ocher expanses, it is clear that Las Vegas builders have no intention of stopping there. Once the economy rebounds, the city will resume its relentless expansion. But to do so Las Vegas will need more water.

As currently configured, Pat's Pipe is designed to pump 134,000 acre-feet of water from five rural basins by 2020, which is enough water to provide for 270,000 homes. Yet the University of Nevada estimates that the population of SNWA's service area will grow to 3.6 million by 2035, nearly double what it was in 2009. The agency hasn't said how it plans to hydrate so many people or how it will win the legal right to build the pipeline.

To critics, the SNWA's plan to provide low-cost water to twice as many customers in a few years is tantamount to promoting irresponsible development. "Cheap water is what fuels growth," charged Nevada assemblyman Joe Hogan, an SNWA opponent. "There is no appetite in the water community to even consider charging what the water is worth, or charging higher rates to . . . water wasters."

Pat Mulroy contends that her pipeline is designed not to expand Las Vegas but to protect Clark County from extended drought. Her defenders say that she is not pro-growth, nor is she a policymaker; she is merely a civil servant whose job is to provide Las Vegas with water. Blame politicians or developers for the state's water woes, they say, but don't blame Pat Mulroy.

But this is disingenuous. Pat Mulroy is the highest-profile water manager in the nation, with influence that extends throughout Nevada, the six other Colorado Basin states, Mexico, and into the US Senate. Every time she argues for low water rates, purchases rural water rights, funds controversial pipelines, and avoids discussion of the environmental impact of her ideas, she is making policy—if not in name, then in fact. Her larger message is that Las Vegas will use whatever legal means it can to ensure a plentiful supply of affordable water in coming years. Plainly, if that policy is not linked to restrictions on development, it will only encourage growth.

She is shrewd and not to be underestimated, but even Pat Mulroy can't have it both ways forever. Unless she adjusts her actions to match her rhetoric about the realities of the New West, then her greatest strength—her ability to get the water she wants, regardless of the consequences—may lead to her undoing and, in a worst-case scenario, to the undoing of "the city that wasn't supposed to be."

As controversial as water pipelines have been, the damming of rivers is an equally, if not more, emotionally charged subject. By the turn of the twenty-first century, few of the world's rivers remained undammed. According to a study by *Water Alternatives,* an academic journal, there were forty-five thousand large-scale dams in 2010, which, despite their many benefits—hydropower, flood control, water storage, recreation, and the like—had displaced some 40 to 80 million people, altered natural river flows, disrupted aquatic ecosystems, and led to a buildup of silt and the release of greenhouse gases.

Although dam building in the United States has been greatly curtailed because of these concerns, it has not been stopped. As I discovered in California, dam building remains a potent symbol of mankind's ability to harness nature to his needs, and a political tool that tends to pit farmers of the Old West against the cities and industries of the New West. The debate has swung wildly back and forth, with billions of dollars in the balance.

CHAPTER 16

The Dammed

Beneath this building, beneath every street, there's a desert. Without water the desert will rise up and cover us as though we'd never existed! . . . The Alto Vallejo [dam] can save us from that, and . . . is a fair price to keep the desert from our streets, and not on top of them!
—Los Angeles mayor Sam Bagby, *Chinatown,* 1974

THE GOLDEN AGE OF THE WATER BUFFALOES

The history of the West is that you never *kill* a dam, you just postpone the debate. Dams have a way of coming back, like the undead.
—Peter Gleick, the Pacific Institute, 2009

On a Wednesday afternoon in May 2007, the Association of California Water Agencies (ACWA), the nation's largest coalition of public water managers, met in the Sacramento Convention Center. Hundreds of water managers filled the room, some dressed in sharp suits and glossy shoes, others in dusty hats and cowboy boots. They were responsible for 90 percent of the water used in California, but thanks to an extended drought and a host of attendant problems, the ACWA men (there were hardly any women in the crowd) were on edge.

Just before 2:00, a tall, pale, toothy man with a corona of wavy dark hair swirling over a long face rimmed by a salt-and-pepper beard slipped through the crowd toward the stage. This was Peter Gleick. Fifty-one years old, Gleick was raised on upper Park Avenue in New York City. A graduate of Yale, a Berkeley PhD, a MacArthur Fellow, and as the president of the

Pacific Institute for Studies in Development, Environment, and Security, Gleick had become perhaps America's foremost independent water expert.

Since founding the Oakland-based Pacific Institute in 1987 with three friends, Gleick had carved out a unique career as a high-profile pundit, gadfly, and counterweight to the pro-dam, pro-agriculture, antifish policies of the ACWA men and politicians such as former governor Arnold Schwarzenegger. Gleick had a reputation as a provocative, at times combative, personality. He usually squared off against his opponents from a distance—in speeches, newspaper opinion pieces, e-mails, blog postings, and through a steady stream of reports issued by the Pacific Institute. This would be the first time he had attended the ACWA conference in person.

Gleick had come to debate Lester Snow, the director at the California Department of Water Resources (DWR), on the question "Does California Need More Buckets?" To the uninitiated, this topic might sound trivial, or like a good sleeping aid. But the ACWA men knew better. They knew Gleick and Snow were longtime, if cordial, antagonists, and they were looking forward to a good old-fashioned water fight.

In the argot of Western water managers, *buckets* means "wet water," or the actual water stored in a reservoir, like money in a bank. This is distinct from *paper water,* or *water rights,* a legal concept about who-gets-how-much-water-when, written into a deed. *Surface storage,* meanwhile, is another way of saying "reservoirs." *Reservoirs* is another way of saying "dams." And *dam* is the D-word: an engineer's dream and an environmentalist's dystopian nightmare.

The debate over dams, and all they stand for, had stretched over most of the previous century.

A dam is a structure designed to impound (retain) water. Of the nation's eighty-five thousand dams, about six hundred of them were built in the West in the twentieth century. Dams—Western dams in particular—are an emotionally charged subject.

A well-considered, well-built dam is a great accomplishment. Dams capture rain and snowmelt that would otherwise be "wasted" as runoff. They protect against flooding and store water for future use. They provide hydroelectric power and beautiful lakes for swimming, fishing, and waterskiing. They offer proof of man's capacity to control nature. The water stored by Western dams is cheap because it is subsidized by the government. Dams in the West allowed cities to grow, vegetables and cattle to be raised, and people to thrive. Without vast reservoirs created by dams—

such as Lake Powell and Lake Mead—Las Vegas, Los Angeles, and San Diego would not have become flourishing cities; California would not be the nation's leading dairy state or the fifth-largest supplier of food and agriculture in the world.

But to some, dams are a blight on the landscape, constipators of natural watercourses, destroyers of salmon runs and killers of endangered species, dislocators of communities, eroders of wetlands and riverbanks, triggers for mudslides, behemoths that impair water quality through the buildup of salts and other dissolved solids, white elephants that cost too much to build and maintain and occasionally fail catastrophically. To critics of dams, it made no sense to build farms and cities in the desert; people should work and live where water is plentiful. By storing millions of gallons of water in reservoirs and aqueducts, dam builders lost thousands of gallons to evaporation and seepage. Silt that normally flows downstream is trapped behind dams, which chokes the flow of nutrients and water, clogs hydroelectric turbines, and dooms reservoirs to short life spans.

Dams require constant maintenance, and without it they become hazardous. Between 2005 and 2009, there were 132 dam failures across the United States, and a further 434 serious "incidents," which could have led to disaster without intervention, according to the Association of State Dam Safety Officials (ASDSO). From 1998 to 2008, the number of dams considered "deficient"—meaning they are susceptible to collapse—rose 137 percent, from 1,818 to 4,308.

Dam opponents point to a few dramatic failures as proof that dams are not to be trusted. The most infamous was the Johnstown Flood, caused by the rupture of the South Fork Dam in western Pennsylvania by heavy rains in 1889: when the dam burst, it sent 4.8 billion gallons of Conemaugh River water rushing downstream, which killed over 2,200 people and caused $17 million worth of damage. (The flood was named after a town wiped out by the flood.) Another notorious flood was caused by the collapse of the St. Francis Dam, northwest of Los Angeles: it gave way at three minutes before midnight on March 12, 1928, sending twelve billion gallons crashing towards the Pacific, and killing about 600 people. The St. Francis was designed by William Mulholland, the legendary head of the Los Angeles Department of Water and Power; he accepted responsibility for the tragedy, which destroyed his career.

The chance of a twenty-first century Johnstown Flood or St. Francis disaster are minute, government officials say, and state and federal agencies have put emergency plans and safety regulations in place. But "the lack of funding for dam upgrade has become a serious national problem," ASDSO charges. "The number of dams identified as unsafe is increasing at a faster rate than those being repaired." To repair the most critical dams will cost $16 billion, and take a dozen years, the association estimates; the price to recondition all US dams could be $50 billion. At this writing, Congress was debating a massive economic stimulus package that contained a $40 billion investment in infrastructure, including dams, roads, bridges ports, rail and water systems.

An early debate over dams stands as a defining moment for the environmental movement. In 1912, San Francisco proposed building the Hetch Hetchy Reservoir, inside the remote northwestern corner of Yosemite National Park, to meet the city's growing demand for power and water, including for fire protection (in 1906, the devastating San Francisco earthquake and an ensuing conflagration killed some three thousand people). But damming a valley on national parkland required federal approval, and the decision to grant it was sharply disputed. The fight galvanized dam opponents and split the nascent environmental movement into two factions: protectionists, led by John Muir, who held that nature is sacrosanct and that humans are intruders; and the more established conservationists, led by President Theodore Roosevelt, who believed that man should maximize the use of natural resources over the long term. At congressional hearings, Gifford Pinchot, the first chief of the US Forest Service and a staunch conservationist, argued in favor of the reservoir on the grounds that natural resources would best be served by careful management. But Muir, founder of the Sierra Club, led the opposition with the famous cry "Dam Hetch Hetchy!"

The battle seesawed, but Hetch Hetchy was finally approved by President Woodrow Wilson in 1913, and the O'Shaughnessy Dam was completed a decade later. Today Hetch Hetchy Reservoir provides 85 percent of San Francisco's water, which comes from the Tuolumne River and, like New York's, is so clean it does not have to be filtered. But the reservoir has remained a lightning rod. In 2010, groups such as Restore Hetch Hetchy declared that the dam was an environmentally destructive nineteenth-century boondoggle and agitated for a ballot measure to remove it; the water from the reservoir, the group said, could be replaced by water from a restored groundwater basin and aggressive recycling. The city countered that tearing down Hetch Hetchy would be expensive and polluting and maintained that the existing system is "one of the greenest systems around."

• • •

In the American West, a cadre of engineers and bureaucrats known as Water Buffaloes enjoyed a golden age of dam, reservoir, and aqueduct building that lasted from the Depression through the late 1970s. Water Buffaloes tend to speak in telegraphic bursts studded with acronyms— IID (Imperial Irrigation District), MAF (millions of acre-feet of water), CVP (the federal Central Valley Project). They wax lyrical about spigots, pumps, and pipes. They love nothing more than to blast rock apart and erect giant "water storage structures."

Water Buffaloes are synonymous with the US Bureau of Reclamation, also known as the Bureau of Rec, or just the Bureau. It is one of ten divisions within the Department of the Interior (DOI), which was established in 1849 to manage, preserve, and develop natural resources and public lands across the country. The Bureau of Rec was founded by the Reclamation Act of 1902, to "reclaim" land—i.e., to establish reliable water supplies and counter desertification; to drain swamps and restrain water with dikes and levees to make new land available for housing or farming; to build and manage enormous irrigation projects; and to help resettle people across the seventeen Western states.

In its first decade, the Bureau was focused on creating reservoirs and canals designed to improve agricultural irrigation. By the 1930s, it had expanded its portfolio to include flood-control and municipal water projects and had become a major provider of hydroelectric power. Since then, it has branched into industrial water supply, water quality issues, navigation, fish and wildlife protection, recreation, and water research projects. But the Bureau is best known for the dams it built across most major Western rivers.

The golden age of the Water Buffaloes began in 1928, when Congress authorized the bureau to build Hoover Dam, which impounds over 9 trillion gallons of Colorado River water in Lake Mead. Hoover Dam—originally called Boulder Dam, after Boulder Canyon, the steep gorge in which it was built, and controversially renamed for President Herbert Hoover, who personally ensured its funding and construction—is a magnificent structure designed with refined art deco touches. It is an "arch-gravity" dam (a dam that curves upstream, which directs water pressure against the canyon walls), with a thin top and a thick bottom, which allows brittle concrete to withstand immense water pressure. Its construction was an epic undertaking, requiring 66 million tons of concrete (the most ever for a project at the time) and the invention of innovative engineering techniques, such as special coils that cooled the concrete as it was poured into trapezoidal forms so that it would cure without cracking. The dam caused the deaths of 112 men during construction and led to the rise of Las Vegas as a center of gambling and drinking in a traditionally Mormon region. The largest dam in the world when it was built, Hoover produces about 4 billion kilowatt-hours of hydroelectric power a year, enough to service 1.3 million people in Arizona, Nevada, and California.

Like most large dams, Hoover Dam was controversial from the moment it was conceived. Arizona saw it as a water grab by California; East Coast legislators saw it as a drain on the treasury; the power industry saw its hydroelectric turbines as unwanted competition; and wealthy landowners saw it as a threat to the irrigation they depended on.

Hoover Dam and its reservoir, Lake Mead, block the Colorado River's natural flooding, which scours the riverbed and helps plant and animal species reseed. The dam proved devastating to native plants and fish along the river—such as the razorback sucker, the humpback chub, the bony-tail chub, and the Colorado pikeminnow, all of which are now listed as endangered species. It took six years to fill Lake Mead in the late thirties, and during that time virtually no water reached the mouth of the Colorado River, where it should empty into the Sea of Cortés. The delta's estuary once boasted a mixing zone (where freshwater mixes with salt water, producing a rich ecosystem) that stretched forty miles south of the Colorado's outflow. But dams along the river, especially Hoover, choked the freshwater flow so fiercely that the estuary's salinity was raised to unprecedented heights, which wreaked havoc on estuarine flora and fauna; the last time the Colorado reached the Sea of Cortés was in 2003.

The Bureau of Reclamation was unmoved by the environmentalists' protests. With the triumphant completion of Hoover Dam, substantial funds began to flow from Washington, DC, to Bureau projects across the arid West for the next half a century.

Much of the midlife success of the Bureau of Reclamation's dam builders can be attributed to Floyd Dominy, the ur–Water Buffalo who served as commissioner of reclamation from 1959 to 1969. Dominy's worldview was defined by a search for water. Raised on an isolated, parched ranch in Nebraska, he grew into a Stetson-wearing, cigar-chomping, pro-fane rancher-politician and indefatigable self-promoter. To the dismay of environmentalists, he was a shrewd operator who held great sway in both the hot deserts of the West and the cool marbled hallways of Congress. Almost every project he favored got built. He was responsible for the Yellowtail Dam, the Trinity Dam, Flaming Gorge Dam, Navajo Dam, and most famously—and infamously—Glen Canyon Dam, which impounded the Upper Colorado to create Lake Powell, on the Utah/Arizona border.

Dominy's foes were legion. The most vociferous of them came from the increasingly powerful environmental movement of the 1960s and 1970s, led by charismatic evangelicals such as David Brower, the Sierra Club's first executive director, and Mark Reisner, author of *Cadillac Desert*. Dominy alternately ignored Brower and his ilk or debated them with great relish—most famously when he accompanied Brower on a raft trip down the Colorado River, during which they argued the merits of damming the river as they splashed through white-water rapids, a scene recounted in John McPhee's book *Encounters with the Archdruid*.

By the late 1970s, however, the Bureau of Rec was confronted by a series of shifts in the public mood that conspired to diminish its scope and alter its focus from construction of new projects to management of existing ones. In the 1960s and 1970s, environmentalists became newly energized and well funded. Rachel Carson's 1962 book, *Silent Spring*, drew attention to chemical pollution, while Paul Ehrlich's *Population Bomb*, of 1968, addressed the question of how many people the earth can sustain. Anxiety over nuclear radiation began with the poisoning of fishermen after a nuclear test in the Bikini Atoll in 1954 and peaked with the partial meltdown of a reactor at the Three Mile Island nuclear plant in 1979. Concern about oil spills, acid rain, and mercury poisoning built support for new laws such as the National Environmental Policy Act of 1969, the Federal Water Pollution Control Act of 1972, and the Endangered Species Act of 1973, which hindered the Bureau of Rec's infrastructure-building projects. Public perception of dams was beginning to change, too.

Teton Dam was a $100 million earth-and-rock-filled structure built by the Bureau of Rec in 1975 to impound the Teton River, in southeastern Idaho. On June 5, 1976, it collapsed, killing eleven people and thirteen thousand head of cattle, and causing some $2 billion worth of damage. (It was not rebuilt, although the Bureau has considered it.)

In the intervening years, water management was becoming a flash point between powerful constituencies—agriculture, industry, cities, Native American tribes, recreational users, environmentalists—and the Bureau was caught in the cross fire. As the seventies wore into the eighties, President Carter, faced with a global energy crisis set off by the Iranian revolution of 1979, began to curtail the number and scope of the Bureau's projects. By the end of the 1980s, the Bureau was subject to major downsizing and reorganization.

In 1993, Reclamation had almost eight thousand employees; by 1996 it had shed nearly two thousand workers, and its annual budget was slimmed down to $772 million. The Water Buffaloes who had engineered and built more than six hundred dams and reservoirs throughout the West in the twentieth century had essentially been turned into caretakers, devoted to the operation and maintenance of about 476 dams, plus canals and hydroelectric facilities.

In 2008, the Bureau of Reclamation was the largest wholesaler of water in the country, providing water to 31 million people, including 140,000 farmers who irrigated 10 million acres of land that produced 60 percent of the nation's vegetables and 25 percent of its fruit and nut crop. The Bureau generated $1 billion a year in revenues operating fifty-eight hydroelectric plants that provided 40 billion kilowatt-hours of energy for 6 million homes.

Shrunk and repurposed, the Bureau nevertheless declared victory: "The arid West has essentially been reclaimed," an agency statement read. "The major rivers have been harnessed and facilities are in place or are being completed to meet the most pressing current water demands and those of the immediate future."

"BUCKETS": A CALIFORNIA WATER FIGHT

In 2000, the World Bank, a backer of dam projects worldwide, joined the World Conservation Union, a protester of dam projects worldwide, to publish a definitive and unprecedented study of large-scale dams. Their joint report concluded that dams have made a significant contribution to human development and have led to considerable benefits, but too often these advances come at "an unacceptable and often unnecessary" price. Dams ruin forests and fisheries, have displaced as many as 80 million people around the world over the last century, and often fail to achieve their objectives for irrigation, flood control, or hydropower, the report concluded.

By the time the report was issued, the antidam crusade had grown so loud and effective in the United States that dam building had dramatically slowed. Governor Schwarzenegger liked to complain that one reason California's "water system is extremely vulnerable . . . [is] we haven't built any dams in thirty years."

"Wrong, wrong, wrong!" Peter Gleick recoiled in a blog post. In fact, Gleick pointed out, since 1969 California had added the New Melones Dam, Warm Springs Dam, and Los Vaqueros Dam. And the last significant dam to be built in the United States was the Diamond Valley Reservoir, in Riverside County, which was completed in 1999. All told, these dams impound some 8.6 million acre-feet of water, which is a far from negligible amount.

Just before the 2007 ACWA conference in Sacramento, Lester Snow and Governor Schwarzenegger had proposed a multibillion-dollar bond offering, largely designed to fund "more surface storage." Translated, this meant that in response to the worsening drought, they proposed to build two new dams—one at Temperance Flat, east of Fresno, and the other at the Sites Reservoir, on the western side of the Sacramento Valley—and expand a third dam, at Los Vaqueros in Contra Costa County. In addition, they proposed building a forty-three-mile-long Peripheral Canal around the troubled Sacramento Delta.

The latter idea was not new, or popular. When a similar canal project had been proposed in 1982, it became the focus of an intense political battle and was resoundingly crushed by voters. But now the Delta was facing more problems than ever: crumbling levees, development in flood zones, and court-ordered restrictions on water withdrawals from the estuary to stem the decimation of salmon, smelt, and other marine life.

"The history of the West is that you never *kill* a dam, you just postpone the debate," Gleick told me. "Dams have a way of coming back, like the undead."

Gleick believes that Schwarzenegger's proposed dams would cost too much, would not provide the benefits they promised, would be environmentally destructive, were political sops to powerful agricultural interests, and were short-term answers to the real long-term issue, which is that Californians use water wastefully and unsustainably.

"I'm not against all dams, per se," Gleick told me. "I just think there are smarter, cheaper ways for California to achieve its goals, and we ought to try those first."

To him, placing huge bets on massive infrastructure projects is a twentieth-century conceit that should now be discarded in favor of a new approach: relatively low-cost, low-impact, long-term, high-technology solutions, such as drip irrigation, low-flow showerheads, front-mounted washing machines, and other water conservation techniques. Pairing this with financial incentives (i.e., raising water rates to reduce consumption) and new regulations, he said, will nurture a more efficient and sustainable use of water.

"We already know how to do more with less water," he said. "It's incontrovertible. In fact, the United States today uses far less water per person than we did twenty-five years ago. People find this shocking, but it's true."

According to a USGS study that looked at fifty years' worth of statistics, water use in the United States steadily increased between 1950 and 1980; it was expected that as the population continued to rise, so would water use. But water use began to decline in 1985, the study found, and has remained relatively stable ever since, despite a steadily growing population. This was the result of water conservation efforts, mainly by industry, along with the government's 1992 laws mandating the use of conserving technologies— such as low-flow showerheads and toilets—in new homes.

For those who share Gleick's view, the question is, how do you convince the public, which largely takes its water supply for granted, and the Water Buffaloes, who are entrenched, to think about and use water in a new, intentional way? How do you make water efficiency and conservation the new ideal?

In May 2007, Gleick decided it was time to go outside his usual comfort zone and speak directly to those in charge: Lester Snow and the ACWA men who run California's water systems.

At 2:05, inside the cavernous auditorium at the Sacramento Convention Center, Peter Gleick stepped onto the stage and took up his position behind a lectern, stage right.

At 2:06, he raised his fists, which were now encased in a pair of bright red boxing gloves, and threw a few punches in the air—*whiff, whaff!*

The crowd's chatter suddenly stopped, and perhaps a thousand eyes turned at once to focus on the stage. After pounding the red mitts together a few times, Gleick cleared his throat and said, "When I asked my wife what I should wear today, she said, 'Something that doesn't show blood.'"

The crowd chuckled appreciatively, settled into seats, crossed tanned arms, adjusted hats, and raised chins in anticipation.

Winding his voice up like a game-show host, the moderator, the journalist Tom Philp (who won a Pulitzer Prize for editorials about the Hetch Hetchy controversy), pointed to the lectern on the opposite side of the stage and said, "And in this corner of the Aqua Dome, ladies and gentlemen, please welcome ... Mr. ... Lesterrrr ... Snooooooww!"

Snow is stocky, with thinning hair and a mustache the color of sand. He gave a barely perceptible smile and took up his position behind a lectern. Like Peter Gleick, Snow was a transplant from the East: originally from Pittsburgh, Pennsylvania, he was now California's main water expert, a man considered by many—even Peter Gleick—to be one of the smartest water managers in the country.

At 2:20, Gleick, now gloveless, took the first verbal jab: "California's water infrastructure has brought enormous benefits to us today, but it comes with some costs. The time may come when we *do* need new surface storage, but I don't believe that time has come yet. You don't spend billions of dollars to build something you think *might* be needed before it actually *is* needed. We should spend our money and effort to create new conservation and efficiency measures first. That would free up far more water, for far less money, and with far less environmental harm than the governor's new dams."

Lester Snow counterpunched, "We currently don't have the storage capacity to capture runoff in big-flow years. When we get a heavy rain, we're losing on average 450,000 acre-feet of water straight into the ocean. Last year, we lost 1.2 million acre-feet. If you wait to build infrastructure *today*, it's going to cost you more to do it *tomorrow*."

Gleick: "We spend a lot of money to capture, treat, and deliver water that we use inefficiently. New dams are an outdated solution. Assembly Bill 2496 [a bill to improve toilet efficiency], which the governor unfortunately vetoed, would have saved *far* more water than these new da—"

Snow: "California has already spent two hundred million dollars on conservation and efficiency. But no single water management action can meet all of our challenges. The future is *here*. We need to use a 'portfolio' approach, which includes conservation, recycling, desalination, water transfers, reoperation of existing reservoirs, groundwater management, new surface storage—"

Gleick: "With all due respect, the water policy of the twenty-first century *cannot* be the water policy of the twentieth! We don't know what the benefits of surface storage will be, who will use it, or who will *pay* for building these expensive dams. . . ."

The debate went back and forth in this vein for some time. When I spoke to the combatants later, they agreed to continue disagreeing. "Lester is a smart guy, but all he really said was 'We have to do everything,'" Gleick complained. "It is a way to pretend to be balanced, a way to avoid making decisions that piss off one constituency or another. But we can't afford to do *everything*, and fortunately I don't think we have to."

Lester Snow said, "Yes, I *do* think we ought to try 'everything.' We have no choice. Climate change is here, and it is the single biggest challenge we face in water management. We can't afford to take any strategies off the table."

Both Peter Gleick and Lester Snow agree that California faces a serious and growing threat to its water supply. But their very different solutions to the problem have wide implications for the state, the West, the nation, and much of the world.

CHAPTER 17

Snowpack:
The Canary in a Coal Mine

GEHRKE AT THE ROSETTA STONE

Gin Flat is a small meadow surrounded by pine and cedar trees that sits in the thin air at seventy-two hundred feet above sea level in Yosemite National Park, in California's Sierra Nevada. In winter it is covered with layer upon layer of deep snowpack, the snow that accumulates at high altitude in regions that are cold for most of the year. Snowpack "stores" water like a giant reservoir, which it then slowly releases during the spring and summer snowmelt. Snowmelt from the Sierra flows into streams and rivers that empty into the Sacramento and San Joaquin Rivers, which flow through the Sacramento–San Joaquin Delta, a vast estuary near the state capital. The Delta supplies freshwater to millions of Californians and thousands of acres of farmland around San Francisco, Los Angeles, and as far south as San Diego. The Sierra snowpack is California's most important source of freshwater.

Gin Flat has been called the Rosetta Stone of the California water supply because it has just the right conditions—a balance of snow, sun, and air temperature—to help scientists predict snowmelt, water flows, and potential floods and droughts in coming seasons. Because it is just above the altitude where snow turns to rain, Gin Flat is an ideal spot to test the theory that global warming will lead to more rain and less snow at higher elevations. Such a shift, climatologists hypothesize, will result in major hydrological changes: less water stored as snowpack, and more runoff, flooding, and evaporation, which could in turn lead to less freshwater flowing to arid Southern California in the spring and early summer, when it is needed most.

Every winter Frank Gehrke clips into his cross-country skis, harnesses himself to a sled loaded with equipment, and slips and slides his way up a three-mile-long trail to Gin Flat. Gehrke is chief of California's Department of Water Resources' (DWR) Cooperative Snow Surveys Program. He is considered the dean of the state's snow studies experts, and thus an expert on the future of California's water supply. Gin Flat (named after a former speakeasy) is a "snow course" that has been providing DWR with valuable snowpack data since 1930. California has two hundred and eighty similar sites, eighteen of them in Yosemite. Because of its location and long data record, Gin Flat is always the first and most important site for testing.

Having skied out of the close-wooded trail and onto the white expanse of Gin Flat, Gehrke took a moment to catch his breath. Then he and a colleague began to check scientific instruments that had been placed around the meadow to monitor conditions year-round. The devices, which automatically transmit data to laboratories in Sacramento and Virginia every three hours, measure the depth, temperature, and weight of the snow, the moisture of the soil under the snow, the humidity and wind speed, and the intensity of the sun's rays. Gehrke used a long aluminum tube to measure the water content of the thick drifts of powder and to check the snowpack's depth.

As California struggled in 2008 with the effects of a second year of drought, Gehrke's readings from Gin Flat and other sites helped to determine California's water rates, how much water farmers and industry could use, and whether homeowners' car washing and garden watering would be restricted.

Though he is a careful scientist, reluctant to make bold statements or far-reaching predictions, Gehrke noted that in twenty-seven years of taking measurements he'd noticed snowpack levels becoming "erratic"— meaning that California winters had become "either really dry or really wet." Sierra-wide, snowpack was only 40 percent of average in 2007, but in 2008 it would rise to 118 percent.

Gehrke measures snow water equivalent (SWE), which is the amount of water in snowpack: the depth of water that would result if you melted the entire snowpack. The average SWE at Gin Flat is thirty-two inches a year. In 1988, during the previous drought (1987 to 1992), Gin Flat's SWE dropped severely, to only 5.1 inches. Since then it had risen. In 2007, Gin Flat's SWE was 11.4 inches; in 2008 it was 33.8 inches; and in 2009 it was 30 inches. In 2010, heavy rains seemed to ease the latest drought, and Gin

Flat's average SWE was 43 inches. But Gehrke cautioned that La Niña conditions (low ocean surface-water temperatures) were expected, and that 2011 would be dry again.

When climatologists talk about a hotter climate, they often depict a world of too much water, an era in which the coasts of today are submerged by rising oceans. But in recent years they have begun to focus on a different aspect of climate change, and to imagine a world in which the snowpack of the Sierra, the Rockies, the Himalayas, and other important mountain ranges liquefies earlier in the year, faster than ever.

In 2006, Steven Chu—the Nobel-winning physicist whom President Obama named secretary of energy in 2009—said that decreasing supplies of freshwater from snowmelt might prove a far more significant problem than slowly rising oceans. "There's a two-thirds chance there will be a disaster," Chu told the *New York Times Magazine*. "And that's in the best scenario." By disaster he meant the possibility of a modern Dust Bowl in the Southwest, which would cause grave ecological harm and cause millions of people to evacuate desert cities.

Even the most optimistic climate models for the second half of the twenty-first century indicate an alarming 30 to 70 percent chance that snowpack could disappear, Chu added.

Other experts are just as concerned about the Sierra's 497 glaciers. While snowpack is made up of seasonal layers of snow, glaciers are relatively permanent features of the landscape. They flow, extend, and retreat according to changes in climate, which makes them important indicators of long-term trends.

Among those studying glaciers in Yosemite are Hassan Basagic and Andrew Fountain, climatologists from Portland State University, in Oregon, who studied ten glaciers in the park, comparing their size in 2007 to that of a century earlier. They hiked up to the ice fields to measure, then compared modern photographs to those from 1883, 1944, and 2004. They found that all ten glaciers were in retreat. To take just one example, the west lobe of Lyell Glacier had been reduced by 30 percent since 1883, and the smaller east lobe had been reduced by 70 percent. The Basagic and Fountain report points to an unavoidable conclusion: the climate is warming and the ice is melting.

The US Forest Service has characterized the Sierra Nevada as a "canary in the coal mine," an early-warning system for the effects of a hotter, drier future.

The four-hundred-mile-long range in Northern California has many different ecosystems: as altitude changes, so does the climate, soil, and plant life (it is believed the Sierra houses some ten thousand to fifteen thousand different species); each of these zones wraps around the peaks like a belt. As the climate warms, the bands are forced upward; eventually, some of the bands will run out of room and disappear. There is already evidence of this. By 2008, ponderosa pine trees were growing five hundred meters upslope from the top of their traditional elevation. Sugar pine was also advancing upslope, as the lower elevations became too warm for comfort. Wildlife species that depend on the trees followed. This uphill march will change the ecosystem: with sustained aridification, vulnerable species could become extinct, invasive species could move in, and the risk of fire could spread—thanks to more dry underbrush, dead trees, and an increase in lightning strikes.

When he checked on the Phillips snow course in March 2008, Frank Gehrke was surprised to find a pencil he'd dropped on a previous trip. It was lying in the dirt, in an area that would usually be covered by snow at that time of year. After checking his instruments, Gehrke found that the snowpack was only 67 percent of normal, significantly lower than it had been only a few months earlier. Over the summer, the drought deepened. Governor Arnold Schwarzenegger asked people to cut back on water use by 20 percent. "It's pretty grim," observed the usually laconic Gehrke.

"WE COULD USE LESS WATER"

On June 4, 2008, two months after Gehrke's trip to Phillips, and a year after Peter Gleick and Lester Snow jousted over dams at the ACWA conference, Governor Arnold Schwarzenegger leaned into a bristle of microphones in front of the statehouse in Sacramento and said, "This March, April, and May have been the driest ever in our recorded history. Some local governments are rationing water. Developments can't proceed. Agricultural fields are sitting idle. We must recognize the severity of the crisis."

After the driest spring in eighty-eight years, California's rivers and reservoirs had dropped to 41 percent of their average depth. Governor Schwarzenegger issued the state's first drought proclamation in sixteen years and declared a state of emergency in nine of the state's fifty-eight counties. Schwarzenegger also directed Lester Snow and the state Department of Water Resources to improve efficiency and coordination among local water districts, facilitate water transfers, and expedite grant programs. The governor said these measures would aid water conservation and struggling farmers. But if people didn't voluntarily cut back on water use, he warned, every California resident would face mandatory water rationing.

Then, with great urgency, he proposed an $11 billion bond to underwrite the construction of new dams at Temperance Flat, at Sites and Los Vaqueros Reservoirs, and a Peripheral Canal around the ailing Sacramento–San Joaquin Delta, just a few miles from where he stood. "Water is like our gold," Schwarzenegger said. "We have to treat it like that. There is no more time to waste."

When I asked Peter Gleick about this, he responded tartly, "No new dams are needed! Efficient toilets would save California more than 130 billion gallons of water every year—more than the annual yield of the Hetch Hetchy Reservoir."

The battle occasionally grew personal, as when Michael Wade, executive director of the California Farm Water Coalition, wrote to the *San Francisco Chronicle,* "Peter Gleick demonstrates his disdain for California farmers by claiming the taking away of water . . . and adding a few more low-flow toilets . . . is the solution to our state's water woes. . . . He thinks cotton doesn't contribute enough to California's economy because other crops have the ability to generate more income. What's next on the chopping block, cheaper varieties of lettuce? . . . Does his thinking include jobs?"

As Gleick saw it, Governor Schwarzenegger, Lester Snow, the ACWA men, the agricultural lobby, and their mostly rural sympathizers remain fixated on the idea that dams *have* to be part of the solution to California's water problems simply because that has always been the answer in the past. "It's a mind-set, an inability to believe that serious water problems can't be solved by *more* storage," Gleick said. "I get frustrated by this formulation. After so many years, it's still a fight about dams versus no dams. But if that was really the solution, then why haven't our problems gone away before?"

Even if Schwarzenegger succeeded in funding the Sites and Temperance Flat Reservoirs, Gleick predicted, California's water problems would remain. "Our water problems will be exactly the same tomorrow, only we'll be billions of dollars poorer," he said, eyes blazing. "My question is, why hold up other solutions just because you want to make dams part of the package?"

As he zips from water conferences in California to Senate hearings in Washington, DC, and global forums in Sweden, China, and Dubai, Gleick's mantra is always the same: "Almost everything we do on earth, we could do with less water."

Humans cannot prosper without a clean, reliable supply of H_2O. But is there enough freshwater to sustain the world's growing population?

In a 2006 report, the UN declared, "There is enough water for everyone" but added a caveat: "Water insufficiency is often due to mismanagement, corruption, lack of appropriate institutions, bureaucratic inertia, and a shortage of investment in both human capacity and physical infrastructure." These human failings are not likely to disappear, and as water stress grows, they will have exponentially greater impacts than ever before.

Water is unevenly distributed and strategically important, and it confers great temptations of power: it will almost certainly be at the center of rising political, economic, and environmental tensions this century. The imbalance between water supply and demand has already led to societal unrest around the world, and experts fear that as the effects of population growth intersect with those of global warming, tensions will ratchet up further and could become violent.

CHAPTER 18

Water Wars

Too often, where we need water, we find guns. . . . As the global
economy grows, so will its thirst. . . . Many more conflicts lie
over the horizon.
—UN secretary general Ban Ki-moon, 2008

RIVER/RIVALS

Closely related to the word *river* is *rival*, originally "one who
uses the same stream (or 'one on the opposite side of the
stream')" . . . the notion is of the competitiveness of neighbors.
—the Online Etymology Dictionary

The last time one American state took up arms against another was over
river water. In 1934, Arizona governor Benjamin Moeur dispatched
National Guardsmen to patrol the Colorado River on two ferryboats
armed with machine guns, dubbed "the Arizona Navy," to stop the construction of Parker Dam and the "theft" of river water by California. In a
stirring court case, the US Supreme Court ruled that California had acted
illegally and halted construction of the dam. But the ruling was undone
when Congress passed a retroactive bill legalizing California's water
expropriations. This ended the fight, if not the rancor, over the Colorado,
which lingers today.

Although water-sharing agreements—such as the Delaware River
Compact, which the Supreme Court brokered among New York, New Jersey, and Pennsylvania—outnumber conflicts, plenty of states are waging
water battles in the courtroom. Kansas and Nebraska have squared off
over billions of gallons of water each wants from the Republican River.

The US Supreme Court has appointed a special master to adjudicate Montana's lawsuit that contends Wyoming violated terms of the Yellowstone River Compact of 1950 by pumping too much water from aquifers for use in coal-bed methane drilling. And Texas has warred with Oklahoma over the Kiamichi River.

Sometimes these skirmishes cross national boundaries. The five Great Lakes—Superior, Huron, Michigan, Erie, and Ontario—contain about 90 percent of the fresh surface water in the United States and approximately one-fifth of the entire world's supply. Some 42 million Americans and Canadians rely on the Great Lakes Basin water for their drinking supply; the waterways also play a crucial role in the region's multibillion-dollar economy. In 1998 the Nova Group, a small Canadian consulting firm, announced its intention to withdraw 158 million gallons of water a year from Lake Superior and ship it by tanker to Asia. Permits were quickly issued by a local Ontario government office, but when word of the deal spread, officials from the eight US states bordering the lakes—already concerned about overuse, industrial pollution, and invasive species—agreed that a stringent set of rules to protect lake waters was necessary.

In 2008, after nearly a decade of discussion, the eight states and the provinces of Quebec and Ontario signed the Great Lakes Compact, to protect the lakes from large water withdrawals. President Bush signed the bill into law. But some, such as Michigan congressman Bart Stupak, opposed the bill because under the Chapter 11 provision of the North American Free Trade Agreement (NAFTA)—the 1994 trade agreement among the United States, Canada, and Mexico—if a foreign company believes its ability to conduct business is hindered by state law, it can sue for compensation, which could set off an international water dispute. Thus far, cooler heads have prevailed, though the potential for mischief is real.

Rivers, in particular, have the potential to be flashpoints because those upstream can control flows to those downstream. The UN has warned that strife over shared rivers—especially the Nile, Niger, Volta, and Zambezi—has the potential to erupt into armed conflict. Others have pointed to tensions over the Tigris and the Euphrates as a likely catalyst to violence. The rivers snake from the Turkish highlands down into Iraq and Syria, then out to the Persian Gulf; each of these nations has laid claim to the rivers.

In 1998, Turkey and Syria nearly went to war over water. When the United States invaded Iraq, much of Saddam's infrastructure was destroyed, making the regional demand for water all the more acute. Matters have been vastly complicated by the rise of the Kurds, whose ancient homeland straddles the headwaters of the Tigris and the Euphrates, and who have emerged as a potent political force with US backing. A behind-the-scenes struggle has been under way among Turkey, Kurdistan, and Iraq (and the US forces there) over how to collect and distribute water from the Tigris-Euphrates systems in coming decades.

Water has been considered a lethal strategic weapon in Korea. South Korea was first gripped by a "water panic" in 1986, when the North built a massive dam on the Han River, which runs through Seoul, the South Korean capital. To protect itself, the South quickly countered by building the Peace Dam. Then, at two o'clock one morning in September 2009, North Korea opened the gates of a new dam on the Imjin River without warning, unleashing a fifteen-foot-tall wall of water, which swept into South Korea, creating a wide path of destruction and killing six people. It was unclear if the mercurial North had done so by accident or to provoke its neighbors.

Despite these riverine tensions, researchers at the London School of Economics say that rivers have historically provided a good example of "asymmetrical cooperation" between nations of different sizes and strengths.

The Nile is a vast river that has tributaries extending over a tenth of Africa's surface, and a watershed that encompasses ten nations and 160 million people. The largest nations along the river—Egypt, Sudan, Uganda, and Ethiopia—hold the most sway, but these neighbors have spent centuries developing water-sharing agreements, and a water war is unlikely.

More worrisome is the prospect of an outsider's disrupting the established order. China, for instance, has been negotiating with Ethiopia, which lies upstream of Egypt, for use of its agricultural land; one day, China might attempt to divert Nile water to the fields it plants in Ethiopia, which would almost certainly raise tensions.

Indeed, it is nations such as China, India, Pakistan, and the rising "Tigers" of Southeast Asia—nations finding economic success while faced with increasing demands for water and food—whose potential for conflict seems most real.

CONFLICT/COOPERATION

Whiskey's for drinking, water's for fighting.
—attributed to Mark Twain

The Chinese character for "political order" is based on the symbol for "water," and the meaning is clear: those who control water control people. In 1950, China invaded Tibet in part to gain control of the water stored in its Himalayan glaciers. China is planning to create nearly two hundred miles of canals to divert water from the Himalayan plateau to the parched Yellow River. The fate of Himalayan snowmelt is particularly sensitive because it supplies the rivers that bring water to more than half a dozen Asian countries. A large-scale diversion of these waters will lead to a spike in regional tensions.

"Once this issue of water resources comes up—and it seems inevitable at this point that it will—it also raises emerging conflicts with India and Southeast Asia," writes Elizabeth Economy, director for Asia Studies at the Council on Foreign Affairs.

Worldwide, a lack of water leads to low productivity, weak governments, and violent protests that can spill across borders. In 1995, Ismail Serageldin, the World Bank's leading environmental expert, famously predicted that with 263 international river basins and 273 international aquifers "the wars of the next century will be over water."

A 2008 report by International Alert, a peace-building organization based in London, identified forty-six countries with a combined population of 2.7 billion people where contention over water has created "a high risk of violent conflict" by 2025.

Thus far, actual wars over water are more difficult to pinpoint. In the 1980s and 1990s, a dramatic decrease in rainfall was blamed on overgrazing and tree cutting in Darfur, Sudan. Violence flared between farmers and nomadic herders of different tribes, leaving three hundred thousand dead and 2.5 million people displaced. But the war in Darfur, which continues to flare up, was the result of many complex ethnic, religious, and political factors and is not strictly a "water war."

Similarly, droughts were arguably responsible—or, at least, were important contributing factors—for starting the Taliban uprising in Afghanistan and the Maoist insurgency in Nepal. But those conflicts also have complex roots, and neither is an example of a pure water war.

In researching water conflict, Dr. Aaron Wolf, of Oregon State University's Institute for Water and Watersheds, found that the only actual water war recorded between nations occurred some forty-five hundred years ago, between the city-states of Lagash and Umma in the Tigris-Euphrates basin. Since the late 1940s, Wolf found, water-cooperative events have outnumbered water-conflictive events by 2.5 to 1, even in some of the world's most unstable regions.

Nevertheless, diplomats at the UN remain concerned about the building tension around resources and have made water awareness one of the UN Development Goals, a list of initiatives that aim to reduce by half the number of people without safe drinking water by 2015.

It may be that the very thing causing tension between tribes or nations—that they share limited supplies of water while contending with increasing demand—proves the best inoculant against water wars in coming years. If one nation usurps or destroys a neighbor's water supply, then it, too, will suffer, but if both nations work to share water fairly, then both will benefit.

When I spoke to him in 2007, Jan Eliasson, a former president of the UN General Assembly who has made water a personal cause while mediating disputes from Bosnia to Iran, had just returned from Darfur. "Water is *one* of the root causes of war there—not the only one, but a very important complicating factor," he explained. "Water is crucial. If we could solve the situation logically, it would be through efforts to share irrigation and other resources. You have to get people out of their helplessness and hopelessness."

There are historical models for this. From 1948 to 1994, while Israel and Jordan were technically at war, they continued to hold secret talks on cooperatively managing the Jordan River. While India and Pakistan have warred several times, the Indus River Commission has survived; during one of the wars, India continued to make payments to Pakistan as part of its treaty obligations.

"I think water hits us at a profoundly different level than other resources," said Oregon State's Dr. Wolf. "People are willing to do horrible things to each other. What they seem not willing to do is turn off each other's water."

Jan Eliasson fervently hopes this tenuous state can be maintained. "Water is the only indispensable liquid in the world," he said. "Some people use it as a reason for conflict, but it can just as easily be used as a reason for cooperation. If world leaders are smart, they will see that an investment in water, and building an interdependence over water, is an investment in peace."

• • •

Water scarcity is of growing concern to the hydrologists, diplomats, and aid organizations worried about how climate change will impact water and food supplies. But an equally grave, though less publicized, concern is the way global warming will turn parts of the world wetter.

As temperatures rise, climatologists expect rainstorms to become more frequent and intense and sea levels to rise, making communities along waterways vulnerable to flooding. Floods lead to a host of serious problems: the threat of drowning, erosion, waterborne disease, loss of property, disruption of transportation routes, rampant pollution, and mass evacuations. Furthermore, rising tides and fiercer hurricanes will strain the world's rickety hydro-infrastructure, much of which is in poor shape and was built at, or below, the twentieth century's sea level.

In the first years of this century, unprecedented flooding in England has led to concern that the nation is ill equipped for the higher waters predicted for the future. And in the United States, climatologists warn that the devastation wreaked by Hurricane Katrina in 2005, considered "America's worst environmental disaster," was merely a foretaste of deluges to come.

PART III

▼ ▼ ▼

FLOOD

Come Hell or High Water

CHAPTER 19

"A Twenty-First-Century Catastrophe"

TOO MUCH OF A GOOD THING

When water chokes you, what are you to drink to wash it down?
—Aristotle

Throughout history, people have built communities near reliable drinking supplies and created vast hydraulic systems—soaring dams, astonishingly long pipelines, and massive canals—to collect, purify, and distribute drinking water. So successful were these waterworks that by the twentieth century humans began to take water for granted and forgot about its destructive nature. People built in areas previously considered out-of-bounds—deserts, floodplains, filled-in wetlands, and low-lying coastal zones. But conditions are changing in the twenty-first century, and now communities around the world are increasingly vulnerable to rising seas and "extreme weather events," such as flash floods.

While many experts are racing to find ways to avoid our running out of water in coming years, others are deeply concerned about the opposite problem: too much water, of the wrong kind, at the wrong time. Most countries have systems to collect, purify, and distribute water, but few, including the United States, have sufficient infrastructure to keep water at bay.

Floods are a natural occurrence that can be highly beneficial to the ecosystem—by providing nutrients that fertilize soil, cleaning silt from channels, removing invasive species, maintaining biodiversity, recharging groundwater supplies, and providing hydration to arid regions. But floods can also be devastating, tearing boulders and trees from embankments, scouring out old channels and creating new ones, and setting off mudslides. In many cases, human interventions—straightened rivers, destroyed marshes, new canals, old levees, cities built in floodplains—set the stage for catastrophic flooding.

As the world urbanizes, naturally absorbent wetlands, fields, and woods are converted to "hard-scape" paved roads and concrete buildings, which amplify the effects of storm-water runoff. According to the USGS, hard surfaces in urban areas increase storm-water runoff from two to six times over what occurs on unpaved ground. Ill-conceived or poorly built flood-control infrastructure worsens the impact of overflowing rivers. Floodwalls designed to restrain water in one section of a river can push dangerously high water downstream. Poorly built levees, such as those that ringed New Orleans during Hurricane Katrina, can breach and allow the gushing floodwaters to sweep away people and their homes, destroy roads and bridges, and submerge cities.

After high waters recede, flooded communities suffer from contaminated drinking supplies, waterborne disease, ruined crops, washed-out roads, and long-term economic hardship.

In the United States, seven of the nation's ten costliest disasters have been caused by floods. Although death by flooding has declined since the 1950s, thanks to improved weather forecasting and early-warning systems, the USGS estimates that flooding kills 140 Americans a year, on average, and causes $6 billion worth of property damage.

In Britain, where floods have been labeled "a twenty-first-century catastrophe," unusually hard, prolonged rainstorms between 2000 and 2007 caused over 2 billion pounds' worth of damage and left more than a third of a million people without drinking water, and thousands homeless. A single violent stormburst, in July 2007, produced more than a month's worth of rain in one hour; towns were swamped, public transportation was paralyzed, and Prime Minister Gordon Brown declared an emergency. The 2007 flood, according to the nation's Environment Agency, eclipsed the UK's previous benchmark, the floods of 1947, which inundated seven hundred thousand acres and were the worst in two hundred years. "We have not seen flooding of this magnitude before," an agency statement read. While experts were leery of attributing the disaster to global warming, the "extreme rainfall event" of July 2007 was consistent with forecasts of what climate change will bring.

Similar statements were made in Australia three years later. After a decade of drought, torrential rains arrived in Queensland in late 2010, creating record-breaking floods that killed dozens and caused millions of dollars' worth of damage. Scientists blamed La Niña weather patterns rather than climate change, but said it was "indisputable" that global warming was leading to more severe storms. "People have to accept that the game's changed," said Chris Cocklin, an environmental scientist at James Cook University.

But as weather patterns change, communities with poor flood defenses will find themselves increasingly vulnerable. This has already been hinted at by storms in usually temperate regions of the US, such as the Northeast and Southeast.

In March 2010, two immense storms soaked Rhode Island and Massachusetts with record-breaking precipitation. The second storm dumped almost nine inches of rain on Providence, Rhode Island, and the Pawtuxet River crested at 20.79 feet, nearly 12 feet above flood stage, causing rampant flooding. More than four thousand homes lost power; over a hundred people were evacuated to shelters; parts of I-95, the major East Coast artery, were flooded; Amtrak service was suspended; sewage treatment plants failed; and President Obama declared a state of emergency. New Englanders were bewildered. "Nobody was prepared," said a college student. "When it comes to man versus nature, nature wins every time."

As in Australia, years of water scarcity in Atlanta, Georgia, masked the threat of suddenly having too much.

PRAYING FOR RAIN

With over 5.4 million residents, the Atlanta metropolitan area was the fastest-growing, most populous region in the Southeast in 2007, and the city promoted itself as being "the economic engine of the South." But as Atlanta grew rapidly—starting in the mid-seventies, with the city's rise accelerated by its hosting of the 1996 Olympic Games, which led to a construction boom—city and state leaders failed to create comprehensive water policies or invest in water infrastructure.

The spring and summer of 2007 were virtually rainless, and Atlanta's main reservoir, Lake Sidney Lanier, dropped a record fifteen feet. Front-page photographs across the nation showed docks high and dry and boats stranded on the lake's gravel ledges. In April, Georgia was placed under statewide restrictions that limited outdoor watering to three days a week.

In May, Atlanta allowed watering only on the weekends. In August, temperatures reached 104 degrees, one degree below Atlanta's record, set in 1980. In September, officials banned all outdoor watering in the northern half of the state for the first time in history. In October, Atlanta officials asserted that Lake Lanier was less than three months from turning empty, while smaller reservoirs were dropping even faster. In November, Georgia governor Sonny Perdue declared a state of emergency for the northern third of his state, asked President George W. Bush to label it a major disaster area, and cut public utilities' water withdrawals by 10 percent. Then Perdue joined hands with supporters on the statehouse steps to pray for rain.

To some, the calamity was no surprise. Years of pro-growth policies and lax zoning had led to poor water management and urban sprawl; hydrologists had warned Georgia for nearly two decades that such a drought was possible, but legislators had never developed a coherent response. In the 1990s, plans to build a network of state reservoirs were defeated, largely by developers who were angered that they would not be allowed to build homes around the new lakes. A 2003 plan to sell water permits, which would limit water use, was derailed by Georgians who feared that neighboring states would be able to outbid them. A 2004 initiative to build a state-funded regional reservoir was defeated. At the same time, local farmers planted thousands of acres of water-intensive sod to embellish the growing supply of new housing developments, while golf courses and car washes faced no restrictions on water use during the three-year drought.

"There's no question this situation could have been avoided," said former governor Roy Barnes. "We've known this for a long time. We have a state approaching nine million people . . . [and] we have no plan for water."

The Southeastern drought began in late 2005 and lasted through the summer of 2007. Many commentators blamed global warming, which seemed to make sense. But after carefully reviewing historical climate data, experts concluded that global warming was not the culprit. In 2009, a team of climate researchers led by Columbia University's Dr. Richard Seagar (who argues that the Southwest is facing a permanent drying out) undertook a dispassionate appraisal of the Southeastern drought and discovered that the three-plus-year dry spell was "quite typical" for the region and will be repeated.

What Atlantans didn't focus on was the second major finding of Seagar's study: "In the near future, precipitation will increase year around in the Southeast." This prediction was borne out almost immediately.

FLOOD

In June 2009, Governor Perdue's theatrical prayer for rain was finally answered with light precipitation, and Atlanta was able to lift water-use restrictions for the first time in three years. Over the summer, the weather seemed to normalize. Then, on Tuesday, September 15, a low-pressure system crossed Georgia, collided with a high-pressure system over the East Coast, and stalled. It began to rain. As the week wore on, the rain fell harder and then harder still.

On Saturday, September 19, some 3.7 inches of rain fell on the city, which was more than double the record for that date, while over 5 inches fell on the suburbs. By Monday, creeks had overtopped their banks. Forty homes were flooded, power was knocked out across the Atlanta metropolitan area, trees heavy with water crashed to the ground, and the Red Cross began to evacuate people. It rained for eight days straight. In one seventy-two-hour stretch, 20 inches of rain fell on parts of Atlanta.

In what seemed like the blink of an eye, fear of drought turned into fear of drowning.

As Atlanta expanded rapidly in the 1980s and 1990s, its failure to upgrade its water system—by building new reservoirs and other water supplies, limiting growth, and erecting flood defenses—left it vulnerable, first to drought, and then to flood. The drought baked soils hard, making them unabsorbent; when the deluge of 2009 hit, the runoff streamed over the hard soil and the acres of concrete and tarmac that had been laid down, sending storm water crashing through sewers, ditches, and rivers; after eight days of ceaseless drenching, the soils became so saturated that ponds, creeks, and rivers overflowed.

US Geological Survey crews monitored three hundred streamgages—devices that measure the flow of streams in real time—across Georgia. The numbers were stunning. On September 22, the USGS measured water flowing down Sweetwater Creek at twenty-eight thousand cubic feet per second and thirteen feet above flood stage, the greatest flow ever recorded there. The Chattahoochee River rose to heights not seen since 1919. Studying historical patterns, USGS discovered that the chance of a flood of this magnitude hitting this region was 1 in 10,000.

By September 23, the rains eased and the clouds over Georgia began to dissipate. Eleven people were dead, sixteen thousand were homeless, and some thirty thousand were left without electricity. Seventeen bridges across the state were closed, as were stretches of interstate highways. A large sewage treatment plant north of the city was flooded, which caused millions of dollars in damage and released untreated sewage into residential neighborhoods, leading to fears of mass contamination. (The rains also added more than three feet of water to Lake Lanier and returned the reservoir to "full pool" in October. Allatoona Lake, nearby, rose more than thirteen feet over its full pool.) The flood caused at least $250 million worth of damage across seventeen counties, mostly to homeowners who did not have flood insurance. Governor Perdue, who had prayed for rain two years earlier, declared a state of emergency and requested $16.35 million in federal assistance.

"The flooding in Atlanta is certainly near the top of the list of the worst floods in the United States during the last hundred years," said Robert Holmes, the USGS National Flood Program coordinator.

Meteorologists concluded that the eight days of steady rain that caused the 2009 Georgia flood was an unusual storm pattern for the Southeast. It raised the question of whether the region will become more prone to extreme shifts in weather—years of drought followed by prolonged drenching and floods—as the climate warms in coming decades. This is a question people around the world are starting to ask: its answer, as yet unknown, will have major implications for how runoff is managed and how flood controls are built.

In a sign of the new hydrologic reality, as some places grapple with devastating drought, others are facing unprecedented floods, and some—such as Georgia, Texas, or Australia—are facing both.

ACTS OF GOD, ACTS OF MEN

Floods are acts of God; flood damages result from acts of men.
—from a congressional report on flood control, 1966

A flood can be local, or it can affect entire river basins and cover several states. It can arrive slowly and gently, or it can appear with sudden, terrifying violence. There are riverine floods, in which heavy precipitation causes rivers to overrun their channels; estuarine floods, caused by storms or tidal surges; coastal floods, which result from hurricanes or tsunamis; catastrophic floods, which are caused by significant events, such as the breach of a levee; and muddy floods, which are generated by agricultural runoff. The most destructive are flash floods, in which water rises to dangerous levels within hours, and these are typically caused by dam failure, collapsing ice jams, or an intense downpour.

Many factors contribute to flooding, but two key elements are the intensity and duration of rainstorms. The less ground cover or wetland available to absorb rising waters, the more likely a river is to flood destructively.

Ground cover—grass, bushes, trees—can help sop up rising water, as can spongy wetlands, the "kidney of the environment." Wetlands absorb rainfall and waves and help to mitigate the impact of flooding (they also absorb carbon, a greenhouse gas).

In the United States, some wetlands are regulated by states and some by the federal government, under the Clean Water Act. But wetlands are transitional zones that lie between wet or swampy areas and dry upland areas; delineating the boundary between regulated wetland and nonregulated lands has proven contentious and led to numerous court cases (a subject I will return to presently).

An estimated 60 percent of the world's wetlands—and 90 percent of Europe's wetlands—have been destroyed over the past century, according to *Science Daily*. When wetlands are filled in and built upon, the displaced water will try to reassert itself. Often the result is flooding, erosion, and wet basements filled with mold.

Floods hold a special, dark grip on the human imagination. People from many societies and religions have envisaged the end of the world arriving in the form of a "great flood," or "deluge," as told in the story of Noah's Ark in the book of Genesis, or in Ovid's *Metamorphoses,* or the Babylonian *Epic of Gilgamesh.* The single deadliest natural disaster ever recorded was a series of terrible flash floods in central China in 1931. After a prolonged drought, heavy snowstorms arrived, along with rains, causing the Yellow, Yangtze, and Huai Rivers to overflow, killing an estimated 2.5 to 3.5 million people.

Between 1991 and 1999, floods in the United States killed 850 people and caused over $89 billion in property damage, according to the Sierra Club. The deadliest natural disaster in American history was the flooding of Galveston, Texas, by a hurricane in September 1900, which killed about eight thousand people. The Okeechobee hurricane of 1928 killed about four thousand people in Florida, the Bahamas, and Puerto Rico. Hurricane Katrina, which devastated the coastal regions of Louisiana, Alabama, and Mississippi in August 2005, killed 1,836 people and caused at least $150 billion worth of damage—a figure that is still being tabulated and does not include the billions of dollars in insurance payouts and court-awarded damages still being litigated.

Nearly half the world's population—some 3 billion people—live in coastal regions vulnerable to the rising oceans, intensifying storm surges, and less obvious problems such as saltwater pollution of aquifers. Rising waters are already a problem for low-lying nations such as the Maldives, the Seychelles, Bangladesh, and Holland. The World Bank estimates it will take $75 billion to $100 billion to build adequate flood defenses in developing countries. Rich countries—the ones largely responsible for pumping climate-warming gases into the atmosphere—have been reluctant to fund flood protection in poorer nations.

By 2025, when the world's population will be around 8.5 billion, some 6 billion people are expected to live in coastal zones. Predicting future sea-level rise is a murky and inaccurate science, but the National Academy of Sciences (NAS) estimates seas will rise by five to twenty-one inches by 2025, and by 2100, the NAS expects seas to rise from two to eleven feet above current levels. At that point, rising waters will become a far greater danger to humans than they are now.

The United States has a flawed flood-protection system. It relies on a mishmash of federal, state, and local bureaucracies—a dysfunctional system notorious for political turf wars, chronic underfinancing, and a lack of leadership. Moreover, certain policies—such as the federal government's "hundred-year levee" design and its flood insurance program—have unintentionally provided a false sense of security and encouraged people to build on risky sites.

In erecting floodwalls, federal agencies, such as the US Army Corps of Engineers, use a "hundred-year" design criterion to determine how big a levee should be. This does not mean a flood will occur once every hundred years; it means there is a 1 percent chance of the levee's being overtopped each year. (A levee is overtopped when high waves wash over it and swamp the "protected" area behind the levee.) The risk of overtopping increases with time, as levees weaken and subside. Yet, people who build behind a hundred-year levee are not required to elevate their buildings, floodproof their structures, or purchase flood insurance—and as a result, their property is susceptible to flooding.

The levees ringing New Orleans were supposedly built to withstand a hundred-year flood, but the wind and waves of Hurricane Katrina plowed right over, under, and through them. Climate change will exacerbate the problem: a one-foot rise in ocean water levels, scientists estimate, will increase the frequency of a hundred-year storm event to once every ten years.

In certain regions, the federal government requires people to buy policies from its National Flood Insurance Program in order to get a mortgage. Most private insurers don't offer insurance in floodprone areas because the damage from high waters is expensive to clean up. But the government's insurance program keeps premiums artificially low (to make them affordable) and often relies on outdated flood maps (because updating them is expensive and is not a priority), which, perversely, encourages building in risky areas.

In 2006, a year after Katrina, only 20 percent of American homes at risk of flooding were properly insured. Despite years of brave talk about fixing the insurance program, Congress has failed to do so. When major floods occur, federal agencies and the National Guard provide substantial aid—meaning that taxpayers ultimately end up shouldering the homeowners' risks of building in flood zones.

"WE CAN'T SAY WE HAVEN'T BEEN WARNED"

One place that experts agree has a high probability of being hit by a severe hurricane in coming years is the Northeast, including New York City. By 2050, climatologists estimate, the city is likely to experience a three-to-five-degree rise in temperature and a 5 percent increase in rain and snow. As the climate warms, ocean waters will expand and cause the seawater around the city to rise about ten inches by 2050 and two feet by 2080, according to a study by Columbia University. When stirred by a hurricane, high waters could swamp the city.

According to a NASA climate study, if a Category 3 hurricane, like Katrina, were to hit New York, it could create a storm surge of up to twenty-five feet high at Kennedy Airport, twenty-four feet at the Battery, twenty-one feet at the entrance to the Lincoln Tunnel, and sixteen feet at La Guardia Airport. Such a deluge would destroy billions of dollars' worth of property and could shut the city down. While the sandhogs and pencils at the city's Department of Environmental Protection (DEP) are racing to finish Tunnel No. 3 to avoid the city's running dry, other experts at the agency are concerned about the opposite problem: the prospect of Manhattan turning into a modern Atlantis.

In 2006, Max Mayfield, then director of the National Hurricane Center, told Congress, "It is not a question of if a major hurricane will strike the New York area, but when." That same year, just a few months after Hurricane Katrina, an insurance-industry assessment ranked New York City as "the second worst place for a hurricane to hit," after Miami. Another survey that year found that New York residents had taken only a few of eight basic steps—such as getting flood insurance or putting together a disaster evacuation plan—to protect themselves.

In the spring of 2007, New York was deluged in a series of vicious stormbursts; one, in April, saw seven inches of rain fall in hours, the biggest precipitation measured there since 1882. If coupled with a nor'easter storm or a hurricane, extreme flooding could hit the city once every forty-three years by the 2020s, once every nineteen years by the 2050s, and once every four years by the 2080s, the DEP predicts.

To help absorb more precipitation, New York has begun to restore wetlands, promote green roofs and bigger tree pits, and build porous "green-streets," which allow storm-water runoff to filter into the ground. But these are incremental steps. The city relies on an old, already overburdened sewer system and a few catch basins and inflatable flood barriers. Its flood maps, which show areas prone to hazardous flooding, are outdated, and the city has no major flood defenses, large catchments, or storm-surge barriers.

"We've been talking about this lack of preparation since the early 1990s, but before Hurricane Katrina no one would listen to a bunch of academics," said Dr. Malcolm Bowman, a professor of physical oceanography at the State University of New York at Stony Brook. "Now a few people in the city government are returning my calls." Hurricane Katrina, he said, was "a warning to other cities of what kind of disasters could be in store. A temperature shift will change our world, and we'd better be prepared for it." With higher sea levels, he said, weak storms of the future will be as destructive as severe storms are today.

To defend against the catastrophic flooding of New York City, Bowman and his colleagues at Stony Brook's Storm Surge Research Group have proposed building three enormous storm barriers, thirty-five feet high and up to a mile long, to provide "a circle of protection" from surging ocean waves.

In England, the Thames River is outfitted with giant swinging floodgates; in Italy, the Venice lagoon is defended by inflatable gates that rise from the seafloor; in Holland, massive swinging barriers protect Rotterdam from the North Sea.

The enormous gates that Bowman suggests for New York have not been designed yet but are likely to be swinging metal structures, with navigation locks to allow boats and water to flow through. They would be placed at the Verrazano Narrows (the gateway to New York Harbor), the upper reaches of the East River (where it joins Long Island Sound), and across the Arthur Kill (a stretch of water between Staten Island and New Jersey).

A similar scheme, designed by Halcrow Group Ltd., a British infrastructure consulting firm, calls for a single five-mile-long barrier to be built between Sandy Hook, New Jersey, and the Rockaway Peninsula, in Queens. A third floodgate plan, from New York–based engineers Parsons Brinckerhoff, envisions a wall that lies flat on the bed of the East River and would crank upward to block storm surges as high as twenty-five feet. Each of these projects would take years to build, might impact water salinity and aquatic life, and would cost an estimated $1 billion to $6.5 billion.

City officials have called these ideas "intriguing" but "theoretical," and say floodgates will not be needed for several decades. In the event of a major flood, they plan to evacuate some 3 million city residents via overland routes.

"That seems a bit hopeful," said Dr. Douglas Hill, a colleague of Bowman's at Stony Brook, who has been exasperated by the city's lack of interest in their warnings. "We are *expecting* to be flooded. It happens here." He recalled Hurricane Floyd in 1999, when "the data says that was the worst flooding here in the last half century. It also says that we will see more hurricanes like it. [Floyd's 155-mile-per-hour winds hit five East Coast states, causing some $4.5 billion in damages and killing sixty people.] After the disaster in New Orleans, we can't say we haven't been warned."

Hill and Bowman estimate that their three barriers would cost $9 billion, a figure that sounds scary. But Hill believes it is a relative bargain. (By comparison, a proposed railroad tunnel from New Jersey to Penn Station could cost $8.7 billion, and a plan to raise railroad infrastructure above flood levels might cost $5.6 billion.) "New York City is the financial center of the world. It is uniquely valuable, and vulnerable," said Hill. "If New York floods, it will cost the nation at least 1.9 *trillion* dollars. If you look at it that way, 9 billion dollars for floodgates isn't so bad."

CHAPTER 20

Forensic Engineering

The Deepwater Horizon was trying to tell us something was wrong in the Gulf of Mexico. And the levees are trying to tell us something is wrong in the Sacramento Delta—if they go, we're all going to be drinking saltwater coffee.
—Professor Robert Bea,
University of California, Berkeley, 2010

THE TWO KINDS OF LEVEES

In places that flood—Holland, central China, the states along the Mississippi River—man has developed various ingenious methods to control water. Dams and reservoirs and canals are built in part, or in some cases primarily, to capture excess runoff. But the most effective and common flood defense are levees, also called dikes: man-made barriers that stand between a watercourse and human development.

Levees come in all shapes, widths, heights, and angles of incline. Some are made of nothing more than sandbags, boards, and sheets of plastic and run just a few yards long. Others are more elaborate, such as the Sny, a reinforced wall of pilings and concrete that runs for fifty miles along the banks of the Mississippi. But most levees are berms made up of dirt, sand, or clay—and all that gets scooped up with that material—that are dredged and piled up along river edges (such as on the Mississippi) or the coastline (as in New Orleans), to control and restrain water. In some cases (as in the Sacramento–San Joaquin Delta of Northern California), levees are used to push water out of estuaries or wetlands to "reclaim" fertile land for farming or for new building lots. Levees are often partnered with a network of floodwalls, pumps and pipes, drains, gates, canals, and islands—complex systems of hydraulic control that require diligent maintenance to ensure their integrity.

Carefully engineered, solidly built levees have protected millions of people from floods and saved billions of dollars in potential damages. But levees are problematic. They tend to push water away from one area, which intensifies its impact on other, unprotected areas. They are often poorly built and are expensive and time-consuming to maintain. And they are only as strong as their weakest point.

Experts say—only half-jokingly—that there are only two kinds of levees: those that have failed, and those that will fail. They fail for many reasons: shifting rocks, falling trees, or burrowing muskrats; getting hit by a ship or the tremendous pressure exerted by floodwaters; or because of the weight of storm surges overtopping them, or burrowing through them, or tunneling under them—any one of which can lead to catastrophic flooding.

Levees exist in every state in the nation. The Federal Emergency Management Agency (FEMA), which is responsible for identifying flood hazards, estimates that levees protect 55 percent of the American population, or about 156 million people. The US Army Corps of Engineers (USACE, or the Corps), which is responsible for building and maintaining federal levees, has estimated that the United States has approximately one hundred thousand miles of levees. But more than 85 percent of US levees were privately built, ad hoc, by farmers, developers, or businesses. No one really knows how many of them exist, where they are located, who is responsible for their upkeep, and what their integrity might be.

Many US levees were built 100 to 150 years ago out of whatever material lay close at hand, such as sand and seashells dredged from the bottom of a canal, which are not structurally sound. During construction, other materials—such as rocks, tree roots, and human detritus (such as piles of garbage or old boxcars)—get swept up and entombed inside levees' banks. These materials tend to shift and weaken the structure over time. Private levees are not inspected by the Corps and are often not well maintained, frequently leak, and are sometimes breached.

In a 2007 inventory of the levees that it oversees, the Corps found that 177 of them—about 9 percent of federally inspected levees—were "expected to fail"; 122 of the levees were at risk of "catastrophic failure." California, with 37 at-risk levees, and Washington State, with 19, were the worst off. But the list included levees stretching from Washington, DC, to Hartford, Detroit, Omaha, Albuquerque, Los Angeles, and Honolulu.

A weakened levee can suddenly give way with little or no warning. At four o'clock one morning in January 2008, the residents of Fernley, Nevada, a dusty town east of Reno, were awakened by the sound of a rushing torrent. Stumbling into the night with their flashlights, residents were shocked to discover that a thirty-foot section of levee along the Truckee Canal had ruptured. Within minutes, the breach had released enough water to swamp 450 homes, force 3,500 people to evacuate, and cause millions of dollars' worth of damage. Some residents found their predicament difficult to comprehend. "We live in the desert, you don't think of [a flood] happening here," a Fernley resident said. But there it was: water several feet deep in their basements. The exact cause of the Fernley breach remains unknown. Burrowing gophers are a leading suspect, though poor maintenance likely played a role, too.

The flood in Fernley highlighted the vulnerability of the estimated hundred thousand miles of levees in America and underscored the much larger challenge of aging infrastructure nationwide—from collapsing tunnels to sagging bridges, broken highways, decrepit ports, outdated canals and locks, congested airports, and underfinanced rail systems.

In the 2009 edition of its biennial Report Card on American Infrastructure, the American Society of Civil Engineers (ASCE), the nation's oldest engineering society, rated fifteen categories, from Aviation to Schools, with a grading system that ran from A, for "Exceptional," to F, for "Failing." Overall, ASCE gave the nation's infrastructure a D, or "Poor," grade. Waterworks earned some of the worst grades of all: the nation's dams were given a D, while drinking water, wastewater treatment plants, inland waterways, and levees all received grades of D-minus. The nation's flood defenses were singled out as a growing problem. Of the 85,000 dams reviewed by ASCE, over 4,000 of them were considered "deficient" in 2009, and of those, 1,819 were classified as "high hazard" cases.

Many levees are in poor shape, ASCE noted, and the cost of upgrading them could be "over $100 billion." (That number could easily climb higher, once the Army Corps of Engineers has assessed levees across the country.) But as of 2009, Congress had committed only $1.13 billion to levee upkeep.

Business has also ignored levees. Developers, abetted by a vague Supreme Court ruling, have rushed to fill in wetlands and build on floodplains. In the 2006 *Rapanos* case, which centered on a developer who had filled in a wetland in Michigan, the court's ruling confused regulators about what legally constitutes a wetland and how to enforce the Clean Water Act. Wetlands absorb rainfall and waves and help to mitigate the impact of flooding. When they are filled in and built upon, history has shown, the displaced water will try to reassert itself. The result is flooding.

Flood protection clearly needs to made a national priority. But to fix America's levees and reform its flood-control policies, the nation will first have to fix the Army Corps of Engineers.

AMERICA'S HANDYMAN

The Corps got its start on June 16, 1775, when the fledgling Continental Congress organized an army that included a chief engineer, Colonel Richard Gridley, and two assistants. The three men built up a cadre of soldier-builders who fortified Boston with earthen redoubts around Breed's Hill and Bunker Hill, which helped to repel a British attack. As the Revolutionary War intensified, the engineers played crucial roles in building defenses and bridges during some of the most closely fought battles, including the pivotal Battle of Saratoga in 1777, and the Siege of Yorktown in 1781, the last major battle of the war.

In 1802, Congress officially designated the US Army Corps of Engineers, which was directed to build a new military academy at West Point, on the banks of the Hudson, a few miles upriver from New York City. The Corps literally laid the foundations for the Academy there, and for the next sixty-two years the West Point superintendent was always an engineering officer.

From the start, politicians demanded that the Corps contribute to both military projects and works "of a civil nature." Although the Corps built roads, buildings, and parks, many of its projects have been focused on waterways. The Corps built lighthouses, jetties, harbors, navigational channels, bridges, and coastal fortifications—most notably the naval bases at Norfolk, Virginia, and New Orleans, Louisiana. Leading up to the War of 1812, the Corps fortified New York Harbor and constructed the eleven-pointed fort that now serves as the base of the Statue of Liberty, which helped to convince the British navy not to attack the city.

Congress expanded the Corps's portfolio in 1826 with new legislation that authorized engineering officers to survey, clean up, and deepen rivers and to make improvements to American harbors. Corps engineers developed innovative methods to remove fallen trees and hazardous sandbars from the Ohio River; in the 1870s, the Corps commissioned the nation's first hydraulic dredges and built a system of dams and locks on the Ohio. During the nineteenth century, the Corps undertook the first significant surveys of the Great Lakes and the Mississippi Delta.

The Corps first addressed the risks of flooding in 1850, when a group of Southern congressmen lobbied for federal assistance to defend their states after severe flooding in 1849 and 1850 by the Mississippi River. Ever since then, the Corps has been bound in a love-hate relationship with the Big Muddy.

The Mississippi has the third-largest drainage basin in the world (after the Amazon and the Congo Rivers), which encompasses 1.245 million square miles. The basin draws water from an area stretching from Montana to New York, and funnels it down to a spout that empties into the Gulf of Mexico below New Orleans.

In 1850, the Corps undertook a survey of the Mississippi Delta near New Orleans. Two engineers—Captain Andrew Humphreys and Second Lieutenant Henry Abbot—produced the "Report Upon the Physics and Hydraulics of the Mississippi River" (known as "the Humphreys-Abbot report") in 1861, which, despite a few technical mistakes, was a crucial document in the development of river engineering as a discipline.

Humphreys and Abbot developed the theory that "levees only" could control flooding along the lower Mississippi. They believed that dams, reservoirs, and cutoff canals were no longer necessary. The levees-only policy profoundly influenced everything the Corps did on waterways across the country up through the Second World War.

In 1879, Congress established the Mississippi River Commission, a panel of experts who oversaw the construction of dozens of miles of levees along the river, the dredging of its shallows, and the building of "mattresses" made of woven willow branches, to prevent erosion of riverbanks and to improve navigation and flood control.

But flooding persisted. In 1882, one of the most devastating floods on record destroyed the delta region. Major flooding hit again in 1912 and 1913, when two terrifying floods overwhelmed levees and devastated the lower Mississippi Valley. In 1916, the region was swamped yet again. Still, the Corps and the Mississippi River Commission continued to rely on levees as their primary defense.

In the fall of 1926, heavy rains swept across the Midwest, and by the following spring a large region, stretching from Minnesota to Missouri, was soaked. In the spring, heavy snowmelt and persistent rains set the stage for the Great Mississippi Flood of 1927, one of the worst disasters in American history. In late March, rivers across Kansas and Iowa swelled over their banks as tons of water rushed downstream. By mid-April, the flood crest had worked downstream to Mississippi and Arkansas, and the Big Muddy rose to unprecedented heights. The Mississippi spread a mile wide, a hundred feet deep, and flowed downstream at a fast nine miles per hour. On Good Friday, April 15, the Mississippi was flooded along most of its 2,320-mile course and in some places had spread eighty miles wide, according to a report by the Goddard Space Center. On April 22, levees near Greenville, Mississippi, broke; a tremendous gush of water flowed inland through the breach—at a rate twice the flow of Niagara Falls, by one estimate—and the city was sunk under ten feet of water.

Along the riverbank, levees broke in 145 places, flooding twenty-six thousand square miles in nine states—Arkansas, Illinois, Kentucky, Louisiana, Mississippi, Missouri, Tennessee, Texas, and Oklahoma—up to a depth of thirty feet in places. In portions of the lower Mississippi Basin, water remained above flood stage for two months. The Flood of 1927 destroyed cities, towns, and farms, killed 246 people, and led to the dislocation of nearly 700,000 more. Many of the refugees were African Americans, who were moved to 154 temporary camps and conscripted, sometimes at gunpoint, to shore up levees and excavate piles of silt deposited by the flood.

Until Hurricane Katrina hit New Orleans in August 2005, the Great Mississippi Flood of 1927 was the nation's worst natural disaster. One of its lessons was that levees alone are insufficient for flood control.

The 1928 Flood Control Act was drawn up in response to the disaster. The act led to what is now called the Mississippi River and Tributaries Project, the nation's first comprehensive flood-control and navigation provisions. The act also approved a controversial plan, designed by the Corps's Major General Edgar Jadwin, to require that flooding rivers be equipped with outlets that spill floodwaters out of the main channel into floodplains. The 1928 act also contained a provision that immunizes the Corps from prosecution when its levees fail, a provision at the center of much Katrina-based litigation today.

In 1936, Congress passed an updated Flood Control Act, which for the first time declared that floods were a menace to the national welfare and that flood control was a federal responsibility. Since then, the Corps has built 375 reservoirs and hundred of miles of levees, floodwalls, and channel improvements. These significant engineering projects compose one of the largest single additions to the nation's infrastructure, rivaled only by the federal highway system.

Today, the Corps is known as the nation's handyman and performs all manner of governmental odd jobs—from hazardous-waste cleanup at former military sites, to warfare logistics, ice management, power generation, and building horseshoe-crab nests. It played key roles in the First and Second World Wars, in Korea and Vietnam. But in recent years the Corps has been "streamlined" by Congress and has slowly become a demoralized and balkanized agency that is mostly staffed by civilians.

In the aftermath of Katrina, the Corps was heavily criticized by civilian engineers for not knowing how many levees exist in the United States, where they are, and what their integrity might be. In 2006, the Corps began to compile the first national levee database. It took another two years for the agency to secure enough funding to include private, nonfederal levees. By 2009, the index contained just ninety-eight hundred miles of levees, or less than 10 percent of the estimated total. Tammy Conforti, manager of the Corps's levee safety program, hoped to add another forty-two hundred miles to the inventory within a year or so, which would complete the fourteen thousand miles of levees over which the Corps has legal oversight. To assess the nation's remaining, privately built levees—an estimated eighty-six thousand miles' worth—the Corps will have to negotiate with state and local government offices to share data and inspect levees.

The rehabilitation of America's levees has not begun and won't until their cataloging is finished. That could take years. For now, the information used to predict how, when, where, and why the next levee breach might occur is mostly anecdotal. Some levee systems are breached again and again, though, regularly causing deaths, mass evacuations, and millions of dollars' worth of destruction. To the experts, this pattern is infuriating and avoidable.

THE MASTER OF DISASTER

In the summer of 2008, the Mississippi flooded again.

A snowy winter and a wet spring led to high moisture levels in the Midwest, and on June 1 the first rains of early summer arrived. The Iowa, the Cedar, the Mississippi, and many smaller rivers began to rise. The rain kept falling, and the rivers began to overtop their banks. The swollen Mississippi swept away bridges, breached levees, submerged the sandbagged fortifications built around small towns by frantic citizens and the National Guard, and overwhelmed the locks and dams operated by the Corps of Engineers. Lakes designed to capture excess runoff overflowed. Up and up the waters rose, for two weeks, sinking large swaths of Illinois, Iowa, and Missouri.

In Missouri, the owner of a house built on stilts high above the floodplain told a group of engineers investigating what was left of the home, "My first house here was flooded out in 1956, so I built a second one. That was flooded out in 1993. This here is my third house. Now it's flooded out, too. They keep tellin' me it's okay to build here, that the levees will protect me. But I think somebody's been lyin' to me."

Like many people who built in the Mississippi's floodplain, the man had been wiped out. "I don't know what to do," he said. "This time I've got nothing left."

The leader of the investigating engineers, a bald, rapier-thin seventy-four-year-old with a military bearing, a silver mustache, and piercing eyes, nodded. This was Dr. Robert Bea, a professor of engineering and codirector of the Center for Risk Mitigation at UC Berkeley. Bea calls himself a "forensic engineer," and he is famous within engineering circles as a kind of master of disaster.

In 2003, he was a principal investigator of the *Columbia* space shuttle disaster for NASA, and in 2005 he led the National Science Foundation's investigation of levee breaches in New Orleans by Hurricane Katrina. He has studied the causes of over six hundred engineering failures—from perforated submarine hulls to collapsed tunnels and upended oil rigs—and found that most of these accidents were caused by human error. In particular, he discovered, engineers failed to address so-called residual risk: those things people believe "will not" and "cannot" fail. Most engineers, he said, "only look at part of the risk and don't take the whole picture into account. But this is not careful engineering, it's 'imagineering.'"

After the Mississippi flood of 2008, Bea and eight graduate students, professors, and engineers had flown into the rising heat and dense humidity of St. Louis, then made their way through flood-wracked towns, washed-out roads, and ruined fields across the Midwest, like detectives scouring a crime scene. Just two weeks after the flood, they were looking for clues as to why the levees had breached, where, and when, to prevent such disasters from happening again.

A forensic engineer is very different from a design engineer, a building engineer, a maintenance engineer, or a decommissioning engineer; it is akin to being an investigative reporter. "You look at the dirt, the steel, the concrete, the water, to find out what happened," Bea explained. "And, crucially, you talk to the *people*, to find out who did what, when, and where. I have done at least fifty of these investigations, and every one has been chillingly interesting."

Bea used lidar (a laser-based measuring tool) to take careful measurements of breached levees and snapped photographs to document the different ways that the river bored over, under, or through flood defenses. "Water is a beast," said Bea. "It scours and erodes and rips apart anything in front of it. It deepens channels faster than you can believe. It cannot be stopped. We humans need to understand that we will never 'beat' water, so we'd better learn to work *with* it."

Which means building homes in sensible places, not in floodplains, and protecting ourselves with sensible flood defenses, not "piles of sand and shells, like the levees the Corps built here, and in New Orleans, and a lot of other places."

When the man in the stilt house expressed his distrust and anger at the US Army Corps of Engineers, Bob Bea knew exactly how he felt. "It was déjà vu," Bea said in a distinctive high, fluttery voice. "We've heard this tune before."

As he toured the man's flooded house, Bea couldn't stop thinking about the Great Flood of 1993. In the aftermath of that deluge, a committee of well-regarded experts issued a 272-page report that described Midwestern flood defenses as "a loose aggregation of federal, local and individual levees and reservoirs"; it predicted that "many levees are poorly sited and will fail again in the future." The report recommended that management of floodwaters along the Mississippi be made the sole responsibility of the Corps and that the agency make levee improvements a priority. The report was widely hailed, but once the politicians and TV cameras left, no meaningful change occurred. The flood of 2008 exposed the same institutional failings.

Now, Bea said, the Corps was trying to dodge its responsibility by tailoring and retailoring its message about levee failures in 2008. First, the Corps said, "No federal levees failed" in the flood. Then the message was adjusted to "Levee failures were due to overtopping," which was another way of saying that the Corps had built the levees correctly, but the water had simply risen too high, and thus any failures were not the fault of the Corps.

Bea did not see it that way. He was angered by what he discerns as a long-standing pattern: the Corps builds poor levees, maintains them badly, and, when they fail in a flood, passes the blame or hides behind the 1928 law that protects it from prosecution should its levees be breached. Indeed, the Corps had quietly begun to decertify some of its levees, effectively abdicating responsibility when disaster strikes. "That is a no-sense loophole that should never have been written into law," Bea fumed.

For Bob Bea, the fight with the Army Corps of Engineers could hardly be more personal. His father, "the Colonel," joined the Corps during the Depression and considered it a steady, well-paid job that gave him a respected place in the world. Rigorously disciplined on the job, the Colonel could turn into a Great Santini–like despot at home, where he flew into rages and hectored his son to "conduct yourself like an officer!"

Bea became a Corps engineer himself in 1954, stationed in Jacksonville, Florida. His first job was to build levees on Lake Okeechobee and "drain every drop we could out of the ever-loving Everglades—which is how I first learned about levees, and their problems," he said.

After a bitter falling-out with the Colonel in 1959, Bea quit the Corps and moved to New Orleans to work as an engineer for Royal Dutch Shell. He loved the Big Easy. He kept a boat to sail on the Gulf of Mexico and was in charge of designing and maintaining Shell's giant offshore oil platforms. Part of his job was to assess how the rigs would fare in severe weather.

In 1965 Hurricane Betsy struck: Bea's oil rigs survived 120 mph winds and tanker-size waves, but New Orleans's rudimentary levees failed, and the nation suffered its first "billion-dollar hurricane." When Lake Pontchartrain spilled into the city, Bea's house flooded, and he and his family barely escaped onto the roof; they lost all of their belongings, including their wedding album. "We evacuated vertically," he said, meaning that he moved his wife and children into his office at Shell, in a tall office building. For two months, the Bea family camped out around his desk and cooked meals on a hot plate. Fearing another flood, they relocated to Houston, Texas. "We decided we'd never go through *that* again," he said.

Named head of Shell's Offshore Technology Group, Bea modeled hurricanes, designed arctic pipelines, and built oil platforms off the Australian coast. He loved this work but chafed in the corporate environment. He quit Shell in 1976, helped found and sold two engineering consultancies, studied hydrology in Norway and Holland, and earned a master's degree in Australia and an MBA at Harvard. In 1989 he applied to the PhD engineering program at UC Berkeley. He was turned down because he didn't have the prerequisite courses, but the faculty were so impressed by his résumé that they offered him a job as a professor. Bea accepted on the spot.

The personal tragedy of Hurricane Betsy in 1965 was a formative experience for Bea, a touchstone that he frequently references. Betsy had prompted Congress to authorize the Corps to ring New Orleans with sixteen-foot-high levees—a project that was still under construction when Hurricane Katrina hit, in 2005. "In 1965, we said we'd never repeat the disaster of Hurricane Betsy. And yet forty years later, almost to the day, I go back to the site of my previous home in New Orleans—and what are the new owners doing? Dragging wet mattresses out the door to dry in the sun. What does that mean? That with all the struggle and money and resolution, we still failed to get the job done. The Corps is misleading people into false self-confidence about the level of protection they have from flooding."

New Orleans has long been dominated by politicians and their cronies who allegedly control the city's flood defenses and water systems through patronage. The designing and building of flood defenses was directed by local political considerations as much as by a desire for public safety. The Corps plays along, critics charge. "Corps officials, under pressure, repeatedly justify unworthy projects, which displace limited funds needed by more critical projects elsewhere," the Environmental Defense Fund (EDF) wrote in a 2007 report. In the five years before Katrina hit, for instance, Louisiana received far more federal funding—$1.9 billion—than any other state for water projects, according to the EDF. Yet only a small percentage of that money was spent on strengthening New Orleans's levees.

"Good engineers are good worriers, just like good doctors are," said Bea. "I worried a lot about New Orleans before Katrina hit. A Category Three storm was predicted, but people didn't want to hear it. They care about where the fish are biting, or how the Saints are doing—'Laissez les bons temps rouler!' It's endearing, I guess. But it can have tragic consequences."

"NOT A 'NATURAL' DISASTER"

On September 27, 2005, four weeks after Hurricane Katrina submerged the Gulf coast, Bob Bea and his UC Berkeley colleague Dr. Raymond Seed arrived in New Orleans to lead the most prominent independent investigation of the disaster that killed over eighteen hundred people and swamped the Big Easy. The result was an encyclopedic report on what they deemed the "catastrophic" and "unnecessary" failure of the flood defenses that were supposed to protect lives and property.

By the time the hurricane crossed Plaquemines Parish, a peninsula that juts out into the Gulf below New Orleans, it had weakened from a Category 5 to a Category 3 storm, yet Katrina still managed to punch through nine "secure" levees and overtopped or undercut many others. Bea's investigation revealed that the levee failures were caused by faulty design, shoddy workmanship, poor maintenance, and a culture of "hubris and arrogance" that prevented Corps engineers from listening to constructive criticism from outsiders. When the Corps protested that it had done all it could to protect New Orleans, Bea scoffed, "This was not a 'natural' disaster. It was a manmade disaster. And, sadly, much of the blame can be pointed at the Corps. I really hate to say that, but it's the truth. If they can't learn from experience, they are doomed to repeat the same mistakes over and over again."

Bea and Seed's report on Katrina became the focal point of a massive class-action lawsuit against the Army Corps of Engineers, which was filed in 2006: sixty-five thousand New Orleanians have charged that the Corps ignored its own flood-protection guidelines and left the city vulnerable to the ravages of the hurricane. (Another three hundred thousand plaintiffs have filed separate claims. Taken together, the litigation over Katrina represents the biggest legal action in the nation's history.)

This suit involving Bea is the most significant challenge yet to the web of laws stemming from the 1928 Flood Control Act, which grants the Corps immunity from prosecution when its levees fail. As the case slowly crawled through the courts, Bea was frequently called upon as an expert witness. His overall goal, however, was to build effective flood control, and he continued to offer the Corps his expertise.

In December 2007, Bea flew into New Orleans for an unprecedented, off-the-record meeting with Corps leaders. The weather was sultry. The sun was a bright disk in the gray sky as it warmed the afternoon; in the evening, lightning flashed and thunderstorms drenched the streets. Bands tooted along alleyways, as the city prepared for Mardi Gras. Bea's man on the ground, Jimmy Delery, a community activist, radio host, gardener, real estate entrepreneur, and gadfly, who had rescued people during Katrina, drove us through the city's poor, mostly African American Lower Ninth Ward. More than two years after Katrina, the neighborhood remained a muddy shambles, as if it had been freshly destroyed. "This should not have happened," Bea said, shaking his head. "We knew Katrina was coming. We did this to ourselves."

I heard many conspiracy theories about what "really" happened during the storm. People said that the levees had "intentionally" been blown up—to save white neighborhoods, some said; or just the rich, said others; or friends of politicians, said yet others. In light of the government's woeful response to the crisis, it is easy to understand such thinking. But as I toured the decrepit levees with Bea, a more likely scenario presented itself. It wasn't that the Corps had intentionally blown up perfectly good levees out of racism or spite or greed; it was just as likely that they had built the minimum amount of flood protection required by law, did so in a hurry and without much of a budget, maintained the levees sporadically, and did not consider the consequences should a major storm hit. Which begs a pointed question: which is worse, intentional destruction or lethal apathy?

The next day, Bob Bea, three senior Corps officers, and local politicians tucked into Cajun food in the back room of a restaurant. It was their first face-to-face meeting, and the conversation seesawed between the jovial and the testy. Bea kept his comments focused on technical engineering issues, and the big, gruff USACE officers seemed genuinely interested in his critique. Some of the local pols debated about money for reconstruction, while others rocked back to eye their BlackBerrys or to whisper. The meeting was deemed a qualified success. "At least we're talking," one participant said. "You gotta start with that."

A few weeks later, federal district judge Stanwood Duval upheld the Corps's immunity from the New Orleans class-action suit—thanks to the 1928 Flood Control Act—while agreeing with Bea's assessment in a tartly worded opinion: "Millions of dollars were squandered in building a levee system which was known to be inadequate by the Corps' own calculations," he wrote. In his lengthy opinion, the judge seemed to lay out a road map for appeal, which the plaintiffs vigorously pursued.

In a significant 2009 ruling, Judge Duval blamed the Corps for mismanagement of the Mississippi River-Gulf Outlet (known as MRGO), a channel dredged by the Corps that flooded St. Bernard Parish and the Lower Ninth Ward, affecting at least one hundred thousand people. The ruling set the stage for judgments worth billions of dollars against the government for damages. "The Corps' lassitude and failure to fulfill its duties resulted in a catastrophic loss of human life and property . . . the wasting of millions of dollars in flood protection and billions of dollars in Congressional outlays," Duval wrote.

The Corps had already spent $7.1 billion repairing New Orleans's flood defenses and had requested twice that amount to defend the entire Gulf

Coast against another Category 3 storm. Bea continued to worry. "If another Katrina were to hit today, the levees in New Orleans would fail just the same way," he said. "It will. The question is not *if*, but *when*."

WHAT KATRINA AND THE DEEPWATER HORIZON
HAVE IN COMMON

According to Bob Bea, the levees in New Orleans are only the third-most vulnerable in the nation. The second-most vulnerable are in Texas City, Texas, near Galveston (which was flooded by the Hurricane of 1900, the deadliest disaster in US history). In Texas City, fifty thousand residents and $6 billion worth of property, including almost 5 percent of the nation's oil-refining capacity, are surrounded by seventeen miles of levees. The consequences of a failure there are high. But of all the levees in America, the most vulnerable are in the Sacramento–San Joaquin Delta—the largest estuary on the West Coast, which lies just north of San Francisco and west of Sacramento, and is not far from Bea's house near Berkeley.

The Delta's waterways and peat bogs have been regulated by eleven hundred miles of levees, which pushed the waters back to reveal acres of rich, peaty soil that is some of the most productive farmland in the country. An intricate system of pipes, pumps, and aqueducts siphons freshwater from the Delta south to the Central Valley, the 4 million residents of the Bay Area, and the 21 million inhabitants of Southern California.

Today, many of these levees are old—some of them, built by Chinese laborers during the Gold Rush, are over 150 years old—and have grown fragile. "Between 1900 and 1950, we saw two hundred levee failures up there in the Delta," said Bea. "Heck, they're leaking right now."

One day I drove along the brow of the Jones Tract, a curving levee that collapsed on a sunny day in 2004 for no apparent reason, causing a tremendous flood that resulted in $100 million worth of damage. The repaired levee I drove along was potholed and decrepit. On my left, the land had subsided at least thirty feet below the top of the levee; on my right, the water had risen almost parallel to the road. The water pressure against the earthen berm beneath me was nearly palpable.

If a large chunk of levee is breached in the Delta, it would set off a cascading effect: salt water would surge inland, destroying lives and property and tainting freshwater supplies for millions of people. Unless drastic measures are taken, Bea said, such a failure is "inevitable."

To make his point, he enumerated the many similarities between the Delta and New Orleans. Each is along the outflow of big rivers—the Sacramento and San Joaquin Rivers in California, and the Mississippi and its tributaries in Louisiana. Both are set in wide, flat floodplains, on landscapes of soft earth made rich by the silt of regular flooding. Both are ringed by old, badly maintained, increasingly infirm levees run by the Corps. Both, he said, "are ticking bombs."

Bea is not alone in this estimation. Federal flood experts have characterized Sacramento, which sits at the northeastern edge of the Delta, as the most flood-prone city in the nation. The levees there, which protect about 60 percent of California's freshwater, are vulnerable to earthquakes or major storms. Seismologists have predicted a 1-in-3 chance of a "catastrophic" earthquake in the region in the next fifty years. Such a temblor could liquidate the earthen levees and transform the Delta to an inland sea. If a major Pacific hurricane caused waves to overtop and collapse the Delta levees, then California, the eighth-largest economy in the world, would suffer catastrophically, and so would the nation.

"In terms of total damage, deaths, and cost, a breach in the Delta would be far worse than what happened to New Orleans," Bea said. "This is a national problem. We are due for a megaflood catastrophe." Yet he might as well be shouting into the wind.

Just days after the April 22, 2010, sinking of the Deepwater Horizon in the Gulf of Mexico, Bea pulled together the Deepwater Horizon Study Group (DHSG), a group of sixty experts from the United States, Australia, Canada, Brazil, and Norway, to undertake an independent investigation of what mistakes had led to the explosion of BP's oil well in the Gulf of Mexico, and to recommend steps to avoid repeating those errors.

Bea has investigated more than twenty offshore rig disasters—including the catastrophic blowout of Ixtoc I, a Pemex platform, in June 1979, which caused the biggest oil spill in the Gulf of Mexico prior to the Deepwater Horizon. Most of these accidents were caused by human error—though Bea prefers the term *human defect*, meaning man's "hubris, greed, and indolence." In studying the causes of over six hundred engineering failures, he found that only 20 percent of such disasters are the result of intrinsic uncertainties, such as floods, tornadoes, and dust storms, while 80 percent are rooted in extrinsic uncertainties, or what Bea terms "the human factor."

In the Deepwater Horizon case, Bea's key finding was that the companies involved—BP, Transocean, and Halliburton—as well as the federal regulators supposedly overseeing the Deepwater Horizon, were "misled by their assumptions about the risks involved" in drilling miles deep, while cutting corners, on a tight deadline.

As a lead independent investigator of both the Hurricane Katrina and Deepwater Horizon disasters, Bea says the two tragedies have "chilling" similarities. "BP underestimated the *whole* risk to their platform and fell into the same damn trap that the Corps did in New Orleans," he said. In both cases, a misunderstanding of the limits of technology combined with a cavalier attitude led to massive losses. "The result is the same: a trail of tears, floating bodies, expensive equipment destroyed. The big difference is that the Deepwater Horizon will impact the ecology of the Gulf for many years to come."

CHAPTER 21

Keeping Our Feet Dry

No policy without a calamity.
—Dutch proverb

BUILDING TEN-THOUSAND-YEAR PROTECTION

"God created the earth, but the Dutch created the Netherlands," the saying goes. Dutch farms, it turns out, were built up much the way the farms of the Sacramento Delta were, and man's interventions in both places have had similar effects on the environment.

The Netherlands originally comprised a lowland of domed peat bogs that rose just above sea level. Around 1200, farmers began digging channels to drain the bogs to grow crops such as wheat. As the peat marshes were drained, lower water levels allowed oxygen to penetrate the soil, which promoted the growth of microbes that consumed organic detritus. The peat dried up and blew away. Thus the land began to sink, or "subside," and emit carbon gas. As the land dropped, water levels rose, and the Dutch turned to increasingly aggressive drainage methods—sluices, dikes, and windmill-powered pumps—to protect their crops. This caused further subsidence, and a degenerative cycle was under way. Holland's thousands of acres of oxygenated peat send millions of tons of carbon gas into the air, causing further global warming, which raises sea levels.

Today, much of the Netherlands—and two-thirds of the population—is almost twenty feet below sea level. Floods have long plagued the nation. Most notorious was the storm of February 1953, which collapsed numerous dikes, swamped 9 percent of Dutch farmland, killed 1,834 people, and caused millions of dollars' worth of destruction. The calamity touched off a period of national soul-searching. Realizing that they suffered from

230

poor storm prediction, badly engineered floodwalls, and miscommunication, the Dutch spent billions of dollars to create a world-class flood-control system. Unlike the United States in countless vulnerable areas such as New Orleans, Sacramento, or Texas City, the Netherlands have now armed themselves against a once-in-ten-thousand-year storm.

Just downstream from Rotterdam, the Maeslant Barrier is ready to shield Europe's biggest port from the next megastorm. The barrier is made of two sets of triangular metal arms, each as long as the Eiffel Tower and twice as heavy, which hold floating gates that swing together to defend the nation from wind-driven waves. Completed in 1997, the barrier—one of the longest moving structures in the world—is a key piece in Holland's $7.5 billion Delta Works, a network of dikes, dams, and locks that were designed to permanently end the floods. With protection from a once-in-ten-thousand-year storm, the Dutch are considered the master builders of flood defenses.

The Maeslant Barrier remained unused until November 2007, when a big storm whipped out of the northwest and pounded the Dutch coast with tall waves. In response, the Maeslant and other barriers, such as the Hartelkering and the Oosterscheldekering, were closed. The barriers worked flawlessly, and the nation was spared. But the Dutch realized that even these enormous storm gates would not be sufficient to hold back the rising seas that will result from a warming climate.

Considering its future risk, the Dutch asked, what is required to flood-proof the nation for two hundred years? A team of experts called the Delta Committee has suggested innovative solutions—abandoning some existing turf to the water; extending other parts of the coast as far as 2.5 miles out to sea; using parks as floodplains; building a new generation of flood barriers, dunes, dikes, and retention ponds; and designing floating houses. This stormproofing will cost about $1.5 billion a year for a hundred years, the Dutch estimate. And the nation is prepared to spend the money.

This is a key point. While Holland's success "looks like science and engineering," said Piet Dircke, a Dutch water management consultant, "the main lesson is funding." Since the Middle Ages, the country has used elected bodies called water boards to levy taxes solely to fund flood defenses. Flood defenses require constant tending, and the Dutch water boards ensure that there is always enough money to "keep our feet dry."

Inspired by the flood-protection systems of Holland, Bea and his colleagues are trying to pioneer a new approach to flood control. One aspect

of this initiative is to change the way the Army Corps of Engineers operates. Some in the Corps remain skeptical of him, but Bea wants to put the
animosity aside, gather all of the nation's leading flood experts, including
those from the Corps, and share technical notes. "That's the only way we're
going to fix this damn thing," he said. "And it is very broken."

He concedes that the Corps has good levee designs on its books and
has occasionally built successful flood-control systems. The Mississippi
River and Tributaries Project (MRTP), for example, has proven largely
effective at flood control, and Bea would like to see its integrated approach
emulated elsewhere. The MRTP has four components: high, strongly built
levees for containing floodwaters; floodways for diverting excess water
past critical sections of the river; canal improvements and stabilization,
to protect levees, increase the water-carrying capacity of the river, and
provide efficient navigation; and tributary-basin improvements, which
include the building of dams, reservoirs, pumps, and channels for drainage and flood control. It is a massive system: the "main stem" levees, floodwalls, and various control structures stretch 2,203 miles (some 1,606 miles
along the river itself, and another 596 miles along the Arkansas and Red
Rivers in the Atchafalaya Basin).

But Bea also believes that even more basic changes to the way America
handles floods are required. While America has plenty of technology to
control rising water in an environmentally sound way, the government
has yet to use it wisely or broadly. We need new state and national organizations to address the infrastructure challenge. And we need to engage
all concerned—commerce, government, and the public—to help the process. "We need a long-term vision for how to deal with water, which we've
never had," he said. "We need much better leadership, from the bottom of
the local level to the top of the federal level."

The United States will face more, and more intense, flooding this century.
How should we react?

The nation can take some basic steps to control high water, eliminate
dangerous levees, and curtail building in flood zones. First, Congress
must rethink land- and water-use policy and connect them more closely.
Second, the Army Corps of Engineers should be reinvigorated and given
a mandate to build and maintain a coherent, robust, nationwide flood-
protection system, as opposed to the ineffective, piecemeal measures that
have tragically failed regularly. As part of this reinvention, the Corps must
be held accountable. This means repealing the laws stemming from the

1928 Flood Control Act that immunize the Corps from prosecution when its levees fail. Third, citizens and businesses that benefit from levees, which is most of the nation, should apply their resources to their construction and upkeep and work hand in hand with the Corps. Fourth, by integrating nature and technology, building only in areas that can adequately be protected, and allowing some wetlands to return to their naturally absorbent and unconstrained state, bioengineered flood defense will provide effective protection.

Most fundamentally, the nation needs to rethink how it accommodates the environment. For years, Americans have relied on "hard" engineering—dredging, bulldozing, and building ever-taller walls—to control floods. But water is an irresistible force, and these efforts are eventually doomed to fail. Instead of trying to beat nature into submission with hard engineering, the Corps should develop a greener and more intelligent system of flood defenses that integrates traditional engineering with natural storm defenses, such as barrier islands, wetlands, and reeds. Such a "soft" approach to flood control is costly to build and maintain at first, but over the long term, it is more effective and cheaper than the hard engineering approach.

The commitment has to be well funded and sustained for at least a hundred years. "That's the way the Dutch think: work *with* nature, and think very long term," Bea observes. "They've been doing this since the thirteenth century. We have a lot to learn from them—if we're willing to listen."

As Congress dithers, and the Corps refuses to listen to outside advice, some people have built innovative solutions on their own.

THE BIOENGINEER

One day I stepped aboard the *Tule Queen II,* a forty-foot-long aluminum catamaran captained by Jeff Hart, to see how he has developed a soft-engineering approach to restoring Sacramento Delta levees that could be a model for other projects. Hart is a tall, bearded, fifty-eight-year-old Harvard-trained evolutionary biologist and the son of a Sacramento River farmer. He runs Hart Restoration, a nursery that sells "California-friendly" plants, which require minimal maintenance, are drought tolerant, and are beneficial to wildlife and insects.

"It is to nobody's advantage to let the levees go," he said. "It could lead to ecological and economic disaster for California."

Hart lives next to a levee, in Steamboat Slough, and sees the Delta levees being tested every day. Some stressors are natural, such as river flow, tidal action, or flooding. Some stressors are man-made, such as boat wake, tree cutting, and roads built on top of levees. Most of the Delta levees were not carefully engineered but were built informally by farmers and laborers. Some were built on top of natural silt deposits—narrow, sometimes infirm spits of land that were enhanced with piles of sand, dirt, and rocks during 150 years of reclamation. Maintaining this fragile "coalition" of materials is a constant, expensive challenge.

Sensitive to criticism that poor maintenance contributed to the breach of the Delta's Jones Tract in 2004, and New Orleans' levees during Hurricane Katrina in 2005, the state of California and the Corps have been "armoring" Delta levees against erosion by dumping boatloads of rock along the levee walls. But the rock is expensive, costing about $8,000 to $10,000 per linear acre-foot, Hart said, and while it looks imposing, it is ultimately only a stopgap.

Furthermore, the Corps has threatened to remove vegetation along hundreds of miles of levees in the Delta (and across the nation), believing that plants weaken the earthen berms. Classically trained "engineers abhor nature," Hart said. "To them, plants are the enemy. They argue that the roots go all the way through a levee and weaken it. That's not true for all plants. You don't want really big trees growing out of your levee, but we have found that layers of different kinds of soil with a little bit of vegetation on top makes a levee much stronger" than the Corps's rock armor.

Hart and Bea don't know each other, but they have arrived at the same conclusion: the integration of traditional engineering—such as levees and floodwalls—and natural defenses, such as reeds, will help restore the Delta and provide effective storm defenses.

Since 1977, Hart has been using plants such as tule—a tall marsh plant, with long, grasslike leaves, pale brown flowers, and strong roots—to revive wetlands, reduce erosion, and buffer embankments around Delta sloughs. Hart's primary "bioengineering" tool is the "brush box," a series of fences made of vertical stakes filled in with horizontal piles of brush that are planted along the sides of channels to break wave action. Planting tule between the brush boxes and levee walls traps sediment, protects fish, and further strengthens levees and embankments.

With government and private funding, Hart has established hundreds of yards of brush boxes in the Delta, which he believes reduce wave energy by 60 to 80 percent; when tule is added, the wave impact is reduced to nearly zero. The bioengineered approach, Hart said, is "far more effective and costs about one-hundredth the price in certain situations," of the Corps's hard-engineered piles of stone.

The larger message of such initiatives is that it is not enough to simply reengineer our water infrastructure; we must reengineer the way people think about water and our relationship to it. As the Dutch have shown, the way man interacts with the environment must change as conditions change. And in the twenty-first century the pace of change is increasing.

In places such as the flooded Midwest or the suddenly dry Southeast, where people have had a foretaste of our hydrological future, a vigorous dialogue about man and water has sprung up, technical innovation is on the rise, and cooperation over shared resources is being promoted. Yet more people are using more water than ever, in new ways, and H_2O is increasingly the focus of conflict. Tension is growing over privatization, and among thirsty resources such as agriculture, power, fuel, and minerals. Frustrations over the growing demand for water and limited supply is boiling up across the country, from hot, dense cities in Florida to chilly, remote villages in the Alaskan tundra.

PART IV

WATER IN THE TWENTY-FIRST CENTURY

Conflict and Innovation

CHAPTER 22

The Sacramento Delta: A Gordian Knot

Who needs water, how much water do they need, what do they need it for, and where is it going to come from?
—Dr. Peter Gleick, the Pacific Institute, 2009

THE "AXIS RESOURCE"

Central to the production of food, energy, and minerals, water is considered an "axis resource." As the demand for goods and services rises exponentially this century, competition for limited supplies of water will grow intense. Governments, industry, and individuals will be confronted by difficult questions, such as, how much water can, or should, man take from the ecosystem? How will we use limited water supplies—for food, power, or manufacturing—and what will the result be? Who makes these decisions; who benefits, and who doesn't? In short, who controls the tap? These are knotty questions, and their answers will have significant, long-term consequences for man and the planet.

Worldwide, irrigated agriculture, which accounts for about 70 percent of water withdrawals, is by far the greatest water user. In California, the number is probably closer to 80 percent. In 2000 (the latest data available), California farmers used 34.3 million acre-feet of water, about four times as much as the state's residential, commercial, and industrial users combined.

Under the West's "law of beneficial use," it is legal for farmers to divert water from rivers, or pump it from aquifers, without paying for it as long as it is used "beneficially," a vague term that essentially sanctions water takings.

239

Irrigation wells are rarely equipped with meters, so there is little information about how much water is being used, and irrigators, leery of "government intervention" in their affairs, resist attempts to find out.* But without that essential information, it is difficult to manage water responsibly.

Many Western irrigation districts impose a flat rate, which allows farmers to use as much water as they want. The Bureau of Reclamation subsidizes water, charging farmers a small percentage of the actual cost of providing it. In the Imperial Irrigation District of Southern California, farmers pay $15 per acre-foot, or $0.0006 per gallon, with no cap on how much they use and no surcharge for higher use. With no financial incentive to conserve, irrigators grow thirsty, low-value crops such as cotton, rice, and alfalfa in conditions better suited to cactus or scrub brush.

Even in the face of serious drought, irrigators resist any hint of government oversight, fearful of rationing or higher water prices. The result is the overpumping of groundwater in California and other agricultural states such as Nebraska, Kansas, Texas, Georgia, and Florida. This *water mining*, the technical term for pumping water from aquifers faster than nature can replenish it, lowers water tables, causes sinkholes, leads to wasteful runoff and evaporation, and, near coastlines, causes the saltwater pollution of drinking supplies. Furthermore, aging aqueducts and canals cannot deliver water to farmers in an efficient "on-demand" way, while overlapping bureaucracies and emotional, politicized water debates have left numerous states in hydrological gridlock. Nowhere is this more apparent than in California, the largest and thirstiest state in the Pacific West, and a bellwether for water issues.

THE DELTA AND ITS DISCONTENTS

Three-quarters of California's water is located in the north, but three-quarters of its population is in the south. The Sacramento–San Joaquin Delta—the vast marshy area ringed by crumbling levees that Bob Bea

---

* The farmers aren't alone in California's water meter "rebellion." Sacramento, the state capital, doesn't have meters; in the 1990s, residents of Fresno used the city charter to ban them, claiming that "meters are taxing machines" (state lawmakers later overrode Fresno's rule); and in 2009, 55 percent of the residents of the San Joaquin Valley were charged a flat fee and didn't have water meters, according to a study by the Public Policy Institute of California. Yet, the Institute found that metered cities use about 15 percent less water than unmetered cities. New laws will require residential water meters statewide by 2025.

fears are at risk of catastrophic failure—is the link between the two. You cannot separate a discussion of water in California, and thus the West, from a discussion of "the Delta."

In the blunt vocabulary of local politics, the Delta pits farmers versus cities versus fish. But in reality, the situation in the Delta is complex.

In the mid-1800s, farmers began to drain the Delta's marshlands, rolling back spongy peat and uprooting marsh grasses to create islands, and erecting about eleven hundred miles of levees to keep the water at bay. In this way, 450,000 acres of fertile land was "reclaimed" by the 1930s, and the Delta became one of the most productive farming regions in the world, with crops ranging from corn to alfalfa, grain, hay, tomatoes, asparagus, pears, and wine grapes.

Two vast water systems, the State Water Project and the federal Central Valley Project, use canals, aqueducts, pipes, and giant water pumps to move Sierra Nevada snowmelt from the northern end of the Central Valley to the southern end, and then south to Los Angeles. While these projects are efficient at moving water from remote sources in the mountains to human communities on the dry coast, they were not built with an eye to protecting the environment. Dams, pumps, and other man-made waterworks have decimated the Delta's once thriving salmon and smelt populations, along with other aquatic species, raising the ire of conservationists and, lately, the courts. A series of rulings in the first decade of the twenty-first century limited the amount of water irrigators could take from the Delta, thus protecting the aquasystem. This provoked a fight between farmers, fishermen, and politicians.

Waterworks are not the Delta's only problem. Natural gas is being extracted by drill rigs from beneath marshland, which adds to the Delta's pollution. With land in the Delta much cheaper than in Sacramento and San Francisco, towns have grown into small cities, and subdivisions have risen behind the old levees, in floodplains, without much regulatory oversight. In a catch-22, cities and counties have the authority to approve development but bear no legal responsibility for flood protection. State agencies are responsible for flood protection yet have no legal control over construction permits. When levees fail or floodplains flood, property owners have successfully sued the state (i.e., taxpayers) for compensation. This has set off another legal tussle.

Each of these constituencies—farmers, cities and counties, energy companies, industry, environmentalists—has laid claim to the Delta's water in an ad hoc way over the years. The result is an unholy mess. As the population expands and demand for water rises, competing claimants are fighting over a resource that is badly deteriorating.

The Delta's levees are aging and leaky; they have drained tidal marshes and exposed peat to oxygen; as the peat decomposes, the land subsides and releases carbon dioxide (a greenhouse gas). Most of the Delta has sunk below sea level, rendering the levees unstable and allowing salt water to intrude. Diversion of about 48 percent of the Delta's freshwater—to supply farms and cities—has profoundly impacted the region's twenty-two fish species. Moreover, CALFED, a federal-state consortium founded in 1994 to handle disputes and monitor the Delta's environmental health, is facing insolvency. As a result, the environmental group American Rivers declared the Sacramento Delta the nation's most endangered waterway in 2009.

Peter Gleick, president of the Pacific Institute, describes the warring constituencies as "hardly monolithic blocs." Consider agriculture: "The reality is that you not only have farmers against developers and environmentalists, you have Northern California farmers versus Southern California farmers in the Delta. San Joaquin farmers versus Sacramento farmers. Cotton versus rice. *Northern* rice growers versus *southern* rice growers. It goes on and on. Every stakeholder has a strong interest in what happens to the Delta's water, but how do you get beyond the impasse? So far, we haven't."

In 1980, as California was recovering from its longest drought since the Depression, state legislators proposed building a Peripheral Canal to route water around the Delta, which would protect the area's sensitive ecology while delivering more water to Los Angeles and the south. The plan was to tap into the Sacramento River below the capital and channel water 43 miles around the Delta into the Clifton Court Forebay, the reservoir that primes the giant water pumps that shoot Sierra snowmelt south. But the Peripheral Canal plan was grandiose and became entangled in a water dispute between Los Angeles and San Francisco. Discussions broke down, and in 1982 the Peripheral Canal proposal was rejected by 62.7 percent of voters in a ballot initiative; in San Francisco, the vote was 95 percent against the canal.

Governor Schwarzenegger revived the plan in 2006 and began to push for a revised Peripheral Canal. But farmers worried that routing large amounts of freshwater around the Delta would turn their fields to dust. Despite record agricultural production in the Central Valley in 2007, farming losses were estimated to be as high as $245 million in 2008. Farmers worried that a Peripheral Canal could remove a further half million acres of farmland from use.

Environmental groups, which split bitterly over the 1982 debate—with some arguing for a Peripheral Canal, to protect the Delta's ecology, and others against it—reached a consensus in 2008 that a Peripheral Canal would siphon too much freshwater from the estuary and destroy habitats and aquatic life.

By mid-2010, California's twenty-nine water agencies had yet to reach agreement about how best to manage the Delta, and the Peripheral Canal, which was estimated to cost some $3–$4 billion, at a time when the state was facing bankruptcy, was politically unpopular.

"We have bad hydrology, compromised infrastructure, and our management tools are broken," observed Timothy Quinn, executive director of the Association of California Water Agencies (ACWA). "All that paints a fairly grim picture for Californians trying to manage water in the twenty-first century."

While in some ways the gridlock over the Delta is specific to California, it exemplifies the kind of complicated multiparty water disputes that are popping up everywhere. As in other parts of the country, where debates over mining, energy, and the "rights" of the ecosystem have flared, the battle over the Delta represents a competition between resources in which water is the focal point. Such "resource wars" will be a signature issue of this century.

With this scramble for water in mind, I invited Peter Gleick to join me on a driving tour, to see the Delta mess from a smelt's-eye view.

INTO THE HEART OF RUBE GOLDBERGIAN DARKNESS

As I parked my rented Prius behind his Prius, Gleick bounded out of his house in Berkeley with a large pair of serious birder's binoculars slung around his neck. He folded his rangy body inside, and the hybrid whirred quietly out of Berkeley, heading northeast. It was alternately sunny and overcast as we slipped past rolling hills, a wind farm with huge spinning blades, and across the bridge at Suisun Bay, where the Sierra snowmelt flows out into San Francisco Bay. Around a sweeping bend, the Delta suddenly spread wide ahead: a biologically rich zone that is home to 500,000 people, 300,000 acres of agriculture, and 750 species of flora and fauna.

It is the largest estuary on the West Coast. Five major rivers, and many smaller tributaries, feed into it. It is California's most important, and vulnerable, freshwater resource.

Since 1940, the Delta has served as the nexus of the federal Central Valley Project (CVP), a water system run by the Bureau of Reclamation that consists of twenty dams, eleven hydroelectric generators, five hundred miles of canals and aqueducts, and countless pumps, pipes, and ditches. The CVP moves Sierra Nevada snowmelt from the northern end of the Central Valley to the southern end, to Los Angeles. The system irrigates 3 million acres of farmland and provides freshwater to 2 million consumers a year. The region's other water system, the State Water Project (SWP), diverts water from the Feather River across the Delta to the Harvey O. Banks pumping plant, in Tracy.

"It all *sounds* like it makes sense, but the Delta system is really a giant Rube Goldberg–esque machine,"* Gleick said, gesturing out the window at a tangle of muddy canals. "They've twisted so many knobs and pulled so many levers here that no one really knows how the Delta's plumbing works anymore. It just goes on and on, somehow. You can't honestly describe the Delta as a *natural* system anymore."

Before the human plumbing system siphoned off most of its water, the Delta carried 25 million acre-feet of water a year; now it gets about 8 million. Grizzly bears—the ones featured on the California state flag—used to roam here but are now gone. Enormous herds of tule elk once thrived around the marsh, but few remain.

During the gold rush of 1848 to 1855 in the Sierra Nevada, prospectors used hydraulic mining—high-pressure streams of water to wash away rock and uncover gold—which led to the mass erosion of the Yuba, Sacramento, and other rivers, with thousands of tons of silt flowing downstream and into San Francisco Bay. The rivers have still not fully recovered.

"It's hard for me not to dream of what it used to be like," Gleick said.

We arrived in Tracy, once a quiet agricultural town that has morphed into an exurb of San Jose. Sprinklers were whirling in the midday heat, turning brown patches into bright green grass and evaporating thousands of gallons of water up into the sky.

---

* Rube Goldberg was an American cartoonist of the mid-twentieth century who dreamed up fanciful devices such as "the self-operating napkin" to perform simple tasks in amusingly convoluted ways.

Two sets of giant pumps near Tracy suck up the Delta's water and propel it south: the federal Tracy Pumping Plant, which serves Central Valley farmers, and the Harvey O. Banks Delta Pumping Plant, which is state-run, and before the gates of which we now stood.

At the Banks pumps, Delta water flows into the Clifton Court Forebay, through a set of fish screens (which are supposed to keep fish away from the pumps), and finally into the pumps, which shove the water 245 feet up a hill and into the California Aqueduct. The aqueduct carries the water 444 miles south, to the Perris Reservoir between Los Angeles and San Diego. It is a magnificent system for moving water, but the pumps are at the heart of a long, bitter controversy over the Delta.

Inside a metal shed, eleven thundering pumps were lined up in a row, the largest of which use eighty-thousand-horsepower engines. "With everything working, we can move 6.7 billion gallons of water per day," said our guide, Doug Thompson. The State Water Project is the single biggest user of electricity in California. Prices are cheaper at night, so the temptation is to do most of the pumping then. But the Delta smelt, *Hypomesus transpacificus*—a small, silvery fish endemic to the Delta that is listed as threatened—prefers to spawn at night, along the channel's edges. In an effort to prevent the fish from being sucked into the pumps' spinning impellers, the Banks plant is mostly run during the day.

Smelt live for about a year, travel in schools, feed on zooplankton, and are an "indicator species," meaning that they act as a natural gauge of the health of the ecosystem. Delta smelt were once one of the most plentiful fish in the estuary, but the Banks and Tracy pumps have been blamed for pulverizing millions of smelt and pushing the fish close to extinction.

Upstream from the Banks pumps, the John F. Skinner Delta Fish Protection System is basically a giant screen that, according to the DWR, diverts an average of 15 million fish a year away from the pumps. The facility consists of an intake channel, a series of V-shaped, louvered blue gates that push away or collect smaller fish, and holding pens for fish. Once enough fish are gathered, they are loaded into silver tanker trucks, which take them to a release point near Antioch.

"The system is effective but not flawless," notes a DWR pamphlet. Not only do the smelt get into the pumps, but big fish and sea lions have figured out how to corral them near the screens and gobble them up.

I could see that Gleick, who had remained preternaturally calm as we toured the pumps, was growing agitated. Back in the Prius, he vented about the pumps and the fish screen: "This thing is the Achilles' heel of the whole Delta system! It's what an engineer would design to move water efficiently, which it does very well, but it doesn't screen fish well at all."

The pumps were built in the 1960s, when DWR's mandate was to supply water. But water managers now have to satisfy a much broader set of needs, including the ecosystem's. "The world has changed," said Gleick, "but the infrastructure hasn't."

In the early twentieth century, the Delta boasted a healthy fishing industry, noted for its chinook (king) salmon. Canneries processed 5 million pounds of salmon a year, plus other valuable fish such as flounder, herring, sardines, and anchovies. By the 1960s, however, overfishing, agricultural pollution, and dams had destroyed fish stocks. Hatcheries introduced new species, such as striped bass, for sport fishermen, which feasted on native species. The Delta's fish populations continue to decline for reasons not fully understood, but scientists worry that if the trend persists, the region's aquatic food chain could crash.

In the spring of 2007, a California court ruled that the DWR had violated the state Endangered Species Act by failing to protect salmon and smelt. US district court judge Oliver Wanger threatened to shut down the pumps altogether. Farmers were outraged, and the decision was appealed. But in May 2007, a survey found only twenty-five smelt—the smallest number ever recorded in the Delta, and 93 percent fewer than the previous year. The pumps were shut down for ten days to allow the fish to recover. Bill Jennings, the executive director of the California Sportfishing Protection Alliance, called the pumps "the smoking gun" in the smelt's demise, quipping, "There are so few smelt out there now that you might as well name them instead of counting them."

The pumps deliver water to some 25 million people, and the court order was met with deep concern in the region, especially by irrigators, who rely on timely water deliveries to sustain their crops.

In August 2007, Judge Wanger ordered water exports from the Delta cut by 6 to 30 percent between December and June 2008. "The evidence is uncontradicted that these project operations move the fish," wrote Wanger.

The decision outraged Governor Schwarzenegger, who declared, "This federal biological opinion puts fish above the needs of millions of Californians. . . . [It is] a devastating blow to our economy." Hundreds of farmers marched through the Central Valley, chanting, "Water! Water! Water!"

and carrying signs that read NO WATER, NO JOBS, NO FOOD. (Some of them were allegedly paid by wealthy farm-owners to march.)

Too many people have been competing for a finite amount of water in the Sacramento Delta, and perhaps inevitably the fishermen and farmers began to throw elbows at each other, as they have done around the Chesapeake Bay. California fishermen have pushed Central Valley farmers to shift to less water-intensive crops; they have demanded that officials regulate pesticides and fertilizer runoff; and they have lobbied state regulators to take conservation and recycling more seriously. It was no mistake, fishermen say, that as water diversions from the Delta increased, peaking at more than 6 million acre-feet in 2005, fish stocks began to decline. That year, almost eight hundred thousand mature salmon returned to spawn in the Sacramento River and its tributaries. By 2009, the number had dropped to about thirty-nine thousand, which Paul Johnson, founder of the Monterey Fish Market, called "far too few to support fishing." California's salmon runs are "collapsing," he wrote, thanks to the water withdrawals by "powerful corporate agricultural interests."

But farmers vociferously disagree, saying there is no proof that water diversions to their fields led to fish kills. Restricting how much water they could use, farmers said, forced them to fallow hundreds of thousands of acres of arable land and led to a 40 percent unemployment rate in towns such as Mendota. By diverting into the ocean billions of gallons of water the farmers desperately need, said Representative Tom McClintock (R–Granite Bay), federal regulators aim "to indulge the environmental left's pet project, the Delta smelt."

In the summer of 2009, farmers erected signs in the west side of the San Joaquin Valley bemoaning a CONGRESS-CREATED DUST BOWL. The Fox News personality Sean Hannity flew into the valley with a camera crew to say, "The government has put the interests of a two-inch minnow before [farmers]!" And Representative Devin Nunes, who was trying to persuade federal regulators to ignore the Endangered Species Act when allocating water to farmers, declared, "The radical environmental groups have ... been trying to turn this into a desert."

But this argument is specious. Commenting on Hannity's proclamation, Jon Stewart noted on *The Daily Show,* "The government should stop meddling in the business of the farmers, who would actually still be living in a desert if not for government meddling."

The west side of the Central Valley did face drought and unemployment in 2009, but it was not facing anything close to Dust Bowl shortages. While Fresno County officials described 2009 as a "dire year" for agricultural production, that was only in comparison to 2008, a record year, when the county produced $5.7 billion worth of products, representing a nearly 6 percent increase over 2007. Mendota suffered unemployment, but that was not new: according to state statistics, the town's unemployment rate has fallen below 25 percent only twice between 2000 and 2010. Perhaps Hannity's most disingenuous argument is that Washington is "sacrificing farmers for fish." There is no question that the many dams, pumps, and aqueducts, and the wasteful use of Delta water by irrigators has destroyed the region's fisheries and those who make their living from them.

"We're looking at an ecosystem that's in severe peril," said Rodney R. McInnis, regional administrator for the National Marine Fisheries Service. "It's not just the Delta smelt that are affected, but the salmon runs and killer whales and coastal communities."

The West Coast fishing season runs from May to October and results in an average harvest of eight hundred thousand fish, from California to Oregon. In April 2008, federal regulators canceled the fishing of chinook salmon for the first time since the birth of the industry 150 years earlier. When state regulators closed the salmon fishery for a second year, in 2009, about twenty-six hundred jobs and $270 million were lost. (The Monterey Fish Market's Paul Johnson calculates that the two-year closure cost the fishing industry some twenty-three thousand jobs and $2.8 billion in revenue.) The commercial salmon fleet dropped from five thousand boats in 1985 to four hundred boats by 2010. A tightly restricted fishing season was open in the spring of 2010, but catches were anemic.

Dave Bitts, a Stanford University graduate who forsook an academic career to fish out of Humboldt Bay, said he wasn't surprised by the bans: "Fishermen are born with an extra helping of hope. But I never had much hope for this season," he told the Los Angeles Times in 2008. "Going fishing this year would be like a farmer eating his seed corn. For a sliver of a season and a tiny catch, it's not worth it. . . . It's painful to watch what's happening to the fish, and the fisherman."

FOOD AND WATER

On our second day in the Delta, Gleick and I were standing on top of Friant Dam, just north of Fresno, which impounds the once powerful

San Joaquin River and creates a fifteen-mile-long reservoir called Millerton Lake. We were here to look at the dam that had destroyed the San Joaquin's chinook salmon fishery and investigate the site of Temperance Flat Dam, which Governor Schwarzenegger wanted to build at Millerton's northern end. If it is built, Temperance Flat will dwarf the dam we stood on.

Friant Dam is a vast concrete crescent, 319 feet high, that bisects the San Joaquin Valley. On either side of the dam, a smooth concrete-lined canal sluiced water to irrigators far away. On the left, the Friant-Kern Canal angled south; to the right, the Madeira Canal bore water to the north. Running from the dam's spillway, the San Joaquin River flowed tamely along a narrow channel in the wide valley, where big rocks had been pockmarked and sanded smooth by centuries of unconstrained torrents. Since the dam was built in 1942, the valley has grown lush with trees and bushes.

The San Joaquin begins as Sierra Nevada snowmelt, pools in three lakes near Yosemite National Park, gathers momentum as it tumbles past Fresno, turns north across the Central Valley, and empties into the Delta, which carries it out to the Pacific. At a length of 350 miles, it is the second-longest river in California and once boasted one of the state's richest ecosystems.

The river's chinook salmon fishery was one of the biggest on the West Coast, and the fish were once so plentiful that farmers used salmon as hog food. But when Friant Dam was completed, and its two irrigation canals began diverting up to 95 percent of the river's water to irrigate about a million acres of agriculture, the salmon run was decimated. By the early 1950s, river diversions were so great that in some places the San Joaquin ran completely dry. The chinook were wiped out.

In September 2006, after an eighteen-year legal campaign led by the Natural Resources Defense Council (NRDC), an environmental advocacy group, a historic agreement was announced to restore San Joaquin River flows to a sixty-mile stretch of river. Under the agreement, river diversions will be reduced by fifteen percent during the spring, chinook (now listed as a federal endangered species) will be reintroduced to the river, fish ladders and screens will be built, and levees will be repaired. NRDC attorney Hal Candee hailed the restoration as "unprecedented in the American West." The project is estimated to cost $250–$800 million (to be shared by the federal government, the state, and the agricultural industry) and is slated to be completed by 2014.

The agreement attempts to protect farmers, as well. It allows irrigators to buy discounted water in wet years, and to buy water from other irrigation districts. But those not covered by the settlement worry that they will be forced to sacrifice more water and incur costly upgrades, and will have less hydroelectric production. The Modesto and Merced irrigation districts have taken their concerns to Congress, decrying the project as "a potential disaster."

A crosswind blew over Friant Dam, ruffling Gleick's beard as we stared at the placid reservoir. In a normal year, this basin can store up to 520,500 acre-feet of water, though on the day of our visit it looked at least a quarter empty; by October, the lake would hold about 40 percent of its capacity, which was lower than average. Even so, it was a serene and beautiful scene, and the dam and its canals were remarkable pieces of engineering. "It's hard not to be impressed," I ventured.

"True," Gleick replied. "I've always said that these dams brought enormous benefits." He paused a beat, then added, "But that doesn't mean we need to build any more of them!"

If the Temperance Flat Dam is built in a gorge just north of Millerton Lake, it will dwarf Friant and create a vast new reservoir holding 1.26 million acre-feet of water, which is close to three times the size of Millerton. Standing on Friant, it was difficult to imagine the size and scope of the proposed structure. Dam proponents said water from Temperance Flats would cost $300 to $400 an acre-foot. But as they hadn't decided on a site or design, or how the dam will be operated, those numbers were merely guesstimates.

"I'm in favor of *designing* dams—that's cheap," said Gleick. "Basic dam design hasn't changed much over the years, although today you have to integrate climate change into your design. But *building* dams is horribly expensive. It always costs more than they say it will. Who is going to pay for Temperance Flat? The people who really use this water, the farmers, never buy water at full cost [it is subsidized by federal and state programs]. And now the state is bankrupt. So where is all of this money supposed to come from?"

Gleick says that agricultural water use in California is unsustainable, although he sympathizes with farmers. "Agriculture uses about eighty percent of the Delta's water, while urban use represents just eight to ten percent. The agriculture industry hates that comparison and always says that 'California produces a big percentage of the world's food.' But the issue is not 'food versus no food.' The issue is, can we grow the *same* food with *less* water, and without crashing our ecosystem? My answer is yes, unequivocally."

If California farmers used more efficient irrigation technology, they could save enough water each year to fill Hetch Hetchy Reservoir sixteen times, the Pacific Institute found. If growers could be persuaded to conserve just 10 percent of the water they use, Gleick said, that would be equal to the total volume of water used by the residential sector.

To accomplish such savings, Gleick recommends three basic improvements. First, crop shifting: grow fewer low-value and water-intensive crops such as alfalfa, rice, and cotton, and grow more high-value, water-efficient crops such as fruits, nuts, and vegetables. Second, smart irrigation: use technology and information to schedule irrigation for key moments, and replace wasteful flood irrigation with sprinklers and drip irrigation. Third, short-term fallowing of crops: if California fallows 10 percent of field crops during a drought, it would save an estimated 1.7 million acre-feet of water and provide revenue for capital improvements.

"Farmers are smart," says Gleick, "and I believe I'm on their side. Given the right signals, they do the right thing."

A common lament, he says, is that "farmers can't change what they grow." But when provided with incentives, farmers are perfectly able to shift from one crop to another. Consider the shift from cotton to corn production in recent years: in 2009, cotton production in California dropped 27 percent, and it dropped 20 percent nationwide, compared to 2008, but corn production rose 83 percent in California and 26 percent nationwide. Why? Because of government incentives to grow corn for ethanol fuel.

What if we provided a similar incentive for planting water-efficient crops and provided farmers with tax credits for using efficient irrigation technologies? I asked. "There's no question we'd save water," Gleick replied.

I asked if he'd proposed the idea to actual farmers. "I've tried," Gleick sighed. "But I can't have that discussion. It depends a lot on who the messenger is. Growers don't want to be told by an academic with a beard what to do. Frankly, I'm happy *not* to tell farmers what to do. They do the best they can."

Mike Wade, of the California Farm Water Coalition, wrote, "The assertion that farmers can conserve 4 million acre-feet of water is absurd and borders on pie-in-the-sky reasoning. Most often, flood-irrigation is the only avenue to irrigate these crops. In addition to providing water for the plant to grow, the water also seeps into the underground and provides a recharge to the groundwater." Pointing to the suggestion that farmers switch from field crops to vegetable crops, Wade added, showed a lack of understanding of how the market works. "If we follow the Institute's suggestion, then grocery stores would be glutted with more vegetables than anyone would want to buy. Prices would collapse, and the crops would be wasted. . . . You can't just wave a magic wand. There are consequences."

At the northern end of Millerton Lake, we inspected one of the canyons where Temperance Flat Dam could be built. The lake and its surroundings are gorgeous. With dramatic beige hills rising around the sun-spangling lake, this is prime vacation country. Some of the older homes were modest, but the newer houses were large and expensive-looking. Yet something was vaguely wrong with the postcardlike view. As we drove along a winding road called Sky Harbor Drive, high above the lake, nearly every house had a FOR SALE sign in the driveway.

"What's going on here?" I asked.

"Well, if *you* suddenly discovered that your vacation getaway was about to be turned into a horrible construction site for the next ten years while they built a seven-hundred-foot-tall dam in your face, you'd probably try to sell, too!" Gleick muttered.

It was bright at noon, and the heat was rising. We drove up and over the ridge, passed a few remote ranches, and eventually nosed the Prius down a hairpin road to a tributary of the San Joaquin. It was stultifyingly hot down there, especially on the river's edge, where wide water-sculpted rocks radiated solar energy next to a venerable pumping station. Gleick and I glanced around, then stripped off our clothes and plunged into the stream. It was so clear and cool that it refreshed me down to my bones. If the new dam is built, this entire valley will be submerged.

Farmers, environmentalists, politicians, engineers, water managers, and citizens are in broad agreement that the Sacramento Delta system is broken, but almost no agreement exists on how to fix it. In 2008 Governor Schwarzenegger declared a state of emergency, convened experts into a Delta Vision Blue Ribbon Task Force, and provided millions of dollars' worth of state funding for levee repair. But at least 220 government agencies have jurisdiction in the Delta; its massive technical problems are further complicated by politics and years of enmity between constituents. Washington has dithered, local politicians have bickered, cities and farmers have demanded more water, and environmental activists have declared war on the salmon- and smelt-killing pumps and the proposed Peripheral Canal. The result is a circular argument that leads nowhere.

WATER IN THE TWENTY-FIRST CENTURY

"It's the ultimate Gordian knot. There's no other system in the world as complex as the Delta," said UC Berkeley professor Ray Seed, who is studying the Delta with his colleague Bob Bea. In 2009, the state legislature passed a broad water package that created the Delta Stewardship Council as a central authority on the matter. But veterans of Delta battles questioned whether anything will change.

In July 2010, California faced a $19.9 billion budget deficit, and Governor Schwarzenegger pushed his $11.1 billion water bond—$3 billion of which was slated for the new dams in the Central Valley and $1.5 billion for the Peripheral Canal around the Delta—back to the 2012 ballot, which may signal its demise. (Schwarzenegger was succeeded by Jerry Brown, a Democrat, in 2011.)

"We've had a sixty-, seventy-year stalemate," said Seed. "The biggest change now is the conjugate level of desperation from all parties. No one is winning, and people are finally realizing that if we all keep fighting each other, we eventually will all lose together."

THE WATER WE NEED VERSUS THE WATER WE HAVE

To Gleick, the central question presented by the Delta—and, by extension, water use in general—is "Who needs water, how much water do they need, what do they need it for, and where is it going to come from?"

Farmers, cities, residents, industry, and aquatic species all have claims on the estuary's limited resources. The dispute over the Delta is about how to satisfy as many of those water users as possible. But perhaps we have been looking in the wrong direction for answers.

"We don't really want *water*, per se," said Gleick. "We want to grow our alfalfa or tomatoes, to make our semiconductors, to clean our clothes, to be happy fish. Large amounts of water is what we have been using to accomplish those things. But we need to rethink that."

The Delta's conveyance system grew ad hoc, over a century, with the undergirding supply-and-demand question being, how do we move water from Point A to Point B? Today, the demand question is, what is the minimum amount of water that will satisfy our needs? The supply questions are, do we have enough water to accomplish those goals? Where should our water supply be, and how do we design a system to move it?

"We need to change the mind-set away from an engineering mentality—'Let's find the water we *need*'—to a management mentality—'Let's manage the water we *have* more wisely,'" Gleick said. "It's difficult. But it's not impossible."

Late in the afternoon, we rolled through slanting light and shadows and billowing fog to Gleick's house, in Berkeley. He showed me his low-flush toilet, his front-mounted washer and dryer, and his gray-water irrigation system for the garden. The house was like a living laboratory for his work, a glimpse inside his mind. It is tasteful but modest, water-efficient, surrounded by greenery, and inhabited by a family that treads lightly on the earth. This environment is very much like the ideal Gleick imagines for the entire state of California, and perhaps the world beyond it.

"Ahhhh," he said, after gulping down a tall, cool glass of Hetch Hetchy water drawn from the kitchen tap. "That tastes really good. You get thirsty out there!"

CHAPTER 23

Liquidity: Privatization and the Rise of Big Water

"WATER IS THE NEW OIL!"

On nearly every continent, groundwater in aquifers is being drained faster than the natural rate of recharge
—*National Geographic*, April 2010

I drained you dry, you boy. If you have a milkshake, and I have a milkshake, and I have a straw and my straw reaches across the room . . . I drink your milkshake. I drink it up!
—Daniel C. Plainview,
There Will Be Blood, 2007

In 1971 the oil and natural-gas entrepreneur T. Boone Pickens bought a 2,960-acre ranch along the Canadian River in the Texas Panhandle. The Panhandle is a rectangular chunk of north Texas that juts up into New Mexico and Oklahoma. The ranch was in Roberts County, a remote area of hills and canyons, prairie grass and mesquite. Although it is roughly forty times the size of Manhattan, the county had only a few hundred residents. Some ranched there, but the topography was too rugged for irrigated agriculture. Pickens didn't care about that. He loved the area's scrubby remoteness. He moved a double-wide trailer onto his property and used it as a getaway. Fueled with cheese, crackers, and six-packs of Big Orange soda, he'd spend hours with his dogs hunting quail on the property, before racing ninety miles back to Amarillo, where he was building Mesa Inc. into the largest independent oil firm in the world.

In the 1980s, Pickens built a reputation as the country's most fearsome corporate raider. He made hostile bids for companies many times larger than Mesa—including Gulf Oil, Phillips Petroleum, and Unocal—which helped to reconfigure the resource business and made him a billionaire. His enemies referred to Pickens as a "greenmailer," and in 1985 *Time* magazine depicted him on its cover as a cagey poker player. But over the next decade Mesa was hobbled by a series of legal battles and business reversals that left it with a $1.2 billion debt. Pickens fought with nearly everyone around him and underwent two divorces. In 1996, he was forced to resign from the company he had founded in 1956. Angered and humiliated, he left Amarillo for Dallas, where he started over again, building up an energy hedge fund called BP Capital Management. The one constant for Pickens throughout the tumult was his ranch, Mesa Vista, in the Canadian River Valley.

By the 1990s he had built a house there, installed electricity, and expanded his holdings to twenty thousand acres. Echoing Maurice Strong, who insisted he had decided to develop the giant aquifer beneath his Baca Ranch in Colorado only as an afterthought, Pickens declared to me, "I never thought twice about the water" that lay beneath Mesa Vista. At least that was the case until 1997, he said, "when I first saw the possibilities."

That year the Canadian River Municipal Water Authority (CRMWA), a local utility, bought the rights to forty-three thousand acres of water for $14.5 million. "I could not believe that number," Pickens said, amazed that people would pay so much for mere water. "I thought it must be a misprint." Two years later, Pickens's ranch neighbor, a thirty-two-year-old money manager named Salem Abraham, assembled a seventy-one-thousand-acre parcel and offered Pickens the chance to join in selling the property's water rights. He declined, but when Abraham sold the water to Amarillo for $20 million, netting a $10 million profit, Pickens was once again stunned.

For a resource specialist, the implications were obvious. Demographers predict the Texas population will leap as much as 43.5 percent by 2030, mostly in urban areas. Texas is the nation's top producer of cattle and cotton and is a leading producer of many other crops. And Texas has suffered a string of drought years, most notably in the early 1950s and again in the mid-2000s.

The former wildcatter had a new mantra: "The hydrocarbon era is over. Water is the new oil!"

• • •

Texas water law distinguishes between surface water and groundwater. Surface water is owned by the state. As in much of the West, Texas property owners can buy and sell the right to groundwater separately from the land above it. But unique to Texas is a law known officially as the rule of capture and unofficially as "pump or perish," by which landowners are allowed to pump as much groundwater as they like, even if it drains adjacent properties. The law, which dates to the early twentieth century, has been controversial and environmentally destructive, but numerous attempts to undo it have failed.

The property Abraham sold Amarillo wrapped around the south, east, and west of Pickens's ranch. Pickens told me he had no choice but to sell the water from beneath his ranch: "If they started pumping, I'd get drained."

In 1999, Pickens formed Mesa Water and began to accumulate water rights to sell to thirsty cities such as El Paso, Lubbock, or San Antonio. But as time passed, Mesa Water focused on the Dallas–Fort Worth (DFW) Metroplex. Already the state's largest water user, DFW's population was growing quickly in the midst of a worsening drought.

Many of Pickens's neighbors were alarmed by his plan to privatize the groundwater, treating it as a commodity like oil or gas, to be sold to the highest bidder. Some of them rallied against him and threatened lawsuits; others joined Mesa Water, hoping to profit.

As water supplies are stretched thin across the country, this scenario is becoming increasingly familiar.

For much of the nation's history, Americans have fought over surface water—who gets to use how much of lake or river water—but most of those disputes have been settled; today, the biggest water wars are over groundwater.

FOSSIL WATER

A hundred times more water is stored underground than in all streams, rivers, and lakes combined, according to the USGS. Groundwater can be found in a marsh, close to the surface, or a thousand feet underground, in aquifers. At shallow depths, water is often only a few hours old; at medium depth it can be hundreds of years old; at great depth, groundwater can be a million or more years old.

Groundwater is often compared to money in a bank account: if it is withdrawn faster than nature can replenish it, it will eventually run dry.

Pumping water out of the ground faster than it is replenished results in dry wells, reduced rivers and lakes, deterioration of water quality, increased pumping costs (to reach ever-deeper aquifers), land subsidence, and the formation of sinkholes that have been known to swallow pets, people, cars, chunks of highway, and entire buildings. Near the ocean, overpumping aquifers can result in saltwater intrusion, which has contaminated aquifers from Long Island, New York, to Hilton Head, South Carolina, Savannah, Georgia, and Orange County, California.

In 2008 Americans pumped 83.3 billion gallons of groundwater every day, a 23 percent increase from 1970, according to the USGS. Globally, groundwater use exceeds 600 billion gallons per day. About half the US population, and most rural communities, use groundwater for drinking supplies, representing 19 percent of the groundwater used annually; 60 percent, or 50 billion gallons of water a day, is used for irrigation, in places such as the Great Plains.

The groundwater beneath Pickens's ranch wasn't from just any aquifer. It was the Ogallala, the largest groundwater supply in North America. The Ogallala (or High Plains) Aquifer holds a quadrillion gallons of H_2O, or enough to cover the entire continental United States to a depth of nearly two feet. If the water beneath Colorado's San Luis Valley presented Maurice Strong and Gary Boyce with "blue gold," then Pickens had found blue platinum.

The Ogallala Aquifer stretches beneath parts of eight states: South Dakota, Wyoming, Nebraska, Colorado, Kansas, Oklahoma, New Mexico, and northern Texas. It is also the most heavily used aquifer in the country, providing 30 percent of all groundwater used for irrigation in the United States, and drinking water for 2 million people. The Great Plains overlays it and supplies 40 percent of the nation's grain-fed beef and one-fifth of the total annual US agricultural output, representing crops worth some $20 billion a year.

The Ogallala's water is estimated to be from ten thousand to several million years old and is known as fossil water. The aquifer was formed when the Rocky Mountains were volcanic and rivers that no longer exist washed pieces of the mountains east. The channels eventually filled with silt and sediment, but the water remained and slowly percolated underground, where it pooled in gravel beds that lie only a few feet thick in the southwestern part of the aquifer to more than a thousand feet deep in the north. Although rain and river flows continue to recharge parts of the Ogallala, it can take many years for the water to make its way underground and move through the system. Heavy pumping has drained the Ogallala's water ten times faster than nature has recharged it. Even if all pumping were to stop tomorrow, hydrologists estimate it would take the Ogallala six thousand years to refill by natural processes.

Before European settlers arrived, roughly 1 billion acres of grasslands covered the Great Plains. With a short growing season, and only twelve to eighteen inches of precipitation a year in parts, hardy plants such as blue grama and green needlegrass sustained bison, pronghorn antelope, swift fox, lesser prairie chicken, and burrowing owl. There was little surface water on the Plains, and it was a difficult place for humans to live. Native tribes used the plains as seasonal hunting grounds but withdrew to river valleys to build their communities. Cattle drives across the plains in the 1860s faced drought and problems from overgrazing. Homesteaders, beset by low rainfall and high soil erosion, were driven away in a mass migration during the Dust Bowl of the 1930s. But as farmers learned to use windmills to pump water from the aquifer in the 1950s, more than half the native grasslands were replaced by crops on the Plains, and permanent settlements took root. The process has accelerated in recent years, and some 25 million acres of cropland have been planted since 1982.

The accelerated planting was the result of diesel-powered water pumps, which replaced windmills after the Second World War and pushed water extractions from a few gallons a minute to many hundreds of gallons per minute. The brown plains turned green, and one of the nation's poorest regions became one of the richest. Between 1937 and 1971, the number of irrigation wells in West Texas leaped from 1,166 to 66,000, according to *Scientific American*. But the heavy use of the Ogallala has resulted in a gradual buildup of contaminants, such as nitrates and dissolved solids, in the soil and the groundwater.

After analyzing samples taken from 370 public and private wells between 1999 and 2004, the USGS reported that unless "substantial changes" were made, the Ogallala would be jeopardized. Most of the water met federal quality standards, but in about 6 percent of the wells, nitrate—which can occur naturally or be the result of fertilizer runoff—was higher than the federal standard of 10 parts per million. (And there are new worries: PCBs dredged by GE from New York's Hudson River, for instance, are shipped to a landfill in Andrews County in the Texas panhandle: the Sierra Club fears the toxins could eventually seep into the Ogallala, though GE and the EPA dismiss these concerns.) Dr. Jason Gurdak, the lead author of the USGS study, warns: "Once contaminated, the [Ogallala] aquifer is unlikely to be remediated quickly" because water underground travels slowly, and it takes years for pollutants to degrade.

A US Department of Agriculture project has compiled data and recommended techniques to avert the aquifer's collapse. Using lasers to measure airflow over fields (which affects evaporation rates), infrared sensors to turn on irrigation systems only when needed, and computer databases to help farmers efficiently manage crops, the project has saved some water—perhaps 10 to 15 percent per crop per season. These are worthy advances, but in West Texas, where the Ogallala is rapidly petering out, such technologies could give farmers only another fifty to a hundred years of use, scientists estimate.

As the population of Great Plains states continues to grow, farmers, eager to capitalize on the global demand for food, have put short-term opportunity ahead of long-term conservation. Some have pumped their groundwater dry and been forced to abandon their land. Meanwhile the federal government has pushed corn-based ethanol production. Corn, which is profitable, is also a thirsty crop. Plans to double the number of ethanol production plants in the region will require an additional 120 billion gallons of aquifer water per year, the Environmental Defense Fund has estimated.

The USGS has studied the Ogallala since the early 1900s and found that yearly groundwater withdrawals quintupled between 1949 and 1974. By 1980, water levels in the region had dropped an average of nearly ten feet. In some parts of the central and southern plains, the drop was over a hundred feet. In southern Kansas, where groundwater dropped one hundred and fifty feet, some people have forsaken thirsty crops, such as corn, to try "dryland farming"—growing sunflowers, wheat, and other drought-resistant plants. "We have optimistic locations" in the aquifer, said David Pope, the former chief engineer of Kansas. "Other places, we can see the end."

By 2009, the volume of depletions from the Ogallala was equivalent to eighteen Colorado Rivers per year, and tensions were flaring. But the most intense fight over Ogallala water is taking place in Texas—thanks to T. Boone Pickens's plan to commodify it.

"DEVASTATING"

The cities of Dallas and Fort Worth are located in north Texas, east of the Panhandle and just south of the Oklahoma border. By the time of the 2003 census, the two cities' suburbs had merged into one megacity, the

Dallas–Fort Worth Metroplex. DFW is the largest metropolitan area in Texas and the fourth largest in the United States, with approximately 6.5 million residents spread over ninety-three hundred square miles—an area larger than the states of Connecticut and Rhode Island combined, with the tenth-largest gross metropolitan product in the world. As DFW grows, so does its need for water.

Between 2000 and 2007, the population served by the North Texas Municipal Water District (NTMWD), the utility for the seven counties north of the Metroplex, increased by half a million, to 1.6 million people. By 2060 the population of the Dallas–Ft. Worth region is expected to leap to 18.6 million, and water demands are estimated to more than double, from 1.4 million acre-feet per year to 3.3 million acre-feet per year. If no new water supplies are added, the cities face a projected shortfall of 1.9 million acre-feet per year, or more. Using revised figures, some experts believe that by 2060 DFW will have 5.5 million more residents than originally predicted, and water demands will exceed estimates by 50 percent.

"Population is just eating us up," Jim Parks, NTMWD's executive director, said. In 2008, he restricted yard watering to one day a week and signed a twenty-year contract to buy additional water from Lake Texoma, a reservoir on the Red River. But Parks, like Pat Mulroy in Las Vegas, is unwilling to take on developers and their political allies. "Limit growth? That's not what we do," said Parks. "My charge is to respond to the needs of the customers I'm committed to serve."

The other problem eating at Texas has been an extreme lack of rain. The worst drought ever recorded in Texas was in 1956, when virtually all greenery disappeared; hot winds kicked up massive dust clouds; stock tanks, creeks, and lakes ran dry; and the cattle industry was devastated. Artesian wells were opened so that desperate people could fill pails with water; swimming holes were pressed into service as makeshift reservoirs; muddy water from the Red River was piped down to Dallas.

In 2005, DFW suffered its second-driest year on record. Lake Lavon, a 21,400-acre reservoir on the East Fork of the Trinity River, and one of the main water supplies for Dallas, dropped to 38 percent of full. Cracked mud lined Lavon's shore, and bleached tree stumps jutted from stagnant pools of brown water. That year, Texas suffered $4.1 billion in crop and livestock losses. The drought continued into the next year, and the next. In 2008 almost 48 percent of Texas suffered severe drought conditions, and cattle producers lost about $1 billion, mostly because their grazing land had turned to dust and they were forced to buy feed. Between November

2008 and July 2009, nearly 80 of Texas's 254 counties faced "extreme" or "exceptional" drought, the worst levels on the US Department of Agriculture's Index, and suffered $3.6 billion worth of crop and livestock losses.

In 2009, Texas suffered a combination of record-high heat and record-low precipitation. Central and south Texas were facing the worst conditions since the 1956 drought; 230 cities, including Houston, Austin, and Dallas, set mandatory water restrictions. San Antonio suffered the driest twenty-three-month period since record keeping began in 1885. Off-duty police officers began patrolling San Antonio's streets for illegal lawn watering.

Todd Staples, the Texas agriculture commissioner, summed up the conditions with one word: "devastating." In July 2009, Governor Perry issued a disaster proclamation, and $3 billion in federal drought relief flowed to the state.

"A FOREVER SUPPLY OF WATER"

One afternoon in October 2006, T. Boone Pickens tilted his lean seventy-eight-year-old body back in an enormous brown leather chair in his Dallas office, propped his pointy-toed black cowboy boots up on a corner of his wide brown desk, and gave me an owlish look. "It's just gettin' drier and drier out there," he drawled in an amused voice. He handed me a sheaf of articles about Mesa Water, many of which were critical of his plans to suck water from the Ogallala. But they also noted that a lack of rain combined with a population boom could push Texas into an unprecedented drought.

Pickens had signed up two hundred landowners, representing four hundred thousand acres in Roberts County, to participate in a deal between Mesa Water and a thirsty metropolis willing to pay his rates. He had no buyer yet, but Pickens is a legendarily patient dealmaker.

The Ogallala Aquifer "is just surplus water," he said as he sketched his pipeline route on a whiteboard. "That water is just stranded out there, doing nothing. It's not needed in the Panhandle, which is very rough country not suited to farming. Why should I store water for nothing? You have an asset here, but it's a dead asset until you create a market for it. Meanwhile, north Texas is just exploding. Why not pipe the water out of Roberts County to help the rest? We have everything in place. Eventually, someone will need to buy our water."

Pickens figured that if he could convince DFW to spend $165 million to buy 65 billion gallons of Ogallala water a year, for thirty years, his Roberts County investments—reportedly $150 million by 2008—would net Mesa Water over $1 billion. Despite many contingencies, such as that Dallas officials remained noncommittal, Pickens crowed, "This could be the biggest deal of my life!"

He said he was motivated less by money, "which I don't need," than by the wish to help his rural Roberts County neighbors. "Our plan is attractive, and they could make about one million dollars per family. That's big. These folks are selling their water but keeping their land. I have tripled the value of their property, and they are tickled to death."

Pickens's $1.5 billion pipeline would bring water over 328 miles, from his ranch, across eleven counties and 650 pieces of private property, to DFW. Along the pipeline, he announced in 2008, he would erect "the largest windmill farm in the world" and ship green electricity on wires strung along the water-pipe corridor. (Citing transmission costs, he dropped the idea in 2009. But his "Pickens Plan" calls for the federal government to invest $1 trillion to build turbines on the Great Plains.)

The Mesa Water pipeline would cross private land. To make this feasible, Pickens will have to negotiate with hundreds of individual property owners or find another way to gain access to their land. It wasn't clear what this "other way" might be until 2007, when a change in state law made by Governor Rick Perry allowed Pickens to form a new water district, the Roberts County Fresh Water Supply District No. 1. This gave him the right to issue tax-free bonds for his water pipe and electrical transmission lines, the power to levy taxes, and, most important, to use the power of eminent domain to claim land for the pipeline. Eminent domain is a controversial legal doctrine, dating back to 1066 and William the Conqueror, by which the government can take, or force the sale of, private property "for the public good."

As the full implications of Pickens's new water district sank in, Panhandle residents reacted with "a mix of anger and awe," the local paper reported. "Many seemed stunned that such a small district could boast such broad reach." The Roberts County Water District "would not have been viable without the recent legislative changes," charged Texans for Public Justice, which opposed it. A Pickens spokesman denied any connection between Pickens's donations to state legislators and passage of the law.

In 2008, the US Department of Justice (DOJ) blocked the new law, saying that Texas had failed to prove that the measure did not harm minority voting rights. But a Mesa Water spokesman said he wasn't concerned because Fresh Water Supply District No. 1 remained unchallenged, meaning Pickens retained considerable leeway to do as he pleases. This is what concerns his critics.

Pickens's opponents fear he will poke the Ogallala with such a long, deep straw that he will suck unsustainable amounts of the groundwater from beneath the Texas Panhandle. Decrying him as a "water hustler" who would "turn the Ogallala into a Dust Bowl" for his own profit, critics—such as Ken Kramer, director of the Texas chapter of the Sierra Club—have deemed Mesa's plan "groundwater mining," the technical term for pumping water from an aquifer faster than nature can replenish it.

According to Texas's 50-50 rule, anyone who receives a new pumping permit can draw down an aquifer by no more than 50 percent over the next 50 years. The rule was put into place by C. E. Williams, who runs the Panhandle Groundwater Conservation District, which manages the region's share of the Ogallala. Mining groundwater is unsustainable, says Williams: "It's like taking dollar bills out of your bank account and putting nickels back in. Even with a big bank account, there's an end to it. That's pretty much what's happening in the Ogallala."

When I pressed the depletion question, Pickens shrugged and said, "Look, the Ogallala recharges five percent a year with rainwater. [Others claim that Texas's portion of the aquifer recharges much less, more like 0.1 percent a year.] In the four counties we're gonna pump, it never ends. I could pump it down to 50 percent and not hurt anybody. We will never pump it dry. And why would I? I live there. I've got about a hundred million dollars invested in my property—it's even got a golf course." He flashed a quick grin. "This is a *forever* supply of water."

Once a buyer is in place, Mesa will acquire the rights to sell between 200,000 and 320,000 acre-feet of Ogallala water per year, which is enough to supply 1 million to 1.5 million Texans. The four Panhandle counties—Roberts, Hemphill, Lipscomb, and Ochiltree—that would take part in such a deal sit over 81 million acre-feet of Ogallala water.

As Pickens sees it, water is like any other resource. "It's a commodity, just like oil," he said, that should be prospected and sold for profit. "I don't think you should cut off people from the Ogallala's water. Everyone deserves a bite of the apple. It will provide us with a secure, drought-proof source for the future."

In the summer of 2009, more than 60 percent of Texas suffered extreme drought. But by February 2010, El Niño weather patterns—characterized by a warming of the Pacific Ocean, and a shift in winds—had brought

WATER IN THE TWENTY-FIRST CENTURY

enough rain to lift the drought from much of the state. Mesa Water had yet to find a buyer, and Pickens had grown distracted by other projects. By then he was worth some $1.2 billion, thanks to his dominance of the West Coast natural gas–fueling business, and to the success of his BP Capital hedge fund. But it would be foolish to believe that Pickens had forgotten about water as a commodity. Through additional land purchases, he had built Mesa Vista Ranch up to sixty-eight thousand acres, which not only made him the largest landowner in Roberts County but gave him control of more permitted groundwater than any other individual in the United States.

"I'm in no rush," he said to me in Dallas. "The people who have the water want to sell it, and people will buy the water when they need it. That's the blood, guts, and feathers of the thing."

A COMMON, OR A COMMODITY?

By 2009, water was a $500-billion-a-year industry in America, and growing, according to the *Wall Street Journal*. Like oil, water has never been equitably distributed. About 50 percent of the world's freshwater is controlled by half a dozen nations. As water becomes an increasingly valuable resource, sodden nations, such as Canada and Norway, could become the wealthiest countries of the twenty-first century, perhaps even forming a water cartel, "the next OPEC." The difference between the two resources is, of course, that while oil is crucially important to the global economy, it is not a necessity and can be replaced by other fuels. Water is an essential resource for which there is no substitute.

T. Boone Pickens understands this and instinctually wants to control, or privatize, the resource "just sitting there" under his backyard. But privatized water pushes an emotional hot button in people. To some, this is just business; to others, it is a moral outrage.

Like Pickens, executives at private water companies maintain that privatizing water utilities is a socially beneficial, technologically advanced "economic good." Companies such as Suez, Veolia, and RWE/Thames manage water utilities and finance hydro-infrastructure around the world. American cities such as Lexington, Kentucky, Atlanta, Georgia, Indianapolis, Indiana, and Riverside, California, have come to rely on private water suppliers—but they have not always been happy with the results.

The debate over privatizing water sometimes teeters over into moral philosophy. Is water just another article of commerce, a "commodity" like

265

oil or natural gas to be extracted from the earth, processed, and traded in the global marketplace? Or is it a "common," a basic human right, like the air we breathe? Another question often raised is, who benefits from privatization, and who doesn't?

In the nineteenth century the majority of US water systems were run by private companies. These companies often favored the wealthy, who could afford high rates, and let the middle and lower classes suffer from impure water and poor service. Eventually, American cities bought out or took over most of the private waterworks and put them under public ownership. Since the Second World War, public water systems have supplied drinking water to 85 percent of Americans. (The remainder use private supplies, such as wells.) But shifting demographics, laws mandating clean water, aging infrastructure, and concerns about global warming have pushed many cities to consider privately run water systems, or public-private partnerships.

Private water companies first emerged in Napoleonic France, and French firms such as Veolia, Suez, and Saur have aggressively exported privatization around the globe ever since. In 2008, according to *Pinsent Masons Water Yearbook,* a water-industry bible, about 10 percent of the earth's population relied on water services provided by private companies, known as Big Water, the most successful of which still come from Western Europe. The figure is higher in cities and continues to rise overall, especially in water-short and polluted developing nations.

Big Water companies provide four basic services: collecting and purifying water, delivering it, treating wastewater and sewage, and maintaining and expanding the pumps, pipes, aqueducts, dams, desalination, and wastewater treatment plants that make up modern water systems. It can be a nail-bitingly complex job to balance the ebb and flow of people's daily tap, shower, toilet, and washing-machine use against fluctuations in water supply, water quality, the soundness of infrastructure, shifting politics, global economics, and the weather.

Water providers are doing their job well when their customers scarcely register their existence. But when tap water runs brown, people suffer from *E. coli,* broken pipes flood streets and basements, and water rates skyrocket, people suddenly grow curious about who is providing their water, and for how much.

Big Water's main selling point is, essentially, that the problem with water management is human nature. When water is given for free—as is usually the case with publicly run utilities (whose water rates cover the cost of infrastructure but not the water itself)—people waste it because they have no incentive to do otherwise. Farmers overpump aquifers and overfertilize crops; factories use wasteful processes and pollute; developers build houses with large lawns, inefficient showerheads, toilets, and washing machines, and don't fix leaking pipes; governments are often corrupt, incompetent, or simply lacking the expertise and wherewithal for complex water projects. Aside from the global elites, privatizers say, water systems are generally underfunded, inefficient, and poorly maintained, and provide bad service. But private companies, they say, have access to resources and know-how, which allows them to build and operate bigger and better water systems.

Big Water and its backers claim that free markets are the most efficient way to determine what people really want and how much they are willing to pay for it. When water is plentiful and clean, its price is relatively low, but as water becomes scarce and polluted, its value rises, and so should its price, the privatizers say. According to this theory, when prices rise, water providers earn money to reinvest in their systems, and their competition for customers incentivizes them to expand services. Indeed, competition protects consumers and promotes accountability in the marketplace: if a public water utility does a poor job, then consumers can often do little, but if a private water company does a poor job, consumers will reject it in favor of another, better company.

This argument has won favor from Albania to Bolivia to China, where municipalities are increasingly turning to private companies to fix and upgrade their systems. The rise of Big Water has been abetted by politicians from wealthy nations—particularly France, Germany, England, and Spain—who encourage poor nations to outsource their utility needs as much as possible. Big Water is also aided by major lending institutions, such as the International Monetary Fund, the World Bank, and the Asian Development Bank, which are largely staffed by free-market economists who favor privatization, and which provide loans for infrastructure projects.

But arrayed against them is a growing movement of antiprivatizers who believe that water should be treated as "a human right." Community and environmental activists say that citizens bear too much burden and see too few benefits from privatization. According to their view, privatization, especially in developing nations, leads to water monopolies that are accountable only to their shareholders. Such monopolies, antiprivatizers charge, make greater profits in times of shortage and are thus enticed to restrict water services. The activists point to a record of occasional price-gouging by water companies and note that corporations destroy ecosystems to make "unnecessary" products, such as bottled water and other packaged foods. But their greatest fear is that privatization leads to a loss of control of an essential resource: that for-profit water companies become, in essence, arbiters of life and death and make such godlike decisions based purely on an economic calculus.

"No one should be denied access to water because they can't pay for it. It's very important that we say water is not a commodity," writes Maude Barlow, a Canadian activist who is the loudest critic of privatization. Barlow has written several antiprivatization books and in 2007 was named the UN's first senior adviser on water issues. While she has agreed that the private sector should be allowed to build pipes, dams, and water treatment plants, Barlow has been adamant that the delivery of water—i.e., control of the tap—be left to public not-for-profit utilities. When the poor cannot afford private companies' rates, she said, they are forced to make a Hobson's choice: either drink contaminated water or face death by dehydration. "No one has the right to appropriate water for profit while other people are dying," Barlow writes. "Water is the most important environmental and human rights issue of them all . . . [but] you can't have a human right to water if there is no water."

This position has gained a widening audience, not only in developing countries but across the United States.

"Why does somebody need to make money on your water?" asked Dick Hierstein, the city manager of Pekin, Illinois, a small city that sold its water system to American Water Works, a private company owned by the German firm RWE AG, but then repurchased it. "Does somebody need to make money on the air you breathe? It is as simple as that."

T. Boone Pickens has a quick rejoinder to that: "People always say to me, 'Water is like air. Do you charge for air? Well, no, course not, and you shouldn't charge for water, either.' I say, 'Okay, go ahead and *don't* charge for water and see what happens. You won't have any water left.'"

Water privatizers have had some laudable successes. The city of Bucharest, Romania, where the French company Veolia took over the water system in 2001, used a combination of infrastructure repair and price incentives to reduce per capita water use from four hundred liters a day in 2001, to two hundred liters a day in 2007. But in other cases, Big Water has promised more than it could deliver or has taken advantage of people, causing protests to spring up in Bolivia, Argentina, Uruguay, Ghana, India, Indonesia, Malaysia, the Philippines, and South Africa, among other places.

The United States has had many private water successes and a few well-publicized failures. After bitter town meetings, editorials, and lawsuits, contracts with private water companies were canceled in Atlanta, Georgia, Stockton, California, and Puerto Rico. New Orleans scrapped plans to privatize its water system just before Hurricane Katrina struck, in 2005. And community groups in Lexington, Kentucky, Indianapolis, Indiana, and Felton, California, have campaigned to regain control of their municipal water systems from private firms.

In the summer of 2008, Akron, Ohio, was gripped by a debate over a plan by Mayor Donald Plusquellic to sell or lease the city's wastewater business for about $200 million. The plan was to use $75 million to pay down existing debt and the remaining funds to support student scholarships; the buyer would recover its investment through revenues from a ninety-nine-year lease. But resistance to the plan was strong from the start. Demonstrators accused the mayor of "disguising" water privatization as "a scholarship program" without explaining to voters that it would benefit "for-profit business corporations who care principally about their shareholders." Akron would have had to replace tax-exempt low-interest public financing with more expensive private financing, which would have raised the price for infrastructure improvements. In November 2008, Akron voters defeated the plan, called Issue 8, by 62 to 38 percent.

"Issue 8 would have . . . amounted to making the residents of Akron guinea pigs of a risky privatization experiment," said Wenonah Hauter, executive director of Food & Water Watch, a Washington, DC–based consumer advocacy group. "Privatization is not the cure to repairing ailing infrastructure systems. The evidence from the 86 percent of [publicly controlled] US water systems shows . . . lower costs for ratepayers. In contrast, corporations' costs are higher. . . . Indeed, the 14 percent of [private] US water utilities charge ratepayers from 13 to 50 percent more than their public counterparts."

Like big banks and pharmaceutical corporations, Big Water companies portray themselves as "boring," "unsexy," just plain old service providers and therefore not worthy of attention. In fact, they are large, sophisticated, powerful, occasionally corrupt, and increasingly lucrative operators.

Veolia, for example, the world's largest water-services provider, is a $38 billion company based in Paris, which serves 108 million people in fifty-seven countries and has seventy thousand employees. Originally called Compagnie Générale des Eaux (roughly "the general company of waters"), or CGE, the company was founded in 1853 by Napoléon III, France's last emperor. With financing from noblemen and business leaders, including Charles Lafitte and Baron de Rothschild, CGE built much of France's key infrastructure and was granted control of the water supply of Paris. Since then, it has built operations around the world and lately has targeted China and the United States for growth.

In the United States, Veolia runs municipal water systems from Tupelo, Mississippi, to Indianapolis, Indiana, and wastewater treatment plants from Woonsocket, Rhode Island, to Wilsonville, Oregon. Yet, in spite of its breadth and history, it is remarkable that Veolia remains in business.

In 1996, a debonair French investment banker named Jean-Marie Messier was named the company's CEO, and he changed its name from CGE to the more marketable Vivendi. In 2000, Messier convinced his board to use Vivendi's solid revenue and low debt to leverage the acquisition of more exciting media firms. Messier went on a dealmaking spree, snapping up TV, film, music, publishing, telephone, and Internet companies. The stodgy Vivendi water utility, which had a debt of only $3 billion, was transformed into the Vivendi Universal conglomerate, with $21 billion in debt. When I interviewed Messier in his sleek office in the former Seagram Building, in December 2001, he assured me, "Vivendi Universal is in better-than-good health." But in July 2002, Messier was forced out of the company, Vivendi's shares were downgraded to junk status, and rumors swirled that the firm might file for bankruptcy.

New management was installed and turned the company around. In a bid to raise cash, the company spun off Vivendi Environment, the original water company, which was renamed Veolia in 2003. In 2006, the company's revenues shot up 12 percent. Veolia's new chairman, Henri Proglio, was the antithesis of Messier—he claimed to have never owned a tuxedo and said that corporations must act as a positive force on the environment.

Veolia's prime competitor is another Paris-based multinational, Suez Lyonnaise des Eaux, which grew out of the group that built the Suez Canal in the 1860s. In 2007, it was ranked ninetieth on the *Forbes* list of the world's largest public companies. In 2007, Suez had water and energy projects in thirty-one countries and annual revenues of $60 billion. Suez gained notoriety when, in 1994, the former mayor of Grenoble was sentenced to a four-year prison term for accepting a $3 million bribe for privatizing the city's water system; three local Suez officials were also sentenced in the case. Suez's then CEO, Jérôme Monod—a close associate of Jacques Chirac, the mayor of Paris and later president of France—was reported to have personally finalized the deal in Grenoble. Monod was never charged and later served as Chirac's senior adviser. A second court ruling showed that Grenoble's Suez subsidiary grossly overcharged customers and used fraudulent accounting, even allowing for a rise in rates to compensate the company when people conserved water. As a result of the scandal, control of the water system was turned over to a public utility, and Grenoble's water rates became some of the lowest in France.

Suez's high-handedness in Grenoble, wrote the International Consortium of Investigative Journalists, "revealed how the privatization of water offered the perfect opportunity for personal gain and corporate graft."

In the United States, Suez owns United Water, a subsidiary that has operations stretching from El Segundo, California—where it runs the West Basin Recycling District, the largest water-recycling operation in North America—to a small treatment plant in the town of St. Johnsbury, Vermont. Most of their contracts have been renewed uneventfully. But a few have not.

In January 1999, United Water began to manage the Atlanta, Georgia, water system. The company had won the city's twenty-year contract with a surprisingly low bid of $21.4 million a year, which was about half the cost of the existing public system. The $428 million deal was the largest water-privatization contract in US history. In explaining the shift from a public to private system, Mayor Bill Campbell told the *Atlanta Journal-Constitution*, "It's virtually impossible to finance the improvements without going to . . . privatization." For Suez, the corporate strategy was to use Atlanta as a "loss leader," a high-profile deal that would entice other cities into more lucrative arrangements with United Water. "Atlanta for us will be a reference worldwide, a kind of showcase," said Suez chairman and CEO Gérard Mestrallet.

But soon Atlantans were complaining of rate increases, brown water coming from their pipes, a dearth of maintenance, and terrible customer service. (From December 1999 to February 2000, it reportedly took an average of seventy-nine days for United Water to fix a broken water main.) The company protested that Atlanta's water system was in far worse shape than it had been led to believe and that it could never hope to make money from the deal. After great acrimony, the two sides issued a joint statement in January 2003 announcing an "amicable dissolution" of the contract. United Water walked away, and Atlanta returned to a public utility. The

following year, Mayor Campbell was indicted on seven counts of racke-
teering, bribery, and tax violations involving several contractors and political supporters—including Suez's United Water, which allegedly provided
him with "undisclosed benefits," such as a $13,000 junket Campbell took
to Paris with his mistress. Campbell was convicted of tax evasion and sentenced to two-and-half years in prison. His successor cancelled United
Water's contract.

The experience of a third European water company in the US provided
an even more cautionary tale. In its 2001 annual report, RWE (Rheinisch-
Westfälisches Elektrizitätswerk) AG, Germany's biggest electricity company, hailed water as "blue gold" and the United States as "the world's most
attractive water market." Just days after 9/11, RWE paid $4.6 billion for New
Jersey–based American Water, the largest water company in the United
States, and assumed some $3 billion in debt. RWE proclaimed its long-
term commitment to reviving municipal water systems in the United States
and to aiding the nation's recovery from the terrorist attacks. In 2001, RWE
also acquired Thames, Britain's largest water company, which was also its
"most hated utility," according to the *Independent,* based on its record of
poor service and pollution. These acquisitions instantly transformed RWE
into the world's third-largest water company, behind Veolia and Suez.

But RWE quickly found that the American water business was nothing like the German electricity business. Water is heavy and difficult to
transport, which made it difficult to build economies of scale. Regulators
moved slowly, and it took the company sixteen months to gain full control
of American Water. When it finally did, RWE was shocked to discover that
rate increases to finance infrastructure improvements were not always welcomed by the communities it served. Although RWE claimed that 90 percent of its US customers were satisfied, opposition to poor service, leaks,
nonfunctioning fire hydrants, and rate hikes—reportedly as much as 2,000
percent in one community—quickly sprang up. Some people didn't like
that RWE was a private company; others, especially older ratepayers with
memories of the Second World War, didn't like that RWE was a German
company. Anti-RWE groups appeared in Charleston, West Virginia, Chat-
tanooga, Tennessee, Lexington, Kentucky, Gary, Indiana, Champaign-
Urbana, Illinois, and Monterey, California. The company was mired in
local political battles, which distracted it from building its water business.

Emblematic of the anti-RWE groundswell was the revolt in Felton,
California, a coastal town in the redwood forest. In 2002 California-
American (Cal-Am), an RWE subsidiary, bought the Felton water sys-

tem from a small private American company and announced plans to fund infrastructure improvements by raising water rates by 74 percent over three years—the town's first rate hike since 1998. This provoked outrage in the small, affluent, and well-educated community. Soon Cal-Am and RWE were besieged by a group called FLOW, or Friends of Locally Owned Water, which held dances, bake sales, and protest marches to demand that control of the water system be turned over to a public utility. Retirees in wheelchairs rolled door-to-door, collecting signatures on an anti-Cal-Am petition. Parades featured chanting seniors holding colorful antiprivatization banners. The local paper ran anti-German cartoons.

Commenting on the fracas to the *Wall Street Journal*, Catherine Bowie, an RWE community-relations manager, said, "People are just kind of weird with water."

In 2002, RWE's stock price dropped 40 percent. (This wasn't unique to RWE. According to a report by Global Water Intelligence, a water-business analyst, a $100 investment in Veolia, Suez, and RWE in 2001 was worth only $60 two years later.) In 2004, RWE pulled out of a water supply contract in Shanghai after Chinese authorities reneged on a guaranteed fixed rate of return. In 2005, RWE wrote down the value of its US water business by about $950 million. Analysts began to grumble that the company wasn't making enough money in water to justify its massive investments. By June 2006, RWE began to dismantle its global water empire, which had cost over $10 billion to build and spanned forty countries. Water is "a very local business," Harry Roels, RWE's chief executive, judged, and a global water company "just doesn't have outstanding advantages."

Many of the American towns that resisted RWE, such as Montara, California, have since "remunicipalized" their water systems. In the spring of 2008, after a six-year fight, ownership of the Felton water system was transferred from Cal-Am to the San Lorenzo Valley Water District, and rates were immediately lowered. The story seemed to end there. But a year later, as residents confronted the need for costly infrastructure improvements, the debate over how much people were willing to pay for water began roiling Felton once again.

Water supplies in Latin America are notoriously polluted or scarce, and Big Water companies, usually with government and/or World Bank assistance, have targeted the region. As always, the privatizers argue that their investments have created more clean water, jobs, and a better distribution system than people in countries such as Argentina, Chile, and Peru have ever had; in return, the companies expect to turn a profit. Since the early 1990s, tensions have grown over privatization and have occasionally turned deadly.

The debate has been framed as a clash of civilizations, or ethnicities. Indigenous people have traditionally viewed water as a "natural right," a gift from the heavens, rather than as a product. "Why should we pay for rain?" they ask.

In the first big water deal in the region, Argentina turned over the Buenos Aires water system to a consortium composed of Suez, Vivendi, Aguas de Barcelona, and several local companies, in 1993. The World Bank funded the project, which served about 10 million people, and used it as a model for similar deals in Australia, Indonesia, the Philippines, and South Africa. But cronyism, rate increases, and broken pipes led to widespread demonstrations in Buenos Aires. In 1998 Argentina was hit by a severe recession, and many people couldn't pay their water bills. Tensions ratcheted up, and in 2005 the Europeans abandoned the project. The Argentine government was obliged to step in; officials discovered that the public utility had been so thoroughly dismantled that it would take years, and millions of dollars, to reconstitute it.

The most notorious illustration of the pitfalls of privatization took place in Cochabamba, Bolivia, that country's third-largest city, located in the dry foothills of the Andes. In 1996, state subsidies aided industry and wealthier neighborhoods, but most of the city's populace—poor rural people, with little income—were not connected to the municipal water system. Instead, they paid inflated prices for often polluted water supplied by entrepreneurs from handcarts and trucks. That year, the World Bank offered Cochabamba a $14 million loan to upgrade its water system. The following year, the World Bank offered another $600 million in foreign debt relief, at a time when the country was suffering from hyperinflation. The loan package was offered under the condition that Cochabamba's notoriously corrupt and lackadaisical water utility, run by the state agency SEMAPA, be replaced by a private company. Because of the challenges of the situation, only one company bid on the Cochabamba concession. In 1999, Bolivian president Hugo Banzer signed a $2.5 billion forty-year lease with a European consortium and with Aguas del Tunari, a subsidiary of Bechtel Enterprise Holdings, a San Francisco-based engineering company. The plan was to provide drinking water to every citizen of Cochabamba and to spread electricity and telephone service throughout the region.

Problems surfaced the first week Aguas del Tunari was on the job, in early 2002. Under its contract, the company had agreed to pay down a $30 million debt incurred by SEMAPA, and to build the long-delayed Misicuni Dam, to bring more water into the city. To afford these obligations, Aguas del Tunari immediately raised water rates an average of 35 percent (and some reportedly as high as 200 percent), to about $20 a month. But in Bolivia, where the minimum wage was only about $70 a month, most people could not afford such a price hike. To make things worse, the company was largely run by engineers who appeared indifferent to the societal impact of rate hikes, or what it meant for people to go without water.

"If people didn't pay their water bills, their water would be turned off," an American manager told the *New Yorker*.

The result was a massive protest. In January 2002, peasant farmers, factory workers, and others took to the streets of Cochabamba, waving banners and barricading roads, in a series of convulsive demonstrations. The homeless, as well as college students and the middle class, joined in, denouncing Bechtel and the World Bank; even a few upper-class business owners, who had been stripped of their water subsidies, joined the protest. Cochabamba was shut down. In early February, thousands of protesters hurling rocks and Molotov cocktails clashed with police and federal troops armed with tear gas, batons, and rubber bullets. In March and April, protest leaders were arrested, but the demonstrations shut down highways and spread to other cities. President Banzer declared the nation to be under a "state of siege," suspended constitutional protections, allowed police wide latitude, restricted travel, and imposed curfews.

After a Bolivian army captain was televised shooting his rifle at a crowd of chanting demonstrators, wounding several and killing a seventeen-year-old boy, crowds erupted in anger. Aguas del Tunari officials were forced to flee Cochabamba. Banzer used this as a pretext to declare that the company had "abandoned" its lease and revoke its $200 million contract.

Bechtel responded by filing a $25 million lawsuit with the International Centre for Settlement of Investment Disputes, an appellate arm of the World Bank, for "lost profits under a bilateral investment treaty."

In 2003, Banzer and other politicians who had brokered the deal resigned or were thrown out of office. In 2006, a settlement was reached between the new government of President Evo Morales (who as a congressman had supported the protesters) and Aguas del Tunari: both sides agreed to drop claims against the other. Responsibility for the city's water returned to the state utility, SEMAPA, which returned water rates to their pre-2000 levels.

In 2007, half of the city's population of six hundred thousand remained unconnected to the SEMAPA network, and even those who did have water received spotty service, sometimes for only three hours a day. Graft, waste, and incompetence remained firmly entrenched.

Speaking to the *New York Times* in 2007, Luis Camargo, the water utility's operations manager, said Cochabamba's aquifer was being drained. Its water-filtration system was built for a much smaller population, yet the city had no choice but to use the obsolete eighty-year-old tanks and a twenty-nine-year-old section of pipe that moved water from tank to tank by gravity. The solution, Camargo said, was to develop high-altitude reservoirs in the mountains that ringed the city. But with an annual budget of only $5 million, SEMAPA couldn't afford to build the project. Instead, many of Cochabamba's poorest residents rely on small, cheap, unreliable wells or the freelance water dealers.

"I was hoping water would get here," said Rafael Rodriguez, a citizen with little good to say about either Bechtel or SEMAPA. "But it just has not happened."

Addressing the debacle in Buenos Aires, and privatization in general, André Abreu of France Liberté, a nonprofit water program, told *Vanity Fair,* "This is one of the hidden costs of privatization. It's very hard to reverse. If a poor city makes a mistake, it is worse off than when it started."

A 2006 UN report judged that privatizing water in developing countries led to price increases that were "creating social and political discontent, and sometimes outright violence." Courts in Brazil, India, and South Africa had reversed decisions by private contractors to disconnect pipes when customers didn't pay. Remunicipalization of water systems had taken place in Africa, Uruguay, Argentina, and Canada. "It now seems like this trend of increased privatization is reversing," the UN report concluded.

Perhaps the most telling development came from France, the ancestral home of Big Water. In June 2009, the mayor of Paris, Bertrand Delanoë, announced that after more than a hundred years of "private monopoly" by Veolia and Suez, Paris would remunicipalize its water services. This was greeted as near heresy. In fact, more than forty other French municipalities had shifted control of their water from private to public ownership over the preceding decade. "We want to offer a better service, at a better price," Delanoë said.

In "Private Water Saves Lives," an essay in the *Financial Times,* Fredrik Segerfeldt, of the Cato Institute, a libertarian think tank, admitted, "Many privatizations have been troublesome. Proper supervision has been missing. Regulatory bodies charged with enforcing contracts have been nonexistent, incompetent or too weak. Contracts have been badly designed and bidding processes sloppy." But, Segerfeldt wrote, such mistakes should not preclude privatization per se, only "bad privatizations." Instead, he and others argue, citizens and companies should focus on how to improve the way the marketplace deals with a commodity that is essential for survival. In addressing the issue of water as a human right, Segerfeldt noted, "Access to food is also a human right. People also die if they do not eat. And in countries where food is produced and distributed 'democratically,' there tends to be neither food nor democracy. No one can seriously argue that all food should be produced and distributed by governments." He pointed to Chile, Argentina, Cambodia, the Philippines, Guinea, and Gabon as places where privatized water systems had helped to save "many lives . . . [and] there are millions more to be saved."

A growing number of water experts believe that privatization is not a zero-sum equation. Some, such as Peter Gleick and Dr. Michael Campana, a professor of geosciences at Oregon State University, argue that a compromise would guarantee people enough free water—say, fifty liters (about thirteen gallons) per person, per day—to ensure survival. Beyond that, public or private suppliers could charge for water use, perhaps with tiered rates so that the heaviest users bear the greatest burden. This formula could be an effective middle path, so long as clear ground rules are set and oversight is rigorous. The devil, of course, is in the details. But if such a system is not instituted soon, then the hard facts of life may assert themselves.

"The idea that water can be sold for private gain is still considered unconscionable by many," James M. Olson, a leading American water-law expert, said. "But the scarcity of water, and the extraordinary profits that can be made, may overwhelm ordinary public sensibilities."

CHAPTER 24

Water and Power

THE WATER-ENERGY NEXUS—AND COLLISION

About 4% of all electricity used in the U.S. is used to move and treat water and wastewater.

—the EPA

Water and power are so closely intertwined that it is virtually impossible to manage one resource without taking the other into account. After agriculture, power generation is the greatest user of water in the world. In the United States, some 190,000 million gallons of water is used every day to produce electricity. Water is used in the production of oil, natural-gas, coal, ethanol, solar, wind, and hydroelectric power, and, especially, to cool power plants. According to the federal Sandia National Laboratories, the production of each kilowatt-hour of electricity using coal—the cheapest, most common, and one of the dirtiest fossil fuels—requires 25 gallons of water.

Americans use as much water indirectly, by turning on lights and heating their homes, as they do directly, by brushing their teeth or spraying their lawns. The simple act of running a faucet uses energy; heating tap water is responsible for 9 percent of residential electrical consumption; water treatment and distribution use about 4 percent of the nation's annual electrical output, and in some regions that number can be much higher.

As the population grows and shifts from the cool Northeast to the hot Southwest, the demand for power is surging and setting off disagreements over how much water to devote to energy. In the East, competition among the power industry, developers, and environmentalists has led to showdowns over Maine rivers, the New York watershed, and the coastal waters of Florida. In the Midwest, competition among irrigation farmers, oil-shale developers, biofuel entrepreneurs, and growing urban populations is helping to drain ancient stores of groundwater. In the Sunbelt, dozens of planned solar power plants—large, high-tech projects in the vanguard of the renewable-energy boom—will require billions of gallons of water to produce steam to run their turbines, for cooling, and to maintain solar mirrors. But in 2009 growing restrictions on water use in Nevada, Texas, and California slowed many of these solar projects. Similar confrontations over resources are rippling throughout the global economy.

The water industry itself uses a lot of energy. The collection, transportation, treatment, and distribution of water by the nation's sixty thousand water systems and fifteen thousand wastewater treatment plants account for about 4 percent of America's total electrical use, according to the Sandia National Laboratories. In a 2007 study by state agencies, California found that "water-related energy use"—i.e., moving the state's water supply across great distances, through the Sacramento–San Joaquin Delta and over mountain ranges—consumes about 19 percent of the state's electricity, 32 percent of its natural gas, and 88 billion gallons of diesel fuel a year. Energy was required for each step of the value chain, from storage to conveyance, treatment, distribution, and wastewater collection. As more long-distance aqueducts and pipelines are planned, regulators will have to factor in the power needed to build and operate them and the water costs associated with that power.

Climate change is affecting power supplies because sudden shifts in temperature lead to surges in power use, and because generators are vulnerable to drought or flood. As Lake Mead's water levels sank in the early 2000s, managers worried that the hydroelectric turbines in Hoover Dam would stop spinning. Farther down the Colorado River, a debate brewed over San Antonio's wish for billions of gallons of water to alleviate the drought in Texas, while Austin requested water to supply new power plants for its expanding suburbs. There isn't enough blue gold to satisfy both demands.

Roughly half of the freshwater drawn from sources in the United States is used by industrial cooling towers. Many older power plants use inefficient "once-through" cooling (OTC) systems, in which large amounts of water are drawn from a waterway, circulated through the system, then discharged. Of the water used to cool power plants, 2 to 3 percent is lost to evaporation, which works out to a loss of 1.6 trillion gallons a year of water that would otherwise be used by the ecosystem. As they suck water into plants, OTC systems kill fish and other aquatic organisms; when the heated water is pumped back out of the plant, it causes further damage.

During the heat wave of 2008, for instance, Texas used approximately 157,000 million gallons of water a year—enough to supply drinking water to 3 million people—just for cooling the state's power plants.

As we approach the limits of how much water can be extracted from the environment, growth may be held in check. By 2050, the US population is expected to reach 440 million, and energy demand will increase by 40 percent, according to the Department of Energy. This will require adding at least sixteen hundred new power plants. But these plants use tons of water, which may not be available unless other users are sacrificed. Most of the new growth is projected for the water-stressed West, and regulators in Idaho and Arizona have denied permits for new power plants because of concerns about water use.

Academics and politicians have grouped the two resources under a single rubric: the *water-energy nexus*. The term makes sense in theory, but in practice, the federal government has split the management of water and power among different agencies, which has led to confusion. When not handled carefully, the water-energy nexus turns into a vicious cycle of rising energy demand, dropping water supplies, and environmental degradation—known as the *water-energy collision*.

Environmental groups have seized on water as a powerful weapon to challenge the permitting of power plants. In 2004, Riverkeeper and six states sued the EPA for permitting once-through cooling in about five hundred older power plants across the country, charging that the inefficient process violates the Clean Water Act by harming aquatic life and failing to utilize the best technology available. The case, which could significantly affect the energy industry, was sent to the US Supreme Court in 2009.

In the spring of 2010, New York State refused to renew the permit for the Indian Point nuclear plant, which sits on the Hudson River, because its cooling towers used so much water, 2.5 billion gallons a day, and released it back into the river at such high temperatures that it was decimating aquatic life. Company officials said it would cost $1 billion to install a less harmful cooling system (environmentalists say it would cost far less) and would force them to raise electrical rates. But the state's refusal to renew Indian Point's permit was hardly a surprise. The EPA had first told the company in 1975 that it would have to replace its cooling system, and the plant's Clean Water Act permits expired in the 1990s. Politicians were loath to take on the power industry, and so, apparently, were regulators. For years, a series of interim agreements, licensing delays, and other obfuscations allowed Indian Point, and other power plants, to keep operating with outdated equipment.

In the meantime, new, far more efficient "closed loop" cooling technology is available. Instead of using huge amounts of water once and dumping it into waterways, the new system uses smaller amounts of water and recirculates it through cooling towers or ponds several times, which reduces evaporation and the discharge of heated water. In 2008, Pacific Gas & Electric opened the first closed-loop power plant in Antioch, California, and it cut water intake from 40,000 gallons a minute to 1.6 gallons a minute.

As our need, or desire, for energy mounts this century, new methods of extracting natural gas and oil promise to unlock previously unattainable resources and could prove a huge boon that will power the nation into the twenty-second century. But these techniques require vast quantities of water, are dirty, and come with numerous costs.

Extraction methods such as hydrofracking and retorting represent the next phase of the water-energy nexus and collision. They will force us to make difficult choices about how we allocate water. Before we do so, it behooves us to understand what is involved and what is at stake—information that energy companies are not happy to share.

FRACK WATER

A society increasingly confronted with water decision-making should at least understand the ingredients of the problem.
—Abel Wolman,
Johns Hopkins University, 1966

T. Boone Pickens has profited handsomely from his investments in natural gas. He has promoted the Pickens Plan on TV and in print ads, urging people to replace "foreign oil"—which he says "America is addicted to" and helps fund terrorists—with "cheap and significantly cleaner" natural gas. Natural gas burns 30 percent cleaner than diesel fuel and is abundant, with an estimated 4,000 trillion cubic feet of reserves in the continental United States. Running the nation's 8 million freight trucks on natural gas would cut down on air pollution and cost about a fourth of petroleum diesel, Pickens says. He and many others, including the Obama White House, have aggressively promoted natural gas as a fuel for this century, one that helps reduce global warming, creates jobs, and provides healthy tax revenues to recession-hurt states.

Yet Pickens and his colleagues don't mention one critical fact: over 90 percent of natural gas wells today use hydraulic fracturing, or *fracking*, a controversial method of accessing pockets of natural gas trapped in underground shale formations.

To frack a well is to inject a slurry of water, sand, and a mixture of chemicals at high pressure into subterranean shale, cracking open fissures, which release the natural gas; the gas then flows into a borehole to the surface. But each fracked gas well uses 3 to 8 million gallons of water, and the process has been blamed for contaminating groundwater and impacting people's health.

Although hydrofracking has been used for decades in the West, usually on a small scale, demand for natural gas is rising, and by 2008 hydrofracking had emerged as a major extraction method. Over the next two years, reports of health problems and environmental pollution associated with fracking led to scrutiny by the press, a provocative documentary film called *GasLand*, a growing sense of alarm in the public, and demands for regulatory oversight. But natural gas companies were handing out jobs and lucrative deals for the right to frack on private land. In a time of global recession, politicians found these enticements difficult to resist.

Streaming into a high school auditorium in downtown Manhattan one evening in November 2009, at least a thousand people arrived for a raucous public meeting as state regulators deliberated plans to frack in the New York City watershed, the vast and heavily protected source that supplies water to over 9 million people a day.

The mountains, fields, and forests of many upstate counties overly the vast Marcellus Shale deposit, which stretches across New York, Pennsylvania, western Maryland, West Virginia, and eastern Ohio. Estimates on the deposit's size vary, but it may contain as much as 500 trillion cubic feet of natural gas. (New York State uses about 1.1 trillion cubic feet per year.)

The stakes are enormous, with gas companies and landowners in a frenzy to capitalize on it. As gas prospectors offered increasingly lucrative leases to landowners, many rural residents lined up to offer their property in what amounted to a natural gas bonanza. Leases to frack property over the Marcellus Shale skyrocketed from $25 an acre plus royalties of 12.5 percent in 2007, to $6,000 an acre plus royalties of up to 20 percent in 2009.

Gas company representatives went door-to-door in New York State, and some people signed leases for a pittance. One poor resident of Delaware County, for instance, leased her 110 acres for $2,750 in 2007, in order to pay her taxes; two years later, she could have leased the same land for over half a million dollars. Others, such as residents of Broome County, leased their property in 2009 and were grateful for the income—over a million dollars per parcel—which helped them weather the recession.

But in the high school auditorium that November evening, city residents said they considered the potential for gas to pollute the city's drinking supply "a nightmare." Armed with stories about poisoned fish, deformed livestock, tap water that smells of gas or ignites when lit with a match, and neurological and gastrointestinal problems, the crowd at the high school—some dressed as fish or mountains—held placards saying KILL THE DRILL and hurled questions at state regulators. Politicians eyed TV cameras and whipped the crowd into a frenzy, saying things like "Why aren't the gas companies required to adhere to the Clean Water Act?" and "There is no plan on how to deal with the fracking wastewater—which is highly problematic!"

If fracking liquids, some of which are toxic, seep into the city's water supply, New York would be forced by EPA regulations to build a filtration plant, which could cost $10 billion. After a century of carefully buying property to nurture and protect its watershed, the city's Department of Environmental Protection was caught in a political bind. While Mayor Michael Bloomberg said that fracking "is not a risk that I think we should run," Governor David Paterson was intrigued by the jobs and income fracking promised.

"New York State has one of the largest deposits of natural gas in the United States," thundered one red-faced legislator that November night. "But the revenues from the gas won't even come close to equalizing the cost of a new treatment plant. Think about it!" The crowd whooped and whistled.

Similarly charged meetings have been held in the upstate towns that would be affected by fracking, as well as in Pennsylvania, Colorado, Wyoming, New Mexico, and Texas. Hydrofracking has split communities and even families.

Fracking is water intensive and dirty. A single hydrofracked well requires from 3 to 8 million gallons of water per day, the rough equivalent of a day's supply for forty thousand people (based on average US use of eighty to a hundred gallons of water per day). In 2009, the New York State Department of Environmental Conservation made a disturbing discovery. In analyzing samples of wastewater brought to the surface by hydrofracking, scientists found it to be radioactive. The water contained radium 226, a naturally occurring uranium derivative, at levels 267 times the limit safe for discharge into the environment and thousands of times the limit safe for drinking water. Tests suggest the amount of radioactivity in the water was far higher in New York than in many other places. While the state's Department of Environmental Conservation found that "well . . . wastes do not constitute a health risk," the federal EPA notes "potential risks."

West of New York City, the Delaware River runs 410 miles long and is considered one of the cleanest rivers in the East, famous for some of the best fly-fishing in the country. About 17 million people—including residents of Manhattan and Philadelphia—rely on its pristine watershed as a drinking supply. But in June 2010, the advocacy group American Rivers named the Delaware "the most endangered river in the country" because of the threat of fracking. Fears of pollution caused regulators to put a temporary moratorium on gas exploration in the Delaware basin until the matter could be studied.

Yet the temptations of natural gas are huge. An industry study released in 2010 suggested that as much as $6 billion in government revenue and 280,000 jobs could be at stake in the Marcellus Shale region alone.

In 2008, hydrofracked gas wells began to pop up all over the Appalachian town of Dimock, Pennsylvania (population 1,400). People's drinking water turned brown and occasionally exploded; pets and farm animals suddenly began to shed hair; dangerous levels of methane, iron, and aluminum were found in wells; kids grew sores on their legs; and their parents suffered frequent headaches. In 2009, the state imposed a moratorium on drilling new wells in Dimock, though existing ones can continue to be used, and fined Cabot Oil and Gas, a Houston-based energy company, $120,000. Residents fear that fracking has made their properties worthless and have banded together to sue Cabot for compensation.

In other places, such as Silt, Colorado, fracking for gas has led to even more serious health problems for people, such as Laura Amos, who developed an adrenal-gland tumor after her water was tainted by hydrofracking for gas.* Colorado gas-field workers believe that the fluids used in fracking have caused cancer, though it is difficult to prove.

Understanding the full extent of the problem has been made difficult by the secretive nature of the gas industry, and its ability to convince people such as Amos to sign nondisclosure agreements, as she did with Encana, the large Canadian gas company that drilled a well less than a thousand feet from her home.

Gas companies counter that such horror stories are simply not true or are not their fault. "In sixty years of hydraulic fracturing across the country, more than a million wells have been fracked, including fourteen thousand in New York," maintained Jim Smith, spokesman for the Independent Oil and Gas Association of New York. The process "has never harmed a drop of drinking water."

BP, the largest producer of natural gas in the United States, with over fifteen thousand natural gas wells, has been expanding through acquisitions, and predicts "a revolution in the gas fields of North America." But just as the 2010 BP oil spill in the Gulf of Mexico—which revealed shortcuts to save time and money, aided by regulators' lack of oversight—brought new scrutiny of deepwater oil exploration, so have a series of accidents in natural gas fields brought attention to the tremendous potential, and risks, of hydrofracking—including a blowout at a Pennsylvania gas well in June 2010 that sprayed gas and wastewater for sixteen hours.

According to Pennsylvania regulators, in Dimock, Cabot Oil and Gas failed to properly cement well casings, which can allow methane and other chemicals to seep out. When gas gets trapped in the headspaces of wells, it can explode. Several wells in Dimock have exploded or been tainted by gas; a house near Cleveland, Ohio, exploded in 2007 when gas infiltrated its water well; and dozens of wells in Colorado were contaminated by methane in 2008. Gas industry representatives point out that methane can be naturally occurring and doesn't always originate from gas wells. With over 450,000 gas wells in the United States, the industry says, incidents of contamination are statistically meaningless. But, as scientists study hydrofracking more closely, and Congress and states weigh tougher environmental oversight of gas drilling, the industry's arguments are being challenged.

· · ·

---

* A state investigation found that a drilling failure had probably led to the commingling of gas and water strata underground.

Natural gas accounts for about a quarter of all energy used in the United States, a percentage that has steadily grown. From 1996 to 2006, shale-gas production grew from less than 2 percent to 6 percent of all domestic natural gas production. Some analysts predict that by 2020, shale gas will represent half of total domestic gas production.

Now the boom is attracting global attention. In April 2010, Reliance Industries, a petrochemical company based in India, paid $1.7 billion for a 40 percent interest in Atlas Energy's gas fields in Pennsylvania. The United States has agreed to help China develop gas shale exploration, while fracking has ignited a debate over water contamination in Queensland, Australia. Energy companies have targeted Sweden, Poland, and Germany for the next gas bonanza.

Originally developed by Halliburton, the oil-field-services company once run by Dick Cheney, hydrofracking was introduced in 1949. But it has never been subject to federal regulation, and state regulations have been spotty. In the Energy Policy Act of 2005—the contested energy bill crafted by Vice President Cheney in closed-door meetings with oil and gas executives—fracking was granted an explicit exemption from the Clean Water Act, the Safe Drinking Water Act, and the Clean Air Act. This is known as the Halliburton Loophole. The act exempts drilling companies from having to disclose what chemicals are added to the frack water, millions of gallons of which can be pumped into the ground near aquifers during drilling.

At the national level, the EPA has undertaken an investigation of fracking, due to be finished by late 2012, as has the House Energy and Commerce Committee.

One concern is that fracking creates terrible air pollution, which is generated by drill rigs and by the trucks used to move fluids, waste rock, and supplies. According to a preliminary 2010 study of the emissions generated in fracking by Professor Robert Howarth, a Cornell ecologist, hydrofracking is dirtier than drilling for oil and possibly dirtier than mining for coal (usually considered the "dirtiest" hydrocarbon). Although his work is incomplete, due to a lack of public data about fracking, Howarth told *Vanity Fair*, "Society should be wary of claims that natural gas is a desirable fuel in terms of the consequences on global warming."

A more insidious concern is the makeup of fracking fluid, and the slurry of wastewater and chemicals that flows in and out of fracked wells. Much like the poultry integrators who refuse to reveal the recipes for the chicken feed that is polluting the Chesapeake Bay, drilling companies claim the makeup of their fracking fluids is proprietary and refuse to divulge their contents. According experts such as Dr. Theo Colborn, an environmental health analyst known for her work on endocrine disruptors, at least half of the chemicals in fracking fluids are toxic, such as benzene, toluene, boric acid, formaldehyde, and xylene. But many other chemicals used in fracking remain secret.

Shale is hard and requires intensive blasting, which can create unpredictable cracks in the rock, potentially allowing gas and toxic water to be released into aquifers. In 2010, James Northrup, a former ARCO planning manager, wrote a memo to the Otsego County (NY) Board saying that existing New York State regulations "are grossly inadequate . . . they are a prescription for disaster." He compared hydrofracking to a hydrobaric underground bomb, "a very powerful dirty bomb," in which pressures approach fifteen thousand pounds per square inch—equivalent to thirty times that of an air bomb, or to water pressure six miles deep. When shale is exploded by hydrofracking, powerful jets of fracking fluid break up rock indiscriminately for a considerable distance underground. This can allow the release of natural gas—which is made up of methane, butane, propane, and benzene—into drinking supplies, along with toxins in the fracking fluid itself. "The fracking fluid contains chemicals that would be illegal to use under the Geneva Convention banning chemical weapons," Northrup wrote. Once those toxic chemicals have entered a drinking supply, there is no way to claw them back.

If these suspicions about hydrofracking are borne out by further disclosures, then the main premise on which natural gas is being sold by Pickens, BP, and even the White House—that it is a cleaner, greener fuel—is badly flawed.

OILY WATER

Water is used to produce oil, and oil is used to produce water, but spilled oil can pollute water and harm the ecosystem. In coming decades, the two resources will become even more tightly bound, and at odds, as demand for energy increases.

To prepare for the extraction of *shale oil*, a new type of fuel not yet on the market, oil companies have developed long-term strategies in which water is a key component. Firms such as ExxonMobil and Royal Dutch Shell have bought up tens of thousands of acres of ranchland, farms, and open space—because of their water rights—in Colorado, Wyoming, Utah, and North Dakota.

Shale rock tends to be rich in kerogens, a mixture of organic chemical compounds, the soluble form of which is a heavy hydrocarbon known as bitumen. Bitumen can be processed into a petroleum product known as synthetic crude. To mine oil from shale, the rock is brought to the surface and subjected to high heat, which melts the oil out of the rock. This process, called retorting, is energy- and water-intensive: one barrel of synthetic crude retorted requires five barrels of water. According to Western Resource Advocates (WRA), an environmental group, the retorting of oil shale in Colorado will require an estimated two hundred thousand to three hundred thousand acre-feet of water annually—equivalent to the yearly water consumption of 25 million people.

The federal Bureau of Land Management (BLM), the agency responsible for managing public lands, estimates that the shale formation under Colorado, Wyoming, and Utah could yield as much as 1.8 trillion barrels of oil, an amount three times the size of Saudi Arabia's proven reserves. At peak production, oil companies could retort 1.55 million barrels of shale oil per day in Colorado, the BLM said, which would require 378,000 acre-feet of water (Denver uses 300,000 acre-feet of water annually).

But western Colorado is naturally arid, its population is growing, and water is in high demand. The nearest significant supply of water is the already stressed Colorado River. So oil companies have done what Los Angeles did in the Owens Valley and what Pat Mulroy did in central Nevada: quietly purchase property with significant water rights, in this case to prepare for the day when it is economical and technically feasible to extract synthetic crude from shale. In 2007 and 2008, Shell went on a buying spree in Colorado, shrewdly focusing on properties with "senior" water rights, those that predate the water rights of businesses, such as farms and ski resorts, and thus have legal precedence under Western water law. Shell acquired a large ranch with water rights dating to the 1860s, as well as a piece of land near Mack with a thirty-thousand-acre-foot reservoir and rights to Colorado River water. It also swapped properties with the state for land along Piceance Creek. By 2009, Shell had thirty-one conditional rights and ownership in five irrigation ditches in the Colorado and White River Basins. Shell also filed for substantial water rights on the Yampa River and began snapping up properties near Grand Junction. ExxonMobil owned forty-nine conditional claims and forty-eight irrigation ditches, mostly in the White River Basin.

Although major oil-shale production is not likely to begin until 2020, and oil companies are working to improve the water-to-oil ratio, ranchers and environmentalists worry that the industry—which has acquired 7.5 million acre-feet of water rights—will suck Colorado dry. If too much water is used to mine shale oil, they fear, the state might be liable—either because it cannot meet its water delivery obligations under the Colorado River Compact or will not meet limits set by the Endangered Species Act. Ranchers have a different worry.

"A shift of water to oil shale will dramatically change the landscape," WRA executive director Karin Sheldon warned. "It could mean an end to agriculture and to the historic economic base of these rural communities."

A few hundred miles north of the Colorado oil shale fields, tension between oil and water has been growing since the discovery of vast deposits of tar sands, another source of synthetic crude oil, in Ontario and Alberta, Canada. Tar sand consists of quartzite, clay, water, and the "tar," which is the heavy hydrocarbon bitumen (similar to what is found in shale oil).

The first commercial operation to exploit it to produce oil was established in Alberta, in 1930. Today, Fort McMurray, a small town set among rippling hills on the Athabasca River, in northern Alberta, is a tar sands boomtown. Since the mid-1990s, residents have taken to calling it Fort McMoney because companies such as Royal Dutch Shell, Conoco-Phillips, Chevron, Imperial Oil (mostly owned by ExxonMobil), British Petroleum, Total, StatoilHydro of Norway, and Suncor have poured $150 billion into processing oil from the tar sands in a fifty-seven-thousand-square-mile area—a region almost the size of Florida. These companies plan to invest an additional $75 billion in the region by 2012.

The extraction of oil from Alberta's tar sands is the world's largest energy project and is expected to contribute nearly $1 trillion to Canada's gross domestic product by 2020. The tar sands contain more oil than the fields of Kuwait, Norway, and Russia combined. If only 10 percent of Alberta's deposits are actually tapped, they still represent the world's second-largest oil reserve, after Saudi Arabia's. By 2007, output from Alberta's fields was topping a million barrels a day, making Canada the United States's number one source of imported oil. By 2015, oil recovery from the tar sands is predicted to triple. It has been estimated that the three major bitumen deposits in Alberta will eventually yield as much as 1.7 trillion barrels of synthetic crude.

But extracting bitumen from tar sands requires tremendous amounts of energy and water, and the Achilles' heel of "Canada's greatest economic project," that there might not be enough water to sustain it, is largely overlooked.

Alberta is one of the driest parts of Canada, containing only 2.2 percent of the nation's freshwater. The province lies in the rain shadow of the Rocky Mountains, where many glaciers have lost a third of their mass and snowpack has been shrinking due to a temperature rise of two to four degrees since the 1970s. Tree-ring studies show that over the millennia the region has suffered extreme droughts that have lasted up to twenty years.

Tar sand mining uses an average of three to four barrels of freshwater to produce one barrel of bitumen, with the water usually being heated to help separate hydrocarbons from the sand and clay. Although some companies recycle their water as many as eighteen times, the industry still takes great volumes from the Athabasca River and nearby aquifers. Even in a drought, the government will allow the tar sand industry to withdraw enough water to fill fifty bathtubs per second. In 2008, tar sand processing accounted for 76 percent of the water taken from the Athabasca, Alberta's longest undammed waterway. Existing licenses allow oil companies to take 3.3 billion barrels of freshwater a year, which is enough to supply two cities the size of Calgary. Planned expansions to tar sands mining could bring the total up to 4.2 billion barrels a year. But, cautioned Natural Resources Canada, this volume "would not be sustainable because the Athabasca River does not have sufficient flows."

Mining bitumen also requires vast amounts of energy and pollutes the air, ground, and water. This has already had health and social impacts on local people. Although the oil companies employ many Athabasca Chipewyan and Mikisew Cree Indians, the tribes have protested the development of their ancestral land. They worry about high rates of unusual cancers that have suddenly cropped up in their villages and wonder if toxins leaking from the mines have flowed downstream from Fort McMurray to Lake Athabasca, where Indian villagers fish.

After a scathing 2007 report by Doug Radke, Canada's former deputy minister of the environment, on Alberta's "inadequate" enforcement of "outdated and incomplete" environmental regulations for tar sands mining, the provincial government produced an interim plan to guide water withdrawals from the Athabasca River. But Alberta prides itself on a freewheeling Wild West ethos, and the development of new tar sand mine sites hasn't slowed a bit.

• • •

As US states try to cut their carbon footprints and search for alternatives to hydrocarbons, the Obama administration has considered building new nuclear power plants for the first time in decades. But nuclear power uses more water—for steam generation and cooling—than any other kind of power plant, which will have to be taken into account.

In 2007–8, a heat wave forced a power plant in Georgia to reduce its output because discharge water could not be cooled enough to stay within the environmental limit. A nuclear plant in Alabama had to shut down for a day to avoid endangering wildlife with heated discharge water. According to the Associated Press, water shortages threaten to curtail the output of up to a quarter of the nation's 104 nuclear reactors.

The debate over disposal of nuclear fuel has also been influenced by concerns about water. A federal plan to store spent nuclear fuel at a repository deep inside Yucca Mountain, about eighty miles northwest of Las Vegas, was suspended by Energy Secretary Steven Chu in 2009 because of a long-running disagreement over whether the radioactive waste would seep into groundwater there and contaminate the area.

To avoid a disastrous water-energy collision and promote a true water-energy nexus, federal and state officials will have to start managing the two resources together, as a holistic system. If they are going to keep ahead of the mineral and energy industries, which are already planning how to use water in the next century, government agencies will have to become less reactive and learn to think the way business does: long term.

CHAPTER 25

"Pop Culture in a Bottle"

PETWATER

MR. McGUIRE, TO BENJAMIN: "I want to say one word to you. Just one word. . . . Are you listening? . . . *Plastics.*"
—*The Graduate,* 1967

Manufacturing plastic water bottles consumes water and energy. So does pumping water from underground, filling the plastic bottles with water, and transporting them by truck, rail, airplane, or container ship. Sometimes water and energy are used to recycle or dispose of the bottles. Bottled water is a cultural phenomenon and one of the most popular beverages in the world, but it has also been criticized as a prime example of the misuse of resources.

In 2001, Americans drank over 5 million gallons of bottled water and spent over $6 billion to do so, according to the International Bottled Water Association. In 2007, we consumed over 8.7 million gallons of bottled water, worth $11.5 billion. And though consumption has slipped a bit, due to the global recession and changing tastes, Americans still spent $10.6 billion to drink 8.4 million gallons of bottled water in 2009.

These are phenomenal statistics for any product, but especially for one that is readily available from fountains and nearly free at home. Drinking eight glasses of water a day (recommended for health) costs 49 cents a year, if taken from a New York City tap. The same amount of water costs twenty-nine hundred times more—about $1,400 a year—if it is commercial bottled water, and bottled water adds greenhouse gases and landfill waste. But bottled water's perceived convenience and healthfulness led Americans to drink about 29 gallons of bottled water per capita per year in

292

2007. While soft drinks remain the most popular beverage overall, bottled water is the fastest-growing beverage category in the world.

The number of independent brands that have appeared in the United States in recent years is mind-boggling. They include, among others, Tibet 5100, water from Tibetan glaciers; Jana Skinny Water, from Croatia, a "no-calorie water . . . to help people lose and maintain their weight"; K9 Water for dogs, including Toilet Water (chicken-flavored), Gutter Water (beef), and Puddle Water (liver); Liquid OM, said to contain vibrations from a giant gong that promote a positive outlook; Holy Spring Water, said to be blessed by a rabbi, a priest, a monk, and a shaman; 018 Fruit Water, "extracted from Australian fruit"; Aquamantra waters, in flavors called I Am Lucky, I Am Healthy, and I Am Loved; Spiritual Water, a purified municipal water sold in bottles with ten different Christian labels, such as the Virgin Mary and the Hail Mary; and Tap'd NY, purified water from the New York City tap that sells for $1.50 per bottle and has a label promising, "No glaciers were harmed in making this water."

Among the strangest bottled waters available is MaHaLo Deep Sea water, taken from three thousand feet beneath the Pacific off the island of Kona, Hawaii. There, Koyo USA, a Japanese company, pumps seawater, desalinates it, and sells it for $5.50 a bottle. Koyo claims that its MaHaLo Deep Sea water is the purest, most nutritious beverage on earth, one that is "older than Jesus." Competitors have sprung up, and bottled water has now become Hawaii's fastest-growing export.

Then there is Bling H_2O, which comes in a corked limited-edition frosted bottle embedded with Swarovski crystals. "Either you bling or you don't bling," said the company's ebullient founder, Kevin Boyd, a Hollywood producer. In 2007, Boyd sold 750-milliliter bottles of his water (from springs in Tennessee) at his Bling store in Los Angeles for $40. The same bottle at the Tao nightclub in Las Vegas was selling for $90. "This is pop culture in a bottle!" said Boyd.

In spite of this seemingly infinite variety of boutique waters, the *real* bottled water business in America—the $10.6-billion-a-year phenomenon—is far more prosaic. It is a consolidated industry dominated by four multinational corporations with names familiar from the supermarket: Pepsi, Coke, Nestlé, and Danone.

Pepsi's Aquafina leads the market, with 13 percent, and Coca-Cola's Dasani controls 11 percent. Evian is owned by Danone, the French food company known for its yogurt, and is distributed in America by Coca-

Cola. But the biggest player in the United States is Nestlé Waters of North America (NWNA), which built a collection of springwater brands across the country that together controlled 38 percent of the US market in 2010, more than Cocoa-Cola and Pepsi combined.

Aquafina and Dasani are classified by the FDA as "purified water," which is code for tap water that has been filtered. In 2007, Nestlé introduced Nestlé Pure Life, which is also a purified water. Approximately 44 percent of all bottled water is purified water; 56 percent comes from springs or groundwater. In other words, nearly half the bottled water consumed by Americans is tap water that has conveniently been packaged in plastic.

Bottles of lightweight polyethylene terephthalate, or PET plastic, are automatically "blown" by machines from resins made from fossil fuels, usually petroleum and natural gas. In 2006, Beverage Marketing Corporation reported, Americans bought 31.2 billion liters of water, requiring some nine hundred thousand tons of plastic to bottle. Another study showed that 50 billion plastic water bottles were used in the United States that year, or 167 bottles for every citizen. To make a typical one-liter plastic bottle, cap, and packaging, according to the European plastics industry, requires about 3.4 megajoules of energy. In 2006, it took 106 billion megajoules of energy to make enough bottles to contain the 31.2 billion liters of water Americans drank.

In a widely cited editorial in 2007, "In Praise of Tap Water," the *New York Times* reported that it takes about 1.5 million barrels of oil to make the water bottles Americans used. But that number was incorrect, it turned out, the result of a misunderstanding between a journalist and a researcher. After conducting a thorough study, Peter Gleick's Pacific Institute found that it took far more oil—about 17 million barrels of oil equivalent—to produce the plastic water bottles used by Americans in 2006. That, the institute reported, was the equivalent of enough energy to fuel more than 1 million American cars and light trucks for a year. By contrast, the energy required for local tap water is typically about 0.005 megajoules per liter, or around a thousandth as much. A further benefit of tap water is that it does not produce tons of plastic litter or require enormous transportation costs.

Indeed, every ton of PET manufactured results in about three tons of carbon dioxide. The production of plastic bottles for water in 2006 resulted in more than 2.5 million tons of CO_2, a greenhouse gas.

Filling the bottles of water at bottling plants, transporting it by flatbed truck, rail, freighter, or cargo plane, used more energy. So did chilling it in store coolers and home refrigerators. The Pacific Institute concluded that the total amount of energy used for a bottle of water could be represented by filling a plastic water bottle a quarter full of oil. Because producing energy requires water, the institute concluded, every liter of bottled water sold required three to four liters of water to produce.

PET is recyclable, but the great majority of water bottles—about 38 billion a year, worth over $1 billion in 2008, by one estimation—end up in landfills. This is a terrible waste, but it is not an easy problem to fix.

In the United States, many different grades of plastic are used for beverage bottles, but in spite of well-meaning education programs, the public has yet to embrace recycling in a serious way. No national network of recycling plants that will accept a wide range of plastics exists; financial incentives for consumers to recycle are poor; and there are no national guidelines for recycling. The problem requires federal leadership to solve.

It took Western European nations years to work out recycling strategies, but many countries there now have relatively effective systems in place. In France, Italy, and Germany, governments and industry have partnered to educate the public: large multicolored containers at supermarkets or in town centers accept a wide range of products to be recycled by a network of advanced recycling plants, and compared to the five-cents-a-bottle return fee paid by a few states in America, financial incentives to recycle are much higher in Europe.

"If they can do it there, why can't we do the same here?" American activists have demanded.

US beverage companies have responded with recycling initiatives, by purchasing carbon credits, and by developing thinner bottles that use less plastic. Although biodegradable, corn-based plastic bottles exist, their shelf life is limited, and they tend to go soft in the sun. For better and for worse, PET lasts almost infinitely.

After growing at a rapid clip, about 5 to 15 percent a year, bottled-water sales in the United States declined for the first time in thirty years in 2008. But not by much, only about 1 percent, a barely perceptible drop. In 2009, bottled-water revenues declined another 5 percent and volume dipped 2.5 percent.

Bottled water now faces a backlash against its economic and environmental costs. Some consider it a luxury, while others object to the amount of water the bottlers take from aquifers, the energy used to transport heavy water from Fiji or the Alps to America, the plastic used in bottles, and the carbon footprint of the product.

WHAT IT MEANS TO BE FROM MAINE

Beneath the dark green fir trees, wide ocher fields, and rolling purple-blue mountains of western Maine lie deep aquifers filled with billions of gallons of pristine water. The state gets an average of 24 trillion gallons of rain a year; about 50 percent of that runs off into rivers and lakes, 30 percent evaporates, and 20 percent—or 2 to 5 trillion gallons—filters through bedrock or glacial sand and gravel deposits and collects underground. The Maine Geological Survey has mapped over thirteen hundred square miles of aquifers, which are annually recharged by 240 billion gallons of precipitation. Maine's water is consistently ranked at, or near, the highest quality in the nation.

Since Hiram Ricker built a spa here in the mid-nineteenth century, the Poland Spring Water Company has advertised its wares as "the best tasting water on Earth . . . since 1845." Poland Spring bottled water is undeniably refreshing. To my palate, it doesn't taste particularly good or bad; it tastes like what it is: purified springwater. It lacks that distinctive minerally flavor water aficionados prize. But the water Poland Spring sells is clearly what most Americans want: it is the bestselling springwater in the nation, and the third-bestselling water brand overall, behind Aquafina and Dasani. Poland Spring is the largest bottler in Maine and uses about 700 million gallons of water annually—enough to cover the Mall in Washington, DC, to a depth of six feet.

About thirty miles away from Poland Spring, in the town of Hollis, sits an enormous industrial building in what used to be a potato field. Inside the gleaming half-million-square-foot highly automated factory, seven bottling lines produce some 900 million PET bottles a year and fill them with water directly from a spring. The water has been filtered, treated with ultraviolet light, and inspected, remaining untouched by human hands. This is the largest water-bottling plant in North America. It produces 65 million cases a year. At the rear of the building are double-stacked pallets, loaded with 24 million bottles—2.5-gallon jugs, half-liter and half-pint bottles, and eleven-ounce "Aquapods" for kids—spread over six acres and extending eight feet high. This virtual sea percolated through the aquifer beneath the plant only a few days earlier and will soon be trucked throughout the Northeast and replaced by the next plastic-encased virtual sea. The plant processes water twenty-four hours a day, every day of the year.

Poland Spring's advertising slogan is "What it means to be from Maine." But as the dimensions of the Hollis facility indicate, the company is no longer a homespun, family-run operation. In 1980, Poland Spring was bankrupt when Perrier purchased it; a dozen years later, Perrier and Poland Spring were taken over by Nestlé, the largest food-products company in the world, based in Switzerland. Some Mainers welcomed the multinational for the jobs it brought; others resented it as a greedy corporate interloper.

"As oil is to Saudi Arabia, water is to Maine. And Nestlé wants to control it," said James Wilfong, a resident of Stow, near Poland Spring.

In December 2004, H_2O for ME, a citizens' group led by Wilfong, questioned why Poland Spring has the right to take state water without having to bid for it or pay much for it. "We spent twenty-five years, and millions of dollars, cleaning up the groundwater in this state," said Wilfong. "I was part of that effort when I served in the legislature in the seventies. We made sure every single underground gas tank in the state was dug up, and polluted ground near aquifers was remediated. That took a lot of work, let me tell you. And after all that, to say we citizens don't have an interest in our own water? I don't think so."

In 2004, H_2O for ME launched an initiative to impose a first-in-the-nation 19.3-cents-per-gallon tax on the water that Poland Spring pumped. Based on the Alaska Permanent Fund, which puts oil-extraction fees into a public trust, a portion of Maine's water fees would be used to enhance the state's environmental protections, while a larger percentage would be invested in small businesses, to grow the state economy. The idea had nationwide—perhaps worldwide—implications. Over the winter of 2004, Wilfong and an army of volunteers worked to get the 50,700 signatures required to put the issue on the ballot. Momentum built slowly. Wilfong's allies complained bitterly about Nestlé's fleet of fifty to one hundred silver tanker trucks that rumble through town at all hours, and the resulting road wear and traffic accidents. Others griped about Maine's water being siphoned off by "foreigners" who enjoyed large tax breaks; still others muttered darkly of alleged bribery, quiet secret land deals, and influence peddling—claiming that "the long tentacles" of Nestlé had co-opted the state. (I have seen no evidence to support these claims.)

Meanwhile, Kim Jeffery, CEO of Nestlé Waters North America (based in Greenwich, Connecticut, incorporated in Delaware), unleashed a PR offensive. Flying to Portland, Jeffery hired Maine's leading law firm and the former state geologist as consultants—or, as Wilfong charged, "to take them off the table, so we couldn't use them." Jeffery argued that with all the rain that Maine gets, Nestlé's withdrawals were too small to have any negative impact on aquifers, and, besides, they were renewable. He stressed that Poland Spring plants were "clean, modern, and environmentally responsible" operations that provide well-paid jobs and give generously to their neighbors. He said that H_2O for ME and other groups were a "threat to jobs" and that their proposed "$100 million tax" would exceed Poland Spring's annual profit and could very well "drive us out of Maine."

Wilfong stiffened his resolve. "Nestlé is very sophisticated," he told me. "They say, 'What's good for Nestlé is good for Maine.' They've been tossing money at the big environmental organizations, who have remained curiously silent on the water issue. They give money to local schools and volunteer fire departments. You need books at the library? A new sign on the road? How about a cross-country ski trail? Nestlé is happy to help. This is how they have worked their way into local water districts. They do the same thing all across the country. How can local people fight against *that*?"

The dispute over Poland Spring exposed social fissures in Maine, pitting blue-collar workers against the increasing numbers of retirees, environmentalists, and white-collar baby boomers moving to the state. The commissioner of the state Department of Conservation said that Maine has "an endless supply of water." Governor John Baldacci equated Poland Spring to L.L. Bean as a promoter of Maine as a symbol of quality to the nation.

In early 2005, Wilfong's petition drive failed. In 2007, he and his allies proposed a new system that would give the state greater control in monitoring and controlling its water and would require water companies to bid against one another for the right to sink new wells, with proceeds going to the state. Poland Spring and Governor Baldacci pushed back hard against the plan. But the debate led to a discussion in the state legislature, which resulted in greater transparency about water-bottling operations, and enhanced data collection about the impacts of the growing business on aquifers and wells.

The question of who owns groundwater has only recently been debated in the eastern United States, which doesn't have the West's long history of water wars. "We have the 'absolute dominion' rule here, which, like in Texas, means that even though surface water is protected, you can pump all the groundwater you want, regardless of the impact on your neighbors," Wilfong explained. "It's an ancient relic from the age of hand pumps, and most states have abolished it. We should go to 'reasonable use' laws for water, like in New Hampshire and Vermont. But so far we haven't. The state legislature has disregarded its own studies and refused to put our water in a public trust."

New Hampshire and Vermont have tightened restrictions on large-scale water withdrawals, while anti-bottled-water groups in Michigan and California have proposed similar bills for those states.

In 2005, Nestlé submitted an application to build a Poland Spring trucking facility in Fryeburg, Maine, near Wilfong's home. If approved, fifty tanker trucks would fill up there every twenty-four hours and drive along Route 302, a narrow, undulating country road where the tarmac is in poor condition. Alarmed by this perceived incursion, a group of Frye-burg citizens hired an attorney and filed an appeal. In 2006, the town's zoning board denied Nestlé's permit. The company responded by filing a countersuit against the citizens of Fryeburg and the protest group; not content with that, Nestlé then filed suit in state supreme court. The two sides traded legal broadsides through 2007 and 2008, during which Nestlé was denied a permit to build a Fryeburg pumping facility three times. Finally, in March 2009, the Maine supreme court ruled in favor of Poland Spring and cleared the way for a Fryeburg pumping station. "One town after another is falling to Nestlé," lamented Wilfong.

By 2010, Poland Spring owned 5,500 acres of land and operated twenty wells in Maine. A third bottling plant, near Kingfield, had opened, and the company's water hunters were on the lookout for new sources. "Things have quieted down," said NWNA's Kim Jeffery. "We've invested millions into Maine, pay our taxes, and are totally transparent with communities."

Jim Wilfong predicted that the state supreme court had launched Maine down a slippery slope. "I see this huge demand for water growing world-wide," he said. "Pretty soon it's not going to be just companies like Nestlé that take our water away in little bottles. It's going to be railroad-tanker-trains-ful. It's going to be pipelines. Shiploads. Let's face it, the world needs water, and Maine's got it. I don't know *when* this will happen, but I know it *will*. And we citizens, apparently, cannot control it."

"A TRAIN SPEEDING OVER A CLIFF"

Bottled water can cost between 240 and 10,000 times as much as tap water, the Natural Resources Defense Council (NRDC) found. Bottled water even costs more per gallon than gasoline, as Gustave Leven, the former chairman of Perrier, noted with satisfaction: "It struck me that all you had to do was take the water out of the ground and sell it for more than the price of wine, milk—or, for that matter, oil."

A 2005 study by the World Wildlife Fund discovered that a $2.50 bottle of water shipped from a "pure European aquifer" is no healthier or tastier than water from a city faucet. While providers of public water, which are overseen by the EPA, are required to post the bacteriological and chemical content of their water, producers of bottled water—which is considered a "food product" and is overseen by the Food and Drug Administration—are not required to list such information on their labels. Many bottled waters have labels, but they list things such as "Zero grams of fat, cholesterol, sodium, carbohydrates, dietary fiber, sugars, protein, vitamin A, vitamin C, calcium, and iron." This is not only meaningless and unhelpful, it's confusing to the consumer.

In France or Italy, water is prized for what minerals are in it; in the United States, we prize water for what is not in it. All waters (except distilled water, which is not healthful to drink) contain some minerals, such as naturally occurring salts. Minerals give water its distinctive flavor. In Europe, each brand of "mineral water" proudly proclaims a specific taste, mineral content, laxative power, level of calcium (which helps strengthen bones), and so on. The FDA allows bottlers to say that an American springwater has "0 sodium," which is not accurate. In an effort to feed their children the "purest" food available, some parents mix bottled water with infant formula, unaware that the high mineral content of certain bottled waters makes them unsuitable for infants, or the elderly.

The FDA also does not require bottlers to explain where the water comes from, how the water was purified, the results of water-quality testing, or where such information might be found. There is virtually no oversight of the design of water labels, which usually feature a misty grotto, a snowy peak, or a dense rain forest—images that conjure up pristine aquifers far removed from polluting civilization—when in fact the water is taken from municipal supplies, e.g., the taps of non-Alpine Los Angeles, New York, or Texas.

Questions about the purity and source of certain bottled waters have occasionally led to a loss of consumer confidence. In 1990, Perrier was found to contain excess benzene, which led to a costly and embarrassing recall. Other bottled waters have been found to contain mold, algae, glass, fecal coliforms, and—in Texas in 1994—crickets. In 2007, Pepsi was pilloried for identifying the source of Aquafina water as "P.W.S."; now its labels explain that means "public water source"—aka tap water.

Most controversially, the definition of springwater has been modified numerous times. What is a spring? Technically, it is a water source that originates from underground that is not directly influenced by rain or runoff. In 2003, Poland Spring faced a class-action suit alleging its water was not springwater but "treated groundwater," a seeming splitting of hairs but an important legal and marketing distinction. Without admitting fault, Nestlé agreed to settle the case with a $10 million payment to charity.

Protests against bottled water periodically flared in big cities and on college campuses, but the movement gained national attention when Alice Waters, the celebrated chef of Chez Panisse, a restaurant in Berkeley, CA, joined Corporate Accountability International's "Think Outside the Bottle" campaign, to encourage restaurants and cities to eschew bottled water in favor of tap. She objected to a multitude of sins: corporate ownership of water resources; the use of plastic bottles; the quality of the water in bottles; the many hidden costs of pumping, shipping, storing, and serving bottled water; and the carbon footprint created by shipping heavy loads of water over great distances.

"Bottled water is a blight on the globe—it's a train speeding over a cliff!" she told me. "We have to stop using up all of our resources and get off that train. I know that restaurants are certainly making money on bottled water, no question. But you have to balance these things out. For me, it's become a matter of principle."

Chez Panisse used to serve San Pellegrino, an Italian mineral water, by the caseload. But as of late 2007, the restaurant has used only filtered tap water, which it serves in glass decanters. Other restaurants in the Bay Area have done the same thing. Like New York, San Francisco has such high-quality water (from Hetch Hetchy) that it doesn't have to filter it. Alice Waters filters all the water used at Chez Panisse "just to be sure" and bought a machine that adds nitrogen bubbles for those who prefer their water fizzy.

When I asked what prompted her to sacrifice San Pellegrino, which was a popular moneymaker, Waters explained that bottled water took up a lot of storage room, but the main reason was that "San Pellegrino was bought by Nestlé. They want to portray themselves as 'environmentalists,' but I just can*not* take Nestlé's money. They give with one hand and take with the other."

Kim Jeffery, CEO of Nestlé Waters North America, disputed this. "I called her and said, 'Alice, if you're attacking bottled water for its carbon footprint, how come you're bringing all those wines from Italy? [Sonoma] has great wines close to you. Why not use them? And if you don't want to bring water from Europe, why not use a local brand?' " Waters, he said, replied, "Italian wine prices are just *so* good, we can't *not* use them." Jeffery harrumphed, "C'mon, man, that's not a serious response."

He characterized Waters's stance as typical of well-intentioned but ill-informed anti-bottled-water activists. "In America we get a little bit of information and we want to save the world, but we don't attack the root problems," said Jeffery. "We should not try to adjudicate who's got a license to operate their business. We should focus on using less resources in general. That would make a lot more difference than boycotting bottled water."

Alice Waters has inspired other restaurateurs, such as Mario Batali and the Bastianich family, whose restaurants, such as Del Posto and Babbo, serve tap water in New York. But not everyone is convinced. Drew Nieporent, whose Myriad Restaurant Group operates Nobu, Tribeca Grill, Corton, and many other restaurants in New York, Miami, Las Vegas, and California, said, "The politics are taking over. Whether it's serving foie gras, or veal, or bottled water, there's all this shouting. As a restaurateur, what am I going to do—*not* sell wine because it has sulfates in it? That's crazy! The fact of the matter is, the public wants wine from France, and it wants bottled water. And guess what? We're making money on it. Personally, I like the convenience. At home in New Jersey we have terrible municipal water. So we have a big dispenser of Poland Spring—even the dog drinks it. I think the anti-bottled-water stuff will blow over."

Indeed, many restaurateurs rely on the bottled water markup to help cover their rent. Clark Wolf, a Manhattan restaurant consultant, walked me through the math. If a restaurant can buy water for, say, $.98 a bottle wholesale and retail it for $6 to $8 a bottle (prices shift constantly)—or more, such as the $90 a bottle Bling can charge for its water in Las Vegas—the appeal is obvious. "I'd estimate that the restaurant industry takes in about $200 to $350 million a year from bottled water," Wolf said in. "That's a lot of money. So I'm not surprised that all chefs are not jumping on Alice Waters's bandwagon."

But the anti-bottled-water campaign has gained. In 2007, Tappening, an activist marketing group, created a series of ads asserting falsehoods such as "Bottled Water Causes Blindness in Puppies" and "Bottled Water Makes Acid Rain Fall on Playgrounds," with the tagline "If bottled water companies can lie, we can too." In 2008, the US Conference of Mayors adopted a resolution to bring attention to the issue. New York launched an ad campaign to promote the benefits of tap water; Boston and Salt Lake City signed on to the campaign, and San Francisco banned city-funded purchases of bottled water. Faith-based groups, such as the National Coalition of American Nuns, have joined the anti-bottled-water campaign in the belief that water, like air, should be considered a God-given resource that should not be sold for profit. "Our faith tells us to be just and not exploit the poor," said Sister Mary Ann Coyle, who regards drinking bottled water "a sin." In 2010, Congress considered a bill that would impose a 4 percent tax on bottled water to pay for improvements to municipal water systems, after a broken water main left 2 million Massachusetts residents without potable water.

In the mid-2000s, Nestlé's water business saw annual growth rates of 15 percent a year, as Americans' per capita consumption of bottled water spiked from sixteen gallons in 2000 to twenty-nine gallons in 2007. But its US sales fell 13 percent, to $4.2 billion, between 2007 and 2009. The company's efforts to open new bottling operations have been contentious in some parts of the country. After six years of attempting to use a spring in Northern California, Nestlé bowed to critics and left. It took six years of litigation for the company to reach a settlement over using a spring in Michigan, and it had to agree to forty-four conditions before it was allowed to use a source in Colorado. In 2010, Nestlé was fighting activists over the use of springs in Oregon and Idaho.

Kim Jeffery of NWNA bristled at the criticism and complained that emotion had clouded the facts. A typical Nestlé plant, he says, draws 150 million gallons of water annually—about the same as a golf course or a large farm—and is too closely watched by state regulators for it to deplete water supplies. "We use less water per gallon of finished product than any other beverage," Jeffery said. "Soft drinks use three gallons of water to make one gallon of soda. Beer uses a four-to-one ratio. Milk and hamburgers use a lot more. Agriculture uses seventy percent of the nation's water. We use an infinitesimal amount compared to them. Let's not attack the ass end of the elephant here."

As for the plastic problem? "Thousands of beverages come in plastic bottles—Gatorade uses a thick plastic bottle that weighs five times what Nestlé bottles do. Has anybody suggested that we should stop drinking Gatorade? I don't think so." The half-liter bottle Nestlé introduced in 2010 is the lightest on the market, using 9.1 grams of plastic instead of the usual nineteen grams, representing a 20 percent reduction in plastic. "Recycling is something we take very seriously," said Jeffery. "But why should bottled water carry the whole load? If you want to get serious about plastic, you need to look at the entire packaged-food business."

It is a fair point, and it gets at a deeper issue.

Society has prized convenience over all else and has been willing to pay exorbitant amounts for seemingly cheap, healthful products such as bottled water. But today, as Americans contend with a soft economy, have taken an interest in high-quality food, and have adopted a less consumerist and more environmentally aware lifestyle, the value—perceived and actual—of bottled water is shifting. Only a few years ago, Hummers and Marlboro cigarettes were status goods; now they are regarded as symbols of poor judgment, at least among the intelligentsia. Bottled water hasn't quite fallen into that category yet, but it runs the risk.

As Robert Glennon, a water-law expert at the University of Arizona, notes, "The problem of bottled water is it's a new, unexpected, and hundred-percent consumptive use—unlike irrigation, for instance, which allows some water to return to the soil. Once you put water in a bottle, it's gone. Because of this, it raises the issue in the most profound way: 'Whose water is it?'"

The latter is an essential question, and it lies at the heart of the growing resource wars gripping many parts of the country. In Alaska, which is proud to identify itself as a "resource state," the water needs of the mineral, fishing, and fuel industries have collided in a struggle that made national headlines, thanks in part to Sarah Palin's involvement, and has global implications.

CHAPTER 26

The Battle for Bristol Bay

Perhaps it was God who put these two great resources right
next to each other, just to see what people would do with them.
—John Shively, CEO of Pebble Ltd. Partnership

A FLASH IN THE PAN

In the fall of 1986 a bush pilot named Tim La Porte picked up a crew of
Canadian geologists from a remote spot between Lake Clark and Lake
Iliamna, near Bristol Bay, on the Alaska Peninsula. As he pushed the
throttle forward, his Cessna 206 floatplane lifted off the water with a roar,
and the pilot turned to the lead geologist, Phil St. George, to ask a fateful
question: "Whatcha been lookin' for out here?"

St. George eyed La Porte. Experienced geologists, like experienced fishermen or poker players, tend to go monosyllabic when asked what they
are seeking. But the two had known each other for years, and St. George
eventually offered, "Coloration in the ground."

"Like an orangey-green color?"

"Mmm-hmmm."

"Shoot, I know a place like that right around the corner." Banking the
Cessna around, La Porte said, "Let me show you. Won't take but a coupla
minutes."

The spot of colored ground La Porte had in mind was only about five
miles from the geologists' camp, near a hilly area between the Koktuli
River and Upper Talarik Creek. It was known as Pebble Beach. A large caribou herd had established itself there, and La Porte had flown hunters up
to Pebble dozens of times. As they drifted over Frying Pan Lake, La Porte

pointed off his port wing, where the lower slope of hillside had an orange-and-green cast. Then he pointed off the starboard wing, where a bigger hill also showed distinctive streaks of color along its flanks.

"What's it mean?" La Porte asked.

The geologist took in the view, nodded noncommittally, and said, "It means there could be a mineral deposit under the surface." Then he stared out the window.

La Porte shrugged and set a course back to the town of Iliamna, on Lake Iliamna. "It was no big deal," he recalled. "Phil just looked out the window. He didn't jump up and down or say much of anything. I really didn't think any more about it."

On Thanksgiving Day, not long after the flight, St. George and a crew returned to the colored hillsides by Pebble Beach—the land is owned by the state and is between Lake Clark and Katmai National Parks—where he staked out a mining claim on behalf of Cominco Alaska Exploration (CAE), a Vancouver-based mineral company. In 1988, St. George took a drill rig up to Pebble, sank a few holes, and hit more than one vein of high-grade gold. The following year he sank more drill holes and found traces of copper.

He had no way of knowing the enormity of the forces that he had set in motion because he had no way of knowing that this was one of the richest mineral deposits in the world.

Bristol Bay is an austere, silvery-gray expanse of briny water that lies 180 miles southwest of Anchorage, between Cape Constantine to the north, and the Alaska Peninsula to the south. It is fed by five major rivers and empties into the Bering Sea, south of the Arctic Circle. The terrain is green, yellow, ocher, and often snow-streaked, with wide, flat tundra, rolling hills, and dark, sharp-edged mountains. It is stunningly beautiful, home to Native tribes that have lived off the land for three thousand years, and is endowed with a rich trove of natural resources—including the last pristine salmon fishery in the world, fifteen species of whale, and four migratory flyways that bring birds from Africa, Asia, the Pacific, and the Americas, making it one of the most diverse avian habitats on the planet.

As the human demand for minerals, food, and energy rises to new heights, Bristol Bay has become the focal point of a resource war—pitting constituents for each resource against each other and against those who oppose commercial development of the ecologically rich zone. At the heart of the controversy is water: how much of it could be used, how it could be used, and what could end up in it.

By the time I arrived on the Alaska Peninsula in the summer of 2008, geologists had revealed that the Pebble Deposit—which sits on state-owned land—holds the single richest load of copper, gold, and molybdenum (used in alloys for armor-plating and airplane parts) ever discovered in the United States. As exploration of the site continues, estimates of the resources in the deposit have steadily been revised upward. As of 2010, Pebble was said to contain at least 80.6 billion pounds of copper, 107.4 million ounces of gold, and 5.6 billion pounds of molybdenum, in addition to "commercially significant" amounts of silver, rhenium, and palladium. These minerals are estimated to be worth some $250 billion to $500 billion, and perhaps more.

Since 2002, a multinational group called the Pebble Limited Partnership (PLP), a partnership between Northern Dynasty Minerals and Anglo American PLC, which owns the mineral rights to 153 miles of mining claims around the site, has spent close to $400 million conducting soil and seismic tests, monitoring groundwater, and drilling over eight hundred exploratory boreholes up to a mile deep, in preparation for mining the site. If the Pebble mine is built, it will become the largest in North America and one of the largest mines in the world. Its giant open pit would spread nearly two miles wide at the top and sink over seventeen hundred feet deep at the bottom. (The Empire State Building, at 1,250 feet high, could easily fit inside.) It would bring thousands of workers to what is now a remote and largely uninhabited region, and the mine could operate for fifty to a hundred years. To extract minerals from the Pebble Deposit, at least 8 billion tons of rock would be crushed, of which only 0.6 percent would be useful ore. The remaining 99.4 percent of the tailings, or waste rock, would be deposited in massive dumps and covered with water "in perpetuity," to prevent toxic chemicals in the tailings from reacting with oxygen and creating sulfuric acids. The water and tailings would be contained behind five massive dams, including one of the tallest dams in the United States, at 754 feet tall, and the tallest earthen dam, at 740 feet tall, both of which are taller than the Three Gorges Dam in China (607 feet high).

The immense cost of building these facilities is not the only hurdle to building Pebble mine. Also standing in the way are a series of state environmental permits, the possibility of federal intervention, and a rising wail of protest that has reached around the globe.

Pebble's supporters argue that the mine will create well-paid jobs in an impoverished region; it will generate large tax revenues for the state; and it will provide significant amounts of precious metals, which will lessen

America's reliance on foreign supplies. Environmental protections and safety measures at the mine will be state-of-the-art, PLP has promised.

But Bristol Bay is a special place, a natural jewel that is home to one of the last pristine salmon habitats left in the county, and the mine's critics believe that PLP's promises are too good to be true. The risks of destroying such an ecologically rich zone are too great, detractors say, and they would like the federal government to step in and preserve the region as a wildlife sanctuary or national park.

Opposition sprang up in the early 1990s, almost as soon as the mine was announced. A loose collection of Natives, fishermen, environmentalists, academics, cannery operators, ordinary citizens, NGOs, state legislators, and businessmen began to ask pointed questions about the size and impact of the project. They were concerned that an earthquake from nearby faults could destroy Pebble's massive dams, unleashing a wave of toxins. They wondered how the mine's explosions and giant rock crushers would affect the caribou and moose herds that Natives rely on for food. They fretted that new roads and power lines and people would destroy the delicate tundra. Most of all, they worried about how much water Pebble would use and what sorts of toxins the mine could release into local waterways.

"If our people knew that Pebble would truly benefit them, with no risk to the environment or water, then I think they'd listen," said Lisa Reimers, a Yupik woman on the board of the Iliamna Development Corporation, a for-profit Native corporation that is working with the PLP. To the Natives who live near the mine site, Pebble represents the possibility of a steady income and an enhanced, modern way of life, but many Natives are ambivalent about the mine, fearing it could spell the end to their traditional lifestyle. "We are a small community. We are not wealthy. We are fishermen. But fishing is not sustaining our community," said Reimers. On the other hand, she added, "The mine is a complete unknown, and people are not sure about it."

Alaska is proud to define itself as a resource state. But in Bristol Bay, two of its defining resources, minerals and fish, have come into direct conflict on a large scale. While the mining giants behind PLP have defined their claim, many smaller exploration companies are sampling the area nearby for precious metals. If Pebble is permitted, dozens of other companies will file mining claims, which will radically change the region. The oil and gas industries are also hoping to drill offshore in Bristol Bay.

Pebble has created deep schisms, splitting families, disrupting state politics, and, thanks to Sarah Palin's involvement, making national headlines during the 2008 presidential election. While many Native Alaskans are tempted by the mine's jobs, many others are troubled by Anglo American's record in South Africa, where ten thousand local people were allegedly moved from two villages to make way for an Anglo platinum mine (the company blamed local officials and denied it had told police to use force against protestors). In 2009, a delegation of Native elders flew to London to protest the Pebble project outside Anglo American's annual meeting. A few months later, environmental activists dressed up as salmon protested the Pebble mine outside Congress in Washington, DC. Activists pressured Tiffany & Co, Fortunoff, and prominent independent jewelers in the United States and England not to use gold extracted from the Pebble mine.

The debate over Bristol Bay, with its wide implications for the US and the global economy, mining, and water politics, is being closely monitored by investors and environmentalists in Anchorage; Vancouver; Ottawa; Seattle; New York; Washington, DC; London; Zurich; São Paulo; Johannesburg; Melbourne; Bombay; and Tokyo.

Lying about a hundred miles upstream of Bristol Bay, the Pebble site is spongy and wet. Forty inches of rain and snow falls there annually, and so much groundwater surrounds the deposit that it is difficult to quantify. Indeed, the site is so remote and physically challenging that the government has never attempted to map it. As you fly overhead, long blue-black lakes and brown ponds glint in the sun, kettle holes dot the landscape, braided streams cut across the tundra, and rivers crash between blue-white glaciers and steep ravines. All the while gravity pulls trillions of gallons of nutrient-rich freshwater into Bristol Bay.

Every June, some 60 to 70 million salmon flow into Bristol Bay to spawn—the largest number of salmon to spawn in any drainage area in the country. This tsunami of fish is a highly anticipated event around which the entire ecosystem is scheduled. Ichthyologists, commercial and sport fishermen, lodge owners, cannery operators, floatplane pilots, former governor Sarah Palin, the rare freshwater seals in Lake Iliamna, bears, eagles, wolves, gulls, fish, and even the forests look forward to the annual influx of protein. As the salmon die at the end of their journeys, their rotting carcasses flush nutrients into rivers that support aquatic life and fertilize the areas alongside those streams.

Aside from oil and gas, fish are Alaska's biggest export. The fishing industry is the state's largest employer, accounting for more jobs than mining, oil, gas, forestry, and agriculture combined. By 2001, some fifty-four thousand people earned all or part of their annual income from fishing in Alaska. Yet mining is a not-inconsiderable business, too, employing some fifty-five hundred Alaskans, many of whom are Native. When it comes down to whose interests will prevail, the mineral industry is better organized and has a lot more money and clout than fishermen do.

Hard-rock metal mining is water-intensive, and the fishing industry is deeply suspicious of the impact Pebble could have on the water around Bristol Bay. In 2006, Northern Dynasty (now part of the PLP) applied to use some 35 billion gallons of water a year, more than the annual consumption of Anchorage, to process minerals, run operations, and store toxic tailings. Critics believe that the withdrawal of such a tremendous volume of water will harm the caribou, elk, moose, bear, fox, birds, plants, fish, and humans that rely on it. They also fear the two likeliest sources of water pollution: acid mine drainage, which is the outflow of acidic water from hard-rock mining, and poisonous chemicals used to leach gold from crushed rock, which could slip into local waters.

The geology around the Pebble Deposit is complex and allows surface water and groundwater to intermingle. If metals extracted from the mine, particularly copper, or a toxin used in the mining process, such as cyanide or arsenic, enters the water in one place, it could easily reemerge in another place, and flow downstream into Bristol Bay.

Copper and fish, particularly salmon, do not mix well. Salmon have a keen sense of smell that they rely on for navigation and to identify predators, prey, kin, and mates. As they return to their natal streams, salmon follow telltale chemical signatures in the water. Copper is naturally occurring, but if present in just two to ten parts per billion over natural levels, it acts as a neurotoxin. Copper can disorient salmon, impair their immune system, or kill them. "Copper is *the* most toxic element to fish, even at very low levels, and salmon are some of the most sensitive fish around," said Carol Ann Woody, a former USGS fisheries biologist. "If the state permits the Pebble mine, it will be putting public resources—which the salmon and the water *are*—at stake. That is just plain wrong."

Bob Moran, the Colorado hydrogeologist, who has advised some of Pebble's critics, said, "Even when a mine is well run, it is unavoidable that chemical contaminants will be released into the environment. I know of no comparable large-scale ore body that has been mined without release of significant concentrations of contaminants into nearby waters over the long term. And I don't know of any other mine built near such a valuable and potentially vulnerable fishery anywhere in the world."

WATER IN THE TWENTY-FIRST CENTURY

Sean Magee, PLP's former director of public affairs, acknowledged, "In many respects, it's the water issues that are the most challenging. . . . If we can't protect the fish and the water and the wildlife, then we won't proceed with the project." In spite of such reassuring words, PLP has continued to invest in Pebble, explore the deposit aggressively, and prepare itself for the state's permitting process, which is slated to begin in 2011 or 2012.

THE RICHES IN THE ROCK

In the late 1990s, several years after Phil St. George first staked out a mining claim for Cominco Alaska Exploration, the company, renamed Teck Cominco, spent $8 million to drill exploratory core samples around the Pebble mine site, to get a sense of what lay beneath the tundra. The company estimated the minerals there were worth about $10 billion. Teck Cominco continued to sink boreholes into the site until 2001, when, for reasons that have never been made public, the company, which has years of experience mining in the difficult conditions of Alaska, decided to sell off its Pebble holdings. Teck Cominco blamed "environmental reasons," which presumably meant that conditions at the site were too daunting, or that operating a mine there would have such a negative impact on the ecosystem that it would be prohibitive. The company sold its rights for $10 million, a relative pittance, and, unusually, did not keep a share in the project.

The buyer was Northern Dynasty Minerals (NDM), a subsidiary of the global mining giant Hunter Dickinson, which is based in Vancouver. (Rio Tinto, based in London and Melbourne, owns 19.8 percent of NDM, and Mitsubishi, the Japanese conglomerate, owns 6.1 percent.) In 2007, NDM formed a fifty-fifty partnership with Anglo American PLC, the world's second-largest mining concern, based in Johannesburg and London. Anglo American has been mining around the world for over a hundred years, has operations in forty-five countries on seven continents, and with a near-majority stake in the controversial diamond company De Beers and with metal mines stretching from Zimbabwe to Ireland to Nevada, has an environmental record that has been roundly criticized. The joint venture was named the Pebble Limited Partnership.

PLP's first CEO, Bruce Jenkins, was a Canadian mining veteran with strong opinions and a tin ear. When Native families asked how Pebble would affect them, Jenkins replied, "We're committed to preserving your subsistence way of life. Does that mean there will be no effects on your subsistence way of life? No, of course not. How could you have an open pit tailings pond with zero effect on your subsistence way of life? The real question is, what's the nature, the timing, and the magnitude of the effect?"

The locals were horrified by Jenkins's candor, and so were some of his colleagues. In April 2008, Jenkins stepped down as CEO. His replacement, John Shively, was cut from a very different bolt of cloth and came from outside the mineral industry. "He's really bad news for us," one Pebble opponent confided. "Shit, I actually *like* the guy. He's a very smart hire."

For five years in the 1990s, Shively was commissioner of the Alaska Department of Natural Resources (DNR), the agency responsible for permitting mines, oil and gas exploration, agriculture, and parks on 80 million acres of state-owned land. In other words, John Shively knew very well how Alaskan regulators evaluated projects such as the Pebble mine.

One day in June 2008, I found myself at a small airport on the outskirts of Anchorage, waiting for Shively, who had offered to fly me out to the Pebble site for a tour. (I am leery of accepting favors from people I am writing about, but this was the only practical way for me to see the mine site and spend time with PLP's CEO.) In the airport waiting room were a Native girl dressed in pink and a young, buzz-cut guy holding a rifle case, but nobody who looked like a corporate suit.

As I waited, a guy in a wrinkled brown shirt, rumpled blue jeans, and an old hat wandered into the waiting room and looked around distractedly. He pulled a cell phone from a leather case decorated with Native beads and mumbled into it, "Yeah, hey, this is John Shively. I'm at the airport and I'm supposed to meet a writer. You heard from him?" When Shively hung up, I introduced myself.

PLP's vaunted new CEO was not at all what I expected. Soft-spoken, with big eyes that stared at the world with apparent curiosity, he'd occasionally flash a half grin. He was friendly, low-key, and disarming. *He's Columbo,* I thought. *Disheveled in the way that Peter Falk's seemingly absentminded detective was in the old TV series.*

Shively came to Alaska in 1965, by way of the VISTA program (Volunteers in Service to America), an antipoverty initiative championed by President John F. Kennedy. He was posted to the town of Yakutat, where he befriended Byron Mallott, the young Native mayor. Later, they worked together in community action organizations that sponsored rural Alaskan regional development corporations. For about eight years in the late 1970s and early 1980s, Shively worked at NANA (formerly the Northwest Arctic Native Association), one of thirteen for-profit Native corporations, where he educated shareholders about the landmark $1 billion Alaska Native Claims Settlement Act of 1971, which conveyed some 44 million acres to Native corporations to resolve disputes over the trans-Alaska oil pipeline. Shively spent a lot of time in villages and rural areas, teaching people how to empower themselves. Shively served as chief of staff to Governor Bill Sheffield, a Democrat (in 1985, Shively resigned under a cloud, while Sheffield narrowly avoided being impeached for alleged perjury over an office lease). Shively's wife is an environmental writer and organic farmer, and they have an adopted Native Alaskan daughter. All of which seems to peg Shively pretty firmly in the "hippie Left" camp. But there is a zealous side to his activism, dedicated to bringing Natives into the mainstream white world.

Before taking the job at PLP, Shively was working for the Holland America cruise line and was contemplating a quiet retirement. "If [PLP] had wanted to hire a mining guy, they could have done that. I admit I don't know much about metals. But one of the skills I do have is negotiating," Shively said. In the early 1980s, while working for NANA, Shively led the negotiations that resulted in the permitting of Red Dog, the largest zinc mine in the world, which is in the Brooks Range of northwestern Alaska. NANA's partner in the deal was Cominco, the Canadian mineral company that originally developed Pebble. "Red Dog created a lot of Native jobs. It was one of the highlights of my career," Shively said. "My hope is that maybe we can do the same thing at Pebble. There's just not a lot of economic opportunity in rural Alaska. To me, this project is about improving people's lives."

From 2001 to 2007, federal environmental regulators listed Red Dog as the worst toxic polluter in the United States for six years in a row. Much of that pollution was mined waste rock, which is strictly regulated to prevent toxic metals from leaching into the ground and water. (In 2009, the EPA would fine Teck Alaska Inc., Red Dog's operator, $120,000 for other cases of water pollution.) "Well, no question, there have certainly been some of those issues," Shively replied, happy to discuss this touchy subject. "There was a case of acid-mine drainage when we first opened Red Dog. But it is safe and being tested now. That area never supported fish before, and now there are actually fish in Red Dog Creek."

But what happens if there is a toxic spill at Pebble, near the headwaters of two of Bristol Bay's most important salmon rivers? I asked. Wouldn't that have far worse consequences than what happened at Red Dog?

"If I am not convinced that the Pebble mine is well designed and safe, I'll walk away," Shively said. "It is a very attractive prospect, and it concerns me that people are trying to stop it before we even have a proposal. Obviously, it is in a sensitive area. But we are confident we will address the fisheries issues. If we can't mine it safely, okay, then let's turn it into a wildlife refuge or something."

But as well-intentioned as he may be, it hardly matters if Shively walks away from the project. The companies behind PLP—Anglo American and Northern Dynasty—have invested years of work and hundreds of millions of dollars in developing the mine; Anglo executives are deeply experienced with controversy over their global mining operations and are not likely to give up on such a rich prospect unless forced to by the state or the federal government.

At that airport outside Anchorage we boarded a single-engine plane and flew up to the village of Iliamna, on the edge of Lake Iliamna, Alaska's largest lake and an important salmon breeding area. Iliamna, with a population of about one hundred, is PLP's local headquarters. There we transferred to a sleek company helicopter for the eighteen-mile trip to the mine site. I sat in the left front seat, next to the pilot. Shively sat in back with Nicky, a cheerful Canadian engineer, who narrated through a headset. Below us, the tundra swooshed by like a movie—rolling green-brown hills, glintingly wet depressions, and patches of snow. There were no roads, or any sign of humanity.

We came upon an area of tall, undulating hills and broad meadows: Pebble. "There are two contiguous deposits, Pebble East and Pebble West," Nicky explained. "The exact nature of the mining activities has yet to be finalized." While Pebble West is slated to be mined as an open pit, the geology of Pebble East is less well understood, but it would probably be mined by the block-caving method, in which interlocking chambers are excavated deep underground. The logic was clear: most of the minerals here are of such a low grade that only a huge mine that could benefit from economies of scale made economic sense.

The vast operation could include the construction of a new port at Iniskin Bay, on Cook Inlet, about 104 miles to the east. A haul road running along the north side of Lake Iliamna would connect the port to the mine. A pipeline next to the road would carry a slurry of metal concentrate from Pebble. The slurry would be dewatered, loaded onto ships, and sent to a smelter, while a second pipe would return the used water to the mine, where it would be treated. Underground mining requires more electricity than aboveground mining, and it is estimated that Pebble will require about 250 to 350 megawatts of electricity, which is more power than is used by the entire Kenai Peninsula and would require transmission lines.

While Nicky explained the layout, I stared out the windshield, trying to imagine this pristine landscape split open by a yawning pit, alongside two of the largest dams in the world holding perhaps 2.5 billion tons of toxic tailings, with miles of roads, bridges, pipelines, and power lines snaking here and there. PLP now estimates the mine will cost over $6 billion to build, a figure three times the initial estimate.

After we passed over Frying Pan Lake, the chopper lost altitude, bucked in a crosswind, and landed about two hundred yards from a temporary drill rig.

The rig and a small wooden shack had been placed here by helicopter and sat on wooden skids, so as not to harm the tundra. With a loud clatter, it was extracting core samples from deep underground. We jumped out and watched three scruffy men pulling sections of pipe out of the bore-hole, carefully removing rock-core samples and placing them in cardboard sleeves (the samples would be taken to a lab in Iliamna, inspected, and cataloged), then running new sections of pipe down the hole again. A hose snaked from a nearby pond, to supply the rig with water. The drill was noisy and the men worked quickly, with few words. Then the wind kicked up, and it was time to fly.

To help gain what John Shively calls the "social license" to mine here—industry jargon for obtaining permission from the local community—the Pebble Partnership maintains that it has gone "beyond the state's environmental guidelines" to maintain a light footprint on the land. Instead of etching new roads into the fragile tundra with bulldozers, for example, the PLP ferries most of its people and equipment by helicopter or snowmobile. Groundwater is monitored. By 2008, the partnership had spent "in excess of $100 million" on assessing the mine's potential environmental and sociological impacts, as is required by the permitting process.

Pebble mine, its developers say, will be good for Alaska: it probably won't use all of the water it has requested, the explosions used to loosen rock will be contained, the gigantic dams will be engineered to withstand earthquakes, the poisonous tailings will be perfectly safe forever, and Pebble will bring nothing but good fortune to an impoverished corner of the state. This is a potent message, and many Natives support the mine.

The PLP has issued a steady stream of reassuring scientific reports about air, soil, and water quality at the site that have been posted on the company's website. Shively noted that the mine site is on public land (PLP owns rights to the minerals, not the land) and that skeptics are welcome to visit it and perform their own tests there, as the Nature Conservancy has done.

But, critics counter, PLP's tests are performed by consultants, its reports are written in-house and are not peer-reviewed, and the company refuses to detail its mining plans for independent review, making its reams of data useless. Critics are suspicious that the company is pretending to be open, while spinning the story to suit its agenda.

Mining is considered one of the dirtiest industries in the world. The chemicals used to process minerals are often poisonous, including lime and sodium hydroxide, sodium cyanide, hydrochloric acid, sodium metabisulfite, copper sulfate, polypropylene glycol methyl ether, xanthates, dithiophosphate and thionocarbamate, and methyl isobutyl carbinol.

The EPA estimates that hard-rock mining has contaminated the headwaters of over 40 percent of watersheds in the American West. In 2006, the agency estimated that the cost of cleaning up the worst of many abandoned mine sites in the United States would be at least $20 billion, or almost three times the EPA's budget for 2007. Long-term water treatment is often the costliest aspect of mine cleanup, and an increasing number of large mines like Pebble require water treatment of tailings "forever."

Mining's dirty legacy is due in large part to the General Mining Law of 1872, passed by Congress to encourage economic development in the West. Calling mining the "best use" of public land, it allowed miners to extract precious metals for a token fee and made no provision for environmental cleanup. Now an estimated sixteen thousand miles of streams are polluted, as are lakes and reservoirs. Mining industry officials vigorously defend the statute and say the absence of federal guidelines has given rise to a tight regulatory framework and state laws that protect water, air, and endangered species. But the evidence is not reassuring.

In June 2009 the US Supreme Court ruled, 6 to 3, to allow the Kensington gold mine, northwest of Juneau, to dump as much as 4.5 million tons a year of mine-waste slurry into Lower Slate Lake—even though it would certainly kill the lake's fish. The Kensington ruling was based on a 2002 Bush administration rule that allowed the dumping of mine waste into previously protected waters. Until that rule, the Clean Water Act had stipulated that the Army Corps of Engineers could dump "fill material" in waters while building levees and bridges. The Bush rule enlarged the definition of fill to include contaminated mining waste. As of this writing, it

316

is unclear whether the court's ruling on Kensington set a precedent that would affect water use at Pebble. But Bristol Bay residents have long worried about the PLP's plan to dump mine waste into Lake Iliamna. "We will not put tailings into Lake Iliamna," Shively told me. "There's no lake big enough up there for the tailings." The company claims this idea has been shelved. (According to the *Anchorage Daily News*, Pebble could conceivably fill in a different lake with clean dirt and load mining waste on top of it without breaking the law. Other mines in Alaska have used this tactic, including the Pogo and the Fort Knox gold mines.)

The mine that most resembles the open pit proposed for Pebble is the Bingham Canyon Mine (aka the Kennecott Copper Mine), near Salt Lake City. It is the largest copper, gold, and molybdenum mine in North America, for the moment, with an ore body only half the size of Pebble's. Pollution from Bingham Canyon has contaminated sixty square miles of groundwater in Utah. This resulted in the building of the largest wastewater treatment plant in the United States: it is designed to treat 2.7 billion gallons of polluted water annually for at least forty years.

RED TIDE

Every spring, millions of salmon fry emerge from the gravel of the Bristol Bay region's streams and lakes, migrate down to the bay, and swim out into the Bering Sea and beyond. Once they have matured, after two to six years of roaming the ocean, the salmon return to their natal streams, fin their way to the pool they were born in, and spawn.

In dry years, you can find stretches of waterway where a thin layer of brown water—as little as an inch deep—churns with a seething mass of red torpedoes wriggling furiously toward home.

"It's a force of nature," the locals told me. A "biblical flood of fish." Because the prized sockeye develop red sides by the time they spawn, their onslaught is known as the red tide, or red gold.

Alaska has some of the most valuable fishing grounds in the world (if it were a nation, the state would be the ninth-largest seafood producer), which generated a catch worth a record $533.9 million in 2010. Bristol Bay is Alaska's richest commercial fishery and the world's most productive commercial sockeye fishery. All five species of Pacific salmon—pink, chum, sockeye, coho, and king—spawn in the bay's rivers.

In 2008, 29.3 million salmon, valued at $113.3 million, were harvested in Bristol Bay; in 2009, 30.9 million salmon, worth $144.2 million, were taken; in 2010, bay fishermen hauled in 28.6 million salmon, worth a record $148.2 million.

In early June 2008, I flew into Dillingham, a weather-beaten fishing port on Bristol Bay, just as the sockeye were about to arrive en masse. A large silver sculpture of a salmon is suspended between two poles in a small park in the middle of town. Dillingham has three canneries, and everywhere you looked was the message NO PEBBLE MINE—on bumper stickers, posters, lapel pins, camouflage baseball caps, and flags flying from the radio masts of the fishing fleet. One guy wore a black sweatshirt emblazoned with the message PUCK FEBBLE!

People spend hundreds of thousands of dollars on equipment for the Bristol Bay fishing season, which lasts only about six weeks. A fisherman can expect to pay, on average, $325,000 to buy a new gill-netter, the thirty-two-foot fishing boats that are the monster trucks of the sea: wide, squat, stainless steel, blunt-nosed salmon-killing machines, armed with enormous engines and big spools of netting at bow and stern. That doesn't include the cost of gas, crew, nets, and supplies you need to survive for days at sea in a harsh climate. But such is the nature of salmon fever.

June 1 is opening day for king salmon in Bristol Bay. A few days later, the sockeye arrive and begin to make their way up local rivers. When enough of them have passed the counting stations—tall towers set up along the rivers, from which fisheries biologists monitor the red tide—the governor goes on the radio to say something like "Okay, all you folks out there in Bristol Bay, it's time to start fishing—good luck!"

By the end of the 2008 season, the Bristol Bay fishery was down 6.7 percent compared to 2007. Alaska's statewide salmon harvest of 146 million fish brought in $400 million, 31.4 percent below the year before. Even so, it was still the sixteenth-largest catch since 1959 and was far healthier than the salmon fisheries in the Lower 48 states.

Thanks to overfishing, pollution, and the construction of dams on spawning streams, the Atlantic salmon of New England are listed as endangered species. On the West Coast, the California salmon season was canceled in 2008 and 2009 by federal regulators. Central Oregon fishermen were granted a nine-thousand-fish catch in 2008, and Washington State fishermen were granted only a short season in 2009. Millions of sockeye once spawned along Idaho rivers, before hydroelectric dams were built. Now the salmon have to swim nine hundred miles from the

Pacific, surmount eight dams, and climb sixty-five hundred feet up to lakes in the Sawtooth Valley. In 2006 fisheries biologists suggested that Idaho sockeye were "functionally extinct." In 1995, not a single salmon returned to the Sawtooth; in 2007, only four salmon were reported to have survived the trek. A hatchery program is promising, but whether hatchery-bred fish can survive the grueling life cycle of an Idaho salmon is an open question.

Today, far more farm-raised salmon exist in the world than wild salmon. Farming salmon adds pollutants, such as PCBs (the chemical that pollutes the Housatonic River), to the ecosystem, where they enter the food chain. The threat of domesticated salmon escaping and crossbreeding with native fish, and the amount of wild fish required to feed farmed salmon, add to the environmental stress. Salmon advocates across the country have petitioned Washington for sweeping changes in the way wild salmon stocks are managed, and in 2009, they asked President Obama to appoint a national salmon czar to oversee the care, maintenance, and rescue of fish populations.

Aside from limiting the catch, the best way to help wild salmon is to remove dams that block their spawn runs. In 2008, American Rivers reported that 430 outdated dams had been removed in the last decade. The first was the Edwards Dam, on the Kennebec River, in Maine. On the Penobscot, also in Maine, fish ladders will open one thousand miles of river to salmon. In the West, three dams in Washington State are slated for removal in 2011, while four dams on California's Klamath River will be removed by 2015. But in Alaska dams aren't the issue: salmon advocates fear contamination of the water, particularly by Pebble mine.

ODD BEDFELLOWS

The anti-Pebble coalition is broad and loose and does not always work in sync toward a common goal: liberal-leaning groups, such as Trout Unlimited and the Nature Conservancy, certain Native groups, and most commercial and sport fishermen, oppose the mine. But so do many of the cannery operators, and a few conservative businessmen.

On the outskirts of Dillingham, Bobby Andrew, a diminutive Yupik man in a plaid shirt, was unloading a dozen freshly caught salmon from his skiff. He showed me around his smokehouse, where long, greasy strips of deep orange salmon hung from the rafters, curing. "I know an elder who found a place on a river in this area—and I'm not gonna say where—where you could pull out finger-sized pieces of gold," he said. "My friend knew what they were worth, but he threw the gold back into the river. He didn't want people to know about it. Gold only creates problems. The more you have, the more you want, and then the less you have. Gold creates greed."

Speaking slowly, in a soft voice, Andrew opined that Pebble mine will make things worse, not better, for Natives. "The resources we subsist on, like salmon, are *there*. They are renewable. We've been fishing them for more than a thousand years, and we haven't run out of salmon yet. So why would we ever want to risk losing that?"

I was introduced to Andrew by Bob Waldrop, who served as the Special Assistant for Natural Resources under Jay Hammond, Alaska's famous "Bush Rat Governor," and now helps to run the Bristol Bay Regional Seafood Development Association, which assists commercial fishermen. One day, Waldrop took me across Lake Clark, inside Lake Clark National Park, which is adjacent to the Pebble site, to meet Bella Hammond at the log cabin she built with her husband, the governor. When I asked about Pebble, her gentle smile flipped into a scowl and her dark eyes flashed. "Jay always said, 'I couldn't imagine a worse location for a mine, unless it was right here in my own kitchen!'" the first lady said. "I couldn't put it any better myself."

One of the curious details of the battle over Pebble is that while the industrial mining giant PLP is led by the rumpled Democrat John Shively, the save-the-salmon opposition is (nominally) personified by Bob Gillam, an archconservative money manager who believes it is "stupid not to drill" for oil in the Arctic National Wildlife Refuge but has become a powerful behind-the-scenes force against the Pebble mine. An avid fisherman, Gillam has built an enormous lodge on Keyes Point, on Lake Clark, just downstream from Pebble, where he entertains clients. Gillam—who likes to say, "Only two things matter in life: getting rich and catching fish!"—denies that his lodge has anything to do with his opposition to Pebble, though the claim stretches credulity.

Gillam first heard of the mine in 2005. Inspecting the site from his private plane, he underwent a conversion. "You don't have to be particularly smart to know that if you take away the water, the fish go away," Gillam told the *Wall Street Journal*. "I cannot sit by and let this happen to my state."

Said to be Alaska's only billionaire, Gillam funds a nonprofit organization called the Renewable Resources Coalition, which runs anti-Pebble print and TV ads. He has hired an army of attorneys, lobbyists, pollsters, hydrologists, geologists, and fisheries researchers to build a scientific and legal case against the mine. His detractors estimate that he spends about $3 million a year on his anti-Pebble effort and seek to portray him as a rich man "throwing around his money . . . to protect his playground." There is no end to the conspiracy theories about him, and several websites, such as The Bob Gillam Initiative to Kill Mining in Alaska, are dedicated to revealing the "real" Bob Gillam.

Even some of his supposed allies are suspicious of Gillam and have been trying to distance themselves. His investment management firm, McKinley Capital, holds more than $1 billion in mining stocks: when the firm bought over $7 million worth of shares of Anglo American PLC (the 50 percent owner of PLP) in 2007, the pro-Pebble faction snickered, while the mine's critics grew alarmed. Some began to wonder, paranoically, whether Gillam might be a double agent for the mining industry, sowing confusion to split the opposition. Or perhaps, they theorized, he is a cynical opportunist playing both sides off each other for his own advantage. Only Gillam knows, and he declined to speak to me.

In 2008, Gillam was pushing Measure 4, a public referendum to disallow any new large metal mine from releasing chemicals that would damage salmonoid fish (a standard not included in Alaskan law), and a vote was scheduled for August 26. Pebble supporters complained that the referendum was designed only to stop Pebble, though Gillam denied it.

On August 20, polls showed that the two sides were neck and neck. That morning, Governor Sarah Palin called a news conference with no specific agenda, during which she said, "Let me take my governor's hat off for just a minute here and tell you—personally, Prop 4? I vote no on that." Bedlam ensued. The pro-mining side ran full-page ads featuring Palin's photograph and the word NO.

On August 26, 57 percent of Alaskans voted against Measure 4, defeating it. Opponents blamed Palin for tipping the balance. Alaskan law forbids officials from using state resources to advocate for or against ballot initiatives. Tony Knowles, a former Democratic governor, charged that Palin broke the law by issuing her statement. "Being governor is not a costume—you either are the governor or not," he said. "The only reason the press was there was that they were called by the governor."

Three days later, Senator John McCain surprised nearly everyone by naming Sarah Palin his vice presidential nominee.

Just before Thanksgiving in 2008, Bob Moran flew from a water pollution conference in Papua New Guinea to Tyonek, an Athabascan village on Cook Inlet. The salmon fleet was gone, and a bitterly cold wind whistled through the quiet, snow-streaked streets. Standing in front of about twenty-five Native Alaskans in a classroom, he ran PowerPoint slides and said, "Companies routinely claim that they can operate a modern metal mine without environmental impacts. This is simply false."

Talking to me later, he explained that Anglo American and Northern Dynasty have been in business for a long time, in some of the most difficult environments in the world, and had been very successful. "The truth is, they don't really care what happens this year, next year, or even five or ten years from now. They are playing for the long term, fifty years, maybe one hundred years down the road. They know that the minerals in Pebble will just get more valuable over time. They can afford to be very, very patient."

John Shively had told me essentially the same thing, noting that the Pebble Deposit could be mined for eighty to one hundred years but that PLP would apply for only twenty-five-year permits for its first phase. Once the first stage is successful, he said, permits for further work would not be as controversial. "The minerals are in there," he said. "They're not going anywhere."

Moran looked at the crowd of concerned faces in Tyonek and said, "If the mine is built, the wastes will remain on the site forever, available to be released into the water. The question you need to answer is, is that risk acceptable to you?" The crowd muttered, then shuffled out into the cold to think it over.

SACRIFICING ONE RESOURCE FOR ANOTHER

Miners and fishermen are not the only ones with their eyes on Bristol Bay. In 2007, President George W. Bush lifted a moratorium on drilling for oil there, which had been imposed by his father in 1990 in response to the *Exxon Valdez* disaster. The 2007 decision was yet another reminder of the growing competition for resources, and it enraged fishermen, environmentalists, and Native groups, who sued and delayed oil exploration in the bay.

Drilling in Bristol Bay would generate an estimated $7.7 billion worth of oil and gas over twenty-five to forty years, which is a relatively modest return. Taking the bay's notorious storms, ice, and cold into account, the former Minerals Management Service predicted that drilling there would result in at least one major oil spill. Environmental groups such as the World Wildlife Fund charge that it makes "no sense" to drill in Bristol Bay and argue that large oil and gas rigs could pollute the bay's $2 billion fishery, disrupt the migratory patterns of salmon, and disturb whales and migrating birds.

On March 31, 2010, President Barack Obama proposed opening vast new areas on the East and West Coasts, and in the Gulf of Mexico, to oil and gas drilling. Under the plan, the Chukchi and Beaufort Seas in Alaska would be opened to drilling, while Bristol Bay would be designated as a sanctuary in which no drilling would be allowed. Three weeks after the president's controversial announcement, the Deepwater Horizon, an exploratory drill rig leased by BP, exploded and sank in the Gulf of Mexico, creating the largest oil spill in US history and touching off a furor over offshore drilling.

As of this writing, it remains unclear if Obama's proposal will be enacted, or whether the BP disaster in the Gulf will have any impact on oil, gas, or mineral exploration in Alaska. Over the summer of 2010, Interior Secretary Ken Salazar and EPA administrator Lisa Jackson flew to Alaska on fact-finding trips and held meetings with proponents and opponents of the Pebble mine, though they were careful not to tip their hands.

Unless the federal government steps in, Pebble will live or die by the sixty-seven state and federal permits it is required to get. The mine site lies on state land (Shively refused to speculate about what sort of taxes or fees PLP would pay to mine the claim). State mining coordinator Tom Crafford said that while acid rock drainage and metal leaching are "a major issue of concern" if the mine is permitted, PLP's exploration of the site by about two hundred people a day "will have no significant impact on fisheries." The Alaska Department of Natural Resources is in charge of permitting mines, and only rarely does that agency not grant permits. Critics note the "revolving door" of personnel between regulatory agencies and mining concerns, which, the critics say, stacks the deck in favor of miners.

"Industry has hijacked the regulatory process," snorts Carol Ann Woody, the former USGS fish biologist. "The state's permitting process is set up to *permit*. I worked on about thirty permits in my career at USGS. Once they file their Environmental Impact Statement (EIS) for Pebble, we'll get their environmental data, but by then it will be game over. As far as I know, there has never been a mine that filed an EIS that was not permitted."

Over a halibut lunch in Anchorage, John Shively tilted his head to one side, as if something had just occurred to him, and said, "Alaska is a natural resource state. It's what we do here. I don't want to wreck things in the environment, but I don't believe our resources should be locked up forever, either. We'd never trade fish for mining. Our challenge is to see them coexist, and I believe we can do it. There's no sense in sacrificing one resource for another."

In the twenty-first century, humans' previously unbridled use of natural resources is yielding to a new era of limits, pressures, and restrictions. Just as geologists are looking for new mineral prospects, so hydrologists are searching for new water supplies. For water managers, the focus of this search has led to a quest to find a limitless, "drought-proof" supply of freshwater: the hydrologic Holy Grail.

CHAPTER 27

In Search of
a Drought-Proof Source

NO SUCH THING AS NORMAL

In America, events can move from the impossible to the
inevitable without ever stopping at the probable.
—Alexis de Tocqueville

In the spring of 2008, a hot wind blew out of the Sonoran Desert, blasting
sand through the air and rolling tumbleweeds across the streets of Phoenix, Arizona. The temperature was nearing one hundred degrees, and
the air was bone-dry. The few people caught outside shielded their eyes,
hunched their shoulders, and ran through the flying grit from one air-
conditioned sanctuary to another. On the third floor of a large beige office
building downtown, Herb Guenther, the director of the Arizona Department of Water Resources, and one of the last of the classic Water Buffaloes
of the Floyd Dominy school, was committing near-blasphemy. "Climate
change is for real," he said. "We can't keep doing things the same old way."

I was there to find out how a man of his experience was coping with
increased water demands in a state that was already the hottest in the
nation, and how it would adapt to even hotter, drier, more crowded conditions in the future.

For an old-school water manager such as Herb Guenther to acknowledge "climate change" and the need for "sustainability" was a major leap.
He joined the Bureau of Reclamation as a wildlife biologist in 1971 and
inherited Commissioner Dominy's legendary harpoon-size electrical
pointer from the bureau. Guenther has no use for what he calls "environmental extremists" who have saddled Americans with "a Chicken Lit-

tle mentality," in which "everything man does is considered bad" for the planet.

But in discussing climate change, the sometimes reactionary Guenther sounded almost as progressive as Peter Gleick: "We can't just pray for more rain. We need to develop creative strategies that will allow us to use our limited water in a sustainable way."

Guenther walks with a slight limp and tilts to one side as he sits. "It's from flood fighting in the desert," he explained. "It's ironic, but that's life in Arizona." In 1993, fighting a flash flood on the Gila River, he blew out two of his cervical disks trying to save his airboat in a biblical downpour. "We're either in drought or flood here. There's no such thing as normal," Guenther said. "They tell me that's what it's going to be like in climate change"—more violent shifts in weather, causing droughts one minute and floods the next. "Life is getting to be a whole lot more interesting."

Although Arizona is defined by its deserts, it had "banked," or stored underground, a surprising amount of water, some 3.1 million acre-feet, or about one trillion gallons. Guenther has ensured that Phoenix has a diverse portfolio of water supplies: the Central Arizona Project (CAP), a massive 336-mile aqueduct that annually siphons 1.5 million acre-feet of water from the Colorado River and jags across the desert like a dark scar; the Salt River Project, a series of canals and hydroelectric dams on the Salt River; and from aquifers. Begrudgingly, Arizonans have accepted what Guenther calls "the low-water-use lifestyle"—which includes xeriscaping (replacing grass lawns with cacti and rock gardens), strict limits on lawn watering, the restoration of rivers, interstate water deals, and using treated effluent for irrigation—which has allowed Arizona to use less water per capita every year.

But the problem in Phoenix is the same as in Las Vegas, Los Angeles, or Dallas: as the state's climate warms and population climbs, so does its need for water. By 2009, Arizona had 6.6 million residents, and by 2030 that number is set to double. "I understand why people want to come here. It's a nice place to live," said Guenther, himself a transplant from Long Island, New York. But sometimes, he said, "people have to be reeducated" about water use in the desert.

In 1980 the USGS estimated that groundwater beneath Phoenix had dropped 220 feet in places, sometimes causing sinkholes. With the threat of a federal ultimatum looming, the state legislature restricted groundwater use in parts of the state and mandated that new homes have a hundred-year supply of renewable groundwater. But people accustomed to cheap, plentiful supplies have found ways around the regulations.

In 2008 Arizona used about 8 million acre-feet, or 2.3 trillion gallons, of water. Demand continued to increase, as weak zoning laws promoted growth. In over 80 percent of Arizona, developers can build subdivisions with hundreds of houses even if water supplies are known to be insufficient. Planned communities such as Verrado, on the western edge of Phoenix, would not have been built under the original water laws because they were too far from renewable supplies; but with help from the legislature, Verrado worked around the renewable-supply requirements. Rural wells—many of which are not required to use meters—are steadily drawing from the same aquifers that cities use for water banking. "That really scares us," said Kathryn Sorensen, water resources director for Mesa, a city that has banked water for years. "We hope [the water] is there when we need it. But we don't have control over the [rural] water pumping."

Phoenicians, many of them from snowbelt states, insist on artificial lakes, green lawns and golf courses, shopping malls kept at arctic temperatures, and other resource-intensive methods of beautification. One of the most popular cooling methods for restaurants, shopping centers, and even homes is to use outdoor misting systems, which create a light fog on patios. (Misters are popular in other desert cities, most notably Palm Springs, California.) A typical home misting nozzle uses about one to fifteen gallons of water per hour, equivalent to running a large load of laundry. But a fifty-foot misting system on a restaurant patio might consume as much as fifteen hundred gallons of water per night, which is equivalent to a week's worth of water for a household of two. It is so hot in Arizona that water misted during the day "flash evaporates" almost immediately. The state does not regulate misters, though there are "plans" to ban them in case of severe water shortage.

Arizona doesn't know exactly how much groundwater it has, or how fast it is being used, and, according to the Bureau of Reclamation, it could face a water crisis by 2025.

With a glint in his eye, Guenther disputed that assessment and said that while he was concerned about climate change, he fully expected man to engineer himself out of trouble "as we always have in the past." He believes that by refining existing technologies such as "weather modification" and desalination, we already have drought-proof water sources in hand. People have used these technologies for years, but results have been mixed, and skeptics question whether they are worth the effort.

THE RIPPLE EFFECT

TURNING THE RAIN ON AND OFF

I will give you rain in due season, and the land shall yield her
increase, and the trees of the field shall yield their fruit.
—Leviticus

When rain falls from clouds, it does not always arrive when and where it is useful to man. But what if we could control the weather and produce rain whenever we like? This question has consumed people for years.

Meteorology was considered a black art until the nineteenth century, when James Pollard Espy, aka the Storm King, transformed it into an empirical science. Through careful study of weather, he developed a convection theory: air rises as it heats, expands, then cools; water vapor condenses in the clouds, then falls to earth as rain, snow, sleet, or hail. Espy believed that he could summon rain on command and tried to convince Congress to pay him to start forest fires so that he could demonstrate how his on-demand precipitation would snuff them out. Congress declined to fund Espy's project.

In the late nineteenth and early twentieth centuries, "pluviculturists" promised they could draw rain from clouds by "puncturing" them with pointed balloons, blasting them with percussive artillery barrages, releasing steam from chimneys, or sprinkling clouds with "electrified sand" from a plane.

In 1946, two General Electric chemists in Schenectady, New York—Vincent Schaefer and Irving Langmuir—discovered that when dry ice was dropped into a cold cloud, it produced crystallized water vapor, better known as snow. Bernard Vonnegut, another GE chemist (and the older brother of novelist Kurt Vonnegut), found that silver iodide created snow in clouds. Their insight was that they didn't have to create new clouds; rather, they could induce precipitation by adding crystallization to existing rain clouds. They termed their methods cloud seeding. Langmuir, who won the 1932 Nobel Prize in Chemistry, believed that this was his most important discovery and spoke of the potential to end drought and hail, control snowfalls, and turn the Southwest into a verdant garden.

The trick is to fly above already moisture-laden clouds in an airplane and "seed" them with a trail of silver iodide or dry ice (frozen CO_2) particles, which causes the precipitation to fall. Some scientists estimate that under perfect conditions spreading silver iodide into a cloud can increase precipitation by 10 to 15 percent.

Cloud seeding has been used to produce rain around the world for over sixty years, and today numerous dry nations—Morocco, Saudi Arabia, countries of West Africa—are researching the technology as an answer to their chronic lack of water.

The Xinjiang region of China is home to the world's largest cloud-seeding initiative. The China Meteorological Administration fires tens of thousands of rockets and cannon rounds loaded with silver iodide into the skies to promote rain. From 1999 through 2006, China claims to have produced 36 billion metric tons of artificial rain per year, reduced the size of hailstones (which destroy crops and houses), and suppressed forest fires caused by lightning strikes. China's latest five-year plan calls for increasing artificial rainfall to 50 billion metric tons a year.

But tinkering with the weather can go badly wrong. In November 2009, clouds were seeded over China to alleviate a drought, but the temperature suddenly dropped, and the resulting blizzard closed highways and the Beijing airport, while heavy snows in other cities collapsed roofs, injured scores, and killed at least eight people.

Does weather modification really work? Proponents such as Herb Guenther believe it does. But critics say it is impossible to distinguish cloud-seeded rain from natural rain, that the amount of precipitation created by silver iodide cannot be measured, and that controlled experiments to answer these questions are impossible to construct.

In the 1970s, the federal government was spending $20 million a year on cloud-seeding studies, but its scientists concluded that most "moisture accelerators"—cloud-seeding entrepreneurs who charged farmers hefty fees to produce rain—were charlatans, and federal research money disappeared. In 2003, the National Research Council of the National Academies issued a report that stated, "There is still no convincing scientific proof of the efficacy of intentional weather modification efforts."

Nevertheless, industry groups such as the Weather Modification Association have continued to lobby for federal support, and adherents persist. By 2006, sixty-six weather-mod research programs were under way in ten states. Ski areas, such as Vail, contract private firms to seed clouds for snow. A five-year $8.8 million experiment in Wyoming is under way to determine, once and for all, whether rain and snow can be squeezed from clouds on demand, and when and where people want it. At the conclusion of the study, lawmakers will have to decide if research should continue.

"If this is shown to increase the [water] supply by ten percent, it would be very valuable," said Mike Purcell, director of the Wyoming Water Development Commission.

The evidence suggests that cloud seeding works to a limited extent, when conditions are right, but that it is difficult to control. It could be a useful tool but will not be a major new source of water. Other, more proven technologies for creating new drinking supplies hold much greater promise.

A SEA OF POSSIBILITY

> Water, water, everywhere,
> Nor any drop to drink.
> —Samuel Taylor Coleridge,
> *The Rime of the Ancient Mariner*

> If we could ever competitively, at a cheap rate, get freshwater from salt water, that would be in the long-range interests of humanity which would really dwarf any other scientific accomplishments.
> —President John F. Kennedy, 1962

Ninety-seven percent of the earth's water is too salty for human consumption, yet dreams of turning salt water into a "new" supply of freshwater keep Herb Guenther up at night. "It is the municipal water supply of the future," he said. The technology could provide a "limitless supply" of drinking water, on demand.

The oceans hold 321 million cubic miles of water. When salt is dissolved in water, it breaks the ionic bonds that bind salt crystals together; removing those resulting salt ions requires a lot of energy. The problem with distilling seawater is that it requires so much energy that it can be used only in small shipboard systems, or in places such as the Middle East where money and fuel are plentiful and freshwater is scarce.

A few "multi-effect" distillation plants, which use a cascading system of chambers, were built in the early nineteenth century, but mineral deposits on heat exchangers hampered the system. By the mid-twentieth century, a second method was developed that pushed salt water through a set of fine semipermeable membranes, which remove most of the salts. The best-known form of this process is called reverse osmosis, or RO.

In 1965, an experimental RO plant was built in Coalinga, California. And in 1980, the world's first municipal seawater desal plant opened in Jidda, Saudi Arabia. These early plants required huge amounts of energy to run (the Jidda plant needed more than eight kilowatt hours [kwh] of electricity to produce one cubic meter of drinking water) and were considered too expensive and technically complex to be widely popular. Furthermore, the membranes were expensive to make and difficult to keep clean.

But the dream lived on. Cruise ships and aircraft carriers, arid seaside resorts in the Caribbean, and wealthy petro nations in the Middle East began to desalinate water regularly. This pushed down prices and led to the development of new technologies. Today, greater economies of scale, improved energy-recovery devices, and more sophisticated membranes have lowered the cost further, making desal on a larger scale more feasible.

During the extended drought of the late 1980s, several desal plants were built along the California coast. One was operating in Santa Barbara, but three months after the plant was completed, the drought abruptly ended with a series of drenching rainstorms referred to as the "March miracle." The Santa Barbara plant was mothballed. (Much of the equipment has been sold off or is obsolete, and the city's homeless have taken up residence around the plant's perimeter.) Since then, refinements have brought down the cost of desalting ocean water from about $2,000 an acre-foot in 1990 to about $800 in 2007, which was slightly above the cost to coastal California cities of importing water from the Sacramento Delta and the Colorado River.

By 2005, more than two thousand desalination plants were operating in the United States, and today many more are on the drawing boards. The American Water Works Association, a trade group, predicts the desalination business will grow by $70 billion over the next two decades.

Not all desal plants are built on the ocean. About a quarter of them, such as the planned American Waters plant on the Hudson River, just north of New York City, process river water. Others, such as the Bureau of Reclamation's Yuma Desalting Plant in Yuma, Arizona, process brackish inland water. Because inland water has less salt and other pollutants than ocean water, desalting it requires less power and fewer membranes than ocean desal and is therefore less expensive. The Yuma plant was built to reduce the salts in the Colorado River water that the United States is obliged by treaty to deliver to Mexico. It took twenty years and $250 million to build the plant, but thanks to design flaws and changing environmental circumstances, it has been idled since 1993. When I visited Yuma in the spring of 2007, the plant had just undergone a $30 million upgrade and was being run at 10 percent of capacity. It may be used for its original purpose in the future, but at present the Yuma desalter is run as the nation's only full-scale RO research-and-testing facility, to help answer the question, is desal the magical tool that will solve the world's quest for a drought-proof supply of water?

Saudi Arabia, where temperatures hover at 130 degrees in the desert, and the population is rising to an expected 36.4 million by 2020, once considered towing an iceberg from Antarctica or filling oil tankers with water from Norway to slake its people's thirst. But as prices and technology have improved, the Saudis have become the world's largest users of desalination, with twenty-eight plants supplying 70 percent of the kingdom's water. In April 2009, King Abdullah pushed a button to start up the world's largest desalter: the $3.4 billion Shoaiba Desalination Plant, in Jubail Industrial City, on the Persian Gulf, which produces eight hundred thousand cubic meters of water a year and generates electricity for 1.5 million people. But the nation's desal plants consume 1.5 million barrels of oil a day, and the Saudi government plans to open the world's largest solar-powered desal plant in 2012.

One lesson learned in Saudi Arabia is that the high cost of a desalter can be reduced when built next to a coastal power plant, which typically uses over a million gallons of seawater a day and can supply relatively cheap electricity. This was the theory behind choosing Tampa, Florida, as the site for the largest desalination plant outside the Middle East.

In 1998, twenty local governments in Florida, locked in a fierce competition over dwindling groundwater supplies, put their differences aside and established Tampa Bay Water (TBW). It is now the largest water wholesaler in the state, serving over 2.5 million people. In 1999, TBW approved a plan to construct a large desalination plant at Apollo Beach. The company driving this plan was a small firm called Poseidon Resources Corp., based in Stamford, Connecticut. Poseidon and its partner, the engineering giant Stone and Webster, estimated the desalination plant would cost $110 million to build and would produce water costing $677 an acre-foot.

Walter Winrow, Poseidon's cofounder and president, was an engineer who had spent most of his career working on power projects around the world for GE. "I travel a bit," he said blandly, by which he meant he was in near-constant motion, monitoring desal projects and drumming up new business for Poseidon (he declined to be specific about where he travels). "Freshwater," he said, "is a growth opportunity."

In 1994 Winrow saw an unfilled need: "On one side, the equipment and service providers were looking to sell power and their services; on the other side were public agencies; but there was nobody in between to mediate." He quit GE to help form Poseidon Resources, where he put together small water deals that eventually led to bigger deals. He forged a partnership with Pemex, Mexico's giant state-owned petroleum company, and Ionics, an American company experienced in membrane technology, to develop desal plants in Mexico.

In 1999, in Tampa, Winrow saw another opportunity: a bay with water of low salinity, a supply of cheap energy from Big Bend Power Plant, a growing population, and generous tax breaks. The desal plant he envisioned would be privately owned and operated. According to the plan, it would begin producing a steady supply of freshwater in 2002, at the unprecedented wholesale cost of $1.71 per thousand gallons. (At the time, big desalination plants could produce a thousand gallons of water for $4 to $6, under ideal conditions, and for as much as $10 in less ideal conditions.) Groundwater pumping, by contrast, cost about $1 per thousand gallons wholesale but was subject to the vagaries of supply, which in turn depended on the weather, pollution, and other people's pumping. But after Winrow's partners went bankrupt, Tampa Bay Water grew restive and bought out Poseidon in 2002. TBW hired other companies to finish and operate the plant, but there were numerous problems. Finally, in December 2007, five years behind schedule and $48 million over budget, the Tampa Bay desalination plant began to produce 25 million gallons of drinking water a day for $1,100 an acre-foot ($423 per acre-foot more than Poseidon had estimated it would cost).

The $158 million plant is the largest desalinator in the country. It aims to produce 25 million gallons a day (mgd) of freshwater, but during the drought of 2009 it was limited to 14 mgd by a cracked pipe, a blown transformer, and other issues. In 2010, the plant was producing 15 mgd, but with heavy rains and an 18.4 percent slump in demand since 2007, caused by Florida's mortgage crisis, the plant was temporarily shut down to save money; this angered state regulators, who threatened to penalize Tampa Bay Water for failing to live up to its agreement.

An industry expert told the *Wall Street Journal* that everyone involved in the Tampa project was guilty of "sloppy work." Ken Herd, TBW's operations director, said that the plant is "mostly" running smoothly, and that while desalination "is not the cheapest source of supply, it is drought-proof."

Winrow, meanwhile, was looking for the right combination of demand, location, and financing to cobble together his next big desal deal. He found it in Carlsbad, California.

In 2002, California passed Proposition 50, which provides grants for desalination, and in 2005 the state's Department of Water Resources underwrote $25 million worth of desalting projects. About twenty of these have been proposed for the coast, but they are all waiting to see what happens to Poseidon's latest gamble. If the Carlsbad desalination plant is built, it will supplant Tampa's as the largest desalter in the western hemisphere.

Carlsbad lies between San Diego and Los Angeles. For the moment, Poseidon's operation is not much to look at: a wide green lagoon, the old Encina Power Station, a shimmering black parking lot, a mobile home, and a long blue contraption that is mostly tanks, pipes, and valves—a scaled-down version of a reverse-osmosis desalinator.

Peter MacLaggan, the Poseidon senior vice president in charge of the project, looks like a surfer but speaks like an industrialist. He toured me along the scaled-down desalinator: it is about as long as a railway car, begins with a couple of tanks, proceeds to a panel full of gauges, then to two long white tubes, and ends with a water fountain. It is essentially a mechanical intestine. Seawater used for cooling the Encina Power Station is piped through a series of filters to remove impurities. Purifying chemicals are added, then the water is pumped through reverse-osmosis membranes (the white tubes), which remove salts and other microscopic impurities. (If the plant is built, it will use a slightly different process developed in Israel by IDE Technologies.) It takes two gallons of salt water to make one gallon of "ultra-high-quality freshwater."

At the end of the tour, MacLaggan offered me a drink at the fountain. I leaned down and took a sip. What was ocean water about half an hour earlier now tasted like cool, clean tap water. Actually, it tasted more like the RO-cleansed bottled waters made by Aquafina and Dasani, which is to say it has been so thoroughly stripped of minerals that it doesn't have much identifiable character at all. MacLaggan said that the total dissolved solids in this water are about half that of the existing water supply, which pleases local biotech and other high-tech industries that rely on superclean water for their manufacturing.

It will cost an estimated $450 million to build the full-scale plant in

Carlsbad, which will be housed in a low, square one-story building across the lagoon. The plant will produce 50 million gallons of drinking water a day, enough for three hundred thousand residents, or about 8 percent of San Diego County's water consumption in 2020.

In keeping with the new emphasis on "blue," or water-smart, technology, Poseidon will offset its footprint by building or remediating 66 acres of wetlands, planting trees, using efficient pumps, and purchasing renewable energy credits. The company intends its Carlsbad desalinator to be the first major infrastructure project in California to be completely carbon-neutral.

MacLaggan had been pushing the plant through the permitting process for five and a half years, facing down protests, lawsuits, and negative editorials. The Carlsbad project is the test case for desal in Southern California, and many people were still following its stop-and-start progress with zealous interest.

Critics such as Food & Water Watch noted that due to spiraling costs, Poseidon might need to sell its water for as much as $2,000 to $3,000 an acre-foot, which is far more than the $950 an acre-foot the company said it would charge in 2008. (MacLaggan said his water would cost about $1,690 an acre-foot. By comparison, local water agencies charge $1,150 per acre-foot.) They also complained that desal requires finicky, expensive membranes to remove salts from seawater, and that desal requires tremendous amounts of power, which will be costly as fuel prices rise and adds greenhouse gases.

"Ocean desalination, quite frankly, is the SUV of water," Mindy McIntyre, of the Planning and Conservation League, editorialized in the *Los Angeles Times*. "It requires more energy to desalinate a gallon of ocean water than it does to pump water from Northern California over a mountain range all the way to Southern California."

In a counter-editorial, MacLaggan replied, "McIntyre's Model T–era assertion [is] incredible and outdated. . . . Yes, energy is one of the cost variables associated with the production of desalinated water; however, the same is true for the transportation of imported water and the treatment of reclaimed water. In truth, the escalating energy costs . . . will affect all means of new drinking water."

A broader environmental critique holds that desal plants use enormous amounts of seawater, which presents two problems: first, seawater provides habitat for plankton, fish, seaweeds, and other marine life, some of which are killed as the plant inhales water; second, seawater is considered a public resource, one that desalinators want to use for private profit.

To build the plant, Poseidon must get permits from numerous bodies, including the powerful California Coastal Commission, whose staff scientists rejected Poseidon's proposal four times and recommended that the commissioners not approve the project because of the potential destruction of marine life. MacLaggan grew frustrated and in an unguarded moment snapped to local newspapers, "Our intake will kill about two pounds of fish a day. That's less than the daily consumption of one pelican." (A few months later, a scientist with the San Diego Regional Water Quality Board found that, due to mathematical errors, Poseidon had underestimated the number of fish it would kill by a factor of four.)

Perhaps the most contentious aspect of desal, however, is how to dispose of the highly concentrated salt brine left over from the plant's water-cleansing. Every hundred gallons of desalinated seawater yields fifteen to fifty gallons of drinking water (depending on the process, and how salty the water is to begin with), and fifty to eighty-five gallons of brine. When the highly concentrated brine is flushed back to sea, it can destroy aquatic species, particularly those in the egg or immature phase. One environmentalist described the brine as "like the blood of the creature in *Alien*— it'll eat through anything. The desalinators don't know how to get rid of it, and they don't want to talk about it."

At the Carlsbad plant, the plan is to mix the brine with seawater discharging from the Encina Power Station and pump it offshore; Pacific wind, tide, and currents will mix and diffuse the brine, MacLaggan said. "A thousand feet offshore, we will get [the brine salts] down to thirty-six parts per thousand. By the time it reaches the kelp beds two thousand feet offshore, it's down to thirty-four parts per thousand. It quickly dissipates. The impact on the marine environment will be de minimis."

Surfers, fishermen, and environmentalists don't buy the argument. The Surfrider Foundation has filed several lawsuits to stop Poseidon, claiming that the Carlsbad project would "kill everything that floats," in the words of Surfrider's Joe Geever—including the garibaldi, the state marine fish—and that it is not required to use the best water-intake technology available.

In 2009, the state's coastal commissioners overrode their staff scientists and approved Poseidon's permit, albeit with a list of twenty conditions attached. After a decade of contentious debate, which included fourteen public hearings and five revisions to the plan, the Carlsbad plant cleared its final regulatory hurdle when the San Diego Regional Water Quality Board unanimously approved permits for the Carlsbad desalter. Environmental groups have vowed to keep fighting the Carlsbad project and a sister plant in Huntington Beach, just south of Los Angeles. MacLaggan says that the fight over the Huntington plant has been even more vituperative than the one in Carlsbad. But as wildfires raged and the public worried about drought, Governor Schwarzenegger said of desalination, "We need it. It's not a choice," and in 2009 he green-lit both Poseidon projects.

By late 2010, the company had all its permits for Carlsbad in place when a deal for nine cities and agencies to buy its water fell apart over the issue of financial guarantees. The San Diego County Water Authority, a water wholesaler, stepped in. But the city of Carlsbad balked and demanded a guarantee that it wouldn't lose money. As of this writing, Poseidon is negotiating with the county and is preparing to offer at least $530 million in tax-exempt bonds to private investors in 2011 to finance construction.

It remains to be seen whether the two plants will be built, and, if they are, how that will impact numerous other desalination projects proposed across the country.

Herb Guenther in Phoenix and Pat Mulroy in Las Vegas predict that a greater use of desal in America is "inevitable." But with the enormous costs to build and operate a plant, the politics of desalination, and the energy and environmental hurdles, it won't be easy. Some of the more ambitious programs require the use of nuclear power, which will entail further complications. As landlocked states, Arizona and Nevada intend to build a nuclear-powered facility on the Mexican coast, which would add diplomatic, trade-pact, and environmental considerations. (Freshwater created by the plant would be used in Mexico, in exchange for giving the states greater use of Colorado River water.)

"At the end of the day we will use desalters, but they will only be one tool in the toolbox," Mulroy concedes, in what has become a common refrain.

The growing need for freshwater and the rising costs of procuring it from distant sources has raised the stakes for desal. In 2008, according to the *Wall Street Journal*, 13,080 desalination plants around the world produced some 12 billion gallons of water a day. Even some longtime critics have been won over. "Ten years ago desalination was the crazy aunt in the attic.

That's changed. It is now entering the mainstream and being taken seriously," NRDC's Barry Nelson said in 2003.

Desal has yet to gain wide acceptance, but the technology is being refined and costs are dropping. This has led some of the nation's leading companies, such as the computer-chip-maker Intel, to aggressively pursue desal as a viable alternative to water imported from the overextended Colorado River and Sacramento Delta. To those who can afford it, then, desalination provides a relatively "drought-proof" (if not entirely green) source of freshwater.

A GLIMPSE OF A WATER-SMART FUTURE

For many years, Intel was so focused on creating the world's smallest, fastest microprocessors and building its presence in the global marketplace, that the company didn't pay close attention to the impact its chip manufacturing had on the environment. Intel is responsible for three Superfund sites in California, and the company has faced messy public opposition in New Mexico, where state regulators cited Intel for violations of wastewater and air-emissions-equipment rules, and residents worried that its chip-making plants were using millions of gallons of water while impacting air quality and the fragile desert ecosystem near Albuquerque. In the early 2000s, Intel built two new "fabs," or semiconductor fabrication plants, Fab 12 and Fab 22, in a place even hotter and drier than New Mexico: Chandler, Arizona, next door to Phoenix. Then, in late 2007, the company opened a "mega-fab" in Chandler, Fab 32, which cost $3 billion to build and is a state-of-the-art facility: it recycles or stores about 75 percent of the water it uses and is among the most water-efficient plants in the company's global operations.

Fab 32 is a behemoth in the desert: a long, low, wide building clad in gray metallic tiles. Big enough to fit seventeen football fields inside, the 1-million-square-foot factory employs over a thousand people, some of whom spend their days clad in full-body white suits, like Woody Allen in *Sleeper,* padding up and down white hallways and etching computer chips in 184,000 square feet of clean rooms. Fab 32 was Intel's first high-volume producer of its forty-five-nanometer (45 billionths of a meter) transistors, which are so small that more than 2 million of them can fit on the period at the end of this sentence. Millions of these transistors are used in processors for computers and servers. They are produced on three-hundred-millimeter silicon wafers, which cost less, and use 40 percent less water, than the older two-hundred-millimeter wafers. Fab 32 produces some of the most advanced computer chips in the world. (Though, in a demonstration of Moore's law, Intel was producing twenty-two-nanometer transistors at other plants by late 2010. To keep pace, Intel plans a $7 billion upgrade to its Arizona fabs to manufacture its latest chips there.)

To many observers, Chandler seemed an eccentric place for Intel to build such a large, costly, high-tech fab. For one thing, the city was not much to look at. Chandler began as a ranch, grew into a small town, and eventually expanded into a pleasant, bland satellite of Phoenix. *Forbes* ranked Chandler as "one of the most boring cities in America," based on how rarely it was mentioned in the press (it is best known for its Peacock Day parade); it hardly seemed like a natural fit for a sophisticated, global, bleeding-edge technology firm such as Intel. More important, Chandler sits adjacent to the hottest city in the nation, in the shimmering Valley of the Sun, in the blazing Sonoran Desert, where water and the ecosystem are constant worries.

Computer-chip fabrication is water intensive. In Silicon Valley, California, the center of US microchip production, fabs from several companies account for a quarter of the water consumed and have faced complains about air and groundwater pollution. Of the twenty-nine Superfund sites in Silicon Valley (the most concentrated number in the United States), nineteen were contaminated by TCE, PCBs, and Freon from computer-chip manufacturers. Fabs are thirsty because as each of several dozen semiconductor layers is applied and etched to a silicon wafer, it must be rinsed by an atomized spray of water to keep it clean. Water has unique properties that remove molecular contaminants. Microprocessors are so sensitive that even minute particles in the water—traces of perfume or cologne, lotion, mold spores, or even smoke particles—can destroy a wafer. Computer-chip fabrication requires "ultrapure water," which acts as a sponge for microcontaminants, such as colloidal solids, particles, total organic carbon, bacteria, pyrogens (fragments of bacteria), metal ions, and the like.

A few years ago, the three Intel fabs at the Ocotillo campus in Chandler would have required at least 7 million gallons of water per day to produce their transistors. But in the pointy-headed world of Intel, experience shapes ideas, ideas lead to actions, actions have consequences, and consequences provide further experience, which feeds back into the learning loop. Or, as Len Drago, Fab 32's environmental health and safety director, put it, "We learned from our mistakes."

As it was being criticized in Albuquerque in the late 1990s, Intel apparently underwent an epiphany and made green technology a corporate priority. The company invested heavily in conservation, pollution control, renewable energy, emission reductions, and recycling initiatives—all of which saved resources and emphasized efficiency, provided environmental credibility, and ultimately saved it money. "It's about doing the right things right," says Intel's CEO, Paul Ottolini, who has linked employee compensation to achieving environmental goals.

"Water conservation was a big, big focus here from the get-go," said Tom Cooper, a cheerful blond hydrologist who runs the company's water programs worldwide, as he toured me around Fab 32.

Between 1998 and 2006, Intel invested about $100 million on water conservation projects, $20 million of that in Chandler alone, which saved over one hundred thousand acre-feet of water, equivalent to about 36 billion gallons. By using recycling and conservation technologies, and streamlining their manufacturing processes, the fabs in Chandler have reduced water use to about 2.5 million gallons a day.

Intel is still the largest water user in Chandler, by far, but these numbers are remarkable and set a standard for other manufacturers to emulate, or at least to aim for, as water demand rises and supplies grow stretched across the country.

Worried about industrial espionage, Intel bars outsiders such as me from touring the inside of its fabs, so Cooper showed me around the outside of Fab 32's futuristic circulatory system. City water, which originates from the Colorado River, is squeezed through a series of membranes until its mineral content is a hundred-thousandth that of water in the river. The ultrapurified water goes into the fab to wash chips. Brine, left over from the water cleansing, is fed into a tall silver evaporating tower that looks like a toy rocket. It sends rinsed water back into the system and the salts to a series of evaporation ponds. The rinsed water is treated, and the resulting gray water is used in cooling towers and air scrubbers, and to irrigate the campus's xeriscaped grounds. Finally, Intel sends 1.5 million gallons of water a day to Chandler's $19 million RO desal plant, which the company paid for. After being cleaned to drinking standards, this water is injected six hundred feet underground into a sandstone aquifer beneath the city, which has enough stored to survive a major drought.

Intel hopes Fab 32 will become a LEED (Leadership in Energy and Environmental Design, a green building standard)-certified manufacturing facility. It has room to build two more fabs on the Ocotillo campus and has already worked their water budgets into its calculations. The company has invested some $9 billion in Chandler; it employs ten thousand people statewide, and it pays an average of four times the median salary. Its three fabs recycle tons of waste, and the company donates wooden packing boxes to local nurseries, used copper to sculpting classes, and tons of coffee grounds as mulch to the local botanical garden. In Chandler, Intel had extensive negotiations over water use with the city before building its fabs, built a desalination plant and brine-evaporation ponds for the city, and has been a model corporate citizen. But one of the lessons of the greening of Intel is that such innovation is not easy, or cheap.

Wired points out that the company's environmental record doesn't take into account the energy required to operate the pumping, recycling, and recirculating of water on the Ocotillo campus. The three fabs there use enough power to supply fifty-four thousand homes a year, much of which comes from the Palo Verde nuclear plant, which uses 20 billion gallons of water a year in its massive cooling towers. Nor do Intel's numbers take into account the water footprint of its workers.

Nevertheless, the chips Intel builds at Fab 32 help power the computers used to keep American water supplies abundant and clean. And the company has produced a "tool kit" on water use developed by a "virtual team" (every Intel fab around the world contributes at least one employee to the virtual team) to use internally—and, in theory, with other companies willing to share information about costs, return on investment, problem solving, and the like.

Some Arizonans worry that Chandler is more beholden to Intel than the other way around, and that if an environmental problem arises the company could easily steamroll city leaders. (Though when an evaporation pond—built by Intel and run by the city—began to stink, upsetting neighbors, Intel bent over backward to fix the problem.) Traditionalists worry that Intel is changing the nature of the region and supplanting them, though this is a common reaction to the shifting demographics and rising urbanism of the Southwest.

In places such as Chandler, the past, present, and future of water come together. Here the New West and the Old West are learning to cohabitate and share, and water is the key resource that brings them together and could split them apart.

In *Unquenchable*, Robert Glennon writes approvingly of Intel's economies of scale at the Ocotillo campus, but his words might send a chill down the spine of local agriculturists: "It takes roughly 135,000 gallons of water to produce one ton of alfalfa, but it takes fewer than 10 gallons to produce [an Intel] Core 2 Duo microprocessor. . . . Each acre-foot [of water] used to grow alfalfa generates at most $264. That same acre-foot used to manufacture Core 2 Duo chips generates $13 million."

Fab 32's futuristic circulatory system must have seemed like a nearly unattainable dream a few years ago, when its critics sniggered at Intel's environmental missteps. But just as it transformed itself into the world's largest semiconductor maker, Intel refashioned itself into a leading environmental steward and built one of the most water-efficient factories in the world.

I asked Tom Cooper if Intel could ever become "water neutral," meaning that it would recycle or offset all of its water use so it had zero net impact on the environment, as Coca-Cola and others aspire to do. Cooper stared off into the distance, then changed the subject. Clearly, the question bugged him. A few days later he e-mailed me: "To be candid, we don't know yet. What we can be sure of is that the solution will boil down to: collect and analyze lots of data, communicate internally and externally, have persistence, and use a *lot* of patience."

Cooper doesn't believe Intel will revolutionize the way Americans use water overnight. There is no systems theory of water, no silver bullet to solve every water problem. But the efficiencies built into Fab 32 indicate a "blue" path to follow in coming decades. As Cooper put it, "Lots of little, constant improvements eventually add up to big improvements." And in this drying century, every drop counts.

The Ripple Effect

Till taught by pain
Men really know not what good water's worth.
—Lord Byron, *Don Juan*

VALUING WATER

In 1776, the Scottish economist Adam Smith wrote of the diamond-water paradox, "Nothing is more useful than water; but it will purchase scarce anything; scarce anything can be had in exchange for it. A diamond, on the contrary, has scarce any use-value; but a very great quantity of other goods may frequently be had in exchange for it." Two and a half centuries later, it should be obvious that this valuation is imbalanced. While diamonds—and other commodities such as oil, copper, and natural gas—are important, they are not essential for survival. Water is vital and has become inextricably linked to many other crucial issues, including health, diet, trade, urbanization, globalization, energy, and the state of the ecosystem.

Oil was the defining resource of the twentieth century, but the hydrocarbon era was an exception: for most of human history water has been the crucial resource; in coming years, the critic Alan Moores writes, it will reassume its natural dominion. H_2O will be the defining resource of the twenty-first century.

Every time man uses water, it sets off a widening ripple effect that has consequences few people understand. But we no longer have the luxury of ignoring our impact on water supplies. We must acknowledge the new hydrologic reality and adapt. The good news is that water, unlike oil, is renewable: humans may pollute it, overuse it, or allow it to evaporate into

343

the hot sky, but we cannot destroy water. The challenge is to learn how to manage the earth's limited supply more efficiently and sustainably.

The bad news is that people usually resist change until a crisis is underway. In the 1930s, Americans ignored warnings about drought and poor farming practices until the Dust Bowl drove 2.5 million people off the Great Plains. In the 1970s and 1980s, Americans ignored warnings about water pollution until the Cuyahoga River ignited and people were poisoned at Love Canal and elsewhere. In the first decade of this century, Americans ignored warnings that they were polluting and draining important supplies such as the Colorado River, the Everglades, the Great Lakes, the Mississippi, and the Sacramento Delta. Today, water scarcity, population growth, and environmental degradation have combined to force the kind of reckoning that the United States has not seen in forty years.

In the 1970s, the American environmental movement forced the passage of the Clean Water Act and the Safe Drinking Water Act, and the founding of the Environmental Protection Agency. Thus began a remarkable period of collective action when Americans, for the first time, agreed on the need to protect the nation's water supply. But since then, the nation's attention has drifted, and many important hydrologic lessons have been forgotten or no longer apply.

Laws designed to protect drinking supplies have become outdated, and the agencies responsible for enforcing them have been marginalized.

Since 1981 (at least), when President Ronald Reagan named James Watt as his secretary of the interior and Anne Gorsuch as his administrator of the EPA—both of whom were antiregulation and business-friendly—presidential administrations of both parties have weakened environmental protections. The EPA has been underfunded, politicized, and demoralized. The US Army Corps of Engineers has failed to build effective flood defenses. Employees of the Minerals Management Service were found literally and figuratively in bed with the company representatives they were supposed to regulate, allowing industries to cut corners, and resulting in such disasters as the 2010 sinking of the Deepwater Horizon in the Gulf of Mexico.

In mischievous rulings such as the 2006 *Rapanos* decision, the US Supreme Court has undermined the Clean Water Act, muddied the definition of which waterways can be regulated, and tacitly sided with developers who fill in wetlands to build shopping malls. Congress has likewise turned a blind eye to polluters, failed to invest in crucial hydro-infrastructure, encouraged waste (by providing irrigators with federal subsidies while not requiring them to measure how much water they use), and generally taken a short-term, uncoordinated approach to water governance.

Nearly half a century after the Clean Water Act was signed in 1972, America and the world face a second defining period in which our actions, and inactions, will have serious consequences for water supplies for years to come.

There are plenty of suggestions, and sharp disagreements, over how to respond. One camp favors building up water supplies by increasing the nation's reservoirs, canals, and pipelines (as the Schwarzenegger administration pushed for in California); this is essentially an updated version of nineteenth- and twentieth-century strategies. Another group favors a new water ethic built on the opposite approach: conserving existing water supplies and limiting new demand through efficient technologies, stringent regulation, price incentives, and broad public education.

These dueling visions have pitted some of the nation's leading water experts against one another, especially in the West, where hydro-politics has been described as "a blood sport." But the debate is more complex than headlines about "cities versus farms" or "concrete versus fish" would lead you to believe.

Today's water arguments reflect a growing unease about how to proceed when old certainties are being pushed aside and new options seem limited or unappealing. But the stark warnings implicit in Wisconsin's poisoned wells, the intersex and dying fish of Chesapeake Bay, Lake Mead's record-low waterline, the decay of levees across the country, and the resource war in Alaska's Bristol Bay, cannot be ignored.

THE HARD PATH, AND THE SOFT

In January 2010, Pat Mulroy, the celebrated water manager of Las Vegas, suggested that President Obama consider a plan that would solve the riddle of water supply for the entire nation with one deft move. In 2008, she had tried the idea out on me: "We need to look at the really big picture. The West is growing drier. The Midwest is growing wetter. We've ignored our infrastructure for decades. But why can't floodwaters in one part of the country be used as a water supply in another part of the country, through a series of exchanges?"

Water mavens have been asking this kind of question for years. If we can move oil from northern Alaska to Southern California, then why not move water from the Mississippi to the desert West?

Mulroy proposed dusting off a decades-old plan to collect surplus flood-water from the Mississippi River and export it to dry regions in the West. "If the West is growing drier and the Midwest is growing wetter, I see that as an opportunity," she said. One scenario envisions piping excess Mississippi water to recharge the Ogallala Aquifer. Another plan is to use the relatively plentiful water from the East to sate Denver and farmers on the Front Range, which would free them from pumping water across the Continental Divide, allowing more water to remain in the Colorado River for use by the basin states, Indian tribes, and Mexico. Mulroy believes that such massive water transfers would launch a cascade of smaller water projects across the country, creating jobs, stimulating the economy, providing water security for millions, and "making an investment in the future"—just as the building of the interstate highway system did in the 1950s.

Known as Flipping the Mississippi, the project would be the largest water diversion in American history. Like a twenty-first-century version of the national effort to send men to the moon, it would take thousands of workers at least a decade to build; it would dwarf the construction of Hoover and Glen Canyon Dams. Mulroy suggests the project be funded with some of the billions of federal stimulus dollars earmarked for infrastructure improvements.

While the Colorado River carries about 13 million acre-feet of water annually, the Mississippi and the Ohio Rivers carry 436 million acre-feet a year where they converge. "You could take six million acre-feet out of the Mississippi, and they wouldn't even know it's gone," said Mulroy.

Flipping the Mississippi is a wildly ambitious idea that critics say may be technically feasible but politically impossible, and that Mulroy's hometown antagonists—such as Bob Fulkerson, of the Progressive Leadership Alliance of Nevada—worry is a Trojan Horse that Mulroy could use to convince Washington to spend "billions of dollars to dry out rural Nevada." (Mulroy said she has no intention of using her Mississippi plan to influence the Nevada pipeline debate.) It would certainly be expensive, environmentally disruptive, and politically fraught. And with global warming changing conditions in unpredictable ways, such a project could prove to be a multibillion-dollar boondoggle. Yet Mulroy remains committed. "If you want to *really* think outside the box, and *really* solve our water problems? Then we need to talk about solutions we've never had the courage to talk about before," she insists.

Give Mulroy credit for asking the right questions and pushing for new, sometimes disconcerting answers. But at heart Flipping the Mississippi is a flashback to the costly, grandiose projects championed by Floyd Dominy and the Water Buffaloes. While conceptually intriguing, the scheme doesn't provide a realistic answer to the nation's new water challenges.

A cheaper, less risky, though no less ambitious, alternative is to adopt a new approach to managing water that emphasizes conservation and working with nature, rather than constantly trying to bend it to human will.

According to the proponents of this new water ethic, such as the British environmental writer Fred Pearce, the best way to ensure a healthy water supply and enough food, while protecting people from floods and droughts, is to undo many of the "improvements" people have made to natural water systems in the last century, and to re-embrace certain traditional methods of water management.

This approach requires people to stop building giant dams, allow artificially straightened rivers to reassert their natural courses, replenish aquifers and wetlands, and disassemble old levees and dams. These measures will occasionally be disruptive and expensive, but their backers say they will ultimately provide a more dependable, affordable, and sustainable supply of water than gargantuan concrete and pipe structures.

Instead of flood-irrigating fields—a notoriously inefficient practice that leads to the evaporation of water, the buildup of salt in the soil, and polluting runoff—Pearce and others recommend using traditional methods of water collection once popular in India, China, and throughout the Middle East (which were often undone by colonial occupiers, who didn't understand how effective they were).

Chief among these methods is "rain harvesting," which is the collection of rainwater in cisterns, qanats (vertical shaftways connected to horizontal tunnels), and ponds that allow water to percolate underground and replenish aquifers. Some 800 million acre-feet of water falls from the clouds every day, and over half the world's crops are already watered by rain. "Harvested" water is stored underground, which limits evaporation, and is carefully doled out. With wider use, rain harvesting could replace expensive, inefficient irrigation systems in many places.

Similar techniques could also improve life in urban settings. In Los Angeles, a desert city said to be the world's most paved area, activists are pushing to build catchments and porous streets in order to collect the city's scant precipitation, avoid floods and storm-water runoff when the skies do open, and lessen the city's dependence on expensive water imported from distant sources, such as the Colorado River. In 2010, Mayor Michael Bloomberg announced a twenty-year $1.5 billion initiative to make New York a "permeable city" that will use more trees, green roofs, porous roads, and revived wetlands to capture and retain storm water, reduce sewage overflows, clean waterways, cut costs, and green the Big Apple.

Such initiatives are gaining popularity and dovetail with new questions about the ecological impact of human water use. Bob Hirsch, of the US Geological Survey, has noticed a growing "societal shift in values over water." While people need H_2O for health and economic growth, the ecosystem—what Hirsch refers to as "the fish"—also needs water to survive. "The question used to be 'How much water can we take *out* of the river?'" he said. "Now people ask, 'How much water can we leave *in* the river?' There is no question that 'the fish' has a seat at the negotiating table."

But balancing the water needs of man and the fish is complex. One of the most promising solutions is so-called Soft Path water management, developed by Peter Gleick and other academics.

The Soft Path was a phrase coined by one of Gleick's old friends, the physicist, mountain guide, and inventor Amory Lovins, best known for founding the Rocky Mountain Institute, an environmental think tank in Colorado. In a 1976 essay in *Foreign Affairs,* Lovins first laid out his notion of a future powered by "soft energy," by which he meant solar, wind, and geothermal power. The Soft Path assumes that efficiency and renewability are paramount, and that creating power is only a means to an end, not the end itself. It presupposes that man should use whatever methods will achieve his ultimate goal in the most efficient way.

Applying this ethos to water, Gleick reasons that the Hard Path, as practiced by the Water Buffaloes, treats water problems as simple engineering questions: How do we extract more water from the environment as quickly as possible? How do we remove water from rivers and lakes and aquifers and move it farther and farther away, to make deserts bloom? This approach does not take into account how we move water (by building giant salmon-killing dams and pumps), what the environmental effect might be (silt buildup, depleted supplies, destruction of wildlife), or how we use it (to supply thirsty crops, golf courses, or housing developments in the desert).

"In engineering school, I was taught how to design a dam on a virgin river to build a reservoir that will meet the needs of one hundred thousand people," Gleick said. "But I was never taught to think about how those people actually *use* the water. Now we are changing the nature of our economy, and we are becoming more efficient. This is good news: it means we can do better."

The Hard Path worked well, initially, to provide water supplies that built the nation. But now it is widely recognized that large dams are expensive, inefficient, and environmentally destructive. The Water Buffalo ethos is becoming obsolete. As global warming and demographic shifts change the way water is managed, experts are searching for ways to build smaller, cheaper, less intrusive means of supplying water. Seemingly small efficiencies, such as low-flush toilets and low-flow showerheads in homes, and relatively modest infrastructure projects, such as drip-irrigated farming, underground waterbanking, and toilet-to-tap sewage recycling, can save more water, and money, than new dams can provide.

"Maybe I'm naive, but I believe we can conserve more and more. We just need to think harder about it," said Gleick.

CHARTING THE WATERS

Everything we do, we could do with less water.
—Peter Gleick,
the Pacific Institute, 2009

Looking back at the major questions examined in this book—water quality (pollution), water quantity (drought and flood), and how we manage water today and in the future (infrastructure and governance)—lessons have emerged that will help people make informed, thoughtful decisions for the future. There are no universal answers to the planet's water problems. But we can take concrete steps on the personal, local, national, and global level to use water more wisely and sustainably.

Water quality is declining around the world and is stealthily becoming a major health, economic, and environmental issue. In 2010, a billion people lacked access to clean, safe drinking supplies, and over 2.6 billion (mostly children) lacked proper sanitation, a crucial health indicator.

In the United States, the volume and complexity of pollutants flowing into waterways is on the rise. As water quality worsens, it has become glaringly obvious that federal environmental laws such as the Clean Water

Act, the Safe Drinking Water Act, and the Endangered Species Act, as well as many state regulations, require updating. Just as important, the agencies in charge of enforcing these laws must be reinvigorated and given the backing to do their job properly.

With little oversight, industrial polluters such as BP, ExxonMobil, and GE have allowed toxins and suspected carcinogens such as benzene or PCBs to linger in the environment for decades. Stocks of salmon, smelt, oysters, and other aquatic species have been decimated by agricultural runoff, dams, mines, and other human interference. Ineffective federal laws, combined with an inability of state governments to work collectively against water pollution, have allowed rich fisheries and commercially important waterways, such as the Chesapeake Bay or the Mississippi River, to become severely impaired.

If the nation's "worst environmental disaster," the 2010 BP oil spill in the Gulf of Mexico, has taught any lasting lesson, it is that the desire for corporate profits combined with lax oversight will result in environmental catastrophes that neither man nor the environment can afford. Society relies on fossil fuels and minerals: it is not realistic to expect resource exploration to stop in the near future, but it can be limited, monitored, and made safer with better regulation and oversight.

Certain glaring omissions—notably the Halliburton Loophole, which exempts natural gas drillers from major environmental laws or having to disclose what chemicals are used to hydrofrack shale—court environmental disaster. It is pure hubris to allow the injection of toxic chemicals into the ground, at explosive pressure, with no real idea of the effects. If a resource as valuable as the New York City watershed, which provides drinking water to over 9 million people and adjoins the heavily fracked Marcellus Shale deposit, is polluted for the sake of profit, there will be no way to undo the damage.

Regulators must be given the political and financial backing to curb such practices; industry and individuals should be incentivized to participate in slowing the tide of poisons leaching into waterways; and the nation should make the cleansing of toxic waters a priority. Without action, human and environmental health will suffer, and the nation will set itself back in many significant ways.

When it comes to personal responsibility for water pollution, it bears repeating that whatever substances we pour into our drains, flush down our toilets, or spray on our lawns end up in the water supply. According to a study by Johns Hopkins University, 75 percent of ingredients washed from homes survive wastewater treatment. These chemicals impact the ecosystem, including humans.

Even seemingly benign products, such as perfume or soap, contain endocrine disruptors that are suspected of causing fish intersex and death and may impact human health in ways that are not yet understood. Antibacterial soaps are increasingly popular, but once chemicals in them, such as triclocarban, are flushed into streams, they may act as immunosuppressants that weaken fish's ability to ward off disease.

When the USGS fish biologist Vicki Blazer explained how emerging contaminants are suspected of killing fish, or causing intersex, in the Chesapeake Bay watershed, a group of seventh graders wondered how they should respond. "Ask your parents about the products they use," Blazer said. "'Do we really need antimicrobial soaps? Does it really matter if a few dandelions sprout on our lawn?'" We know that these chemicals affect fish, and the human endocrine system is similar to that of fish, Blazer said. "It is possible that these chemicals could have some of the same effects on humans as on fish."

In 2010, the Obama administration provided the EPA with its largest budget in history, $10.5 billion a year, a 34 percent increase over 2009, but it remains an open question whether the agency will be able to shoulder its growing regulatory burden. While EPA administrator Lisa Jackson appears to be doing the best she can at a time of divisive politics and economic recession, she has been only partly successful in standing up to powerful industrial lobbies, and needs to build greater public support for the environmental battles ahead.

Bold action is called for to protect water quality. To gain the public's trust and backing, government leaders must do a much better job at educating taxpayers about why water is important, which problems need fixing, and why they should be willing to pay for them. As the water managers of Orange County, California, showed when they convinced the public of the benefits of toilet-to-tap sewage recycling, the success of new initiatives hinges on making a strong case to the citizens who will be asked to pay higher water rates and back public bonds to underwrite river cleanups, treatment plants, and other pollution controls.

The same could be said of government efforts elsewhere. India and China, which together comprise 40 percent of the world's population, have seen a spike in water pollution as they scramble for economic growth, but neither government has made meaningful investments in pollution controls. The Asian Development Bank predicts the region will need at least

$8 billion of new infrastructure just to meet the UN's 2015 target of reducing by half the number of people without access to clean drinking water. That kind of investment is unlikely to appear.

It is comforting to imagine that the United States and other industrialized countries, as well as the UN and the World Bank, private industry and wealthy individuals, will share knowledge and fund major global cleanup efforts. But the evidence suggests this is wishful thinking.

As populations and pollution skyrocket around the world, the prognosis for the earth's water quality, and thus human and environmental health, is grim.

The issue of water quantity—whether people will have too little water or be faced with too much of the wrong kind of water this century—is equally pressing.

THE SINGAPOREAN SOLUTION

By 2025, the global demand for domestic and industrial water use is predicted to rise by two-thirds. Experts disagree on whether there will be enough accessible freshwater to meet this requirement. While improvements in efficiency and conservation will help reduce water stress, parts of the world will face localized drought, if not widespread cataclysm.

An increasingly worrisome question is whether there will be sufficient water for food supplies.* According to the Organization for Economic Cooperation and Development, 70 percent of global water use is devoted to irrigated agriculture, which is notoriously unproductive. As emerging nations adopt more meat-centric diets, pressure on water supplies will heighten: it takes 634 gallons of water, mostly for cattle feed, to produce an eight-ounce piece of beef.

Between 2010 and 2025, the world's population is expected to grow from 6.7 billion to 9 billion. Yet water scarcity in that same period is expected to cut global food production by 385 million tons a year, which

---

* Scientists at the UN's Food and Agriculture Organization have categorically stated there is "no water crisis" and maintained that while the world faces "serious" water issues, the real problem is "a future food crisis." But to point out the obvious, food production requires water, and it is impossible to separate the two. If humanity suffers an environmental crisis, the underlying issue will be water.

is more than the average yearly US grain harvest. More people with less food and water is a potentially explosive combination.

As with water pollution, water supply in Asia is a particular concern. Some experts worry that by 2030 the region's water needs will exceed supply by 40 percent, though others say those fears are overblown. The historian Steven Solomon predicts that a lack of water could hobble India and China's phenomenal growth. These two nations have already faced domestic unrest over water scarcity, are arguing with neighbors over transboundary waters, and are vying with each other for Himalayan glacial melt. As the climate warms, and populations expand, these simmering tensions could easily flare into broader problems, even violence.

These are the kinds of water challenges the world will face in coming decades. In response, people will have to adopt a combination of old and new techniques to use water more efficiently than they do now.

No country uses water as carefully as the city-state of Singapore. With a population of just 4.8 million, Singapore is built on a marshy island surrounded by swamps and has limited natural water supplies. In 1942, invading Japanese troops blew up the island's main water pipeline as a way to subdue the populace. In the 1950s, the island faced water rationing, floods, and rampant contamination. But since the mid-1960s, Singapore has built up a world-class water system.

Demand is controlled by high water taxes and tariffs, the use of efficient technologies—such as low-flow toilets, taps, and washers—and exhortations by the government, which educates and constantly reminds citizens about the importance of conserving every drop. Supply comes from a variety of sources: 40 percent is piped in from Malaysia, while a remarkable 30 percent is provided by desalinated ocean water and recycled wastewater (Singapore's recycled wastewater is so thoroughly cleansed that it is used by the nation's booming high-tech industry, which, like Intel's fabs, requires ultrapure water). The rest is drawn from large-scale rainwater harvesting and other local sources. This tightly controlled hydrological system is overseen by a well-funded, highly educated, politically autonomous water authority. Its members invest in dams, bioreactors, and desalination technology as they see fit. As a result, Singapore's per capita domestic water use fell from 165 liters a day in 2003 to 155 in 2010, and the nation's supply is clean and relatively secure.

Most nations are much larger and more complex than Singapore, but the core lessons of the island's water efficiency are transferable.

THE RIPPLE EFFECT

America, for instance, could make rainwater harvesting a priority, desalinate and recycle wastewater on a much larger scale, and, especially, do a far better job of educating its citizens about which water problems need fixing, why, how, and when. Like Singapore, the United States could create a federal water agency to administer a national water policy.

America has never had a central water authority or a comprehensive water policy. Partly due to historical legacy, and partly due to sensitivities over federalism and states' rights, the nation's waters are overseen by a jumble of agencies that by one count includes six cabinet departments and twenty federal agencies, directed by thirteen congressional committees with twenty-three subcommittees and five appropriations subcommittees. With so many people and jurisdictions involved, overlap, redundancies, and rivalries are inevitable.

For America to take water management as seriously as Singapore does, it will have to streamline its byzantine governance system and create a new office at the federal level—perhaps a water czar or an interagency national water board*—to develop a framework for federal, state, and local agencies (many of which struggle in isolation) to operate in sync. A federal water office could set new quality standards, work with existing regulators, coordinate agencies on all levels, and fund research into new ways to adapt to changing conditions.

THE OTHER WATER PROBLEM

In a century destined for increased water scarcity, climatologists say, the world will also face more flooding.

In 2010, protracted rains sent high water surging down China's Yangtze River, straining the Three Gorges Dam—the world's largest hydroelectric project—setting off mudslides, and causing deaths and evacuations. In just that year, over a thousand people were killed and $21 billion in damage was caused by floods across China. In Indonesia, meanwhile, a tsunami killed at least four hundred people, and in Pakistan, where flooding was the worst in eighty years, more than sixteen hundred people were lost to floods. In the United States, high rains caused the Red, James, and Missouri Rivers to

---

* An alternative is to have the White House coordinate federal, state, and local agencies to create integrated water policies, though this approach is vulnerable to political wind-shifts and is not a good solution.

overflow and flooded thousands of acres throughout the Midwest, forcing mass evacuations in Fargo and Bismarck, North Dakota, and Moorhead, Minnesota. People were rescued by helicopter, and the National Guard was once again called on to build emergency flood defenses with sandbags.

While worries about flooding often take a backseat to fears of drought, the projected rise in precipitation and sea levels this century will become a serious problem that needs to be addressed with stricter oversight and greater investment.

The United States can learn much from the example of Holland (as detailed in chapter 21), which has the world's best flood-defense system. As with Singaporean water conservation, the key to Dutch flood control is a serious, national commitment. For America to build effective flood controls, the 1928 Flood Control Act, immunizing the US Army Corps of Engineers from prosecution when its levees fail, must be rewritten. The Corps itself must be revamped, and given support to replace the failing infrastructure with robust flood defenses that integrate traditional concrete and steel structures with natural storm-barriers, such as reeds, wetlands, and islands.

THE LAW OF DEMAND

Another significant issue going forward will be the economics of water. "Water flows towards money," hydrologists such as Bob Moran say, implying that the rich control the tap. While this is often true and can be abused, it is not always a bad thing.

In recent years, more H_2O has been flowing from low-value crops (cotton and alfalfa) to high-value ones (nuts and berries). Ailing farms are selling their water rights to productive industry and burgeoning cities. Food grown in wet, green climes (the northeastern United States, Brazil) is increasingly being exported to dry, brown ones (Arizona, India), allowing their water to be conserved for drinking supplies, for maintaining aquifer levels, or for other high-priority uses.

Yet people have tended to dance around the question of pricing water in a way that reflects scarcity.

Because water is an essential resource, it has no "market value," as, say, oil does. But with no price incentive to use it efficiently, people often squander water by flood-irrigating farmland, using vast quantities for energy and mineral projects, and polluting it. In many places water is free, or priced so low that the revenue it generates is not enough to maintain, or upgrade, reservoirs, distribution pipes, and treatment plants. While citizens have good reason to be wary of water privatizers, cheap water invites waste.

Many resource economists believe that in the twenty-first century the price of potable water will have to better reflect its availability.

The law of demand states that people demand less of a good as it becomes more expensive. This theory was validated in Santa Barbara, California, when, during the drought of 1987–91, the city raised water prices to help reduce consumption. Before the drought hit, Santa Barbara water was priced at a flat rate, meaning that the cost did not change when people used more water. In 1990, after three years of extremely low rainfall, prices shifted to a block rate: as water supplies dwindled, prices were raised in price "blocks," and consumption dropped by 50 percent. After the drought ended, water use rose, but only to 62 percent of predrought levels. "These prices permanently changed people's habits and attitudes," UC Berkeley economist David Zetland wrote of Santa Barbara. "People change their behavior when the price of water increases."

To allay fears that wealthy interests will take unfair advantage of the poor by jacking up water rates, the sensible compromise is to guarantee people enough free water to ensure survival—experts recommend a minimum of thirteen gallons per person, per day—and to charge for use beyond that, using tiered rates that put the cost burden on the heaviest users.

Water and money will be closely entwined in other ways this century: the need for significant investments in water infrastructure will force painful choices.

"THE DAWN OF THE REPLACEMENT ERA"

Most of the world's hydro facilities were built in the last century, are aging, and will need to be upgraded in the not-distant future. But these crucial facilities tend to be built out of sight, or buried, and are largely ignored even as they malfunction or disintegrate.

In the United States, some 240,000 water pipes burst every year, according to the EPA. By another estimate, from the USGS, 650 water mains break every day—a rate of one every two minutes. These leaks result in a loss of 1.7 trillion gallons of water a year, which is worth $2.6 billion annually and is enough water to supply 68 million people.

Many municipal water pipes are fifty to a hundred years old; some were built at the time of the Civil War; a handful of pipes in Alaska, Pennsylvania, South Dakota, and Washington are made of wood. Dilapidated sewer systems spew untreated sewage into waterways, while corroded water mains allow toxins to contaminate drinking supplies or rupture into floods that wash out roads, strand people, and cause millions of dollars' worth of damage.

With so many bits of water infrastructure aging across the country, the American Water Works Association has deemed this "the dawn of the replacement era."

Water infrastructure is expensive, is often large, and can run for miles underground, making it difficult to maintain or replace—especially for older industrial regions with weak economies. In 2009, America's water systems cost $1 trillion a year to operate; the Obama administration's federal stimulus bill provided $6 billion for water projects, with $2 billion of that earmarked for improvements to drinking-water systems. But that money is a mere drop in the ocean. The EPA estimates that, just for drinking-water systems, repairs and upgrades will require a $334 billion investment over the next two decades, mostly to improve aging pipelines and pumps.

This is an onerous and politically unpalatable cost. But utilities provide essential services, and without repairing and replacing old parts, water systems will face a general collapse. Furthermore, water infrastructure is a good investment. According to the US Conference of Mayors, every dollar invested in water and sewer improvements has the potential to increase the long-term gross domestic product by more than $6.

THE AGE OF RESTORATION

The greatest threat to freshwater supplies is human indifference. It has allowed disease, poverty, conflict, and environmental destruction to proliferate. Some fear that humans have already passed the world's hydrologic tipping point.

In an influential 1968 article in *Science,* titled "The Tragedy of the Commons," Garrett Hardin, a leading American ecologist, wrote of "the damage that innocent actions by individuals can inflict on the environment" and described the pattern by which people acting in their own self-interest destroy shared resources. The hypothetical example he used focused on medieval farmers who shared a field, "the commons," and allowed their cattle to graze indiscriminately. As each farmer added more and more cows to the field, he reaped benefits, but with each cow added, the field became more degraded; eventually, all of the grass on the common was eaten, at which point all of the farmers and their cows suffered. The shared resource was destroyed by individuals concerned only with their own well-being.

The field in Hardin's parable is a metaphor for the unrestricted use of modern "commons," such as the earth's atmosphere, national parks, and fish stocks. Lately, Hardin's theme has been taken up by water experts. By allowing virtually unlimited access to water, and by focusing on individual success rather than on collective benefit, they fear, humans are running blindly into a tragedy of the hydrologic commons.

Unless people snap out of their apathy, no amount of investment, regulation, lofty goal-setting, or technical breakthroughs will save the planet from a hydrological tragedy. Success, even partial success, in overcoming ignorance and inaction will help end many of the root causes of the problems discussed in this book and allow people to live healthy lives. Surely, this is worthy of our time, interest, and resources.

There is reason for hope. Because humans cause most of the world's water problems, we have a degree of control over them, and we can choose to solve them.

In the summer of 2008, Bob Hirsch presented the annual M. Gordon "Reds" Wolman Lecture to the Consortium of Universities for the Advancement of Hydrologic Science Inc., in Boulder, Colorado.* For an audience of some 250 of the nation's leading water scientists, USGS's former chief hydrologist described how Stephen Ambrose's writings about Lewis and Clark had shaped his thinking about the evolution of American hydrology. The historian characterized the nineteenth century as an era of "discovery and description," and the twentieth century as an era of "command and degrade"; he hoped the twenty-first century would be regarded as "the century of restoration."

In his lecture, Hirsch drew parallels to this historical scheme. In the nineteenth and early twentieth centuries, American hydrologists measured stream flow, the behavior of groundwater, and the chemistry of American rivers. "When we look back [at those studies] now, they help us

---

* Wolman, who died in 2010, was one of the nation's most respected hydrologists. Hirsch earned his PhD under Wolman at Johns Hopkins, in 1976.

understand how our nation's rivers have changed chemically over a hundred years," Hirsch told the audience. The twentieth century, the period of "command and degrade," witnessed massive degradation of surface-water quality (epitomized for the nation by the burning of the Cuyahoga, and for me by the poisoning of my local waters, such as Newtown Creek and the Housatonic River). This was also the time of significant groundwater depletion, such as the draining of "fossil water" from the Ogallala Aquifer by high-capacity pumps and center-pivot irrigation systems, while point-source pollution and the environmental impact of large dams emerged as national issues. In 1971, Wolman published a seminal paper in *Science* entitled "The Nation's Rivers," in which he pointed to how little we knew about the degradation and improvement of rivers and underscored the need for long-term data collection on which to build informed decisions.

"Our science has followed [Wolman's] pattern and needs to continue" to do so, Hirsch said, to applause from the crowd.

Hirsch ended his talk by echoing the hope that this will be the century of hydrological restoration. He emphasized the importance of "integrated water management," in which the needs of all users are taken into account and where engineered structures are integrated with natural features—as has been done in the New York City watershed, where strict water regulations and aggressive land conservation have maintained water quality and avoided costly treatment plants. "Today we have some of the most exciting pieces of integrated scientific work focused on restoration in the Everglades, the San Francisco Bay Delta, the Grand Canyon, the Platte River, and many other places," said Hirsch. "We know that these systems . . . have been severely degraded. Now, in the twenty-first century, our society has set about to try to restore them—maybe not to a pristine condition, but clearly to a *better* condition."

After years of neglect, signs are that Washington is slowly acknowledging that the nation's waters are in trouble and require the kind of careful attention long advocated by such experts as Bob Hirsch, Bob Moran, Bob Bea, and Peter Gleick.

For now, the nation has only a vague idea of the quality and quantity of its freshwater supply, and whether there is enough of it to meet future demands. Amazingly, the last comprehensive census of US water resources was completed by the Water Resources Council in 1978. But "you can't manage what you don't measure," say hydrologists, who have been pushing for a new national census.

In October 2010, four days after Lake Mead dropped to a record-low water level, Interior Secretary Ken Salazar announced the first small step in that direction: a three-year, $1.5 million study of the Colorado River. Called WaterSMART,* this will be the first study to measure the state of three river basins—the Colorado, the Delaware, and the "AFC" (Apalachicola/Chattahoochee/Flint) systems—where there is "significant competition over water." The study, conducted by the USGS, examines water quality and quantity, climate change, and will predict how much water needs to be left in rivers to sustain aquatic life—"the fish."

The study is belated and modest, but represents the sort of clear-eyed, science-based, integrated approach that is urgently needed to assess the state of the nation's water supply, explain it to the public, and spur action in coming years.

By the second decade of the twenty-first century, most people have not run out of potable H_2O yet, but they continue to take it for granted, waste it, contaminate it, and mismanage it. These practices are unsustainable. A growing number of hydrologists, economists, and diplomats warn that localized water problems could coalesce and tip the earth into a full-blown "water crisis." To forestall an emergency, we must redefine how we think of water and how we use it. In short, we must learn to treat deceptively simple H_2O for what it really is: the most valuable resource on earth.

* WaterSMART stands for Sustain and Manage America's Resources for Tomorrow.

"Water!"

> Water, thou hast no taste, no color, no odor; canst not be defined, art relished while ever mysterious. Not necessary to life, but rather life itself, thou fillest us with a gratification that exceeds the delight of the senses.
> —Antoine de Saint-Exupéry, *Wind, Sand and Stars*, 1939

One summer in the early 1960s, a drought hit the coast of Maine, where my grandparents had built a log cabin on a point of land thirty years earlier. The water level in their usually reliable well suddenly dropped, and their pipes began to cough and go dry. Worried, they contracted a dowser, or water witch, to search for a new source.

The best dowser in the neighborhood was Mrs. Martha Willis, a young city-born woman who had married a Mainer and discovered that she possessed the power to divine veins of freshwater hidden deep underground. Her only tool was a freshly cut twig of swamp alder. Holding the trilimbed twig by its forked ends, with the longest limb pointed forward and level, she picked her way around the property, alert for a signal. Occasionally the stick would dip in a shallow indication of a source, but Mrs. Willis wasn't satisfied. Eventually, she found two spots where the stick lunged toward the ground. "These look like good places," she said. "Mark those spots with stakes." Then, handing the twig to my grandmother, she said, "Here, you try it."

My grandmother Fredericka Child wandered about with the stick but had only haphazard luck. Then my grandfather Charles Child tried it. Within a few paces, he recalled, "The fork plunged so hard in my [hands] it tore the bark off the twigs. It was a strange, rather compelling sensation. . . . I didn't quite believe it even when it happened . . . but one must leave the door open to mystery. . . . The sensation is one of having an invisible hand reach up suddenly and pull the stick toward the ground as you pass over certain areas."

Mrs. Willis was satisfied with the spot my grandfather found. Soon, a drill rig arrived and spent several days boring a hole into the granite. My grandparents hovered expectantly as the rig drilled 50 feet down, 75 feet down, then 100 feet down. Heaps of dust and mud were extruded from the borehole, but no water. The property was close to the ocean, and the drillers warned it was possible that they'd find nothing or undrinkable, brackish water filled with iron and silt.

After the second day of drilling, the hole was 150 feet deep but still dry, and the charm of the water witch began to fade. On the third day, my grandparents gave up and went out for lunch. When they returned home, the workmen were whooping and hollering: at a depth of 165 feet, they had hit a bulb of cool, fresh H_2O, without a trace of silt or salt. There was so much freshwater that it gushed over the top of the drill casing in a steady stream.

"Water! Pure water! Limpid, liquid, looping, lovely water!" my grandfather wrote. "The first measurements showed we were getting a flow of more than six gallons a minute, or about 10,000 gallons a day. . . . we had a water-tasting ceremony in which all gulped in turn. . . . Hooray! . . . It was pure, clean and cold."

My grandfather's joy at finding a new source rings a bell, as he would say, deep inside. His reaction was instinctual and universal, something every human can relate to: *Water!*

Yet his glee is also a reminder of what is at stake every time we take a drink from the tap, wash off in the shower, hose our lawn, turn on the computer, douse a fire, or manufacture a computer chip. His exuberance at finding a new supply in a time of drought—"pure, clean and cold"—was also a sigh of relief, a shout of triumph over the primal terror of having nothing left to drink.

Acknowledgments

"Chance favors the prepared mind," Louis Pasteur said, and so it was with this book. I have always had a special fascination with water and have spent a lot of time in, on, and around it. But I didn't think of writing a book about H_2O until the day Julia Child and I shared a bottle of water at lunch. We were collaborating on her memoir, *My Life in France*, and she explained how the French consider spring water a healthy "digestive" and enjoy its mineral *terroir*, while Americans consider bottled water a refreshing "beverage" and prefer it without any taste. Later, her niece's husband, Bob Moran, a hydrogeologist, told us that water supplies are under growing pressure around the world, and that H_2O will be the defining resource of this century. Suddenly, water seemed all-important, and without realizing it, I had launched into writing this book.

Water is a vast subject and I had a steep learning curve. I am grateful to the experts who guided me through the four sections of this book: Dr. Robert Hirsch of the USGS, Dr. Robert Moran, Professor Robert Bea of UC Berkeley, and Dr. Peter Gleick of the Pacific Institute. All four were generous with their time and knowledge and were excellent company.

I owe deep gratitude to the many scientists, engineers, activists, and citizens who told me their stories and patiently answered my questions: the Angara family, Sister Francis Gerard Kress, Sebastian Pirozzi, Basil Seggos, Tim Gray, Dave Gibbs, Judy Treml, James Pynn, Dr. Ettore Zuccato, Dr. Vicki Blazer, Carole Morison, Jeff Kelble, Earl Greene, Mike Markus and Gina DePinto, Ted Dowey, Dr. Richard Seager, Mike Prather, Pat Mulroy, Dean Baker, Lester Snow, Frank Gehrke, Ambassador Jan Eliasson, Dr. Malcolm Bowman, Dr. Douglas Hill, Jimmy Delery, Jeff Hart, T. Boone Pickens, Jim Wilfong, Kim Jeffery, Alice Waters, Drew Nieporent, Clark Wolf, Tim LaPorte, John Shively, Carol Ann Woody,

ACKNOWLEDGMENTS

Bobby Andrew, Bob Waldrop, Bella Hammond, Herb Guenther, Walt Winrow, Peter MacLaggan, and Tom Cooper.

At Scribner, Nan Graham and Paul Whitlatch were incisive editors who showed great forbearance and made large and small suggestions that greatly enhanced this work. Tina Bennett was invaluable: a sharp literary agent with great editorial instincts, who helped me craft the book proposal, acted as a sounding board, and encouraged me to keep paddling when the river seemed long. My thanks also to Bill Patrick, who helped trim and focus a manuscript that had grown overburdened.

I greatly appreciate the advice of Matthew Snyder at CAA, and am indebted to my friends Carol Baum and David Helpern. I thank Diane Weyermann, Jonathan King, and Ricky Strauss at Participant Media, and Jessica Yu and Elise Pearlstine for their support.

I want to thank the editors on the *New York Times* editorial page, who ran two pieces I wrote—"There Will Be Floods" (about levees) and "An Oil Spill Grows in Brooklyn" (Newtown Creek). These editorials helped focus my reporting and led to useful feedback from readers.

I interviewed over fifty people for this book, and am grateful to those who were generous with their time but ultimately did not appear in these pages, or did so only fleetingly. I learned much from Brad Udall, Emily Lloyd, Susan Leal, Marilyn Gelber, Meisha Hunter, Chick Donoghue, Dr. Harry Browne, Terry Spragg, Geoffrey Y. Parker, Rick Halford, John Branson, Bruno Bowles, Amy Kenyon, Ken Jaffe, Neal Drawas, Jim Stevens, Bruce Nevins, David Daniel, Ahad Afridi, Walter Robb, Peter Thum, Jonathan Greenblatt, Kimball Chen, Arthur von Weisenberger, Professor Anders Nilsson, Professor Richard J. Saykally, and Judy Maben at the Water Education Foundation.

For moral support, housing, meals, and stimulating conversation, I thank Hector and Erica Prud'homme, Emily Prud'homme, Michael Pollan, Bill McKibben, John Seabrook, Corby Kummer, Henry Labalme, Phila Cousins, Heidi Nitze, Jill and John Walsh, Dana Burke, Dan Fitzgerald, Brian Thomas, Elise Pettus, David Schwab, Curtis Cravens, Bill Shebar, Bill Robens, Tim O'Brien, Luis Jaramillo, Diego Miralles, Mark Friedman, and Caroline and Alexandra Paul.

Writing this book took me across the country and sank me deep into my computer. I was away from my family for extended periods, and I know my absence was difficult for them. I would not have been able to write this book without the support, good humor, and excellent questions of my wife, Sarah, and my children, Hector and Sophia. Thank you.

Notes

Although I did a great deal of original reporting for this book, I also benefited from the efforts of others. In these notes I've tried to give credit to the many people whose work helped to inform my research and writing.

PROLOGUE: UNDER PRESSURE

1 *Thirty-five feet down:* Author's interviews with Angara's family, coworkers, and investigators on the case. See also Douglas Crouse and Amy L. Kovac, "Confusion follows in death of chemist," *Bergen Record,* February 11, 2005.

2 *the Hackensack Water Company:* "United Water Resources Inc," Fundingverse.com.

2 *rancorous arguments broke out:* "Emerson Woods Preserve," NJUrbanforest blog: http://njurbanforest.com/tag/emerson-nj/. See also Bergen Save the Watershed Action Network: http://www.bergenswan.org/about.aspx.

3 *Angara family filed a wrongful-death suit:* John Petrick, "Judge sets mediation deadline in wrongful death suit," *Bergen Record,* September 14, 2009.

3 *a history of accidents:* John Cichowski, "State to Study Sabotage Reports—water officials doubt labor link," *Bergen Record,* May 14, 1993. See also Douglas Crouse, "Water sabotage preceded killing," *Bergen Record,* May 30, 2006.

5 *triclocarban:* Steve Curwood, "Hormone Disruptors Linked to Genital Changes and Sexual Preferences," *Living on Earth,* January 7, 2011.

5 *Atrazine:* Ibid.

CHAPTER 1: THE DEFINING RESOURCE

10 *by 2000 some 1.2 billion people:* These are the latest figures available: cited in the UN's *The Global Water Supply and Sanitation Assessment 2000.*

10 *by 2025 as many as 3.4 billion people:* Jan Eliasson and Susan Blumenthal, "Dying for a drink," *Washington Post,* September 20, 2005.

10 *Between 2004 and 2009, the Clean Water Act (CWA):* Charles Duhigg, "Clean water laws are neglected, at a cost in suffering," *New York Times,* September 12, 2009. This is one part of "Toxic Waters," Duhigg's remarkable series of articles about the declining state of American water quality.

11 *contaminated by 316 different pollutants:* http://www.ewg.org/tap-water/home.

11 *bottled water . . . contained traces of thirty-eight pollutants:* http://www.ewg.org/health/report/bottledwater—scorecard.

NOTES

11 *By 2008, the world's consumption of water:* "Running Dry," *Economist,* August 21, 2008.

12 *thirty-six states will face water shortages by 2013:* GAO: http://www.gao.gov/new.items/d03514.pdf.

12 *McKinsey & Co. forecasts:* http://www.mckinsey.com/clientservice/Water/home.aspx.

12 *some 332.5 million cubic miles of H₂O:* "The Water Cycle: Water Storage in Oceans," US Geological Survey: The Water Cycle.

13 *The body weight of an adult:* Answers.com: http://wiki.answers.com/Q/How_many_gallons_of_water_are_in_the_make-up_of_an_average_person's_body#ixzz17YKjjv90.

13 *Human bones are about 22 percent:* While there are various estimations of these numbers, I have drawn from a list posted by Lenntech, a Dutch water-treatment firm: http://www.lenntech.com/water-trivia-facts.htm.

CHAPTER 2: THE MYSTERY OF NEWTOWN CREEK

15 *At 12:05 p.m. on October 5, 1950:* Riverkeeper, "A Slippery Past," http://www.riverkeeper.org.

15 *rainbow-hued oil slick:* Personal observation.

16 *at least 17 million:* Author's interviews of Basil Seggos, Riverkeeper, in 2007–08. See also NewtownCreekAlliance.org.

16 *the largest in US history:* Melissa Grace, "ExxonMobil Taint Suit," *New York Daily News,* January 25, 2007.

16 *black mayonnaise:* Julie Leibach, "Black Mayonnaise," *Scienceline,* Jan 24, 2007.

17 *more than one hundred homes:* "Greenpoint Oil Spill on Newtown Creek," Riverkeeper.org.

17 *Greenpoint has a lower overall cancer rate . . . Tom Stagg:* Daphne Eviatar, "The Ooze," *New York,* June 3, 2007.

18 *Chicago, for example . . . 6 percent of the city's population:* Marcelo H. Garcia, "Hydraulics in the Time of Cholera: The Chicago River, Lake Michigan and Public Health," remarks from Hydrology Days conference, American Geophysical Union, Colorado State University, 2009.

19 *Between 1961 and 1970, according to the EPA:* "25th Anniversary of Safe Drinking Water Act," remarks by Carol M. Browner, administrator, Environmental Protection Agency, December 16, 1999.

19 *it "oozes rather than flows":* "America's Sewage System and the Price of Optimism," *Time,* August 1, 1969.

19 *William Ruckelshaus was named:* William Ruckelshaus, "A New Shade of Green," *Wall Street Journal,* April 17, 2010.

20 *In 1978, President Jimmy Carter:* Eckardt C. Beck, "The Love Canal Tragedy," *EPA Journal* (January 1979), and Sam Howe Verhovek, "After 10 Years, the Trauma of Love Canal Continues," *New York Times,* August 5, 1988.

20 *Carol Browner announced that:* Browner, "25th Anniversary of Safe Drinking Water Act."

20 *But a year later, the EPA revealed:* "Water Quality Conditions in the United States: A Profile from the 2000 National Water Quality Inventory," EPA, August 2002.

NOTES

21 *By 1860, New York was the nation's leading manufacturing center:* Andrew Hurley, "Creating Ecological Wastelands: Oil Pollution in New York City, 1870–1900," *Journal of Urban History* (May 1994).

21 *Astral Oil:* Jen Phillips, "The Brooklyn Oil Spill: A Timeline," *Mother Jones,* September 13, 2007.

21 *In 1872, John D. Rockefeller's Standard Oil Company:* Hurley, "Creating Ecological Wastelands," p. 346.

22 *three hundred thousand gallons of gas:* Ibid., p. 348.

22 *"a quivering envelope of nauseous fog":* Andy Newman, "Fouled Creek's Improvement Inspires a Site for Respite," *New York Times,* September 27, 2007.

22 *most expedient . . . Fifteenth Ward Smelling Committee . . . "fully developed stenches":* Hurley, "Creating Ecological Wastelands," p. 340.

22 *residents had pumped so much . . . Brooklyn Aquifer:* DEP, BQA study http://www.nyc.gov/html/dep/html/drinking_water/bqa.shtml, and Eviatar, "The Ooze."

23 *Sister Francis Gerard Kress:* Author's interview with Sister Francis on September 9, 2006, at the Maria Regina Residence, in Brentwood, New York, and subsequent correspondence.

24 *Sebastian Pirozzi:* Author's interview of Sebastian Pirozzi, November 30, 2010, and subsequent correspondence.

24 *osteosarcoma, a rare form of cancer:* http://www.cancer.org/Cancer/Osteosarcoma/DetailedGuide/osteosarcoma-key-statistics.

24 *in 2006, only twenty-four new cases:* Angela Montefinise and Susan Edelman, "Cancer Outrage Near Oil Spill," *New York Post,* October 15, 2006.

24 *the woman who replaced them contracted bone cancer:* Ibid. and Pirozzi interview.

25 *ExxonMobil took the position:* Eviatar, "The Ooze."

25 *Basil Seggos, who worked:* Ibid., and Seggos interview.

26 *If the company assumed responsibility for cleaning up the spill:* Eviatar, "The Ooze."

26 *Riverkeeper's FOIA requests:* Ibid.

26 *oil companies denied the allegations:* Ibid.

26 *no terminal operations there since 1993:* Karen Freifeld, "Exxon to Pay $25 Million to Settle Brooklyn Spill Suit," *Bloomberg Businessweek,* November 18, 2010.

26 *Peter Sacripanti:* Daphne Eviatar, "Out in the oil patch with McDermott Will Partner," *American Lawyer,* April 3, 2007.

27 *Environmentalists characterized the remediation efforts as "rudimentary" . . . twenty-eight thousand gallons:* Riverkeeper.org.

27 *In a related but separate case:* DEP, BQA study.

27 *In 2003, the city sued twenty-three oil companies:* Mireya Navarro, "City Awarded $105 Million in ExxonMobil Lawsuit," *New York Times,* October 20, 2009.

28 *When a dolphin was spotted:* Erin Durkin, "Dolphin spotted in Brooklyn's polluted Newtown Creek," *New York Daily News,* March 4, 2010.

28 *an "estuary of national significance":* "EPA Makes Final Decision: Newtown Creek Is Added to Superfund List," EPA press release, September 27, 2010.

28 *removed 11 million gallons of oil:* Mireya Navarro, "ExxonMobil Settles State Suit on Newtown Creek Cleanup," *New York Times,* November 18, 2010.

28 *creek was designated a Superfund site:* Mireya Navarro, "US Cleanup Is Set for Creek Long Polluted by Industry," *New York Times,* October 28, 2010.

NOTES

29 *pay $25 million in penalties . . . Paul Gallay . . . "an historic turning point"*: "Cuomo Announces Settlement with ExxonMobil to Provide for Comprehensive Cleanup of Greenpoint Oil Spill," attorney general press release, November 18, 2010.

30 *"the worst environmental disaster in the nation's history"*: From numerous press accounts, including the *New York Times* hub: http://topics.nytimes.com/top/reference /timestopics/subjects/o/oil_spills/gulf_of_mexico_2010/index.html?inline=nyt -classifier.

31 Oil in the Sea III: James Coleman, et al., *Oil in the Sea III: Inputs, Fates, and Effects* (No. 3) (National Academies Press, 2003). See also Alan Levin, "Land-based oil spills add up, too," *USA Today*, June 30, 2010.

CHAPTER 3: GOING TO EXTREMES

32 *The Housatonic contains some of the highest levels:* US Environmental Protection Agency site history: http://www.epa.gov/ne/ge/sitehistory.html. The Housatonic River Initiative (HRI): http://housatonic-river.com/blog/. Save the Housatonic (STH): http://savethehousatonic.org/?page_id=57. John Nicas, "The Housatonic Cleanup," Boston University College of Communication, May 20, 2009.

32 *the General Electric (GE) plant in Pittsfield:* Housatonic River Initiative: http://www .housatonic-river.com/links2.php and Nicas, "Housatonic Cleanup."

32 *former senior GE employees, and the watchdog group:* Ibid. See also EPA site history.

33 *over 1.5 billion pounds of PCBs:* US Environmental Protection Agency reports, including http://www.epa.gov/epawaste/hazard/tsd/pcbs/pubs/about.htm, and http://www.epa.gov/NE/ge/thesite/restofriver/reports/456069.pdf.

33 *PCB concentrations of up to 206 ppm:* US Environmental Protection Agency reports: http://www.epa.gov/region1/ge/thesite/halfmile/reports/m1998 memorandum emorandum/242242.pdf and http://www.epa.gov/NE/ge/thesite/restofriver/reports /456069.pdf.

34 *GE, which had been founded by Thomas Edison:* GE company history: http://www .ge.com/company/history/edison.html.

34 *GE first used PCBs in Pittsfield:* Nicas, "Housatonic Cleanup."

34 *so much PCB-contaminated oil:* Author's interviews with Tim Gray, November 17 and 28, 2009. HRI website. Bryant University report, "PCB's and the River": http://web .bryant.edu/~langlois/ecology/pcb.html.

34 *The Harvard School of Public Health:* Bryant University report, "PCB's and the River."

35 *free "clean fill":* Gray, HRI. Complaint filed against GE by residents of Lakewood, Massachusetts, and the Residential Environmental Action League, March 20, 2000: http://www.berkshireeagle.net/lakewood.html. For GE's use of fuller's earth and PCB contamination of the Hudson River, see David Gargill, "The General Electric Superfraud," *Harper's Magazine*, December 2009.

35 *"There have been a lot of studies":* GE ad of September 30, 1997, cited in http://www .housatonic-river.com/rapids_spring99.php.

35 *it was discovered that the soil:* Gray interview. Gargill, "General Electric Superfraud."

36 *Gray first encountered PCBs in 1976:* Gray interview.

37 *Standing in his kitchen, Dave Gibbs:* Author's interview with Dave Gibbs, November 28, 2009.

NOTES

37 *For years, a grassy field there:* Gibbs and Gray interviews. Anthony DePalma, "GE Moves Ahead on Removal of PCBs from 2 Rivers, but Frustrations Remain," *New York Times,* May 1, 2007.

37 *1948 memo:* Michael Cohen, "GE Knew of Pittsfield 'Liability' for Years," *Boston Globe,* August 10, 1997.

38 *"increases in cancer mortality in workers":* "GE Fights Back with Full Page Ads," HRI, Spring 1999 newsletter.

38 *One major roadblock was Jack Welch:* Gray interview and HRI; Gargill, "General Electric Superfraud."

38 *Welch earned $83.6 million a year:* Berkshire Eagle, April 9, 1999.

38 *"PCBs do not pose health risks":* "God versus G.E.," *Harper's Magazine,* August 1998.

38 *The company's lawyers devised a clever argument:* Ibid. See also Gray interview and DePalma, "GE Moves Ahead."

38 *GE used the same argument to deny:* Andrew C. Revkin, "Dredging of Pollutants Begins in Hudson," *New York Times,* May 15, 2009.

39 *Laurence Tribe:* Gargill, "General Electric Superfraud."

39 *In May 2009, a dredge:* Revkin, "Dredging of Pollutants Begins in Hudson."

39 *the company is wholly or partially responsible:* Gargill, "General Electric Superfraud."

39 *Cleanup of the Housatonic has gone more slowly:* Gray interview and HRI; DePalma, "GE Moves Ahead."

40 *Instead, activists propose a ten-point plan:* Gray interview. HRI: "Ten Principles for a Better River Cleanup," blog post, February 4, 2009.

41 *Anaconda Copper Mining Company:* William Langewiesche, "The Profits of Doom," *Atlantic,* April 2001.

41 *342 snow geese:* Duncan Adams, "Did Toxic Stew Cook the Goose?" *High Country News,* December 11, 1995.

41 *Since 1998, BP-ARCO and regulators:* Justin Post, "Waterfowl land in pit, die," *Montana Standard,* November 30, 2007. See also PITWATCH: http://www.pitwatch .org/2004.htm.

41 *Donald Peoples:* Langewiesche, "Profits of Doom." See also Gerard O'Brien, "Don Peoples: the man behind mining city," *Montana Standard,* February 3, 2008.

42 *Mine Waste Technology Program for the DOE:* Mountain States Energy (MSE): http:// www.mse-ta.com/index.html.

42 *37 billion gallons of toxic seepage:* Montana Bureau of Mines and Geology, "Berkeley Pit Facts," http://www.mbmg.mtech.edu/env/env-berkeley.asp.

42 *extremophiles:* Christopher Maag, "In the Battle Against Cancer, Researchers Find Hope in a Toxic Wasteland," *New York Times,* October 9, 2007.

42 *Huntington's disease:* PITWATCH.

CHAPTER 4: THE NUMBER ONE MENACE

43 *85 percent of water pollution:* Ruckelshaus, "New Shade of Green."

44 *Ninety-six percent of all health violations:* EPA: http://cfpub.epa.gov/eroe/index .cfm?fuseaction=detail.viewInd&ch=47&subtop=203&lv=list.listBy Chapter&r=188226.

44 *43 million Americans—15 percent of the population:* US Geological Survey: http:// water.usgs.gov/nawqa/vocs/national_assessment/report/chapter4.html.

NOTES

44 *Samantha Treml:* Author's interview with Judy Treml, May 20, 2010, and with Melissa Scanlon, of Midwest Environmental Advocates, on May 17, 2010. For background, see http://www.midwestadvocates.org/archive/Treml/index.htm. Judy Treml's congressional testimony: http://transportation.house.gov/Media/file/Full%20 Committee/20091015/Treml%20Testimony.pdf.

47 *agricultural runoff is now:* EPA, "Managing Nonpoint Source Pollution from Agriculture": http://water.epa.gov/polwaste/nps/outreach/point6.cfm.

47 *E. coli are responsible for 35 percent:* "Animal Waste on Factory Farms Comes Under Closer EPA Scrutiny," Environmental News Service, June 1, 2010.

47 *19.5 million Americans are sickened:* Charles Duhigg, "Health Ills Abound as Farm Runoff Fouls Wells," *New York Times,* September 17, 2009.

47 *more than 1 billion tons of manure:* Amanda D. Cuéllar and Michael E. Webbe, "Cow power: the energy and emissions benefits of converting manure to biogas," *Environmental Research Letter* (July–September 2008).

47 *South Florida Water District has spent $2 billion:* Spencer Hunt, "States go soft on polluting farms," *The Columbus Dispatch,* October 12, 2010.

47 *In 2008, US farms held 96 million head of cattle:* "An Urgent Call to Action," Report of the State-EPA Nutrient Innovations Task Group, August, 2009.

48 *Holstein emits 150 pounds of waste a day:* Henry Fountain, "Down on the Farm, an Endless Cycle of Waste," *The New York Times,* December 28, 2009.

48 *19 CAFOs in 1992:* Lee Bergquist, "Taking Care of Cows' Business," *Milwaukee Journal-Sentinel,* March 1, 2009.

48 *Rosendale Dairy:* Ibid. See also "Rosendale Dairy wants to expand," Fox 11 online, December 2, 2009.

48 *Threemile Canyon Farms:* Shirley Wentworth, "Trouble down on the 'farm,'" *Portland Alliance,* September 2005.

49 *many farmers do not file the requisite paperwork:* Duhigg, "Health Ills Abound."

49 *thousands of large CAFOs:* http://www.epa.gov/npdes/pubs/sector_table.pdf.

49 *Brown County, Wisconsin:* Duhigg, "Health Ills Abound."

50 *Holland instituted policies in the 1980s:* Manure and the Environment, the Department of Agriculture, Ministry of Agriculture, Nature Management and Fisheries, the Netherlands, December 21, 2001.

50 *environmental groups sued the EPA:* Natural Resources Defense Council, Sierra Club, and Waterkeeper Alliance filed the suit: Natural Resources Defense Council press release http://www.nrdc.org/media/2010/100527.asp. See also Sindya N. Bhanoo, "Tougher E.P.A. Action on Factory Farms," *New York Times* Green blog, May 28, 2010: http://green.blogs.nytimes.com/2010/05/28/tougher-e-p-a-action-on-factory-farms/.

50 *Judy Treml pointed out:* Treml's congressional testimony.

CHAPTER 5: THE TREATMENT

52 *It was midevening in January 2010:* Author's tour with James P. Pynn, on February 15, 2008, and several phone conversations in 2010.

52 Newtown Creek Wastewater Treatment Plant background: DEP, http://www.nyc.gov /html/dep/html/environmental_education/newtown_wwtp.shtml.

53 *By the time the sewer pipes reach the Newtown plant:* Pynn interview.

54 *as little as one-twentieth of an inch . . . 460 times a year:* "Sewage & Combined Sewage

NOTES

Overflow," Riverkeeper.org: http://www.riverkeeper.org/campaigns/stop-polluters/cso/.

54 *490 outfall pipes:* "Water and Sewer Infrastructure," nyc.gov, May 2010.

55 *forty-four inches of precipitation:* "Sewage & Combined Sewage Overflow," Riverkeeper.org.

55 *more than nine thousand acres of land were paved:* "Draft Sustainable Stormwater Management Plan 2008," plaNYC.

56 *1.4 billion gallons of sewage:* "North River Wastewater Treatment Plant," nyc.gov.

56 *August 14, 2003:* Anthony DePalma, "Sewage Failure in Blackout Puts City Under Court's Thumb," *New York Times,* February 8, 2006.

57 *Americans produce 18 million tons of feces:* "An Urgent Call to Action," Report of the State-EPA Nutrient Innovations Task Group.

58 *Newtown Creek in 1967:* "Newtown Creek Water Pollution Control Plant Expansion and Upgrade, New York, NY, USA," Watertechnology.net.

58 *by 2015, at a cost of some $5.2 billion:* Pynn.

59 *discharge 482 million gallons:* William Angelo, "Raise Brooklyn Batteries," *Engineering News-Record,* July 3, 2006.

60 *CSOs . . . 40 million people in thirty-two states:* John Tibbets, "Combined Sewer Systems," *Environmental Health Perspectives* (July 2005).

60 *Milwaukee, the journal* Pediatrics . . . Archives of Environmental and Occupational Health: Charles Duhigg, "As Sewers Fill, Waste Poisons Waterways," *New York Times,* November 22, 2009.

60 *a third of major US sewer systems*: Ibid.

61 *New York City has invested about $35 billion:* Ibid.

61 *John Lipscomb:* Brian Zumhagen, "Cleaning Up Newtown Creek," WNYC, December 15, 2009.

62 *Philadelphia, for instance, has one:* PlanPhilly, "Green City, Clean Waters," for the city's long-term plan to control sewer overflows: http://www.phillywatersheds.org/what_were_doing/documents_and_data/cso_long_term_control_plan/. See also Brad Linder, "Philadelphia Tackles Rainwater Runoff Pollution," NPR, September 29, 2006.

62 *"porous city"*: Andy Coghlan, "We Can't Hold Back the Water Anymore," *The New Scientist,* January 10, 2003. See also Chris Baines, "I've seen the future and it's a sponge," forumforthefuture.org, October 2, 2001.

62 *$400 billion by 2020:* US Government Accountability Office, "Wastewater Infrastructure Financing," June 2010.

CHAPTER 6: BRAVE NEW WORLD

64 *Lake Erie:* Ruckelshaus, "New Shade of Green."

64 *emerging contaminants:* For background, see US Geological Survey: http://toxics.usgs.gov/regional/emc/.

64 *Paul Freedman:* Elizabeth de la Vega, "Extreme Water Emergencies," *Nation,* August 4, 2008.

64 *sixty thousand different types of chemicals:* Maurice Zeeman, Jerry Smrchek, Joseph Nabholz, and Donald Rodier, "US EPA/OPT and Sediments: Screening New and Existing Chemicals for Potential Environmental Effects," National Sediment Bioaccumulator Conference: http://www.epa.gov/waterscience/cs/library/zeeman

371

.pdf. Charles Duhigg, "That Tap Water Is Legal but May Be Unhealthy," *New York Times,* December 16, 2009.

65 *Christine Todd Whitman:* Duhigg, "That Tap Water Is Legal."

65 *830 of the pollutants most frequently found:* Ibid.

65 *Dr. Jeffrey K. Griffiths:* Griffiths's testimony before the Senate hearing on Federal drinking water programs, December 8, 2009.

66 *46 million Americans drink water:* Patrick Phillips, Herb Buxton, Diane Noserale, "Manufacturing Facilities Release Pharmaceuticals to the Environment," US Geological Survey news release, June 4, 2010.

66 *settlement with five health-care facilities:* "Attorney General Cuomo Announces Groundbreaking Settlements," Office of the Attorney General, January 12, 2010.

67 *triclocarban:* Erik Stokstad, "The Dirt on Sewage Sludge," *ScienceNOW,* January 22, 2009.

67 *"Drugs Found in Drinking Water":* Jeff Donn, Martha Mendoza, and Justin Pritchard, "Drugs found in drinking water," Associated Press, September 12, 2008.

67 *250 million pounds of pharmaceuticals:* Jeff Donn, Martha Mendoza, and Justin Pritchard, "Health care industry sends tons of drugs into nation's wastewater system," Associated Press, September 14, 2008.

68 *In Las Vegas, J. C. Davis:* Author's interview with J. C. Davis, Southern Nevada Water Authority, May 16, 2008.

68 *Roxanne Smith:* Donn, Mendoza, and Pritchard, "Health care industry sends tons of drugs."

68 *Laura Brannen:* Ibid.

68 *"without sufficient evidence of harm":* Donn, Mendoza, and Pritchard, "Drugs found in drinking water."

69 *Dr. Ettore Zuccato and his colleagues:* Author's interviews with Dr. Ettore Zuccato, Dr. Sara Castiglioni, and Dr. Roberto Fanelli at the Mario Negri Institute for Pharmacological Research, Milan, Italy, July 19, 2006, and subsequent e-mails.

71 *"Italian River Flows with Cocaine":* "Italian River Flows with Cocaine," All Headline News, August 6, 2005, and Discovery Channel News: http://dsc.discovery.com/news /briefs/20050815/cocaineriver_zoom0.html.

71 *"The Thames: Awash with Cocaine":* Nina Goswami and James Orr, "The Thames: Awash with Cocaine," *Sunday Telegraph,* November 6, 2005.

71 *they detected 49,066 doses of cocaine:* Zuccato interview.

CHAPTER 7: FROM THE CHICKENS TO THE CRABS

74 *The World Wide Fund for Nature:* "Sin Aqua Non," *Economist,* April 8, 2009.

74 *In the spring of 2002, huge shoals of dead fish:* Potomac Water Watch.org.

74 *Dr. Vicki Blazer:* Author's interview with Dr. Vicki Blazer, September 17, 2009, and subsequent e-mails and conversations.

75 *Intersex in the South Branch:* David Fahrenthold, "Male Bass in Potomac Producing Eggs," *Washington Post,* October 15, 2004.

75 *most comprehensive study of intersex:* US Geological Survey press release, "Widespread occurrence of intersex bass found in US Rivers," September 14, 2009: http://www .eurekalert.org/pub_releases/2009–09/usgs-woo091409.php.

76 *Karen Kidd:* Blazer interview. See also Kidd's web page: http://www.unbsj.ca/sase

NOTES

/biology/kiddlab/. John Roach, "Sex-changing Chemicals Can Wipe Out Fish, Study Shows," National Geographic News, May 21, 2007. See also Martin Mittelstaedt, "Estrogen Threatens Minnow Manhood Released into an Ontario Lake," Northern California River Watch: http://www.ncriverwatch.org/wordpress/2009/05/18/estrogen-threatens-minnow-manhood/.

77 *Dr. Philip Landrigan:* Nicholas D. Kristof, "Do Toxins Cause Autism?" *New York Times,* February 24, 2010.

77 *Endocrine disruptors are found:* National Institutes of Health: http://www.niehs.nih.gov/health/topics/agents/endocrine/index.cfm. US Environmental Protection Agency: "What are endocrine disruptors?": http://www.epa.gov/endo/pubs/edspoverview/whatare.htm.

77 *Anne Fausto-Sterling:* Ariel Levy, "Either/Or," *New Yorker,* November 30, 2009.

78 *Bob Hirsch:* Author's interviews with Dr. Robert M. Hirsch, May 7, 2008; July 9–11, 2008; and follow-up conversations.

79 *failed Virginia's fecal coliform:* US Environmental Protection Agency report: http://www.epa.gov/reg3wapd/nps/pdf/success/va/shenandoah.pdf.

80 *"slightly impaired":* Ibid., and Hirsch interviews.

80 *The Shenandoah Valley has nine hundred poultry farms: What's Growing on in Virginia?* (Virginia Foundation for Agriculture in the Classroom, spring 2002).

80 *Charles W. Wampler Sr.:* Ibid.

81 *Carole Morison:* Author's interview with Carole Morison, June 10, 2009. See also *Food Inc.,* directed by Robert Kenner, 2008, and "Poisoned Waters," Hedrick Smith, *Frontline,* WGBH, April 21, 2009.

82 *nitrate concentrations:* US Geological Survey.org.

82 *1.5 billion pounds of manure:* "Poisoned Waters," *Frontline.*

82 *Bill Satterfield:* Bill Satterfield, "Every Day Is Earth Day for Delmarva's Chicken Industry," Delmarva Poultry Industry press release, April 21, 2009: http://www.dpichicken.org/media/nr_view.cfm?id=336.

82 *"I'm not sure what these studies indicate":* Smith, "Poisoned Waters," *Frontline.*

82 *Jim Perdue:* Ibid.

83 *"Nobody educates farmers":* Morison interview.

83 *Agribusiness has powerful, well-funded lobbyists:* Smith "Poisoned Waters," *Frontline*; Duhigg, "Health Ills Abound."

83 *Leon Billings:* Smith, "Poisoned Waters," *Frontline.*

84 *call "the next global warming":* Hirsch interviews.

84 *applying nitrogen-based fertilizers:* Ibid.

85 *"Every spring since 2004":* Author's interview with Jeff Kelble, July 10, 2008.

85 *Shenandoah has the highest incidence of intersex bass:* Blazer interview.

85 *"fifth most endangered river":* Lara Lutz, "Poorly planned development lands Shenandoah on endangered rivers list," *Chesapeake Bay Journal,* June 2006.

85 *80 percent of smallmouth bass:* Kelble interview.

86 *arsenic in the Chesapeake region:* Jennifer Hlad, "Poultry Farmers Resist Bill to Ban Arsenic in Chicken Feed," Capital News Service, March 16, 2010.

86 *"That's a lie":* Kelble interview.

86 *Keeve Nachman:* Statement of Dr. Keeve Nachman, Science Director, Food Production, Health and the Environment, Center for a Livable Future: www.livablefutureblog.com.

86 *Poultry & Egg Institute:* "Arsenical Feed Additives in Poultry Feed," www.poultry egginstitute.org.

86 *Hobey Bauhan:* "Something Fishy about the Shenandoah River," *Blue Ridge Outdoors Magazine,* March 1, 2008.

86 *Richard Morris:* Ibid.

86 *5.24 million people live in the Potomac watershed:* "Learn About the Potomac Watershed," Potomac conservancy: http://www.potomac.org/site/potomac-watershed/.

87 *2002 National Water Quality Inventory:* Ibid.; "State of the Nation's River," 2007.

87 *Blue Plains:* Blue Plains Advanced Wastewater Treatment Plant, District of Columbia Water and Sewer Authority: http://www.dcwasa.com/about/facilities.cfm.

88 *hypoxic:* "Hypoxia—Definitions," US Geological Survey: http://toxics.usgs.gov /definitions/hypoxia.html.

89 *Chesapeake's rockfish:* Elizabeth Williamson, "Chesapeake's Rockfish Overrun by Disease," *Washington Post,* March 11, 2006.

89 *oyster can exude ten thousand to 60 million eggs:* "Gem of the ocean": *Economist,* December 18, 2008.

90 *Bill Goldsboro:* Ibid.

90 *Great Wicomico River:* Henry Fountain, "Oysters Are on the Rebound in the Chesapeake Bay," *New York Times,* August 3, 2009.

90 *blue crab:* "Maryland crabbers fear blue crab is gone," Associated Press, July 16, 2008.

90 *eighty-three thousand tons of fish:* David Biello, "Oceanic Dead Zones Continue to Spread," *Scientific American,* August 15, 2008.

91 *Paul Kellam:* "Maryland crabbers fear blue crab is gone," Associated Press.

91 *$5 billion had been spent on pollution controls:* David A. Fahrenthold, "EPA threatens states over Chesapeake Bay cleanup," *The Washington Post,* September 24, 2010.

92 *Dick Brame:* Angus Phillips, "The Chesapeake Bay Is Ailing, and This Time It's Serious," *Washington Post,* June 26, 2005.

CHAPTER 8: THE MISSING GREENHOUSE GAS

93 *146 dead zones worldwide:* John Heilprin, "U.N. reports growing number of ocean 'dead zones,'" Associated Press, October 20, 2006.

93 *dead zone off the coast of Oregon:* "Dead Zone," Wikipedia.org.

93 *"missing greenhouse gas":* "The missing greenhouse gas," *Nature Reports Climate Change,* July 10, 2008.

94 *biggest dead zone lurks in the Gulf of Mexico:* Allison Winter, "This Year's Gulf 'Dead Zone' Among Largest Ever," *New York Times,* August 3, 2010.

94 *7 million metric tons of nitrogen:* Donald Goolsby and William Battaglin, "Nitrogen in the Mississippi Basin—Estimating Sources and Predicting Flux to the Gulf of Mexico," US Geological Survey, Kansas Water Science Center, December 2000: http:// ks.water.usgs.gov/pubs/fact-sheets/fs.135-00.html.

95 *a dead zone of 8,500 square miles:* Joel Achenbach, "A 'Dead Zone' in the Gulf of Mexico," *Washington Post,* July 31, 2008.

95 *Robert Diaz:* Biello, "Oceanic Dead Zones Continue to Spread."

96 *Nancy Rabalais:* Seth Borenstein, "Floods to widen 'dead zone' in gulf," Associated Press, June 22, 2008.

NOTES

96 *shrink the Gulf's dead zone:* Bruce Eggler, "Despite promises to fix it, the Gulf's dead zone is growing," *New Orleans Times-Picayune,* June 9, 2007.
96 *TMDLs:* "Impaired Waters and Total Maximum Daily Loads," US Environmental Protection Agency: http://water.epa.gov/lawsregs/lawsguidance/cwa/tmdl/index.cfm.
97 *grown by more than a factor of ten:* Hirsch interview.
97 *Black Sea:* "Dead water," *Economist,* May 15, 2008.

CHAPTER 9: ONE STEP FORWARD, TWO STEPS BACK

99 *Tom Porta:* Congressional testimony, October 15, 2009: http://www.neiwpcc.org/email-newsletter/oct09/ASIWPCA-Porta%20Testimony.pdf.
99 *James Oberstar:* Charles Duhigg, "Clean Water Laws Are Neglected, at a Cost in Suffering," *New York Times,* September 13, 2009.
99 *Underfunded, overly politicized:* Ibid.
100 *fifteen hundred major pollution cases:* Charles Duhigg, "Rulings Restrict Clean Water Act, Foiling E.P.A.," *New York Times,* February 28, 2010.
100 *John Rapanos filled fifty-four acres of wetland:* "Rapanos Will Pay for Clean Water Act Violations," Environmental News Service, December 30, 2008.
101 *Douglas Mundrick:* Duhigg, "Rulings Restrict Clean Water Act."
101 *Peter Silva:* Congressional testimony, December 8, 2009: http://www.epa.gov/ocir/hearings/testimony/111_2009_2010/2009_1208_pss.pdf.
101 *Jay Shimshack:* Congressional testimony, October 15, 2009.
101 *William Ruckelshaus:* Ruckelshaus, "New Shade of Green."
102 *Kingston Ash plant:* Shaila Dewan, "Tennessee Ash Flood Larger Than Initial Estimate," *New York Times,* December 26, 2008.
102 *Jackson, forty-six:* Tim Dickinson, "The Eco-Warrior," *Rolling Stone,* January 20, 2010.
103 *Jeff Ruch:* Ibid., and author's e-mails with Ruch, 2010.
103 *Robert F. Kennedy Jr.:* Dickinson, "Eco-Warrior."
104 *Spruce No. 1 Mine:* "Spruce No. 1 Mine," US Environmental Protection Agency: http://www.epa.gov/region3/mtntop/spruce1.html.
104 *fallen "short of this administration's expectations":* Lisa Jackson congressional testimony, October 15, 2009.
104 *104 chemicals for regulation:* "Contaminant Candidate List 3—CCL," US Environmental Protection Agency: http://water.epa.gov/scitech/drinkingwater/dws/ccl/ccl3.cfm.
104 *Don Parrish:* Duhigg, "Rulings Restrict Clean Water Act."
104 *Gene Whatley:* Senate testimony, December 8, 2009.
105 *Earl Pomeroy of North Dakota:* Dickinson, "Eco-Warrior."
105 *But Jeff Ruch:* Ruch e-mail to author, January 29, 2010.

CHAPTER 10: TIME OF WASTE

107 *Golden Square:* Steven Johnson, *The Ghost Map* (New York: Riverhead Books, 2006).
109 *Arcata:* Gregory Dicum, "The Dirty Water Underground," *New York Times,* May 31, 2007.
109 *Michael Markus:* Author's interview with Michael Markus, December 15, 2009, and subsequent e-mails with Gina DePinto, December 28, 2010.

NOTES

110 *El Paso, Texas, recycled water supplies:* Eilene Zimmerman, "It's Time to Drink Toilet Water," *Slate,* January 25, 2008.

111 *$481 million Groundwater Replenishment System:* http://www.gwrsystem.com/.

111 *"Your golden retriever may drink out of the toilet":* "Yuck!," *San Diego Union-Tribune,* July 24, 2006.

111 *Daniel Okun:* Elizabeth Royte, "A Tall, Cool Drink of . . . Sewage?" *New York Times Magazine,* August 8, 2008.

112 *Bruce Henderson:* Sam Hodgson, "Sanders Wants to Flush Water Reclamation Plans," *Voice of San Diego,* July 19, 2006.

112 *David Spath:* Bettina Boxall, "Doubts Still Swirl to Surface," *Los Angeles Times,* May 7, 2006.

CHAPTER 11: WATER SCARCITY

107 *Tunnel No. 3:* New York City Department of Environmental Protection: http://www .nyc.gov/html/dep/pdf/factsheet.pdf and http://www.nyc.gov/html/dep/html/dep _projects/cp_city_water_tunnel3.shtml.

107 *Ted Dowey:* Author's tour of Tunnel No. 3 with Ted Dowey, March 5, 2007.

119 *The American Society of Civil Engineers:* "Report Card for America's Infrastructure," American Society of Civil Engineers: http://apps.asce.org/reportcard/2009/grades.cfm.

120 *In 2007, 159 leaks:* Anthony DePalma, "Mysterious Leak Provides Hint of Lost Manhattan," *New York Times,* February 5, 2008.

120 *The EPA estimates that 1 trillion gallons:* US Environmental Protection Agency, Water Sense, "The Facts on Leaks," http://www.epa.gov/WaterSense/pubs/fixleak.html.

120 *the water pressure inside:* From David Grann's indispensable article on Tunnel No. 3, "City of Water," *New Yorker,* September 1, 2003.

122 *Standard pay is $35 to $38 an hour:* Ibid.

122 *Hogs have their own language:* Ibid., and Dowey interview. Sandhog website: http:// www.sandhogs147.org/about.aspx. See also the History Channel, "Sandhogs": http:// www.thehistorychannel.co.uk/shows/tunnellers/episode-guide.html.

123 *tunnel-boring machines:* http://www.nyc.gov/html/dep/pdf/tbmfactsheet.pdf. See also Sewell Chan, "Tunnelers Hit Something Big: A Milestone," *New York Times,* August 10, 2006.

123 *corruption plagued the Board of Water Supply:* Grann, "City of Water." This was confirmed to me by a source who asked not to be identified.

123 *$4 billion to the new tunnel:* Chan, "Tunnelers Hit Something Big."

124 *the world had 18 "megacities":* Wikipedia: http://en.wikipedia.org/wiki/Megacity.

124 *In 2007, 336 cities worldwide:* Ibid., and Thomas Brinkhof, "The Principal Agglomerations of the World," www.citypopulation.de.

124 *in 2008, for the first time in history:* UN Population Fund (UNFPA): State of World Population 2007: http://www.unfpa.org/swp/2007/english/introduction.html.

124 *As of 2010, China alone had 43 cities:* Christina Larson, "Chicago on the Yangtze," *Foreign Policy,* September/October 2010.

125 *Bruce Rolen:* "As supplies dry up, growers pass on farming and sell water," US Water News Online, February 2008.

125 *Perth, Australia:* Patrick Barta, "Amid Water Shortage, Australia Looks to the Sea," *Wall Street Journal,* March 11, 2008.

NOTES

125 *America's total water use:* Susan S. Hutson, Nancy L. Barber, Joan F. Kenny, Kristin S. Linsey, Deborah S. Lumia, and Molly A. Maupin, "Estimated Use of Water in the United States in 2000," US Geological Survey Circular 1268, February 2005, and Joan F. Kenny, et al., "Estimated Use of Water in the United States in 2005," US Geological Survey Circular 1344, October 2009.

127 *global population will increase to nearly 8 billion:* "Total midyear world population 1950–2050," npg.org/facts.

127 *more babies were born in the United States:* Erik Eckholm, " '07 US Births Break Baby Boom Record," *New York Times,* March 18, 2009.

127 *as much as 60 percent more water:* "How to feed 2 billion more mouths in 2030? Here are some answers," UN Food and Agriculture Organization, 2002: http://www.fao.org/english/newsroom/news/2002/8280-en.html.

127 *vegetarian diets of Africa and Asia:* "Sin aqua non," *Economist.*

128 *a severe drought and heat wave:* "Drought: the Creeping Disaster," NASA Earth Observatory: http://earthobservatory.nasa.gov/Features/DroughtFacts/.

129 *"creeping disaster":* Ibid.

129 *Dan Nees:* Mark Clayton, "How the World Is Realizing That Water Is 'Blue Gold,' " *Christian Science Monitor,* May 29, 2008.

130 *a fifty-year survey of forests:* "Tree Deaths Have Doubled Across the Western US—Regional Warming May Be the Cause," US Geological Survey news release, January 22, 2009.

130 *USGS's Bob Hirsch:* Hirsch interview.

130 *Nile, Niger, Volta, and Zambezi:* "Rivers and conflict: Streams of blood, or streams of peace," *Economist,* May 1, 2008.

CHAPTER 12: THE AGE OF PERPETUAL DROUGHT

131 *Pablo Valencia:* "Desert Thirst as Disease," Arizona State University's Water Resources Research Center: http://ag.arizona.edu/AZWATER/awr/mayjune01/readings.html. See also Kevin Franklin, "Here's a real sizzler of a story for desert dwellers," *Tucson Weekly,* June 27, 1996; Nathaniel Philbrick, *In the Heart of the Sea: The Tragedy of the Whaleship Essex* (New York: Penguin Books, 2000), p. 126.

132 *temperatures in Phoenix surpass one hundred degrees:* Arizona State University, "Climate of Phoenix: Part 2," http://www.public.asu.edu/~aunjs/ClimateofPhoenix/wxpart2.htm.

132 *average temperature of Phoenix:* Timothy Egan, "The First Domed City," *New York Times,* June 16, 2007.

133 *"we are at ground zero for climate change":* B. William Poole, "Experts: Climate change disasters to hit Arizona hard," *Tucson Citizen,* January 24, 2009.

133 *paleoclimatologists from the University of Arizona:* University of Arizona: Laboratory of Tree-Ring Research: http://www.ltrr.arizona.edu/.

133 *Hohokam Indians:* Jared Diamond, *Collapse: How Societies Choose to Fail or Succeed* (New York: Viking Penguin, 2005), pp. 140–41.

133 *the Rodeo-Chediski wildfires:* US Department of Agriculture Fact Sheet: "Healthy Forests Initiative Update for Arizona," August 2003: http://www.fs.fed.us/projects/hfi/docs/fact-sheet-arizona.pdf. See also Felicia Fonseca, "Tribal Attorney: Fire starter will get fair civil-case trial," Associated Press, May 17, 2009.

134 *a steady decline in precipitation:* Nikhil Swaminathan, "Dust Bowl 2.0: Is the Southwest

Drying Up?" *Scientific American,* April 5, 2007. See also "Hot with Decades of Drought: Expectations for Southwestern United States," ScienceDaily, December 14, 2010.

134 *Dr. Richard Seagar:* Author's interview with Dr. Richard Seagar, May 6, 2008.

135 *Goulburn, New South Wales:* Nick Bryant, "Living with Australia's Drought," BBC News, November 6, 2006. See also Nick Bryant, "Australia drought sparks suicides," BBC News, October 19, 2006.

135 *Goulburn saw only fourteen inches of rain:* Tim Johnston, "Parched in Australia: Drought changes views on warming," *Daily Star,* December 29, 2006.

135 *Australia's three main crops:* Tim Johnston, "A drought alters Australian ideas on global warming," *International Herald Tribune,* November 7, 2006.

136 *Big Dry:* "The big dry," *Economist,* April 26, 2007. See also Daniel Williams, "The Big Dry," *Time,* May 22, 2008.

136 *Dr. Paul Dalby:* David Beasley, "Lessons from Australia: Drought Can Help Georgia Economy," GlobalAtlanta, February 2, 2009.

137 *"virtual water":* Stockholm International Water Institute, 2008: http://www.siwi.org /sa/node.asp?node=282.

138 *Senator Bill Heffernan:* Tim Johnston, "A drought alters Australian ideas on global warming," *International Herald Tribune,* November 7, 2006.

138 *Lisa Jackson:* John M. Broder, "E.P.A. Clears Way for Greenhouse Gas Rules," *New York Times,* April 17, 2009.

CHAPTER 13: REVENUE STREAMS

139 *In its water laws:* For an overview, see: http://en.wikipedia.org/wiki/Water_law_in _the_United_States.

141 *NAWAPA:* Marc Reisner, *Cadillac Desert* (New York: Penguin Books, 1993), pp. 487–94. Michael Campana, "Canadian Water Exports: Will NAWAPA Return?" WaterWired, January 25, 2008: http://aquadoc.typepad.com/waterwired/2008/01 /kennedy-to-cana.html?cid=119725788.

141 *approximately 1 million miles of pipeline:* "Water Trivia Facts," US Environmental Protection Agency: http://water.epa.gov/learn/kids/drinkingwater/water_trivia _facts.cfm.

142 *Roberts Tunnel:* Chris Woodka, "Plumbing the Rockies," *Pueblo Chieftain,* December 21, 2009.

142 *national water fees average about $458:* "Water on Tap: What You Need to Know," US Environmental Protection Agency: http://www.epa.gov/safewater/wot/pdfs/book _waterontap_full.pdf.

142 *Denver's expanding suburbs charge $10,000:* David Olinger and Chuck Plunkett, "Suburban aggression," *Denver Post,* November 22, 2005.

142 *Dave Miller:* "Gunnison River Basin: Union Park Reservoir," Coyote Gulch blog, August 20, 2010: http://coyotegulch.wordpress.com/2010/08/20/gunnison-river -basin-union-park-reservoir/.

143 *Bob Moran:* Author's interviews with Robert Moran, 2006–10.

143 *Maurice Strong (pronounced "Morris"):* Moran interviews. See also Miro Cernetig, "Water wars disrupt New Age valley," *Toronto Globe and Mail,* 1990.

143 *"fire sale price":* Dyan Machan, "Saving the Planet with Maurice Strong," *Forbes,* January 12, 1998.

NOTES

144 *2 billion acre-feet of water:* "Ground Water Resource Potential, Baca Grant, San Luis Valley, South Central Colorado," AWDI, Bishop-Brogden Associates, Inc., April 1989.

144 *pay up to $7,000 per acre-foot:* Cernetig, "Water wars disrupt New Age valley."

145 *Maurice Strong grew up:* Daniel Wood, "The Wizard of Baca Grande," *West,* May 1990.

145 *Kofi Annan until 2005:* "UN gives Maurice Strong his walking papers," Associated Press, July 18, 2005.

145 *Glenn Anderson:* Wood, "Wizard of Baca Grande."

145 *Manitou Foundation:* http://www.manitou.org/MF/mf_index.php.

146 *Great Sand Dunes:* National Park Service: Great Sand Dunes National Park and Preserve, Colorado: http://www.nps.gov/grsa/index.htm.

146 *planned to pump:* Cernetig, "Water wars disrupt New Age valley."

146 *Greg Gosar:* Ibid.

146 *"international conspiracy":* Ibid.

146 *Hanne, who herself had become an obstruction:* Miro Cernetig, "Mystical Hanne Strong likes prophets, not profits," *Toronto Globe and Mail,* July 9, 1990.

147 *a sacred lake lined with crystals:* Ibid.

147 *Colorado Supreme Court denied: Denver Rocky Mountain News,* November 29, 1994.

147 *Strong was paid a $1.2 million settlement by the water company:* Henry Lamb, "Maurice Strong: The new guy in your future!" sovereignty.net.

147 *Gary Boyce:* Ed Quillen, "A water baron takes on the establishment," *High Country News,* October 26, 1998.

147 *Farallon Capital Management:* Mark H. Hunter, "Yale helped fund plan to sell San Luis water. School's secret investment sparks outrage in valley," *Denver Post,* January 24, 2002. Erin Smith, "Yale University silent partner in Baca dealings," *Pueblo Chieftain,* January 20, 2002. See also unfarrallon.info/bacaranch.asp.

148 *"Water is gold":* David Nicholas, "Boyce law suit to be heard in January; Status Conference to be held Nov. 8," *Crestone Eagle,* November 2005.

148 *Stockman's Water Company proposed:* Ibid.

148 *Lewis Entz:* Marty Jones, "High and Dry," *Westword,* November 12, 1998.

148 *agreed to sell their Baca holdings:* "Baca National Wildlife Refuge/Lexam Explorations," San Luis Valley Ecosystem Council, 2009.

149 *Yale University:* Brendan Smith, "Great Sand Dunes National Park and Preserve/Baca Ranch Purchase," redlodgeclearinghouse.org, September 2005.

149 *the Nature Conservancy led the federal:* Ibid.

149 *Lexam and its partner, ConocoPhillips:* "Colorado Oil & Gas Update," press release, lexamexplorations.com, April 3, 2008. See also Erin Emery, "Baca refuge open for drilling?" *Denver Post,* December 19, 2007.

150 *The San Luis Valley Ecosystem Council:* "Baca National Wildlife Refuge/Lexam Explorations," San Luis Valley Ecosystem Council.

CHAPTER 14: DRAIN

151 *Frederick Eaton:* For background, see William Kahrl, *Water and Power: The Conflict Over Los Angeles Water Supply in the Owens Valley* (Berkeley: University of California Press, 1983). See also Reisner, *Cadillac Desert.*

NOTES

153 *citizens dynamited the Lone Pine spillway:* "Whoever Brings the Water Brings the People," Los Angeles Department of Water and Power, ladwp.com.

154 *Mono Lake:* For background, see the Mono Lake Committee site: http://www .monolake.org/.

154 *Mulholland's agents had scouted:* Kahrl, *Water and Power,* p. 330.

155 *backbreaking work by eighteen hundred men:* H. A. Van Norman, "The Mono Basin Project," *Civil Engineering,* May 1936.

155 *in the spring of 1953:* Moran interview.

157 Drain: Author's observations in Bishop on May 5, 2007. For background on the mural, see the website of the artist, John Pugh, http://www.illusion-art.com/bishop _drain.asp. See also Leslie Carlson, "Water Colors," *Los Angeles Times,* November 22, 2005.

157 *dust storms are said to remove:* Molly Peterson, "Owens Lake dust kicks up questions about DWP's eastern Sierra efforts," Southern California Public Radio, December 12, 2010.

157 *LADWP has built a $500 million sprinkler system:* "DWP Chief seeks delay in Owens Valley dust clean-up," *Sierra Wave,* March 16, 2010.

157 *mayor Antonio Villaraigosa:* Deborah Amos, "LA Returns Water to the Owens Valley," National Public Radio, December 7, 2006.

158 *Michael Prather:* Author's tour with Michael Prather, May 5, 2007.

158 *sixty thousand acre-feet of water a year:* Louis Sahagun, "Bird Census at Owens Lake shows nature returning," *Los Angeles Times,* April 19, 2009.

158 *Los Angeles's population:* "List of most highly populated countries," Wikipedia: http:// en.wikipedia.org/wiki/List_of_most_highly_populated_countries.

159 *In 1990, citizens in the Sierra foothills:* John Walton, "Another Owens Valley," Owens Valley Committee, vol. 5, no. 1 (Summer 2009).

159 *Honey Lake Valley fought against:* Ibid.

159 *Fish Springs Ranch, Dr. Harry Brown and Franklin Raines:* Author's tour of the pipeline with Dr. Harry Brown, May 8, 2007.

CHAPTER 15: THE CITY THAT WASN'T SUPPOSED TO BE

160 *starting in 1999, the Southwest:* US Global Change Research Program: http:// downloads.climatescience.gov/usimpacts/pdfs/southwest.pdf.

160 *Lake Mead was formed in 1935:* Bureau of Reclamation, Lower Colorado Region: http://www.usbr.gov/lc/hooverdam/faqs/lakefaqs.html. See also National Park Service: Lake Mead National Recreation Area: http://www.nps.gov/lake/index.htm.

161 *The water level had dropped:* "Lake Mead," Wikipedia.org.

161 *dead pool:* James Lawrence Powell, *Dead Pool* (Berkeley: University of California Press, 2008).

161 *Pat Mulroy, general manager:* Author's interviews with Pat Mulroy, May 16, 2008, and subsequent phone calls.

161 *Dean Baker:* Author's interview with Dean Baker, May 18, 2008.

162 *study by the Scripps Institution of Oceanography:* Tim P. Barnett and David W. Pierce, "When will Lake Mead go dry?" *Water Resources Research,* March 29, 2008. See also "Lake Mead Could Be Dry by 2021," Scripps press release, February 12, 2008.

163 *Using the same data, the federal Bureau of Reclamation:* "Reclamation and Scripps

NOTES

Institution of Oceanography Look to Collaborate," US Bureau of Reclamation press release, June 9, 2010.

163 *population of Clark County:* Mulroy interview.

163 *a $13,000-a-year administrative assistant:* Ibid.

163 *65 percent of the water flowing:* "Conserve Water," Las Vegas Wash Coordination Committee: www.lvwash.org/html/help_waterconservation.html.

164 *76 percent of the water used:* "Turf Wars," Peter Gleick Circle of Blue blog, February 21, 2010: www.circleofblue.org/waternews/2010/world/peter-gleick-turf-wars/.

164 *Steve Wynn:* Mulroy interview.

165 *Each year, the SNWA spends:* George Knapp, "Why Doesn't the SNWA Focus on Water Conservation?" 8NewsNow.com, August 20, 2009: http://www.8newsnow.com/story /10966745/why-doesnt-the-snwa-focus-on-water-conservation?redirected=true.

165 *Vegas grew by four hundred thousand people:* Stephanie Tavares, "Q&A: Pat Mulroy," *Las Vegas Sun,* May 1, 2009.

165 *Las Vegas continues to use more water:* Heather Cooley, et al., "Hidden Oasis: Water Conservation and Efficiency in Las Vegas," Pacific Institute, November 2007, p. 18.

165 *A survey shows the top one hundred:* Henry Brean, "Not a Drop in the Bucket," *Las Vegas Review-Journal,* March 22, 2009.

165 *Mulroy herself uses:* Confirmed by J. C. Davis, SNWA, and *Aguanomics,* March 26, 2009: http://www.aguanomics.com/2009/03/mulroy-channeling-mulhollands-sprawl .html.

165 *Pacific Institute:* Cooley, et al., "Hidden Oasis."

165 *Las Vegan household typically uses seventeen thousand gallons:* Adam Tanner, "Las Vegas Growth Depends on Dwindling Water Supply," Reuters, August 22, 2007: http://www.enn.com/top_stories/article/22117.

166 *David Zetland:* http://www.aguanomics.com/.

166 *Mulroy takes exception to that:* Mulroy interview.

166 *In October 1998, the water level:* "Lake Mead Elevation at Hoover Dam Continues to Fall," University of Nebraska-Lincoln, January 31, 2009: http://www.nebraskaweather photos.org/Lake-Mead-2009.html.

167 *Terry Katzer:* Emily Green, "Owens Valley is the model of what to expect," *Las Vegas Sun,* June 29, 2008.

168 *In October 1989, the Las Vegas Water District:* Ibid., and minutes of the Integrated Water Planning Advisory Committee meeting, November 22, 2004.

168 *Virgil Getto:* Emily Green, "The Chosen One," *Las Vegas Sun,* June 8, 2008.

168 *SNWA spent $78 million:* Emily Green, "Not this water," *Las Vegas Sun,* June 22, 2008.

168 *"Watching the city try to run four thousand sheep?":* Baker interview.

169 *285 miles and cost between $2 billion and $3.5 billion:* Mulroy interview, and news reports.

169 *Robison Ranch in Spring Valley:* Henry Brean, "Spring Valley: water rights, riches," *Las Vegas Review-Journal,* August 14, 2006.

169 *16 billion gallons of groundwater:* Henry Brean, "Groundwater Project: Pipeline hearing postponed," *Las Vegas Review-Journal,* April 25, 2009.

170 *a dozen wild horses died:* Baker interview.

170 *Great Basin National Park:* National Park Service: Great Basin National Park: http:// www.nps.gov/grba/index.htm.

170 *But in 2000, Harry Reid:* Baker interview. See also Green, "Not this water."

NOTES

171 *Utah would like to build a 158-mile pipe:* Mulroy interview. See also "Priming Growth: Questionable Pipeline Should Be on Ballot," *Salt Lake Tribune,* June 16, 2008.

171 *In 2006, Pat Mulroy declared:* Green, "Not this water."

171 *spell the word* conservation*:* "Nevada water director criticizes Utah," transcript of Mulroy interview on KVBC, April 14, 2010: http://www.ksl.com/?nid=148&sid=10 387603&pid=1.

172 *Durbin told the* Las Vegas Sun*:* Green, "Owens Valley is the model of what to expect."

172 *Pat Mulroy shrugs off Durbin and Katzer:* Mulroy interview.

173 *"You're going to live like Amman, Jordan":* Henry Brean, "Nevada Water Authority vote sought on pipeline project," *Las Vegas Review-Journal,* August 7, 2009.

173 *Norman C. Robison:* Mulroy interview. See also Henry Brean, "Pipeline Plans: Judge kills water ruling," *Las Vegas Review-Journal,* October 28, 2009.

174 *the court ruled for the protesters:* Emily Green and Tom Gorman, "The small oversight that threatens the valley's big pipeline proposal," *Las Vegas Sun,* January 31, 2010.

174 *Lake Mead was at 46 percent of capacity:* "Lake Mead Elevation at Hoover Dam Continues to Fall," University of Nebraska-Lincoln.

175 *Oscar Goodman:* Tanner, "Las Vegas Growth Depends on Dwindling Water Supply."

175 *desal remains a viable option:* Mulroy interview.

175 *In a 2007 agreement:* US Bureau of Reclamation: "Colorado River Interim Guidelines for Lower Basin Shortages and the Coordinated Operations for Lake Powell and Lake Mead," December 2007: http://www.usbr.gov/lc/region/programs/strategies /RecordofDecision.pdf.

175 *a "third straw":* Henry Brean, "Third Straw," *Las Vegas Review-Journal,* December 13, 2009.

176 *Nevada has paid Arizona $100 million:* Mulroy interview, and "Arizona Water Bank," Southern Nevada Water Authority press release.

176 *On July 24, 1983, Lake Mead:* Bureau of Reclamation, "Lake Mead High and Low Elevations (1935-2010)": www.usbr.gov.

176 *At 11:30 a.m. on October 17, 2010:* Felicity Barringer, "Lake Mead Hits Record Low Level," *New York Times* green blog, October 18, 2010.

176 *pump 134,000 acre-feet of water:* Henry Brean, "Lake level trigger for pipeline project," *Las Vegas Review-Journal,* June 1, 2009.

176 *Joe Hogan:* Knapp, "Why Doesn't the SNWA Focus on Water Conservation?"

177 *pipeline is designed not to expand Las Vegas:* Mulroy interview.

177 *forty-five thousand large-scale dams in 2010:* Deborah Moore, John Dore, and Dipak Gyawali, "The World Commission on Dams +10: Revisiting the Large Dam Controversy," *Water Alternatives,* vol. 3, no. 2 (2010).

CHAPTER 16: THE DAMMED

178 *On a Wednesday afternoon in May 2007:* Author's observations. For background, see www.acwa.com.

179 *the Pacific Institute:* http://www.pacinst.org/.

179 *the nation's 85,000 dams:* ASCE Report Card for American Infrastructure: Dams http://www.infrastructurereportcard.org/fact-sheet/dams.

180 *132 dam failures across the United States:* the Association of State Dam Safety Officials: http://www.damsafety.org.

NOTES

180 *South Fork Dam:* National Park Service: Johnstown Flood National Memorial: http://www.nps.gov/jofl/index.htm.

180 *St. Francis Dam:* University of Southern California: http://www.usc.edu/libraries/archives/la/scandals/st_francis_dam.html. For background on dam failures, see J. David Rogers, Missouri University of Science and Technology: http://web.mst.edu/~rogersda/dams/.

181 *a $40 billion plan to safeguard infrastructure:* William B. Dickinson IV, "Estimating the cost of Dam Repair," HydroWorld.com, January 14, 2011.

181 *Hetch Hetchy Reservoir:* Quotes about the controversy: http://www.cnr.berkeley.edu/departments/espm/env-hist/espm160/assignments/hetch_hetchy/hetch_qts.htm.

181 *John Muir:* Pinchot's testimony, from "History Matters," the American Social History Project/Center for Media and Learning: http://historymatters.gmu.edu/d/5721/.

181 *Gifford Pinchot:* Ibid.

181 *reservoir has remained a lightning rod:* Daniel Weintraub, "Taking New Tack in Hetch Hetchy Battle," *New York Times*, April 10, 2010.

181 *Restore Hetch Hetchy:* www.hetchhetchy.org.

181 *tearing down Hetch Hetchy would be expensive and polluting:* Susan Leal, former head of San Francisco Public Utilities Commission. See also "Bay Area Council Releases 10-Point Letter Detailing Opposition to Removal of the Bay Area's Hetch Hetchy Water System," Free Library; "Statement of Senator Dianne Feinstein on Proposals to Tear Down O'Shaughnessy Dam," press release, May 18, 2005.

182 *US Bureau of Reclamation:* www.usbr.gov.

182 *Hoover Dam:* US Bureau of Reclamation: http://www.usbr.gov/lc/hooverdam/. See also Wikipedia: http://en.wikipedia.org/wiki/Hoover_Dam. For a gripping history, see Michael Hiltzik, *Colossus: Hoover Dam and the Making of the American Century* (New York: Free Press, 2010).

183 *Floyd Dominy:* John McPhee, *Encounters with the Archdruid* (New York: Farrar, Straus and Giroux, 1971).

184 *the Bureau of Rec was confronted:* "A Very Brief History," US Bureau of Reclamation: http://www.usbr.gov/history/borhist.html.

184 *Teton Dam:* Much has been written on this disaster; see Rogers, http://web.mst.edu/~rogersda/dams/.

185 *In 1993, Reclamation had almost eight thousand employees:* Vernon Dale Jones, *Downsizing the Federal Government* (Armonk, NY: M.E. Sharpe, Inc, 1998) pp. 103–104.

185 *the largest wholesaler of water in the country:* "About Us," US Bureau of Reclamation: http://www.usbr.gov/main/about/.

185 *"The arid West has essentially been reclaimed":* "Very Brief History," US Bureau of Reclamation.

185 *World Bank:* http://www.unep.org/dams/WCD/. World Commission on Dams report: http://www.unep.org/dams/WCD/report.asp.

185 *"we haven't built any dams in thirty years":* "Governor Schwarzenegger Tours Long Beach Aquifer," Office of the Governor, July 23, 2007.

185 *"Wrong, wrong, wrong!":* Gleick interview.

186 *study that looked at fifty years' worth of statistics:* Gleick interview. See also Susan S. Hutson, et al., "Estimated Use of Water in the United States," US Geological Survey Circular 1268, March 2004.

187 *At 2:05, inside the cavernous auditorium:* I have re-created this scene based on my presence at the 2007 ACWA debate in Sacramento, and checked it with Gleick and Snow, though it is not verbatim.

CHAPTER 17: SNOWPACK: THE CANARY IN A COAL MINE

189 *Gin Flat has been called:* Deborah Schoch, "California's water fortune is told at Gin Flat," *Los Angeles Times,* March 3, 2008.

190 *Frank Gehrke:* Ibid., and author's interview with Frank Gehrke, December 1, 2009, and subsequent conversations.

190 *The average SWE at Gin Flat:* Gehrke.

191 *Steven Chu:* Jon Gertner, "The Future Is Drying Up," *New York Times Magazine,* October 21, 2007.

191 *the Sierra's 497 glaciers:* William Raub, C Suzanne Brown, and Austin Post, "Inventory of Glaciers in the Sierra Nevada, California," US Geological Survey report.

191 *Hassan Basagic and Andrew Fountain:* http://www.glaciers.pdx.edu/Thesis/Basagic /mtnclimPOSTER4.pdf.

192 *Sierra Nevada as a "canary in the coal mine":* Greyson Howard, "Climate change: Forests, wildlife, fire danger all expected to be affected by warming Sierra," *Sierra Sun,* May 31, 2008.

192 *By 2008, ponderosa pine trees were growing:* Ibid.

192 *"This March, April, and May have been the driest ever":* "Governor Schwarzenegger Proclaims Drought and Orders Immediate Action to Address Situation," press release, June 4, 2008.

193 *"Water is like our gold":* Jennifer Steinhauer, "Governor Declares Drought in California," *New York Times,* June 5, 2008.

193 *Michael Wade:* Mike Wade, "Water and Crops," *San Francisco Chronicle,* July 25, 2007.

193 *"There is enough water for everyone":* "Water, a shared responsibility," UN World Water Development Report 2, 2006.

CHAPTER 18: WATER WARS

195 *Benjamin Moeur dispatched National Guardsmen:* Marq De Villiers, *Water: The Fate of Our Most Precious Resource* (New York: Mariner Books, 2001), p. 16. See also "The Cowboy Who Went to Tempe as a Doctor and Ended Up Being a Governor," Tempe (AZ) Historical Society.

195 *the Delaware River Compact:* Delaware River Basin Commission: http://www.state .nj.us/drbc/over.htm.

196 *Nova Group:* "The Nova Group and Annex 2001," Great Lakes Water Wars, 2007: http://www.greatlakeswaterwars.com/chapter11.htm.

196 *Great Lakes Compact:* "House approves Great Lakes compact," Associated Press, September 23, 2008.

196 *UN has warned that strife over shared rivers:* John Vidal, "How water raises the political temperature between countries," *Guardian,* June 25, 2010.

197 *Water has been considered:* Choe Sang-Hun, "North Korea Opens Dam Flow, Sweeping Away 6 in the South," *New York Times,* September 6, 2009.

NOTES

197 *"asymmetrical cooperation"*: "Rivers and conflict: Streams of blood, or streams of peace," *Economist*, May 1, 2008.

198 *Elizabeth Economy*: Elizabeth C. Economy, "The Great Leap Backward?" *Foreign Affairs*, September/October 2007.

198 *Ismail Serageldin*: http://www.serageldin.com/Water.htm.

198 *International Alert*: Ban Ki-Moon, "Quenching Global Thirst," *New York Times*, March 21, 2008.

198 *tree cutting in Darfur*: "Darfur deaths 'could be 300,000,'" BBC News, April 23, 2008.

198 *Dr. Aaron Wolf*: Aaron Wolf, "Hydropolitics," Water Encyclopedia.

199 *Jan Eliasson*: Author's interview with Ambassador Eliasson, May 29, 2007.

CHAPTER 19: "A TWENTY-FIRST-CENTURY CATASTROPHE"

204 *increase storm-water runoff*: "Questions and answers about floods," US Geological Survey, 1998: http://ga.water.usgs.gov/edu/qafloods.html.

204 *seven of the nation's ten costliest disasters*: Christine Gibson, "Our Ten Greatest Natural Disasters," *American Heritage Magazine*, vol. 57, no. 4 (August/September 2006).

204 *"a twenty-first century-catastrophe"*: Michael McCarthy, "A 21st century catastrophe," *Independent*, July 24, 2007.

205 *Australian flood of 2010*: Aubrey Belford, "Too Little, Then Too Much in Australia," *New York Times*, January 16, 2011.

205 *Lake Sidney Lanier, dropped*: "Lake Lanier," Wikipedia.org.

206 *Sonny Perdue*: Eleanor Randolph, "Letter from Savanna: Praying for Rain," *New York Times* board blog, November 14, 2007.

206 *former governor Roy Barnes*: "Drought gives Ga. water planning new urgency," Associated Press, October 28, 2007.

206 *Seagar*: Seagar interview.

207 *As Atlanta expanded*: Thomas Wheatley and Ken Edelstein, "Growth, growth everywhere but not a drop to drink," *Creative Loafing Atlanta*, October 17, 2007.

208 *Robert Holmes*: "Atlanta Floods Extremely Rare," US Geological Survey news release, November 9, 2009.

209 *An estimated 60 percent of the world's wetlands*: "Massive Greenhouse Gases May Be Released as Destruction, Drying of World Wetlands Worsen," ScienceDaily, July 21, 2008.

209 *The single deadliest natural disaster*: "List of Deadliest Floods," Wikipedia.org.

209 *floods in the United States killed 850 people*: "1999 Sierra Club Sprawl Report": http://www.sierraclub.org/sprawl/report99/openspace.asp.

209 *flooding of Galveston*: National Oceanic and Atmospheric Administration report: "Hurricane Katrina," December 29, 2005: http://www.ncdc.noaa.gov/special-reports/katrina.html.

209 *Okeechobee hurricane*: Wikipedia: http://en.wikipedia.org/wiki/1928_Okeechobee _Hurricane#cite_note-Gibson-0.

210 *at least $150 billion worth of damage*: Rick Jervis, "2 years after Katrina, pace of rebuilding depends on who pays," *USA Today*, August 29, 2007.

210 *3 billion people—live in coastal regions*: Liz Creel, "Ripple Effects: Population and Coastal Regions," Population Reference Bureau.

NOTES

210 *World Bank estimates:* "The Cost to Developing Countries of Adapting to Climate Change," World Bank, 2009.

210 *By 2025:* "People Head for the Coast," Blue Communities.org.

210 *National Academy of Sciences:* James G. Titus, et al., "Potential Impacts of Sea Level Rise on the Beach at Ocean City, Maryland," US Environmental Protection Agency.

210 *flood insurance:* Cathy Chu, "Should beach towns be rebuilt again and again?" *USA Today,* August 22, 2007.

211 *20 percent of American homes:* "Why We Don't Prepare for Disaster," *Time,* August 20, 2006.

211 *New York City:* "New York's Worst Hurricane Fears Confirmed in New Study," Environment News Service, October 26, 2006.

211 *storm surge of up to twenty-five feet high at Kennedy Airport:* "NASA Looks at Sea Level Rise, Hurricane Risks to New York City," NASA mission pages, October 24, 2006.

212 *Max Mayfield:* Jennifer Peltz, "Hurricane barriers floated to keep sea out of NYC," Associated Press, May 31, 2009.

212 *New York City as "the second worst place for a hurricane to hit":* "Why We Don't Prepare for Disaster," *Time.*

212 *extreme flooding could hit:* Cynthia Rosenzweig and Wiliam Solecki, "Climate change Information Resourcs for the New York Metroplitan Region." http://ccir.ciesin .columbia.edu/nyc/pdf/q2a.pdf

212 *Its flood maps:* Mireya Navarro, "With Flyovers, a Solar Map of New York," *New York Times,* May 9, 2010.

212 *"We've been talking about this lack of preparation":* Author's conversations with Dr. Malcolm Bowman, March 13, 2008.

213 *Halcrow Group Ltd.:* "New York Storm Surge Barrier," Halcrow Group.

213 *Parsons Brinckerhoff:* Peltz, "Hurricane barriers floated to keep sea out of NYC."

213 *Dr. Douglas Hill:* Author's interview with Dr. Hill, May 25, 2008.

CHAPTER 20: FORENSIC ENGINEERING

215 *Federal Emergency Management Agency (FEMA):* Mark Schlefstein, "Levee statistics point up their importance to nation's economy," *New Orleans Times-Picayune,* January 2, 2010.

215 *85 percent of US levees were privately built:* "The Report Card on America's Infrastructure," American Society of Civil Engineers, 2010.

215 *177 of them—about 9 percent of federally inspected levees:* Ibid.

216 *the residents of Fernley, Nevada:* Steve Friess, "Rush of Water Leaves a Nevada Town in Anguish," *New York Times,* January 7, 2008.

216 *Report Card on American Infrastructure:* American Society of Civil Engineers: http:// www.infrastructurereportcard.org/.

216 *Congress had committed only $1.13 billion:* Ibid.

216 *In the 2006 Rapanos case:* John M. Broder, "After Lobbying, Wetlands Rules Are Narrowed," *New York Times,* July 6, 2007. See also Charles Duhigg and Janet Roberts, "Rulings Restrict Clean Water Act, Foiling E.P.A.," *New York Times,* February 28, 2010.

217 *The Corps got its start on June 16, 1775:* "The US Army Corps of Engineers: A

Brief History," US Army Corps of Engineers: http://www.usace.army.mil/History/Documents/Brief/index.html.

218 *The Mississippi has the third-largest drainage basin:* "The Mississippi River and Tributaries Project," US Army Corps of Engineers: http://www.mvn.usace.army.mil/pao/bro/misstrib.htm.

219 *the Great Mississippi Flood of 1927:* "Fatal Flood," *American Experience,* PBS. See also "Great Flood," *National Geographic,* expedition journal, Stephen Ambrose and Douglas Brinkley, May 1, 2001.

219 *The 1928 Flood Control Act:* "After the flood: A history of the 1928 Flood Control Act," *Journal of the Illinois State Historical Society* (Summer 2002).

220 *mostly staffed by civilians:* Author's interviews with Dr. Robert G. Bea, professor, Department of Civil and Environmental Engineering, University of California, Berkeley, 2007–10. See also John McQuaid, "Broken: The Army Corps of Engineers," *Mother Jones,* August 25, 2007.

220 *the Corps was heavily criticized:* Bea interview. See also "The Report Card on America's Infrastructure," American Society of Civil Engineers; and Jim McKay, "Critics Balk at US Army Corps of Engineers Levee Cleanup," *Emergency Management,* August 20, 2009.

221 *In Missouri, the owner of a house:* Bea. For background, see http://www.ce.berkeley.edu/~bea/.

222 *the Great Flood of 1993:* Gerald E. Galloway, et al., "Sharing the Challenge: Floodplain Management into the 21st Century," Interagency Floodplain Management Review Committee report, 1994: http://www.floods.org/PDF/Sharing_the_Challenge.pdf.

222 *the message was adjusted to "Levee failures":* Bea interview.

224 *"Corps officials, under pressure, repeatedly justify unworthy projects":* Jennifer Kefer, et al., "America's Flood Risk Is Heating Up," Environmental Defense Fund report: www.edf.org.

224 *The result was an encyclopedic report:* "Independent Levee Investigation Team Final Report," July 31, 2006: http://www.ce.berkeley.edu/projects/neworleans/.

224 *underfunding of the Corps:* John Schwartz, "Panelist on Levees Faults Army Corps Budget Cuts," *New York Times,* October 19, 2005.

225 *class-action lawsuit against the Army Corps of Engineers:* John Schwartz, "Judge Allows Katrina Lawsuit Against Corps of Engineers," *New York Times,* March 20, 2009.

226 *Bob Bea, three senior Corps officers, and local politicians:* I was granted permission to attend this meeting on the condition that I not reveal details about who was present or what was said.

226 *judge Stanwood Duval:* Susan Finch, "Federal judge rules flood victims can't sue Corps," *New Orleans Times-Picayune,* January 30, 2008.

226 *Judge Duval blamed the Corps:* Mark Schleifstein, "Corps' operation of MR-GO doomed homes in St. Bernard, Lower 9th Ward, judge rules," *New Orleans Times-Picayune,* November 19, 2009.

226 *$7.1 billion repairing New Orleans's flood defenses:* Bea interview, and "New Orleans at risk from Category 2 hurricane," Associated Press, June 16, 2008.

227 *Texas City, Texas:* Bea interview. See also Dan Feldstein, "Texas City's levees contain faults cited in New Orleans," *Houston Chronicle,* July 23, 2006.

227 *the most vulnerable:* Bea interview.

NOTES

227 *built by Chinese laborers during the Gold Rush:* "Levee Repair—Construction," California Department of Water Resources: http://www.water.ca.gov/levees/history /construction.cfm.

227 *Jones Tract:* Author's observations, news reports, and "Jones Tract Flooding Update," County of San Joaquin news release, June 7, 2004.

228 *Sacramento . . . the most flood-prone city in the nation:* Jennifer Kefer, et al., "America's Flood Risk Is Heating Up." See also "Sacramento Flood Threat," Sacramento Area Flood Control Agency.

228 *levees there, which protect about 60 percent:* Kimberly Taylor, "Delta Subsidence in California," US Geological Survey: http://ca.water.usgs.gov/archive/reports/fs00500 /fs00500.pdf.

228 *1-in-3 chance of a "catastrophic" earthquake:* "Bay Area Earthquake Probabilities," US Geological Survey, April 2008: http://earthquake.usgs.gov/regional/nca/ucerf/.

228 *Deepwater Horizon Study Group:* http://ccrm.berkeley.edu/deepwaterhorizon studygroup/dhsg_members.shtml.

CHAPTER 21: KEEPING OUR FEET DRY

230 *"God created the earth, but the Dutch created the Netherlands":* "Netherlands," WorldAtlas.com.

230 *the storm of February 1953:* "The Catastrophic 1953 North Sea Flood of the Netherlands," Suburban Emergency Management Project, January 11, 2006.

231 *the Delta Committee:* David Wolman, "Before the Levees Break: A Plan to Save the Netherlands," *Wired,* December 22, 2008.

231 *Piet Dircke:* Stephan Faris, "What If the Water Wins?" *Time,* November 12, 2009.

232 *The Mississippi River and Tributaries Project:* http://www.mvn.usace.army.mil/pao /bro/misstrib.htm.

233 *Jeff Hart:* Author's Delta tour with Jeff Hart, October 20, 2007. For background, see http://www.hartlandnursery.com/.

CHAPTER 22: THE SACRAMENTO DELTA: A GORDIAN KNOT

239 *irrigated agriculture, which accounts for about 70 percent:* "Crops and Drops," UN Food and Agriculture Organization.

239 *In California, the number is probably closer to 80 percent:* Peter Gleick, "The Denominator Problem; Misleading Use of Water Numbers," Circle of Blue Water News, August 28, 2009.

240 *water meter "rebellion":* Ellan Hanak, "Paying for Infrastructure: California's Choices," Public Policy Institute of California, January 2009. See also Sasha Khoka, "California's Water Meter Rebellion Withers," KQED News, May 17, 2009.

240 *In the Imperial Irrigation District:* Robert Glennon, *Unquenchable: America's Water Crisis and What to Do About It* (Washington, DC: Island Press, 2009), p. 259.

240 *Three-quarters of California's water:* "Of farms, folks and fish," *Economist,* October 22, 2009.

241 *In the mid-1800s, farmers began to drain the Delta's marshlands:* "Delta Subsidence in California," US Geological Survey, April 2000: http://ca.water.usgs.gov/archive /reports/fs00500/fs00500.pdf.

NOTES

241 *In a catch-22, cities and counties:* "Why the Delta Matters to every Californian," Aquafornia, September 3, 2007: http://aquafornia.com/archives/588.

242 *Diversion of about 48 percent of the Delta's freshwater:* Tom Philp, "Delta Watershed Supplies: How Much We All Divert," September 28, 2010: http://www.sfgate.com/cgi-bin/blogs/tphilp/detail?entry_id=73354. See also Delta Blue Ribbon Task Force, "Our Vision for the California Delta," January 29, 2008: http://deltavision.ca.gov/BlueRibbonTaskForce/FinalVision/Delta_Vision_Final.pdf.

242 *American Rivers:* American Rivers report: "America's Most Endangered Rivers of 2009."

242 *Peter Gleick:* Author's tour of the Delta with Peter Gleick, July 15–16, 2008, and subsequent conversations.

242 *farming losses were estimated:* Heather Cooley, Juliet Christian-Smith, and Peter H. Gleick, "More with Less: Agricultural Water Conservation and Efficiency in California," Pacific Institute, September 2008.

243 *Timothy Quinn:* Jennifer Steinhauer, "Water-Starved California Slows Development," *New York Times,* June 7, 2008.

245 *"we can move 6.7 billion gallons of water per day":* Doug Thompson, July 15, 2008.

245 *"The system is effective but not flawless":* "Skinner Fish Facility," California Department of Water Resources, September, 1997.

246 *Canneries processed 5 million pounds of salmon a year:* "Delta Heritage," restorethedelta.org.

246 *judge Oliver Wanger:* Peter Fimrite, "Ruling to protect delta smelt may force water rationing in Bay Area," *San Francisco Chronicle,* September 1, 2007.

246 *only twenty-five smelt:* Patrick Hoge, "Delta smelt numbers plunge," *San Francisco Chronicle,* May 22, 2007.

246 *Bill Jennings:* Glen Martin, "Smelt decline turns off delta water pumps," *San Francisco Chronicle,* June 1, 2007.

246 *Judge Wanger ordered water exports:* "California Judge Helps Declining Fish," Associated Press, September 2, 2007.

246 *"This federal biological opinion puts fish above the needs of millions of Californians":* "Gov. Schwarzenegger Issues Statement on New Salmon Biological Opinion," governor's press release, June 4, 2009.

247 *Some of them were allegedly paid by wealthy farm-owners to march:* From news accounts, such as Malia Wollan, "Hundreds Protest Cuts in Water in California," *New York Times,* April 16, 2009.

247 *Paul Johnson:* Paul Johnson, "The water wars: California's salmon vs. agribiz interests," Grist, March 15, 2010.

247 *Representative Tom McClintock:* Michael Hiltzik, "Deceptive arguments are being made in California's water wars," *Los Angeles Times,* March 14, 2010.

247 *Sean Hannity:* Matt Jenkins, "Breakdown," *High Country News,* January 11, 2010.

247 *Devin Nunes:* Ibid.

247 *Jon Stewart:* "Jon Stewart takes on Sean Hannity over Ca water," *Fresno Bee,* September 30, 2009.

248 *2009 as a "dire year":* Fresno County Farm Bureau, June 5, 2009.

248 *Rodney R. McInnis:* Hiltzik, "Deceptive arguments are being made in California's water wars."

248 *about twenty-six hundred jobs and $270 million were lost:* Mike Hudson, "Protect Endangered Fish, Save the Fishermen," OnEarth.org, August 19, 2009.

248 *Dave Bitts:* Eric Bailey, "US Halts Commercial Salmon Season," *Los Angeles Times,* April 11, 2008.

248 *Friant Dam:* http://www.usbr.gov/projects/Facility.jsp?fac_Name=Friant%20Dam.

249 *San Joaquin River:* http://www.nrdc.org/water/conservation/sanjoaquin.asp.

249 *Hal Candee:* Natural Resources Defense Council press release, September 13, 2006: http://www.nrdc.org/media/pressreleases/060913a.asp.

250 *Temperance Flat Dam:* US Bureau of Reclamation, "Temperance Flat River Mile 274 Dam and Reservoir Site," June 2009. See also John Lindt, "Temperance Flat Cost Pegged at $3.3 Billion," *Valley Voice,* August 6, 2009.

251 *fill Hetch Hetchy reservoir sixteen times:* Peter Gleick, "Saving California Agriculture," *San Francisco Chronicle* City Brights blog, July 22, 2009.

251 *in 2009, cotton production in California dropped 27 percent:* Gleick interview.

251 *Mike Wade:* Mike Wade, "Reality Absent from Report," California Farm Water Coalition, July 20, 2009.

252 *Delta Vision Blue Ribbon Task Force:* http://deltavision.ca.gov/index.shtml.

253 *It's the ultimate "Gordian knot":* Sarah Yang, "Can California fix the Delta before disaster strikes?" UC Berkeley press release, April 20, 2010.

CHAPTER 23: LIQUIDITY: PRIVATIZATION
AND THE RISE OF BIG WATER

255 *T. Boone Pickens:* Author's interview with T. Boone Pickens, October 19, 2007. See also Boone Pickens, *The Luckiest Guy in the World* (Beard Books, 2001), p. 100; and Mesa Water: http://www.mesawater.com/.

256 *Pickens as a "greenmailer":* "Pickens Tells Who Financed Koito Stake," Reuters, December 6, 1990.

256 *Mesa was hobbled:* "Pickens Minding His Own Business," Associated Press, November 10, 1994.

256 *Canadian River Municipal Water Authority:* Forrest Wilder, "Cash Flow," *Texas Observer,* September 9, 2010.

256 *Salem Abraham:* Ibid., and Pickens interview.

256 *Texas population will leap as much as 43.5 percent:* James P. Gaines, "Looming Boom: Texas Through 2030," *Tierra Grande,* January 2008.

257 *Texas water law:* "Groundwater Conservation Districts," Texas Agricultural Extension Service, February 1999: http://www.hpwd.com/downloads/GCD.pdf.

257 *Pickens's ranching neighbors were alarmed:* Pickens interview, and Wilder, "Cash Flow."

257 *A hundred times more water is stored underground:* "Earth's Water: Groundwater," US Geological Survey: http://ga.water.usgs.gov/edu/earthgw.html.

258 *Americans pumped 83.3 billion gallons:* Susan S. Hutson, et al., "Estimated Use of Water in the United States in 2000," US Geological Survey, March 2004.

258 *half the US population:* "Groundwater depletion," US Geological Survey: http://ga.water.usgs.gov/edu/gwdepletion.html.

258 *a quadrillion gallons of H$_2$O:* Andrew Romanek, "Impact of Senate Bill 1 on the Depletion of the Ogallala Aquifer," December 4, 1997.

258 *30 percent of all groundwater used for irrigation:* "High Plains Regional Groundwater Study," US Geological Survey.

NOTES

258 *supplies 40 percent of the nation's grain-fed beef:* Jane Braxton Little, "Saving the Ogallala Aquifer," *Scientific American,* March 30, 2009.

258 *estimated to be from ten thousand to several million years old:* "USGS: Ogallala aquifer water quality currently acceptable," *Lincoln Journal Star,* July 19, 2009. See also Wikipedia.com and Waterencyclopedia.com.

259 *drained the Ogallala's water ten times faster:* Sierra Club, in Michael Milstein, "Beyond Wind Plan, Pickens Eyes Pipelines in Drought-Ridden U.S.," *Popular Mechanics,* October 1, 2009.

259 *roughly 1 billion acres of grasslands covered the Great Plains:* Ned Sullivan, "Protecting Farms Saves More Than Local Food," Daily Green, March 15, 2010.

259 *25 million acres of cropland have been planted since 1982:* Little, "Saving the Ogallala Aquifer."

259 *Dr. Jason Gurdak:* "High Plains Aquifer Water Quality Currently Acceptable but Human Activities Could Limit Future Use," US Geological Survey press release, July 16, 2009.

260 *A US Department of Agriculture project:* Little, "Saving the Ogallala Aquifer."

260 *an additional 120 billion gallons of aquifer water:* Martha G. Roberts, Timothy D. Male, and Theodore P. Toombs, "Potential Impacts of Biofuels Expansion on Natural Resources," EDF.org, 2007.

260 *found that yearly groundwater withdrawals:* Little, "Saving the Ogallala Aquifer."

260 *David Pope:* Ibid.

260 *equivalent to eighteen Colorado Rivers:* Ibid.

261 *the Dallas–Fort Worth Metroplex:* July 1, 2009, Census Bureau estimate, cited by Wikipedia: http://en.wikipedia.org/wiki/Dallas—Fort_Worth_metroplex#cite_note -2009CensusEst-0.

261 *"Population is just eating us up":* Roy Appleton, "N. Texas thirsting for answers," *Dallas Morning News,* September 23, 2006.

261 *The worst drought ever recorded:* http://web2.airmail.net/danb1/records.htm.

262 *$3.6 billion worth of crop and livestock losses:* "Not a cloud," *Economist,* August 13, 2009.

262 *Todd Staples:* Tom Benning, "Texas Scorched by Worst Drought in 50 Years," *Wall Street Journal,* July 28, 2009.

263 *$150 million by 2008:* Susan Berfield, "There Will Be Water," *BusinessWeek,* June 12, 2008.

263 *Pickens's $1.5 billion pipeline:* Milstein, "Beyond Wind Plan."

263 *"the largest windmill farm in the world":* Ariel Schwartz, "T. Boone Pickens Scrapped the World's Biggest Wind Farm. Now What Happens to U.S. Wind Power?" *Fast Company,* July 8, 2009.

263 *"Pickens Plan":* Vaclav Smil, "A Reality Check on the Pickens Energy Plan," Yale Environment 360, August 25, 2008.

263 *Panhandle residents reacted with "a mix of anger and awe":* Elliott Blackburn, "Pickens' energy plans clouded by federal decision," LubbockOnline, August 23, 2008.

263 *Department of Justice (DOJ) blocked the new law:* Ibid.

264 *Ken Kramer:* Milstein, "Beyond Wind Plan."

264 *C. E. Williams:* Berfield, "There Will Be Water."

264 *[Others claim that Texas's portion]:* Pete A. Y. Gunter and Max Oelschlaeger, *Texas Land Ethics* (Austin: University of Texas Press, 1997), p. 46.

266 *supplied drinking water to 85 percent of Americans:* Charles C. Mann, "The Rise of Big Water," *Vanity Fair*, May 2007.

266 *Pinsent Masons Water Yearbook:* Ibid.

268 *"No one has the right to appropriate water":* Alexandra Alter, "How to Quench the World's Thirst," *Wall Street Journal*, November 7, 2008.

268 *Dick Hierstein:* Erika Hobbs, "Low Rates, Needed Repairs Lure 'Big Water' to Uncle Sam's Plumbing," Water Barons, Center for Public Integrity, February 12, 2003.

268 *Bucharest, Romania:* Mann, "Rise of Big Water."

269 *Akron, Ohio:* "Akron Voters Reject Stinky Privatization Measure," Food & Water Watch, November 2008.

270 *Jean-Marie Messier:* John Carreyrou and Martin Peers, "How Messier Kept Cash Crisis at Vivendi Hidden for Months," *Wall Street Journal*, October 31, 2002.

270 *mayor of Grenoble was sentenced to a four-year prison term:* Julio Godoy, "Water and Power: The French Connection," Water Barons, Center for Public Integrity, February 4, 2003.

271 *International Consortium of Investigative Journalists:* Alan Snitow and Deborah Kaufman, with Michael Fox, *Thirst* (San Francisco: Jossey-Bass, 2007), p.77.

271 *United Water:* "Water Privatization Becomes a Signature Issue in Atlanta," Water Barons, Center for Public Integrity, February 12, 2003.

271 *Mayor Campbell was indicted on seven counts:* Richard Whitt and Bill Rankin, "Former mayor Campbell indicted—Feds allege bribery, fraud at City Hall," *Atlanta Journal-Constitution*, August 30, 2004.

272 *to Paris with his mistress:* Snitow and Kaufman, with Fox, *Thirst*, p. 83.

272 *RWE:* Saeed Shah, "Is it really possible to sell Britain's most hated company? You bet it is," *Independent*, August 16, 2006.

272 *claimed that 90 percent of its US customers were satisfied:* Mike Esterl, "U.S. water privatizations fail to pan out," *Wall Street Journal*, June 26, 2006.

272 *Felton, California:* Snitow and Kaufman, with Fox, *Thirst*, p. 49.

273 *Catherine Bowie:* Esterl, "U.S. water privatizations fail to pan out."

274 *in 2005 the Europeans abandoned the project:* Mann, "Rise of Big Water."

274 *Cochabamba, Bolivia:* Ibid. See also William Finnegan, "Leasing the Rain," *New Yorker*, April 8, 2002; and "Timeline: Cochabamba Water Revolt," *Frontline*, PBS, June 2002.

275 *"If people didn't pay their water bills":* Finnegan, "Leasing the Rain."

275 *After a Bolivian army captain was televised:* Ibid. See also "Timeline: Cochabamba Water Revolt," *Frontline*.

275 *Bechtel responded by filing a $25 million lawsuit:* Evo Morales, "From Coca to Congress," Znet, November 11, 2002. See also Mafruza Kahn, "Profits, Profits Everywhere—and Soon Not a Drop to Drink," Corporate Research Project, May 2002.

276 *Luis Camargo:* Juan Forero, "Bolivia regrets IMF experiment," *New York Times*, December 14, 2007.

276 *André Abreu:* Mann, "Rise of Big Water."

276 *"creating social and political discontent":* Esterl, "US water privatizations fail to pan out."

276 *Bertrand Delanoë:* Julio Godoy, "Water flowing back into public hands," Inter Press Service, June 2008.

276 *Fredrik Segerfeldt:* Fredrik Segerfeldt, "Private Water Saves Lives," *Financial Times*, August 25, 2005.

277 *Peter Gleick and Dr. Michael Campana:* Dr. Michael Campana, "The Human Right to Water: The Time Has Come," WaterWired, December 28, 2008: http://aquadoc .typepad.com/waterwired/2008/12/index.html.

277 *James M. Olson:* Berfield, "There Will Be Water."

CHAPTER 24: WATER AND POWER

278 *190,000 million gallons of water:* "Energy-Water Nexus Overview," Sandia National Laboratories: http://www.sandia.gov/energy-water/nexus_overview.htm.

279 *the nation's sixty thousand water systems:* "Energy Demands on Water Resources," Sandia National Laboratories: http://www.sandia.gov/energy-water/docs/121 -RptToCongress-EWwEIAcomments-FINAL.pdf.

279 *California found that "water-related energy use":* Paula Luu, "Pacific Institute Develops Water-Energy-Climate Calculator," C-Win.org, October 2, 2010: http://www.c-win .org/blog/pacific-institute-develops-water-energy-climate-calculator.html.

279 *half of the freshwater drawn from sources:* "Water Use in the United States," National Atlas.gov.

279 *2 to 3 percent is lost to evaporation:* "20% Wind Energy by 2030," Executive Summary, Department of Energy, December 2008.

280 *Texas used approximately 157,000 million gallons:* Ashlynn Stillwell, et al., "Energy Water Nexus in Texas," University of Texas at Austin, Environmental Defense Fund, April 2009.

280 *US population is expected to reach 440 million:* "In Era of Climate Change and Water Scarcity, Meeting National Energy Demand Confronts Major Impediments," Circle of Blue Water News, September 22, 2010.

280 *sued the EPA for permitting once-through cooling:* "Riverkeeper will argue clean water act case before US Supreme Court," Riverkeeper.org press release, November 24, 2008.

280 *refused to renew the permit for the Indian Point:* David Halbfinger, "New York Denies Indian Point a Water Permit," *New York Times,* April 3, 2010.

281 *promoted the Pickens Plan:* http://www.pickensplan.com/theplan/. See also Milken Institute Global Conference 2010: http://www.milkeninstitute.org/events/gcprogram .taf?function=detail&EvID=2085&eventid=GC10.

282 *over 90 percent of natural gas wells today:* "Natural Gas Extraction," ConserveLand.org.

282 *each fracked gas well uses 3 to 8 million gallons:* Christopher Bateman, "A Colossal Fracking Mess," *Vanity Fair,* June 21, 2010: http://www.vanityfair.com/business /features/2010/06/fracking-in-pennsylvania-201006.

282 *Marcellus Shale deposit:* Daniel Soeder and William Kappel, "Water Resources and Natural Gas Production from the Marcellus Shale," US Geological Survey Fact Sheet 2009-3032: http://md.water.usgs.gov/publications/fs-2009–3032/.

283 *$25 an acre plus royalties of 12.5 percent in 2007:* Mireya Navarro, "At Odds Over Land, Money and Gas," *New York Times,* November 27, 2009.

283 *high school auditorium:* Author's observations at Stuyvesant High School, November 10, 2009.

283 *filtration plant, which could cost $10 billion:* Representative James Genarro, "Gas Drilling in Marcellus Shale Is Shortsighted and Unacceptable," *City Hall News,* January 27, 2010.

284 *A single hydrofracked well requires:* Bateman, "Colossal Fracking Mess."

284 *radium 226, a naturally occurring uranium derivative:* Abrahm Lustgarten, "Natural Gas Drilling Produces Radioactive Wastewater," *Scientific American,* November 9, 2009.

284 *"wastes do not constitute a health risk":* "An Investigation of Naturally Occurring Radioactive Materials in Oil and Gas Wells in New York State," NY State Department of Environmental Conservation: http://www.dec.ny.gov/chemical/23473.html; see also US Environmental Protection Agency: "Oil and Gas Production Wastes": http://www.epa.gov/rpdweb00/tenorm/oilandgas.html#whatbeingdone.

284 *Delaware "the most endangered river in the country":* "America's Most Endangered Rivers Report: 2010 Edition."

284 *$6 billion in government revenue and 280,000 jobs:* Eric Wohlschlegel, "New Study Finds Natural Gas in Marcellus Shale Region Worth 280,000 Jobs, $6 Billion in Government Revenue," American Petroleum Institute, July 21, 2010.

284 *Dimock, Pennsylvania:* Bateman, "Colossal Fracking Mess," and news reports.

284 *fined Cabot Oil and Gas:* Abrahm Lustgarten, "Cabot Oil & Gas's Marcellus Drilling to Slow After PA Environment Officials Order Wells Closed," ProPublica, April 16, 2010.

284 *Laura Amos:* Bateman, "Colossal Fracking Mess." Amos tells her story: http://www.earthworksaction.org/cvLauraAmos.cfm. See also Nancy Loftholm, "Breached well fuels feud with gas firm," *Denver Post,* February 18, 2005.

285 *gas-field workers believe:* Dennis Webb, "Worker believes cancer caused by fracking fluids," *Daily Sentinel,* May 11, 2010.

285 *Amos to sign nondisclosure agreements:* Bateman, "Colossal Fracking Mess."

285 *Jim Smith:* Mary Esch, "Advocates: Upper Delaware most endangered U.S. river; upper Colorado on list," Associated Press, June 2, 2010.

285 *BP, the largest producer of natural gas in the United States:* Yahoo!Finance: http://biz.yahoo.com/ic/58/58872.html.

285 *"a revolution in the gas fields":* Mostafa Mabrouk, "US natural gas shale amazes the world," Egypt Oil & Gas: http://www.egyptoil-gas.com/read_article_issues.php?AID=410.

285 *sprayed gas and wastewater for sixteen hours:* Tim Purko, "Marcellus blowout sprays gas in Clearfield County," *Pittsburgh Tribune-Review,* June 5, 2010.

285 *Cabot Oil and Gas failed to properly cement:* Abrahm Lustgarten, "Officials in Three States Pin Water Woes on Gas Drilling," ProPublica, April 26, 2009.

286 *Some analysts predict that by 2020:* Mabrouk, "US natural gas shale amazes the world."

286 *Reliance Industries:* Steve Toon, "Atlas Energy Seals $1.7B Marcellus Shale JV with Reliance Industries," April 22, 2010.

286 *Sweden, Poland, and Germany:* Mabrouk, "US natural gas shale amazes the world."

286 *fracking was granted an explicit exemption:* "The Halliburton Loophole," *New York Times,* November 2, 2009.

286 *Professor Robert Howarth:* Bateman, "Colossal Fracking Mess."

287 *Dr. Theo Colborn:* http://www.endocrinedisruption.com/chemicals.introduction.php.

287 *James Northrup:* Statement by James L. Northrup to Otsego County Board, July 21, 2010: Croton Watershed Clean Water Coalition, Inc.: http://www.newyorkwater.org/pdf/9_24_10CWCWCcommentstEPA.pdf.

287 *shale oil:* Clifford Krauss, "New Way to Tap Gas May Expand Global Supplies," *New York Times,* October 9, 2009.

288 *shale formation under Colorado:* Mike Soraghan, "BLM's OK of oil-shale leases digs up concerns," *Denver Post,* November 15, 2006.

288 *retort 1.55 million barrels of shale oil per day:* David O. Williams, "Oil giants have 'cornered the market' on Western Slope water rights, study says," *Colorado Independent,* March 20, 2009.

288 *In 2007 and 2008, Shell went on a buying spree:* Ibid.

289 *acquired 7.5 million acre-feet of water rights:* Mark Jaffe, "Oil companies 'corner' Western Slope water rights," *Denver Post,* March 18, 2009.

289 *Karin Sheldon:* David O. Williams, "Shell official confirms thirsty nature of oil shale, denies push to 'corner water market,'" *Colorado Independent,* March 23, 2009.

289 *deposits of tar sands:* Elizabeth Kolbert, "Unconventional Crude," *New Yorker,* November 12, 2007.

289 *tar sands is the world's largest energy project:* John Loring, "Q&A: Energy Independence, Obama and Canada's Oil Sands," *New York Times* green blog, February 9, 2009.

290 *Tree-ring studies show:* Laura Nichol, "Tree Rings Tell Story of Ancient Droughts," Natural Resources Canada, February 2009.

290 *three to four barrels of freshwater:* "Canada's oil sands: Water": http://www.canadas oilsands.ca/en/what-were-doing/water.aspx.

290 *76 percent of the water taken from the Athabasca:* "Water Depletion," TarSandsWatch, Polaris Institute.org.

290 *4.2 billion barrels a year:* "Liquid Asset," Polaris Institute.

290 *Athabasca Chipewyan and Mikisew Cree Indians:* "Pollution Flows Downstream," ForestEthics: http://www.forestethics.org/downstream-from-the-tar-sands. See also Gina Solomon, "The Other Oil Disaster: Cancer and Canada's Tar Sands," Natural Resources Defense Council switchboard, May 3, 2010: http://switchboard.nrdc.org /blogs/gsolomon/the_other_oil_disaster_cancer.html.

290 *report by Doug Radke:* Andrew Nikiforuk, "Liquid Asset," *Toronto Globe and Mail,* March 28, 2008.

291 *curtail the output of up to a quarter:* "Drought could force nuke-plant shutdowns," Associated Press, January 23, 2008.

291 *Yucca Mountain:* Peter Behr, "The Administration Puts Its Own Stamp on a Possible Nuclear Revival," *New York Times* ClimateWire, February 2, 2010.

CHAPTER 25: "POP CULTURE IN A BOTTLE"

292 *drank over 5 million gallons:* John G. Rodwan Jr., "Bottled Water 2009," International Bottled Water Association.

292 *In 2007, we consumed over 8.7 million gallons:* From Beverage Marketing Corporation, cited in ibid.

292 *Drinking eight glasses of water a day:* "Bottled Water," *New York Times* topics: http:// topics.nytimes.com/top/reference/timestopics/subjects/w/water/bottled_water /index.html?scp=1-spot&sq=bottled%20water&st=cse.

292 *about 29 gallons of bottled water:* Deborah Ball, "Bottled Water Pits Nestle vs. Greens," *Wall Street Journal,* May 25, 2010.

293 *the fastest-growing beverage category in the world:* "Bottled Water Pricey in More Ways Than One," Worldwatch Institute, May 9, 2007.

293 *MaHaLo Deep Sea water:* http://www.hawaiideepseawater.com/.

NOTES

293 *Bling H₂O:* Dinero, "$90 a bottle 'Bling' water," BX Daily Bugle, March 4, 2007.

293 *Pepsi's Aquafina leads the market, with 13 percent: Beverage Digest,* quoted in "PepsiCo Launches Industry's Lightest Water Bottle," GreenBiz.com, March 25, 2009.

294 *controlled 38 percent of the US market:* Ball, "Bottled Water Pits Nestle vs. Greens."

294 *Beverage Marketing Corporation reported:* "Bottled Water and Energy: A Fact Sheet," Pacific Institute: http://www.pacinst.org/topics/water_and_sustainability/bottled _water/bottled_water_and_energy.html.

294 *3.4 megajoules of energy:* Ibid.

294 *"In Praise of Tap Water":* "In Praise of Tap Water," *New York Times,* August 1, 2007.

294 *about 17 million barrels of oil:* "Bottled Water and Energy: A Fact Sheet," Pacific Institute.

295 *great majority of water bottles—about 38 billion:* http://www.evergreen.edu /sustainability/banthebottle.htm.

295 *bottled-water sales in the United States declined:* Rodwan, "Bottled Water 2009."

296 *24 trillion gallons of rain:* "Water Resources in Maine," Maine Geologic Survey.

296 *Hiram Ricker:* "Poland Spring: History," Poland Spring Preservation Society: http:// www.polandspringps.org/pshistory.html.

296 *700 million gallons of water:* "Shapleigh, Maine, Project Overview," Poland Spring: http://www.polandspringme.com/shapleigh/PDF/ProjectOverview.pdf.

296 *Mall in Washington, DC:* David A. Fahrenthold, "Bottlers, States and the Public Slug It Out in Water War," *Washington Post,* June 12, 2006.

296 *largest water-bottling plant in North America:* Sarah Theodore, "Poland Spring bottling is a Maine event: Nestle's flagship water bottling facility produces 65 million cases of product a year," *Food & Drug Packaging,* October 2004.

297 *James Wilfong:* Author's tour with James Wilfong, July 11, 2006. See also H₂O for ME: http://www.waterdividendtrust.com/.

297 *Wilfong's allies complained bitterly:* Author's conversations with Fryeburg residents.

297 *Kim Jeffery:* Author's interview with Kim Jeffery, February 1, 2008. Wilfong and Jerry Harkavy, "Poland Spring Becomes a Target for Spring-Water Tax," *Buffalo News,* November 16, 2005.

297 *Jeffery hired Maine's leading law firm:* Wilfong.

298 *The commissioner of the state Department of Conservation:* Fahrenthold, "Bottlers, States and the Public Slug It Out in Water War."

298 *Baldacci equated Poland Spring to L.L. Bean:* Virginia Wright, "Troubled Waters," *Down East,* May 2006.

299 *Poland Spring operations in Fryeburg:* http://www.polandspringme.com/fryeburg /index.php?p=project_overview.

299 *Maine supreme court ruled in favor of Poland Spring:* Lisa Williams Ackley, "Nestle gets fill station green light," *Bridgton News,* March 26, 2009; available at: http:// fryeburgmatters.org/pdf/Bridgton-News-3-26-09.pdf.

300 *cost between 240 and 10,000 times as much as tap water:* "Summary Findings of NRDC's 1999 Bottled Water Report," Natural Resources Defense Council.

300 *"It struck me that all you had to do":* Gustave Leven, chairman of the board, Perrier Corporation of France, quoted in P. Betts, "Bubbling Over in a Healthy Market," *Financial Times,* January 13, 1988.

300 *that a $2.50 bottle of water:* "The real cost of bottled water," World Wildlife Fund. See

NOTES

also Catherine Ferrier, "Bottled Water: Understanding a Social Phenomenon," WWF-commissioned discussion paper, April 2001.

300 *The FDA allows bottlers:* Author's observations. See also Peter Gleick, "Bottled water labels: no salt, no fat, no cholesterol, and no useful information," *San Francisco Chronicle* City Brights blog, July 8, 2009.

301 *crickets:* Peter H. Gleick, *Bottled and Sold: The Story Behind Our Obsession with Bottled Water* (Island Press, 2010), p. 47.

301 *Aquafina water as "P.W.S.":* Christina Boyle Daily, "It's tap: Aquafina agrees to spring for truthful label," *New York Daily News,* July 28, 2007.

301 *class-action suit alleging its water:* "Nestle Sued for Falsely Advertising Poland Spring Water," *Water & Wastes Digest,* June 19, 2003.

301 *Alice Waters:* "Think Outside the Bottle," Corporate Accountability International.

301 *"a blight on the globe":* Author's interview with Alice Waters, September 18, 2007.

302 *Kim Jeffery:* Jeffery interview.

302 *Drew Nieporent:* Author's interview with Drew Nieporent, June 2, 2008.

302 *Clark Wolf:* Author's interview with Clark Wolf, December 6, 2007.

303 *Tappening, an activist marketing group:* http://www.tappening.com/ and "Anti-Bottled Water Campaign Tells Lies," *Brandweek,* July 23, 2009.

303 *Sister Mary Ann Coyle:* Rebecca U. Cho, "US: Some faith groups say bottled water immoral," *Chicago Tribune,* 2006.

303 *Nestlé's water business:* Ball, "Bottled Water Pits Nestle vs. Greens."

303 *bristled at the criticism and complained:* Jeffery interview.

304 *Robert Glennon:* Quoted in Fahrenthold, "Bottlers, States and the Public Slug It Out in Water War."

CHAPTER 26: THE BATTLE FOR BRISTOL BAY

305 *Tim La Porte:* Author's interview with Tim La Porte, September 28, 2008.

305 *Phil St. George:* Ibid. See also Patricia Liles, "Pebble facts," *Alaska Business Monthly,* October 1, 2007.

307 *80.6 billion pounds of copper:* "Prospecting the Future," Pebble Limited Partnership: http://www.pebblepartnership.com/project.

307 *at least 8 billion tons of rock:* Dr. Carol Ann Woody, "Bristol Bay & Pebble Mine: Identified Risks," http://www.wildsalmonprotection.com/content/AFS08annotated .pdf. See also Zak Smith, "Anglo American Makes Promises About Pebble Mine It Cannot Keep," Natural Resources Defense Council Switchboard blog, April 9, 2010.

308 *Lisa Reimers:* Author's interview with Lisa Reimers, PLP headquarters in Anchorage, Alaska, June 25, 2008.

309 *South Africa, where ten thousand local people were allegedly moved:* Philip Mattera, "Anglo American's Track Record: Rhetoric or Reality?" Renewable Resources Coalition, Nunamta Aulukstai, July 2008.

309 *Tiffany & Co, Fortunoff, and prominent independent jewelers:* Margot Roosevelt, "Retailers to hold mine to higher gold standards," *Los Angeles Times,* February 12, 2008. See also Nikhil Kumar, "Protest at Anglo's Alaskan quest," *Independent,* November 3, 2010.

309 *Forty inches of rain and snow falls there annually:* Dr. Robert Moran, "Pebble Mine: Technical Background," Pebblescience.org.

NOTES

309 *60 to 70 million salmon flow into Bristol Bay:* Erick Rickstad, "Alaska's Bristol Bay world-famous salmon rivers threatened by Pebble Mine. Help Save Them!" Orvis News: http://www.orvis.com/intro.aspx?subject=4571.

309 *Aside from oil and gas:* "Alaska: Economy," Alaska Public Record Search: http://alaskapublicrecordsearch.org/557/alaska-12/.

309 *fifty-four thousand people earned all or part of their annual income:* Geoffrey Parker, et al., "Pebble Mine: Fish, Minerals, and Testing the Limits of Alaska's 'Large Mine Permitting Process,'" *Alaska Law Review,* vol. 25:1 (2008).

309 *mining . . . employing some fifty-five hundred Alaskans:* "The Economic Impacts of Alaska's Mining Industry," Alaska Miners Association Inc., Jan 2008.

310 *use some 35 billion gallons of water a year:* Dr. Robert Moran, "Pebble Mine: Water-Related Impacts," Pebble Science: http://www.pebblescience.org/pebble_mine/water.html.

310 *The geology around the Pebble Deposit:* Moran interview.

310 *Alaska's water quality standard:* Dr. Carol Ann Woody, "Copper: Effects on Freshwater Food Chains and Salmon," Trout Unlimited, September 2007.

310 *Carol Ann Woody:* Ibid. See also author's interview with Carol Ann Woody, June 25, 2008.

310 *Bob Moran:* Moran interview.

311 *Sean Magee:* Tim Sohn, "Gold Fish," *Outside,* June 2009.

311 *Teck Cominco, spent $8 million to drill:* Paula Dobbyn, "Golden Glitter: Company weighs mining massive amounts of gold, copper," *Anchorage Daily News,* October 17, 2004.

311 *Teck Cominco blamed "environmental reasons":* Dr. Bruce Switzer, "Ballot Initiative #4," Alaskans for Clean Water presentation, July 21, 2008.

311 *Bruce Jenkins:* Lisa Drew, "Prospect of a Mine Near a Salmon Fishery Stirs Worry in Alaska," *New York Times,* April 26, 2005.

312 *John Shively:* Author's interviews with John Shively, June 24–25, 2008.

313 *Red Dog, the largest zinc mine:* "Red Dog UAA," US Environmental Protection Agency: http://water.epa.gov/scitech/swguidance/waterquality/standards/uses/uaa/ak_reddog.cfm.

313 *Red Dog as the worst toxic polluter:* "Red Dog top toxic polluter," SIKU News, March 31, 2007.

314 *Pebble East and Pebble West:* Ibid. See also "Pebble Project," Alaska Department of Natural Resources: http://dnr.alaska.gov/mlw/mining/largemine/pebble/.

315 *gone "beyond the state's environmental guidelines":* Shively interview.

315 *spent "in excess of $100 million" on assessing:* Ibid.

316 *The chemicals used to process minerals:* Moran, "Pebble Mine: Water-Related Impacts."

316 *hard-rock mining has contaminated:* "Liquid Assets 2000: Americans Pay for Dirty Water," US Environmental Protection Agency: http://water.epa.gov/lawsregs/lawsguidance/cwa/economics/liquidassets/dirtywater.cfm.

316 *the US Supreme Court ruled, 6 to 3, to allow the Kensington:* Erika Bolstad, "Supreme Court decides in favor of Kensington mine owner," *Anchorage Daily News,* June 22, 2009.

317 *Pebble could conceivably fill in:* Elizabeth Bluemink, "Pebble says no dumping in Iliamna Lake," *Anchorage Daily News* Pebble blog, July 30, 2009.

NOTES

317 *"We will not fill in Lake Iliamna"*: Shively interview.

317 *Bingham Canyon has contaminated sixty square miles:* Moran, "Pebble Mine: Water-Related Impacts."

318 *In 2005, 26 million salmon, worth $93 million*: Troy Letherman, "They Don't Want Here a Mine City," *Fish Alaska*, July 2008.

318 *$325,000 to buy a new gill-netter*: "Frequently Asked Questions," Alaska Department of Fish and Game: http://www.cf.adfg.state.ak.us/geninfo/about/faq/TMPktm4nju6q .php.

318 *By the end of the 2008 season:* Laine Welch, "Pacific salmon fisheries see 'reduced supply,'" *Capital City Weekly*, December 3, 2008.

319 *Idaho sockeye were "functionally extinct"*: "Don't equate strong sockeye return with recovery," *Idaho Statesman*, August 10, 2008.

319 *Far more farm-raised salmon:* "Paul Greenberg: The Future of 'Wild Fish,'" National Public Radio: *Fresh Air*, WHYY, July 19, 2010.

319 *national salmon czar:* Scott Learn, "Groups want salmon czar in the White House," *Oregonian*, Mar 9, 2009.

319 *430 outdated dams have been removed:* "10 Years, 430 Dams," *New York Times*, July 3, 2009.

319 *Bobby Andrew:* Author's interview with Bobby Andrew, Dillingham, Alaska, June 2008.

320 *Bob Gillam:* Gillam refused to communicate with me, but there have been many articles written about him. See Elizabeth Bluemink, "Businessman's millions bankrolled anti-Pebble drive," *Anchorage Daily News*, November 7, 2010. Gillam expresses his views here at http://www.bobgillam.com/, and here http://www.juneauempire.com /stories/030310/loc_570179730.shtml.

320 *"You don't have to be particularly smart"*: Jeff Opdyke, "Converted, Pebble foe bankrolls opposition," *Wall Street Journal*, March 27, 2007.

321 *the Renewable Resources Coalition:* http://www.renewableresourcescoalition.org/.

321 *he spends about $3 million a year:* Opdyke, "Converted, Pebble foe bankrolls opposition."

321 *McKinley Capital, holds more than $1 billion:* Dorothy Kosich, "Pebble copper/gold project opponent invests in Anglo American," Mineweb, May 12, 2008.

321 *Gillam might be a double agent:* Author's conversations with people who agreed to talk anonymously.

321 *"Let me take my governor's hat"*: Alex MacGillis, "Palin's Stand on Mining Initiative Leaves Many Feeling Burned," *Washington Post*, September 28, 2008.

323 *Drilling in Bristol Bay would generate an estimated $7.7 billion:* "Federal Government Announces Plan to Hold Bristol Bay Oil & Gas Lease Sale," Alaska Marine Conservation Council press release, April 30, 2007.

323 *makes "no sense" to drill in Bristol Bay:* "Campaign to Stop Oil and Gas Development in Bristol Bay Gained Ground," World Wildlife Fund.

323 *sixty-seven state and federal permits:* "Prospecting the Future," Pebble Partnership.

323 *Tom Crafford:* Margaret Bauman, "State confident fish are protected," *Alaska Journal of Commerce*, November 7, 2010.

323 *The Alaska Department of Natural Resources:* http://dnr.alaska.gov/.

CHAPTER 27: IN SEARCH OF A DROUGHT-PROOF SOURCE

325 *Herb Guenther:* Author's interview with Herb Guenther, May 15, 2008. See also Arizona Department of Water Resources: http://www.azwater.gov/azdwr/default.aspx.

326 *In 1993, fighting a flash flood on the Gila River:* Guenther interview.

326 *some 2.7 million acre-feet:* Arizona Department of Water Resources.

326 *the Central Arizona Project:* http://www.cap-az.com/.

326 *Salt River Project:* https://www.srpnet.com/Default.aspx.

326 *groundwater beneath Phoenix:* Shaun McKinnon, "Unabated use of groundwater threatens Arizona's future," *Arizona Republic,* August 2, 2009.

327 *In 2008, Arizona used about 8 million acre-feet:* http://www.cap-az.com/operations /recharge/recharge-in-arizona/water-sources/.

327 *outdoor misting systems:* As explained to the author by Jack Lavelle, Arizona Department of Water Resources public information officer.

327 *The state doesn't know how much groundwater it has:* McKinnon, "Unabated use of groundwater threatens Arizona's future."

327 *it could face a water crisis by 2025:* "Our Water, Our Future: Policy Options to Safeguard Water Resources in Arizona," Arizona Public Interest Research Group: http://www.arizonapirg.org/home/reports/report-archives/our-water-our-future /our-water-our-future/our-water-our-future-policy-options-to-safeguard-water -resources-in-arizona.

328 *James Pollard Espy:* Richard P. Horwitz, "Americans' Problem with Global Warming," *American Studies,* vol. 45:1 (Spring 2004).

328 *Vincent Schaefer and Irving Langmuir:* William Langewiesche, "Stealing Weather," *Vanity Fair,* May 2008.

328 *Bernard Vonnegut:* Ibid.

329 *silver iodide into a cloud can increase:* Joshua Zaffos, "Snow Job," *Colorado Springs Independent,* February 16, 2006.

329 *Xinjiang region of China:* Langewiesche, "Stealing Weather."

329 *clouds were seeded over China:* "China overdoes cloud seeding to end drought . . . and blankets Beijing in snow," *Daily Mail,* November 2, 2009; and Quentin Sommerville, "Scientists 'cause' Beijing snow," BBC News, November 2, 2009.

329 *In the 1970s, the federal government:* Kavan Peterson, "Cloud seedings silver lining hard to prove," Stateline, January 5, 2005.

329 *"There is still no convincing scientific proof":* Dr. Michael Garstang, et al., *Critical Issues in Weather Modification Research* (Washington, DC: National Academies Press, 2003), p. 3.

329 *By 2006, sixty-six weather-mod research programs:* Zaffos, "Snow Job."

329 *Vail:* Ibid.

329 *experiment in Wyoming:* Ibid.

330 *The oceans hold 321 million cubic miles of water:* "The Water Cycle: Water Storage in Oceans," US Geological Survey.

330 *"multi-effect" distillation plants:* M. Al-Shammiri and M. Safar, "Multi-effect distillation plants: state of the art," Water Desalination Department, Kuwait Institute for Scientific Research, 1999.

331 *Santa Barbara:* Daniel Simmons, "Drought-prone regions look to drink seawater, wastewater," *Angie's List,* April 1, 2009.

NOTES

331 *homeless have taken up residence:* Author's observations.

331 *$2,000 an acre-foot in 1990 to about $800:* "Desalination," Beachapeida: http://www.beachapedia.org/Desalination.

331 *more than two thousand desalination plants:* American Waterworks Association.

331 *plant on the Hudson River:* "United Water Prepares Plan for Hudson River Plant," *Water & Wastes Digest,* August 29, 2007.

331 *Yuma Desalting Plant:* Author's tour of Yuma with the Water Education Foundation, March 30, 2007.

332 *the Saudis have become the world's largest users:* "Thirsty for Innovation: Arab Countries Tap Alternative Energy Sources to Quench Water Demands," Arabic Knowledge@Wharton, June 15, 2010.

332 *the world's largest solar-powered desal plant:* Prachi Patel, "Solar-Powered Desalination," *Technology Review,* April 8, 2010.

332 *Walter Winrow:* Author's interview with Walter Winrow, April 7, 2008.

333 *after Winrow's partners went bankrupt:* Ibid., and Cynthia Barnett, "Salty Solution?" *Florida Trend,* May 1, 2007.

333 *five years behind schedule and $48 million over budget:* Craig Pittman, "More problems for Tampa Bay Water desalination plant," *St. Petersburg Times,* March 17, 2009.

333 *Ken Herd:* Kathryn Kranhold, "Water, Water, Everywhere . . ." *Wall Street Journal,* January 17, 2008.

334 *Department of Water Resources underwrote $25 million:* "DWR Recommends $25 Million in Prop 50 Water Desalination Grants," Water Quality Products, April 8, 2005.

334 *Peter MacLaggan:* Author's interview with Peter MacLaggan, March 21, 2008.

334 *$320 million to build the full-scale plant:* Ibid.

335 *Poseidon might need to sell its water:* "Proposed Carlsbad Desalination Project to Cost Up to Three Times More Than Claimed," Food & Water Watch, November 5, 2009.

335 *"the SUV of water":* Mindy McIntyre, "All that water, every drop to drink," *Los Angeles Times,* April 10, 2008.

335 *In a counter-editorial, MacLaggan:* Peter MacLaggan, "Conservation Alone Won't Cut It," *Los Angeles Times,* April 16, 2008.

335 *the Metropolitan Water District:* http://www.mwdh2o.com. See also Peter Gleick, "Giving Desalination another black eye: Poseidon's financial shell game," *San Francisco Chronicle* City Brights blog, November 11, 2009.

336 *"will kill about two pounds of fish a day":* Kranhold, "Water, Water, Everywhere . . ."

336 *(Poseidon had underestimated the number):* Eric Wolff, "Poseidon's long trident," *San Diego City Beat,* April 21, 2009.

336 *Every hundred gallons of desalinated seawater:* Heather Buschman, "Is desalination the answer to SD's water dilemma?" Nature Network–San Diego, August 9, 2008.

337 *Marco Gonzalez:* www.surfrider.org/. See also Noaki Schwartz, "Green light huge desalination plant," Associated Press, May 13, 2009.

337 *Surfrider's Joe Geever:* Author's interview with Joe Geever, April 2008.

337 *the state's coastal commissioners overrode:* Wolff, "Poseidon's long trident."

337 *"We need it. It's not a choice":* "We need it," *San Diego Union-Tribune,* July 27, 2006.

338 *they will likely build a nuclear-powered facility:* Guenther and Mulroy interviews.

338 *"At the end of the day we will use desalters":* Mulroy interview.

338 *13,080 desalination plants around the world:* Kranhold, "Water, Water, Everywhere . . ."

NOTES

338 *Barry Nelson:* Gary Pitzer, "Tapping the World's Largest Reservoir: Desalination," *Western Water Magazine,* January/February 2003.

338 *Intel is responsible for three Superfund sites in California:* Author's interview with Tom Cooper, March 11, 2008, and subsequent conversations. See also "Overview of Intel Superfund Sites in Silicon Valley, CA," intelsuperfundcleanup.com.

338 *messy public opposition in New Mexico:* Daniel Sorid, "Intel Brings N. Mexico Pollution Concerns," Reuters (no date). See also "History of Intel's Toxic Chemical Release in Corrales": http://www.faceintel.com/toxicchemicalhistory.htm and http://www.faceintel.com/nmpollutionconcerns.htm.

338 *Fab 32:* Author's tour of Fab 32, March 11, 2008. See also www.intel.com/pressroom/kits/manufacturing/Fab32/index.htm.

339 *twenty-two-nanometer transistors:* Cooper interview.

339 *"one of the most boring cities in America":* Joshua Zumbrun, "America's 10 Most Boring Cities," *Forbes,* December 10, 2008.

339 *Silicon Valley:* intelsuperfundcleanup.com. See also "Semiconductor Production Pollution," http://www1.american.edu/TED/semicon.htm.

339 *Of the twenty-nine Superfund sites in Silicon Valley:* "Gardening Superfund Sites," futurefarmers.com.

340 *"ultrapure water":* Cooper interview.

340 *7 million gallons of water per day:* Ibid.

340 *Len Drago:* Author's interview with Len Drago, March 11, 2008.

340 *Paul Ottolini:* Intel Corporate Responsibility Report, 2009.

340 *Between 1998 and 2006, Intel invested:* Tom Cooper and Len Drago, "Intel and Water Conservation," August 1, 2007: http://dcdc.asu.edu/K-12Education/INTEL.pdf.

341 *LEED:* http://www.usgbc.org/DisplayPage.aspx?CMSPageID=1988.

341 *the company's environmental record:* Power, "Peak Water."

341 *"tool kit" on water use:* Cooper interview.

341 *an evaporation pond—built by Intel:* Ibid. See also Edythe Jensen, "Intel water recycling stinking up Chandler subdivision," AZCentral.com, July 9, 2008.

342 *"135,000 gallons of water to produce one ton of alfalfa":* Robert Glennon, *Unquenchable* (Washington, DC: Island Press, 2009), p. 201.

342 *"water neutral":* Ling Woo Liu, "Water Pressure," *Time,* June 12, 2008.

CONCLUSION: THE RIPPLE EFFECT

343 *Adam Smith wrote of the diamond-water paradox:* "Adam Smith," Wikipedia: http://en.wikipedia.org/wiki/Paradox_of_value; Adam Smith: "An Inquiry into the Nature and Causes of the Wealth of Nations" (1776), Library of Economics and Liberty: http://www.econlib.org/library/Smith/smWN.html.

343 *Alan Moores:* Alan Moores, "'Water: The Epic Struggle for Wealth, Power, and Civilization': Water as the new oil," *Seattle Times,* January 2, 2010.

343 *the Dust Bowl drove 2.5 million people:* "Dust Bowl," History.com: http://www.history.com/topics/dust-bowl.

344 *by providing irrigators with federal subsidies:* Environmental Working Group: http://reports.ewg.org/content/research/10.

344 *"a blood sport":* Peter Rogers and Susan Leal, *Running Out of Water* (New York: Palgrave Macmillan, 2010), p. 20.

NOTES

345 *Pat Mulroy:* Mulroy interview. See also Henry Breen, "Mulroy advice for Obama: Tap Mississippi floodwaters," *Las Vegas Review-Journal,* January 12, 2009.

347 *Fred Pearce:* Fred Pearce, *When the Rivers Run Dry* (Boston: Beacon Press, 2006), pp. 261–71.

347 *800 million acre-feet of water falls from the clouds:* Ibid., p. 307.

347 *Los Angeles, a desert city:* Ibid., p. 309.

348 *New York a "permeable city":* Mireya Navarro, "$1.5 Billion Plan Would Cut Sewage Flow into City Waters," *New York Times,* September 28, 2010.

348 *Hirsch refers to as "the fish":* Hirsch interview.

348 *The Soft Path:* Gleick interview. See also Amory Lovins, "Energy Strategy: The Road Not Taken?" *Foreign Affairs,* October 1976.

351 *a study by Johns Hopkins University:* Jasmin Malik Chua, "Detox Your Home: Wash Up with Ordinary Soap," Planet Green.com, January 23, 2008.

351 *Vicki Blazer:* Blazer interview.

352 *$8 billion of new infrastructure:* Teresa Cerojano, "Misuse will drain Asia's water supply, experts say," Associated Press, October 12, 2010.

352 *water use is predicted to rise by two-thirds:* "Water: critical shortages ahead?" World Resources Institute.

352 *70 percent of global water use is devoted to irrigated agriculture:* "Water resources in agriculture: outlook and policy issues," Organization for Economic Cooperation and Development: http://www.oecd.org.

352 *"no water crisis":* "No global water crisis—but many developing countries will face water scarcity," UN Food and Agriculture Organization, March 12, 2003.

353 *634 gallons of water:* Rogers and Leal, *Running Out of Water,* p. 3.

353 *cut global food production by 385 million tons a year:* Pearce, *When the Rivers Run Dry,* p. 306.

353 *needs will exceed supply by 40 percent:* Cerojano, "Misuse will drain Asia's water supply."

353 *Steven Solomon:* Steven Solomon, *Water* (New York: HarperCollins, 2010), p. 417.

353 *Singapore:* Rogers and Leal, *Running Out of Water,* pp. 32–37. See also "Every drop counts," *Economist,* May 20, 2010.

354 *which, by one count, includes six cabinet departments:* de la Vega, "Extreme Water Emergencies."

355 *David Zetland:* http://www.aguanomics.com.

355 *experts recommend a minimum of thirteen gallons per person, per day:* Gleick interview. See also Campana, "The Human Right to Water."

357 *240,000 water pipes burst every year:* "Aging Water Infrastructure," US Environmental Protection Agency: http://www.epa.gov/nrmrl/pubs/600f07015/600f07015.pdf.

357 *650 water mains break every day:* "ITT's Value of Water Survey Reveals That Americans Are Ready to Fix Our Nation's Crumbling Water Infrastructure," October 27, 2010.

357 *made of wood:* Michael Cooper, "Aging of Water Mains Is Becoming Hard to Ignore," *New York Times,* April 17, 2009.

357 *"dawn of the replacement era":* "Water infrastructure at a turning point," American Water Works Association, 2010.

357 *America's water systems cost $1 trillion a year:* "FAQ," American Water.com.

357 *will require a $334 billion investment:* Mae Wu, "More money to improve drinking water," Natural Resources Defense Council, May 12, 2010.

NOTES

357 *the US Conference of Mayors:* Bob Herbert, "The Corrosion of America," *New York Times,* October 26, 2010.

358 *Garrett Hardin:* Garrett Hardin, "The Tragedy of the Commons," *Science,* December 13, 1968.

358 *Bob Hirsch:* http://water.usgs.gov/dispatch/2008/podcast/wolman-lecture-transcript.html.

358 *Stephen Ambrose's writings:* Stephen Ambrose, *Undaunted Courage: Meriwether Lewis, Thomas Jefferson, and the Opening of the American West* (New York: Simon & Schuster, 1996).

359 *"The Nation's Rivers":* M. Gordon Wolman, "The Nation's Rivers," *Science,* November 26, 1971.

360 *census of US water resources:* http://water.usgs.gov/wsi/.

360 *Ken Salazar:* Department of Interior press release: http://www.doi.gov/DOI404.cfm; and Amy Joi O'Donoghue, "Salazar announces Colorado River inventory," *Deseret News,* October 21, 2010.

EPILOGUE: "WATER!"

361 *One summer in the early 1960s:* This account is based on my grandfather's book: Charles Child, *Roots in the Rock* (Boston: Little, Brown, 1964), pp. 307–10.

Index

INDEX

INDEX

INDEX

INDEX

INDEX

neurodevelopmental disorders, 77
Nevada, 288
  annual precipitation in, 162
  population growth in, 163
Nevada, University of, 176
Nevada state engineer, 172, 173–74
Nevada Supreme Court, 173–74
Never Summer Range, 162
New Hampshire, 299
New Jersey, 1–2, 195
New Jersey Department of Environmental
  Protection (NJDEP), 102, 103
New Melones Dam, 185
New Mexico, 143, 258, 338
  droughts in, 133
New Orleans, La., 16, 108, 217, 219, 228,
  231
  Hurricane Katrina in, *see* Katrina,
    Hurricane
  levee system in, 204, 214, 221, 223,
    224–27, 229, 234
New South Wales, 135
Newtown Creek, 15–17, 40, 58
  pollution in, 21–24, 25–27, 28, 33, 54,
    61, 359
  as Superfund site, 28–29
Newtown Creek Wastewater Treatment
  Plant (NCWWTP), 52–54, 58–59,
  62
New York, 83, 195, 280–81, 282, 283, 285
  hydrofracking in, 282–83, 284, 285
New York, 17
New York, N.Y., 15, 24, 71
  CSOs in, 54, 55, 56, 61, 119
  daily water consumption in, 120
  environmental suits by, 27–28
  flood threat to, 211–12
  "green" infrastructure projects in,
    61–62, 348
  municipal water quality in, 301, 302, 303
  petroleum-refining business in, 21
  proposed floodgates for, 213
  sewage treatment plants in, 52–54, 56
  sewer system of, 52–57, 61, 119, 212,
    348
  storm-water runoff in, 52, 53, 55–56,
    57, 61–62, 348

  terrorism threat in, 121
  2003 blackout in, 56–57
  watershed of, 66, 278, 282, 283, 350,
    359
  see also specific boroughs
New York City Department of
  Environmental Protection (DEP),
  27, 59, 212, 283
  City Water Tunnel No. 1 of, 119–20
  City Water Tunnel No. 2 of, 119, 120
  City Water Tunnel No. 3 of, 117–18,
    121–24, 211
  water distribution system of, 117–24
New Yorker, 121
New York Harbor, 28, 29, 54, 61, 217
New York Post, 24
New York State Department of
  Environmental Conservation, 284
New York Times, 10, 22, 60, 99, 100, 101,
  276, 294
New York Times Magazine, 111, 191
Niagara Falls, N.Y., 20
Nicky (PLP engineer), 314–15
Nieporent, Drew, 302
Niger River, 130, 196
Nile River, 130, 196, 197
nitrates, 79
nitrogen, 48, 79, 83–84, 85, 90, 91–92
  aquatic dead zones and, 14, 59, 84,
    93–94, 97
nitrogen-fixing bacteria, 84
nitrogen oxide, 95
nitrogen-use technology (NUE), 96
nitrous oxide, 93–94
Nixon, Richard, 19, 63
Norfolk, Va., 217
North American Free Trade Agreement
  (NAFTA), 196
North American Recycling Alliance
  (NARA), 141
North American Water and Power
  Alliance (NAWAPA), 141
North Carolina, 128
North Dakota, 288
Northeast, US, hurricane threat to, 211–12
Northern Dynasty Minerals (NDM), 307,
  310, 311, 314, 322

INDEX

INDEX

INDEX